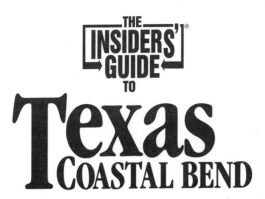

THE
INSIDERS'®
GUIDE
TO

Texas
COASTAL BEND

THE INSIDERS' GUIDE TO

Texas
COASTAL BEND

by
Scott Williams
and
Vivienne Heines

Insiders' Publishing
105 Budleigh St.
P.O. Box 2057
Manteo, NC 27954
(252) 473-6100
www.insiders.com

Sales and Marketing:
Falcon Publishing, Inc.
P.O. Box 1718
Helena, MT 59624
(800) 582-2665
www.falconguide.com

•

FIRST EDITION
1st printing

•

Copyright ©1998
by Falcon Publishing, Inc.

•

Printed in the United States
of America

•

Publications from The Insiders' Guide®
series are available at special discounts for
bulk purchases for sales promotions,
premiums or fundraisings. Special editions,
including personalized covers, can be
created in large quantities for special
needs. For more information, please write
to Karen Bachman, Insiders' Publishing,
P.O. Box 2057, Manteo, NC 27954, or call
(800) 765-2665 Ext. 241.

ISBN 1-57380-061-9

Insiders' Publishing

Publisher/Editor-in-Chief
Beth P. Storie

Advertising Director/
General Manager
Michael McOwen

Creative Services Director
Giles MacMillan

Art Director
David Haynes

Managing Editor
Dave McCarter

Project Editor
Eileen Myers

Project Artist
Bart Smith

Insiders' Publishing
An imprint of Falcon Publishing Inc.
A Landmark Communications company.

Preface

Early visitors to the Coastal Bend called it the Texas Riviera, charmed by its shimmering waters, sea breezes and abundant fishing.

Such ageless attributes still entice thousands of tourists and newcomers to this sunshine-filled hideaway on the Texas Gulf Coast. This is where Texas' larger-than-life ranching heritage blends with the leisure of a beachfront lifestyle, where Stetson-wearing cowboys are as common as bronzed surfers and where a 10-minute drive takes you from a bustling fishing pier to vast acres of fluffy cotton fields.

It's a region rich in history, established by hardy pioneers who came seeking land and wealth and found instead a countryside as beautiful as it was demanding. The blessings of sunshine gave way to the curse of drought, and the cooling bay breezes could also bring deadly hurricanes. And as the settlers endured and flourished on this flat, rich landscape, they learned to appreciate the natural gifts from the land — the bounty of fish and wild game, the graceful shade of towering live oaks and the bright-pink splashes of bougainvillea flowers that accent the greenery.

Today, the area is far more civilized but no less alluring. It promises rest and relaxation, South Texas-style — from windsurfing and sailing to shrimp festivals and fiestas.

The region's largest city, Corpus Christi, boasts a population of more than 250,000, yet most residents and visitors find it has a small-town atmosphere. You'll find a spontaneous warmth and genuine friendliness among the natives, from the waitress at your restaurant to the park ranger who directs you to your campsite.

To say that we're off the beaten path is an understatement. The Coastal Bend is a destination unto itself, not a pit stop on the way to another locale. Still, we're located just hours from both the Mexican border and the big-city bustle of Houston and San Antonio.

To savor the character of our adopted homeland, first take a deep breath and relax.

Then take a drive down Corpus Christi's Ocean Drive and admire the showcase bayfront mansions set against a backdrop of sparkling blue-green water.

Travel to Padre Island National Seashore, the world's longest barrier island, a 55-mile refuge for world-weary visitors as well as more than 350 species of birds and wildlife.

Enjoy the saturated colors of a coastal sunset as you haul in a trophy marlin during a deep-sea fishing trip off Port Aransas.

Watch the *vaqueros* — Spanish for cowboys — corral longhorn cattle during a roundup at the world-famous King Ranch, where the region's ranching traditions meld seamlessly with the cultural heritage of nearby Mexico.

We who have chosen this lush and rugged paradise as our home have learned to celebrate its diversity. We have learned to embrace not only our longtime neighbors, but also the newcomers here and, yes, even the sometimes harsh geology and climate.

And we know that the hot summer sun of this semitropical land warms not only the Gulf waters but the hearts of those who visit here.

About the Authors

Vivienne Heines

Raised in New Orleans, Louisiana, Vivienne Heines is familiar both with the Gulf coast and diverse cultures. Her writing career, however, has been spent mostly in her adopted home state of Texas, where she received a journalism degree from Trinity University in San Antonio and has been a news reporter, features writer and editor at newspapers including the *Houston Chronicle, Corpus Christi Caller-Times, Brazosport Facts, Brenham Banner Press, Wharton Journal Spectator* and the *Colorado County Citizen*. During her 16-year newspaper tenure, she won nearly 30 awards and covered Texas topics ranging from unsolved murders to historical profiles. She has tracked wild mountain lions and javelinas, been attacked by Africanized bees, flown in Navy jets and exposed small-town corruption.

In 1996, Heines decided to swap the fast-paced life of full-time newspaper reporting for freelance writing and spending more time with her three young children. Today, she contributes freelance articles to state and national newspapers and magazines on topics ranging from the military to cuisine. She also serves as assistant leader for her eldest son's Cub Scout den, classroom mother for her other son and is a board member of the Corpus Christi Press Club.

During her 10 years in Corpus Christi, Heines has grown to love the beauty, diversity and brilliance of this coastal city. Jogging along the bayfront, collecting shells at the beach and swimming in the blue-green surf are among the activities that she most enjoys. Most importantly, she has found that the people here are warm, friendly and welcoming, opening their hearts and homes to newcomers with casual ease. She lives with her husband, two sons, one daughter, a dog and a cat in the historic Del Mar area of the city, just three blocks from the bayfront — close enough to catch the evening sea breezes from the swing on their front porch.

Scott Williams

A native Texan who grew up on the outskirts of Dallas, Scott Williams has lived most of his life far from the sandy shores of the Coastal Bend. His lifelong dream of writing took him to the University of Texas at Austin, where he earned a journalism degree in 1985. He began his career at a weekly newspaper, the *Lockhart Post-Register*, where he covered everything from pee-wee football to county government. A year later he accepted a job as a business writer with *The Bryan-College Station Eagle*. In 1988, during his first visit to the Coastal Bend, the sparkling green water and towering palm trees of Corpus Christi convinced Williams to accept a job with the *Corpus Christi Caller-Times*.

He began his *Caller-Times* career on the transportation and economic development beat before graduating to coverage of trials and legal affairs. He later became an area reporter, where he spent hundreds of hours on the roads between the tiny coastal hamlets of Rockport, Port Aransas and Portland. He spent his last four years at the *Caller-Times* as a features writer, profiling prominent South Texans and describing life in the Coastal Bend. He has marveled up close at the Rockport hummingbirds, witnessed two open-heart surgeries by an acclaimed Corpus Christi surgeon, visited a privately owned lighthouse on a small Gulf Coast island and flown with the Blue Angels. He left the *Caller-Times* in 1994 to care for his children full time and finish a novel.

Williams and his wife, journalist Libby Averyt, live three blocks from Corpus Christi Bay with their two children, Avery and Grace. Williams and his family enjoy camping in South Texas parks, building sandcastles at the Padre Island National Seashore and relaxing in the laid-back South Texas lifestyle that accepts shorts and sandals almost everywhere.

Acknowledgments

Vivienne...

Writing this book was a learning experience for me. I discovered much about my community, and I also came to know dozens of people who shared observations, information and insight with me.

Among those who assisted me with this book are all the friendly folks at the Chambers of Commerce in Aransas Pass, Corpus Christi, Gregory-Portland, Ingleside, Port Aransas, Rockport-Fulton, Kingsville, San Antonio and South Padre Island. A special thanks goes to Dick Messbarger at the Kingsville Economic Development Council, who was never too busy to talk to us about his beloved city or to put us in touch with the right people.

Another special thanks goes to my loyal friend Libby Averyt Williams, who provided invaluable research assistance as well as enthusiastic support for this project.

I am indebted to my neighbors, Frank and Cindy Peterson, for their insight into the city's nightlife; to *Corpus Christi Caller-Times* columnist Rene Cabrera for his perspective on the city's Tejano music scene; and to *Corpus Christi Caller-Times* outdoor writer Buddy Gough, who patiently led me through the area's fishing and hunting terrain.

The local and area boards of Realtors helped by sharing their knowledge of the real estate scene, neighborhoods and available properties.

Many friends provided an invaluable resource — babysitting time — to help me conduct interviews and write on my computer. I owe a special thanks to Felisa Garza and Lisa Innins for the loving care they gave to my children during those busy times.

Last, but certainly not least, I owe a debt of gratitude to my family. My two sons, Zachary and Aaron, were great companions during much of the research for this book. When we went to visit all the bed and breakfast inns in the area, they cheerfully pointed out details and shared their opinions.

My daughter, Tessa, actually managed to exhibit patience — a rare attribute for a toddler — when she accompanied me on interviews or played semi-quietly while I talked on the telephone.

Also, I want to thank my co-author, Scott Williams, for his professionalism and his thoroughness in researching and writing this book.

And my husband, Andy, displayed a great deal of tolerance throughout my months of research. He supported, encouraged and generally endured as my files gradually took over most of our filing cabinet, bookshelf and home office.

To all of these people — this book is dedicated to you. Thank you.

Scott...

This book could not have been written without the assistance of several people in the Coastal Bend who shared their knowledge and resources with us. I'd like to thank Ralph Goonan and Gretchen Benkendorfer, both formerly of the Corpus Christi Business Alliance, for their help in acquiring information and some of the photographs for this book.

I'd also like to thank Diane Probst, executive director of the Rockport-Fulton Chamber of Commerce; Kathy Burge, assistant to the director at the Aransas Pass Chamber of Commerce; Cheryl Hill of the Ingleside Chamber of Commerce; Rachel Munson, Ingleside city secretary; Linda Hodge and Santos Villarreal, Corpus Christi Park & Recreation Department; Dick Messbarger, executive director of the Kingsville Economic Development Council; and Lawanda Skrobarczyk, director of the Kingsville Convention and Visitors Bureau. Special thanks to *Corpus Christi Caller-Times* photographer George Gongora for the photograph of Selena Quintanilla-Perez; Elaine Liner,

Corpus Christi Caller-Times media critic, for her assistance on the media chapter; Francisco Tamez of the Laredo Convention & Visitors Bureau; and Gwen Spain, director of public relations at the Austin Convention and Visitors Bureau. I turned to many sources for the History chapter, but none was more helpful than Bill Walraven's *Corpus Christi: History of a Texas Seaport*.

Most of all I would like to thank my co-author, Vivienne Heines, for making this collaboration work without a hitch; friends Del Puckett and Sue Rothschild for babysitting my children while I worked; my wife, Libby, for her love and support and for assisting with research and proofreading; and my two children, Avery and Grace, who saw a lot less of their Daddy during the writing of this book.

Table of Contents

Directory of Maps

Texas Coastal Bend Area

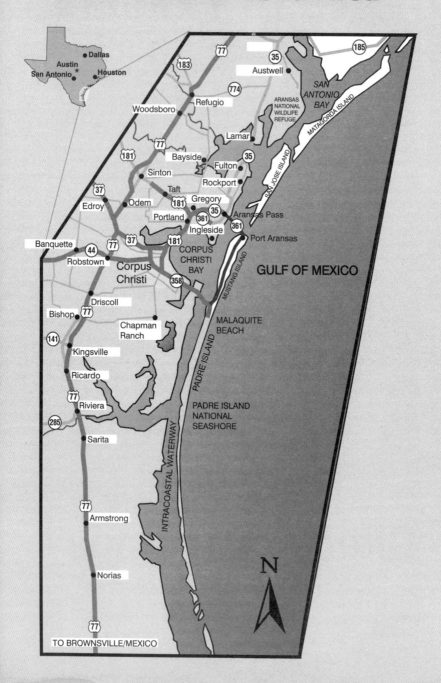

North Bay Area

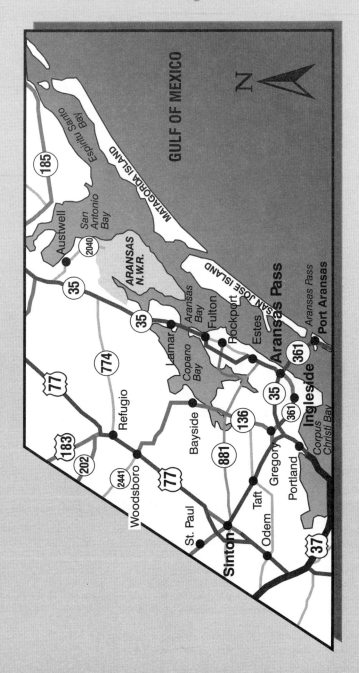

Downtown Corpus Christi

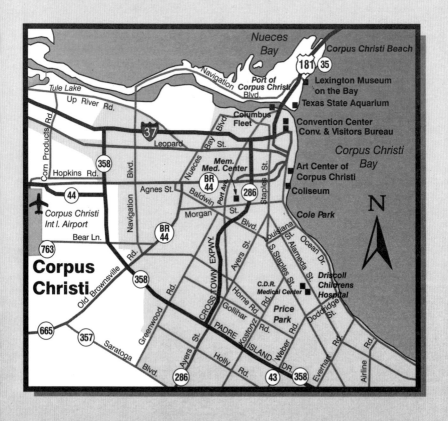

Port Aransas/ Padre Island Area

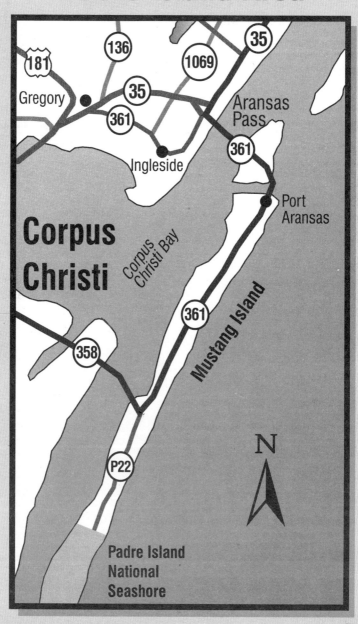

Kingsville Area

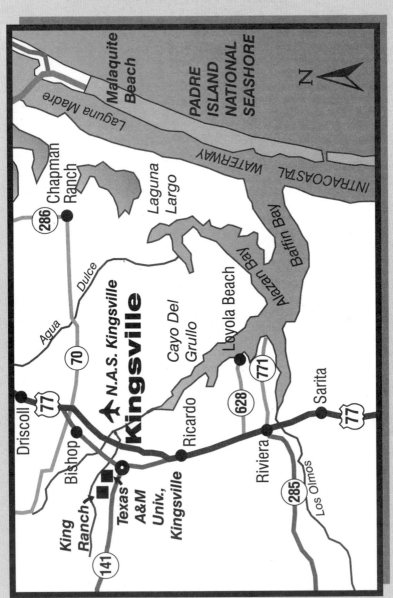

Corpus Christi Bay is one of the premier locations in the world for windsurfing.

How to Use This Book

Like the early explorers who sailed these coastal waters in search of treasure, we find living in Texas' Coastal Bend to be an ongoing adventure. There are so many nooks and crannies to explore, such varied recreational opportunities to experience and so many regional festivals and idiosyncrasies to savor.

Whether you're a summer visitor, a Midwesterner come to escape the chill of winter or a newcomer who plans to settle in and buy a home, we want this book to be your guide. Take along this book, and we'll journey with you to traverse the flora and fauna of state and national parks, to marvel at the minute perfection of a hummingbird in flight, to taste the seafood bounty at local restaurants and to feel the brush of salt spray against your face from a Jet Ski.

You can use the table of contents to flip quickly to the subject you're seeking, be it accommodations or watersports. Or you can use the index in the back of the book to find a specific topic, attraction, museum or shop.

The portion of the Texas Gulf Coast known as the Coastal Bend begins northward at the Aransas National Wildlife Refuge and extends southward along the coast through Rockport, Fulton, Aransas Pass, Port Aransas, Ingleside, Portland and on to Corpus Christi, our largest city. We'll then travel southward along the coast to Padre Island National Seashore and inland to Kingsville, home of one of the world's largest ranches, the King Ranch.

We have grouped many of our listings by four geographic categories. The North Bay area includes the towns of Lamar, Fulton, Rockport, Aransas Pass, Ingleside, Gregory and Portland. The Corpus Christi area encompasses the city and its surrounding towns and communities. In the Port Aransas to Padre Island section, we provide information about the island city of Port Aransas and the area that extends through Padre Island National Seashore. Finally, the Kingsville area includes the city and its surrounding towns, such as Ricardo and Riviera.

In most of our chapters, the headings will be arranged in that same geographic order, from north to south, so you can look for a city name to locate, say, a restaurant or museum. And within each city, the listings will be alphabetical.

Entries for our most visible landmarks and attractions are listed in several different chapters, often cross-referenced for easy access.

We've included maps of this region to help guide you through the state highways and farm-to-market roads that intersect our landscape. The speed limit on interstate highways is 70 mph, not 75 mph. Although you might get away with driving 75, we wouldn't want to encourage law-breaking.

Scattered throughout the book are a host of Insiders' tips — interesting or informative tidbits about the Coastal Bend, its history, its people and its activities that you might not otherwise know or hear about.

In addition, we've included special close-up looks at topics that are particularly important or fascinating, such as the life and death of rising Tejano music star Selena or where to find the world's only flock of whooping cranes that is thriving in the wild.

We hope this book will help you appreciate this place we call home, and that you'll gain a deep insight into the past, present and

future of this region. When you leave, we hope you'll take more than souvenirs and sunburn with you — you'll carry the imprint and memories of our sun-bleached land.

And while we have tried to acquaint you with the multifaceted aspects of the Coastal Bend, we know you may have different opinions about where to go and what to see. Since *The Insiders' Guide®* to the Texas Coastal Bend is updated annually, we want to hear from you so we can include your tips in the next edition. Please contact us at Insiders Publishing, P.O. Box 2057, Manteo, NC 27954. Or check out the *Insiders' Guide Online®* website, at www. insiders.com.

Spanish explorer Alonzo Álvarez de Piñeda, who is generally credited with discovering the Coastal Bend, sailed along the coast in search of a passage to the Spice Islands of the Pacific Ocean.

History

To recount the history of the Texas Coastal Bend is, in large part, to relate the history of Corpus Christi. This city of more than a quarter million people is by far the largest municipality in the region, leading the way in population, commerce and political clout. What began as a tiny trading post in 1839 has grown to the seventh-largest city in Texas.

Compared with other parts of the country, the Coastal Bend is relatively young. The first Anglo-American settlers arrived here in 1828, more than 200 years after the first English colonists landed in Jamestown, Virginia. In the 169 years since those first settlers arrived, the Coastal Bend has grown from a collection of rugged frontier outposts to a thriving mixture of metropolitan, rural and tourist communities. But to focus merely on Anglo-American settlers wouldn't be fair to the explorers, Spanish and Mexican colonists and Native Americans who came before them.

Early Inhabitants

The first people to settle in the Coastal Bend arrived here more than 8,000 years ago. They were descendants of North America's first inhabitants, who crossed the land bridge from Siberia to Alaska at the end of the Ice Age about 20,000 years ago. Little is known of these early settlers other than they used tools, hunted in groups, used flint spears and left during a drought 3,000 years after they arrived. A second group moved into the Coastal Bend 1,000 to 3,000 years later from the Edwards Plateau in West Texas. They ate shellfish, snails and small animals. Camp sites uncovered by archaeologists revealed small spear points, large well-made knives and conch-shell tools. This second group abandoned the area during yet another dry spell 1,200 years ago. For the next century the Coastal Bend remained uninhabited, until a fierce and cannibalistic tribe of Indians arrived on the scene.

The Karankawa Indians

The Karankawa Indians, who may have been descendants of the area's previous inhabitants, occupied a territory from what is now the eastern outskirts of Houston to Baffin Bay, south of Corpus Christi. History has generally painted the Karankawa with a disapproving brush, although it should be noted that they never had a chance to tell their side of the story. Because they were eventually exterminated by settlers, there are no descendants to defend their honor.

Standing 6 feet tall, the Karankawa were considered giants by the more diminutive European explorers who came upon them. They had finely chiseled features, and tattoos covered their faces and bodies. They punctured their lips and breasts with slivers of cane and spoke in guttural tones without moving their mouths. Red-and-black war paint covered their faces, and they smeared their bodies with bear, shark, skunk and alligator grease mixed with mud to repel mosquitoes (and anyone else who came too close).

The Karankawa roamed the Coastal Plain in small bands, hunting deer and javelina (a piglike mammal indigenous to the area) with giant bows made of cedar. They supplemented their diet with cactus fruit, berries, pecans, clams, oysters and fish. European explorers and settlers described them as ferocious warriors and reviled them for their cannibalistic ways. Like other tribes the Karankawa practiced ceremonial cannibalism against enemies killed in battle in hopes of drawing magic from them. Settlers also described the Karankawa as an unlikable lot bent on stealing, robbing and killing. Evidence suggests the hostile actions taken by the Karankawa may have been prompted by the explorers and colonists and that they learned their cannibalistic ways from a Spanish exploration party that ate its dead to keep from starving.

Although there were times when the Karankawa and their visitors got along well, in general they suffered from a severe case of culture clash, including one incident involving religion. The Spanish built missions in the area to convert the Karankawa from sun worship to Christianity. The Karankawa were receptive to their message as long as the missionaries gave them free food and clothing; however, as soon as the enticements ran out, so did the Karankawa, who preferred to continue worshipping the sun as they had for more than eight centuries. The Spanish never forgave them.

The Karankawa's beliefs caused more serious trouble when Texas settlers arrived and began building fences, planting crops and raising cattle. No matter how hard the settlers tried to explain it to them, the Karankawa just couldn't grasp the concept of animal ownership. As skilled hunters they believed the animal belonged to the person who killed it, a belief Texans didn't particularly care for, especially when it was their animal that had been killed. Texans considered cattle theft a crime punishable by death, and it didn't matter to them that the Karankawa had settled the area first.

Empresario Stephen F. Austin, who brought some American families to Texas, ordered the Karankawa exterminated. (Empresarios were people who contracted with the Mexican government to bring Roman Catholic settlers to Texas in exchange for 9,300 hectares, or 23,000 acres, of land for each 100 families.) The Spanish missionaries had long ago given up on the tribe and were therefore unwilling to provide shelter to them. With nowhere to hide and no one to protect them, they eventually fled to Mexico, where they found more trouble. In 1858, at a place known as Tampacuas, 20 miles north of the Río Grande, a band of Mexican rancheros attacked and killed the last small band of Karankawa, extinguishing a culture that for a millennium had called the Coastal Bend home.

The Explorers

Although the Karankawa met their demise little more than a century ago, the beginning of the end may have come 360 years earlier, when Italian explorer Amerigo Vespucci sailed the Gulf of Mexico and made what is believed to be the first map showing the gulf's outline.

Twenty-one years later, Spanish explorer Alonzo Álvarez de Piñeda, who is generally credited with discovering the Coastal Bend, sailed along the coast in search of a passage to the Spice Islands of the Pacific Ocean. Although the passage eluded him, he discovered the Mississippi River and landed at several sites along the Texas coast. Popular myth has it that Piñeda discovered and named Corpus Christi Bay, having supposedly discovered it on the day of the Roman Catholic Feast of Corpus Christi and therefore giving it that name.

The first Europeans to pass through the Corpus Christi area may well have been the survivors of the Panfilo de Narváez expedition that was stranded in Florida in 1528. With their sights set on Mexico, the 242 Spaniards on the expedition constructed crude barges and set sail across the vast gulf, hoping to reach settlements in Mexico where they could find transportation home. The barge commanded by Alvar Núñez Cabeza de Vaca came ashore near Galveston Island. Only four of the original 242 survived. They were immediately enslaved by the Karankawa, who held them captive for six years. They escaped in October 1534 and headed south toward settlements in Mexico, arriving 18 months later in Sonora in Northern Mexico.

Another group fared even worse than Cabeza de Vaca and his friends. They be-

www.insiders.com
See this and many other Insiders' Guide® destinations online — in their entirety.
Visit us today!

INSIDERS' TIP

The Karankawa Indians were fabled marksmen, able to fell wild prey from 100 yards with cedar bows.

Photo: Greater Kingsville Economic Development Council

H.M. King High School was a gift from Henrietta King to the city of Kingsville.

longed to a treasure convoy sailing from Veracruz to Spain that wrecked on Padre Island in April 1554. The Karankawa, friendly at first, attacked without warning. The Spaniards fled toward Mexico, which they wrongly believed to be only a few miles away. A priest lost their package of crossbows as they rafted over an island pass, leaving them unarmed and unable to respond to the guerrilla warfare the Karankawa used against them. Their leaders were felled by arrows, and everyone suffered from hunger, thirst, exhaustion and sunburn. Friar Marcos de Mena, wounded by seven arrows, was buried in the sand and left to die. But the warm sand renewed him and he arose, as if from the dead, to find his friends massacred.

Despite numerous expeditions to the Coastal Bend, no one made serious inroads into the area until Frenchman René-Robert Cavelier, sieur de La Salle, landed on the shores of Matagorda Bay in 1685. He claimed for France all the lands that were drained by the Mississippi River and its tributaries and established a colony named Fort St. Louis. The Karankawa welcomed him with open arms until La Salle made the mistake of demanding the return of stolen items and compounded the problem by stealing their canoes. The Karankawa responded by de-

stroying Fort St. Louis and killing many of La Salle's people.

Spanish explorer Alonso De León left his mark on the area on April 4, 1689, while crossing a stream surrounded by a lovely pecan grove. He named the stream Nueces, Spanish for "nuts," a name eventually given to both the river that empties into Corpus Christi Bay and the county in which Corpus Christi is located.

Spanish Colonization

La Salle and other French explorers who visited the Coastal Bend had little impact on the area other than to frighten the Spanish into sending explorers and colonists of their own. The first was the Marquis de Aguayo, who they sent to expel the French from the territory. Aguayo reached the ruins of Fort St. Louis on March 24, 1722, where he set up a presidio and mission named Nuestra Señora de Zuniga de la Bahía del Espíritu Santo.

It was the captain of that presidio and mission, Joaquín de Orobio y Basterra, who in 1746 made the first official record of Corpus Christi Bay when he discovered Nueces and Corpus Christi bays in his search for possible settlements. He reported that the fresh water, fish, sources of salt and fertile soil made the site ideal for settlement. His favorable reports convinced José Escandón, governor of the newly créated Nuevo Santander state, to start a settlement and mission on Corpus Christi Bay, but the settlers enticed to risk the long journey were beset by a snowstorm, smallpox and the loss of their horses that ended their trip before they left Mexico, and the colony never materialized.

Despite such setbacks Spanish rancheros found the area's rich grasslands appealing and applied for land grants. Among the first Spanish landowners to arrive was Blas María de la Garza Falcón, who between the years of 1760 and 1764 established Rancho Santa Petronilla, 15 miles south of the mouth of the Nueces River. Other Spanish ranchers received grants and joined him, staking claim to vast stretches of grazing lands. In 1764 word of an English settlement on Padre Island brought Spanish Colonel Diego Ortiz Parilla and his troops to investigate. Blas Falcón's son, José Antonio, joined him. He explored the length of Padre Island, and later submitted a report under Colonel Parrilla's name. The report included a sketch of small tents labeled Camp on the Beach of Corpus Christi, the first time the site had been given that name.

Despite their efforts, the Spanish were destined to fail in South Texas. Corruption, government repression, and bureaucratic bumbling contributed to their downfall, as did the Lipan and Comanche Indians, whose periodic looting and killing drove the rancheros to seek safety south of the Rio Grande.

The Irishmen

John McMullen and James McGloin, who in 1830 founded a colony a few miles northwest of what is now Corpus Christi, immigrated to the United States to escape conditions in Ireland. McMullen, who wound up a merchant in Matamoros, Mexico, met McGloin at an English port and convinced him to return with him to Matamoros. In 1828 the two men were granted an empresario contract to bring 200 families to the west bank of the Nueces River.

McMullen and McGloin accompanied the first 58 families that landed in October 1829 near the decaying mission of Our Lady of Refuge in Refugio. A short time later McMullen and McGloin led their party into the wilderness where they eventually established San Patricio de Hibernia on October 24, 1830. Within the year they had built a church, and the first Anglo-American colonists were here to stay. By 1834, San Patricio had stabilized. Crops had flourished, wild game and cattle were plentiful and there was a good supply of drinking water. The only trouble was the growing dissent between Mexico and Texas colonists.

The Texas Revolution

From 1821 to 1836 Texas's population jumped from 4,000 to between 35,000 and 50,000, with most coming from the southern United States. Despite the fact that Mexico owned Texas at that time, these settlers refused to assimilate into Mexican culture and brought slaves to cultivate cotton. Mexicans, having fought recently for freedom from Spain, opposed slavery.

Tensions escalated in 1826 when the Fredonian Rebellion, a failed attempt to create a separate republic, aroused Mexican suspicions that Texas settlers were not loyal to Mexico. The Mexican government stationed troops in Texas and passed a law that both restricted further Anglo-American immigration and banned the importation of slaves. Texans petitioned Mexico to repeal the law, but Austin, their ambassador, was imprisoned when a letter he had written advising Texans to organize a separate state fell into Mexican hands. Mexico rejected the Texans' petition.

In 1834 the Mexican politician and soldier Antonio Lopez de Santa Anna deposed the Mexican government and assumed dictatorial powers, determined to crush the rebellion in Texas. Santa Anna consolidated his power by convincing his enemies that Texans, supported by the United States, were trying to steal Mexican territory. In October 1835 Mexican soldiers arrived in Gonzales, 50 miles east of San Antonio, to reclaim a cannon given to the settlers for use against the Indians. The settlers resisted, firing the first shots in what is considered the opening battle of the Texas Revolution.

A similar incident occurred in the Coastal Bend, although with a different result, when

Capt. Nicolas Rodrigues, Mexico's commander of Fort Lipantitlan across the Nueces River from San Patricio, confiscated the San Patricio colony's cannon. The colony responded by taking Fort Lipantitlan and repelling an attempt by Capt. Rodrigues to retake it. Meanwhile, a convention of Anglo-American settlers formed a provisional government, elected a governor and council, and declared that Texans were fighting for the rights due them under the Mexican Constitution of 1824.

The issue divided the Coastal Bend's Irish settlers. Some wished to remain Mexican citizens in the hope that a liberal government would prevail. Others believed the conservative government and its repressive policies, led by Antonio Lopez de Santa Anna, would inevitably win. Even as they debated these issues, Texans elsewhere proceeded with efforts to break away from Mexico. Austin and two others went to the United States to borrow money, and a quickly formed Texas army marched to attack the Mexican garrison at San Antonio. In December a volunteer force led by Ben Milam defeated the Mexicans and forced them to retreat south of the Río Grande.

On February 23, 1836, Santa Anna's forces entered San Antonio, and the Texans withdrew to the Alamo, a former mission building. William B. Travis, commander of the Texas forces, pleaded for reinforcements, but only 32 men from Gonzales, 50 miles to the east, answered the call. For 13 days the small force defended the Alamo against more than 5,000 Mexican troops until, on March 6, the Alamo fell and its defenders were killed. Among the dead were Tennessee frontier hero, pioneer, and politician, Davy Crockett, and Georgia pioneer, James Bowie. Texans lost several other battles, too, including those in the Coastal Bend towns of San Patricio, Agua Dulce and Refugio.

In a retreat from Goliad, 45 miles north of San Patricio, Col. James W. Fannin and his 283 men surrendered at Coleto Creek and were marched back to Goliad. A few days later, in what has come to be known as the Goliad Massacre, they were executed to serve as an example to other Texans.

On March 2, 1836, during the siege of the Alamo, a group of American Texans met on Washington-On-The-Brazos and declared their independence from Mexico. They also named Sam Houston commander-in-chief and adopted a constitution that protected slavery. The U.S. government supported Texas independence but did not intervene.

Houston retreated toward the coast to entice Santa Anna away from his supply lines near San Antonio. Meanwhile, his army increased daily as volunteers from the United States came to help. He had almost 800 men under his command when he camped at San Jacinto, opposite Santa Anna's force of about 1,600. Santa Anna failed to post guards, and with shouts of "Remember the Alamo! Remember Goliad!" the Texans attacked on the afternoon of April 21, 1836. Most of Santa Anna's troops were killed, wounded or captured in battle. The Texans suffered nine dead and 30 wounded, including Houston, who was shot in the ankle. Captured the next day, Santa Anna eventually recognized Texas' independence and withdrew south of the Rio Grande after his release.

Annexation and the Mexican War

Texas became an independent nation following the war with Mexico and remained one for the next 10 years. Houston defeated Austin to become the Republic's first president, but a host of problems, principally financial, plagued his and subsequent administrations.

The first problem involved a border dispute. Mexico insisted the Nueces River should be the border between the two countries. Texans disagreed. The debate that followed grew so heated that Mexican soldiers invaded Texas, captured and imprisoned a Texas trading expedition and briefly occupied San Antonio, Goliad and Refugio.

Despite problems with Mexico, the population of Texas continued to increase, climbing about 300 percent by 1836. Most came from the United States to claim free land, and most joined Houston and his political supporters, who wanted the United States to annex the republic. Other Texans argued against the U.S. annexation of Texas, preferring to live in an independent republic. Eventually those favoring annexation won out, and on December

Old Nueces County Courthouse

Tourists approaching Corpus Christi's sparkling bayfront often are distracted by a mammoth, five-story building with a crumbling brick facade and boarded-up windows.

Opened in 1914, the old Nueces County Courthouse is one of the city's oldest structures and also one of the most debated. Since it closed in 1977, the building has stood in decay at the city's main entrance just a few blocks from the bayfront.

Close-up

Some describe it as an eyesore that should be bulldozed. Others say its neo-classical style is a historic monument to justice that deserves preservation.

City officials are continuing to study whether the building is structurally sound. It has avoided the wrecking ball because of its designation as a historic site and the high cost of knocking it down.

Proposals for the building have ranged from a Tejano Music Hall of Fame to a satellite campus of Texas A&M University-Corpus Christi. A city councilman once suggested contacting a Hollywood movie mogul to offer the courthouse for a bombing scene.

The Justice Building Inc., a local nonprofit group, took control of the courthouse in 1992 to help raise private funds to restore the building. Several suggestions have been made, but little progress has occurred.

The Texas Historical Commission named the courthouse to the state's 10 most endangered historical properties and imposed a 40-year restrictive covenant on the building. The covenant, set to expire in 2018, mandates that the historical integrity of the building be preserved.

Designed by San Antonio architect Harvey L. Page, the building opened its doors

— continued on next page

Photo: Ralph Goonan

The old Nueces County Courthouse sits at the entrance to Corpus Christi. Critics say the crumbling building should be torn down; others are working to find the funds to restore the landmark structure.

more than eight decades ago to fanfare and applause. Columns and sculpted figures embellished the building, and the lush landscaping included palm and banana trees, oleanders, hibiscus and violets. Goldfish swam in a pond out front.

Along with courts, the old building housed the county jail on its top two floors. Two dark and secluded "death cells" held prisoners awaiting the ultimate penalty.

The courthouse with the imposing steps leading to its front door survived the 1919 hurricane and Hurricane Celia in 1970. Whether it ultimately survives remains to be seen.

29, 1845, Texas joined the union. Mexico immediately broke diplomatic relations with the United States.

U.S. General (and future president) Zachary Taylor marched to the Rio Grande to enforce it as the southern U.S. border, camping in Corpus Christi. The site, now known as Artesian Park, is in downtown Corpus Christi. Mexico considered Taylor's arrival an act of aggression and sent troops across the Rìo Grande. President James K. Polk accused Mexico of invading U.S. soil, and on May 13, 1846, Congress declared war on Mexico.

Taylor and other U.S. generals made quick work of the Mexican army, capturing several cities and putting an end to the war by taking Mexico City. Mexico begrudgingly acknowledged defeat and on February 2, 1848, signed the Treaty of Guadalupe Hidalgo, establishing peace between the two countries. Under the treaty the Rìo Grande was made the southern boundary of Texas, and Mexico ceded California and New Mexico to the United States. In return, the United States paid $15 million and agreed to settle all legal claims of U.S. citizens against Mexico.

The Birth of Corpus Christi

Corpus Christi profited greatly from the Mexican War because it served as a supply point for Taylor's men. When the war ended, it continued as a supply point, shipping goods for operations in the West. The city had begun as a trading post in 1839 on land which Colonel Henry L. Kinney purchased from the former commandant of Fort Lipantitlan. Although subject to raids by Indians, Texas cattle thieves and Mexican troops who suspected Kinney of

harboring border pirates, Kinney prevailed, and a colony slowly grew up around the post. In 1846 the Texas Legislature authorized the formation of Nueces County and a year later — six years before it incorporated as a city — Corpus Christi became the county seat.

The 1850 Nueces County census reported 689 people living in 151 dwellings. There were no schools or churches. More than half of the residents had been born in Mexico and 53 had been born in Texas. Of the others, 51 were from Germany, 32 were from Ireland, 47 were black slaves and one was a freedman. In 1852 immigration peaked with the founding of Nuecestown west of Corpus Christi by settlers from Scotland, Wales, England, Ireland and Germany. That same year Corpus Christi incorporated, and B.F. Neal was elected mayor.

The town entered a brief growth period, which ended in 1854 when a yellow-fever epidemic hit town. Later that year Kinney left town for unknown reasons, and the leaders who remained turned their attention to improving the city. They formed a school and established Catholic, Methodist, Presbyterian and Episcopal churches. But the city's future depended on gaining access to deep water so that large cargo ships could dock there. The problem lay in the Aransas bar, a long ridge of sand near the surface that prevented heavily laden ships from sailing to Corpus Christi. Two attempts to dredge a pass through the bar failed; the problem persisted for the next 72 years.

The King Ranch and North Bay Development

The King Ranch is one of the largest privately owned ranches in the world, covering 825,000 acres southwest of Corpus Christi and adjoining the city of Kingsville. The North Bay is an area north of Corpus Christi encompassing Aransas County and parts of San Patricio and Nueces counties.

The year 1852 was an eventful one in the Coastal Bend, for it was then that Capt. Richard King started a ranch — the King Ranch — on Santa Gertrudis Creek. King spent most of his early life as a seaman, a job that brought him to the Rìo Grande at the age of 23 to captain one of the river steamboats that supplied Taylor's army. In 1852 he quit his job, bought part of a Spanish land grant and started what would become one of the largest ranches in the world.

The town of Kingsville sprung up around the King Ranch, thanks largely to the efforts of King's widow, Henrietta, who donated a large amount of land to help finance the St. Louis, Brownsville and Mexico Railroad. One provision of her financing was that Kingsville be named the railroad's headquarters. The railroad, the King Ranch and the sinking of water wells in 1899 that provided drinking water helped Kingsville prosper.

The King Ranch continues to play a major role in Kingsville's economic and political circles. The city is also home to a pilot-training facility, Naval Air Station-Kingsville and Texas A&M University-Kingsville.

In the mid-1850s, Englishman R. L. Mercer and his family came to the Port Aransas area to fish and raise cattle. Mercer also set up a small dock and warehouse for servicing visiting ships. Others followed, and a tiny community sprouted. In 1870 a New Yorker had bought San Jose Island a few miles north of Mustang Island, and many who had settled there left to join Mercer's settlement, where they made money fishing and catching sea turtles weighing as much as 500 pounds.

Harsh storms have devastated the town twice, but its proximity to the water and the beaches keeps people coming back. Access to Port Aransas was limited to boats and ferries until 1954 when a highway running the length of Mustang Island linked the town with Corpus Christi. The causeway from the town of Aransas Pass to the ferry landing opened in 1960, and three years later the first condominium opened its doors. Port Aransas is now a popular tourist destination for anglers, beachgoers and watersports enthusiasts.

The city of Aransas Pass, a few miles to the west, got its start in a most unusual way. In 1909 a man named T. B. Wheeler and his partner, Russell Harrison, son of former president Benjamin Harrison, decided to hold a lottery to sell 13,000 acres on Red Fish Bay, including the townsite of Aransas Pass. Buyers were attracted to the lottery because the U.S. government was about to finance the dredging of a port in the area, and because the waterway known as Aransas Pass was the closest outlet to the gulf, everyone assumed it would be chosen over Corpus Christi or Rockport.

Lottery tickets sold for $100 each, and buyers from as far away as Kansas and Nebraska arrived on special trains. It was called a lottery although everyone who bought a ticket received land. One ticket was sold for each of the 6,000 lots, and the only gamble concerned the location of the land each ticketholder would receive. As it turned out, they all wound up losers when the U.S. government chose Corpus Christi.

The town of Rockport came into prominence when the Coleman-Fulton cattle companies contracted with the Morgan Steamship Company of New York to supply at least $1,000 worth of hides, tallow, bones and horns every 10 days. As the cattle industry developed after the Civil War, huge herds were shipped to Rockport to be slaughtered, turning the port into one of the largest in the state. But the city's packing industry died as the great cattle drives to the Midwestern railheads became more common. Although the city suffered, residents soon turned to the water for their jobs. Fishing became the major industry; tourism followed. Throughout the years Rockport and its smaller neighbor, Fulton, have grown together to the point that visitors see them as one community. Both continue to serve as major fishing and resort communities.

The Civil War and Beyond

Texans owned slaves, and most sided with the South on the issue of slavery. The Texas Legislature voted to secede from the Union in 1861, and local residents enthusiastically supported the decision at a local meeting. But

Photo: Rockport-Fulton Area Chamber of Commerce

The Fulton Mansion overlooking Aransas Bay was built in 1874, during the time of cattle barons in South Texas.

with the exception of a few cannonballs fired on the city and an occupation by Union Troops of less than six months, Corpus Christi escaped the Civil War unscathed.

After the war, Corpus Christi became a shipping point for Texas cattle moving to eastern markets, and for crops, including cotton, which was first shipped from Corpus Christi in 1883. In 1874 a channel through Corpus Christi Bay was dredged to a depth of eight feet, deep enough to allow steamships to dock at Corpus Christi. In the latter part of the century, the city formed a fire department and acquired a daily newspaper, a hospital and a water system. In 1909 the Texas Legislature formed the Corpus Christi Independent School District, and a year later, trolley cars replaced horse-drawn cars on Corpus Christi streets.

In 1911 the first causeway was built across Nueces Bay, linking Corpus Christi with the North Bay area. Street lights were installed in

1912, and in the following year, a major natural gas field was discovered across Nueces Bay. Gas, electricity and paved streets made life better in Corpus Christi, and the discovery of another gas field assured there would be enough natural gas to supply residents and industries.

At the turn of the century, the city began to attract tourists with tales of cool breezes and a healthful climate. Piers were built along the bayfront, and pavilions offered bowling, dancing, drinking, dining, fishing, bathing and entertainment. Saloons and motion-picture houses popped up everywhere. Drinking establishments became so abundant that in 1915 the City Council passed an ordinance requiring all saloons on three downtown streets to move to the east side so that ladies could walk the sidewalks without having to see inside them.

Hurricanes took a major toll on the city in 1916 and again in 1919. The 1916 hurricane destroyed the Nueces Bay Causeway, damaged the bayfront and left 20 dead. The 1919 hurricane devastated the city, killing 287 people. For the next few years, the tourist industry suffered because tourist facilities had been destroyed and investors were reluctant to invest money in an area vulnerable to hurricanes. At that point Corpus Christi residents decided on two things: They wanted storm protection and a deep-water port. They wanted the former for protection against future hurricanes, and the latter because a deep-water port would bring prosperity to the region. Corpus Christi residents petitioned the federal government for a 21-mile ship channel.

The federal government eventually agreed, and on January 16, 1925, dredge boats began digging the channel while harbor facilities were built with local and state funds. The Port of Corpus Christi opened on September 14, 1926, and Corpus Christi was on its way to becoming a major center for the oil refining and petrochemical industries.

The Modern Era

The deep-water port and an oil boom quickly ushered Corpus Christi into the modern era. By late 1935 Nueces County had 60 oil wells in two oil fields. Two years later there were 894 wells in 15 fields. The boom attracted people from all over, and the city's population jumped from 27,742 in 1930 to 57,301 in 1940. Farmers and ranchers with new oil wealth built expensive homes in Corpus Christi, and young men left jobless by the Depression came from all over the country to work.

Changes came quickly to Corpus Christi during the modern era. The city's first skyscraper, the 12-story Nixon Building (later renamed the Wilson Building), opened in 1927. City voters approved the sale of bonds to finish the $2.5 million seawall along the bayfront, providing storm protection along the downtown area. The 14-foot-tall, 2-mile project was completed in 1940, 20 years after it began.

In 1929 the League of United Latin American Citizens (LULAC) formed with Ben Garza as chairman and president. The group held its first convention in Corpus Christi. Since its inception almost 90 years ago, LULAC has grown from a Texas organization to a national one, and has done much to advance causes important to the Hispanic community.

City residents voted in 1935 to create Del Mar Junior College, now Del Mar College, and U.S. Highway 77 opened through the King and Kenedy ranches south of Corpus Christi. In 1938 Ada Wilson established the Ada Wilson Crippled Children's Hospital, and a year later workers completed the majestic Corpus Christi Cathedral overlooking downtown and the bay.

In 1938, as World War II approached, the U.S. Navy began looking for a site for an airplane training base. The Navy needed 2,000 acres on a sheltered bay with land that sloped to the water for a seaplane base. A citizens' committee met with the Navy and guaranteed roads, water and housing if the Navy would locate its $44 million base in the city. The Navy dedicated the Naval Air Station in 1941 as the largest naval flight-training center in the world. By 1944 more than 20,000 civilians worked at the base, with another 20,000 employed at satellite fields. The city's population almost doubled between 1940 and 1950, rising from 57,301 to 108,287. In 1945 a 12-foot-deep Intracoastal Canal opened from Galveston to Corpus Christi, allowing trade to move quickly between the two cities.

Two years later the Clara Driscoll Foundation bought land for a free clinic and children's hospital that continues to serve sick children throughout the Coastal Bend. In that same year the Baptist Foundation established the University of Corpus Christi (now Texas A&M University-Corpus Christi) at a former Navy facility on the city's southern end. In 1949 the Intracoastal Canal opened from Corpus Christi to Brownsville, and a year later, the 4-mile-long Padre Island Causeway (later renamed

---

INSIDERS' TIP

Before World War I, water carnivals were held on North Beach (now Corpus Christi Beach) each July 4, drawing as many as 20,000 visitors.

John F. Kennedy Causeway) connected the city with Padre and Mustang islands. Del Mar Junior College became integrated in 1952 after the local NAACP challenged school racial policies. The Corpus Christi school district began integrating three years later following the U.S. Supreme Court ruling that separate but equal schools were unconstitutional.

The 1950s ended with a local recession after the Navy Overhaul and Repair Department at the Naval Air Station closed down in 1959, leaving 3,000 people jobless. In that same year, workers completed the towering Harbor Bridge over the Corpus Christi Ship Channel, putting an end to long drawbridge delays.

The 1960s dawned with the dedication of the Corpus Christi International Airport. A year later, the Army Maintenance Center (now called the Corpus Christi Army Depot) opened in space formerly occupied by the Navy Overhaul and Repair Department. In that same year the city annexed Flour Bluff, a subdivision on the city's southside, and in 1962 President Kennedy authorized the purchase of 80.5 miles of Padre Island for a national seashore. Construction began on Interstate Highway 37 connecting Corpus Christi to San Antonio and also on the Corpus Christi Museum. The museum was the first building in the Bayfront Arts and Science Park, a collection of facilities dedicated to art, theater and science. The Art Museum of South Texas opened there in 1972, and in 1976, the city celebrated the bicentennial with a performance of *1776* in the city's new Harbor Playhouse.

By 1970, the population had doubled again to 204,525. Hurricane Celia lashed the city, causing considerable damage and killing 11. In 1972 the state bought land for Mustang Island State Park, and in 1977 county officials moved from the old courthouse near the bayfront to a new one farther inland. The old courthouse, empty and crumbling, continues to greet visitors as they near the bayfront. For the past 20 years residents have debated whether to demolish the building or try to re-store it. See our Close-up on the old Nueces County Courthouse in this chapter.

The 1980s began with bad news when the H.E.B. Grocery Company, founded in Corpus Christi in 1939, announced it would move its headquarters and 450 employees to San Antonio. Hurricane Allen soaked the Coastal Bend that year, driving an estimated 100,000 people from their homes. Like many other Texas cities, Corpus Christi suffered in the early 1980s when the oil and gas industry on which it depended suddenly faltered. Fortunately for the city the oil refineries that had located along the port continued to operate near top capacity as imported oil flowed in to take advantage of sophisticated new equipment. Other industries built facilities along the port and helped make it the sixth largest in the nation in terms of tonnage.

Concerned about the city's overdependency on oil and gas, city leaders began looking for ways to diversify the economy. Although they had always known Corpus Christi was a nice place to visit, city leaders had never thoroughly explored the tourism market. As a new convention center opened in 1981, city officials began looking for ways to attract more tourists. In the meantime, the area's infrastructure received needed improvements; several new public amenities made the Coastal Bend a better place to live.

One of the most important improvements came in 1981 when workers completed the 140-mile IH-37, linking Corpus Christi with San Antonio, a project that was 22 years in the making. A year later officials dedicated the $112 million Choke Canyon Reservoir northwest of the city, establishing a more reliable source of water to the city while creating recreational opportunities for residents and visitors.

In 1985 the U.S. Navy chose the city of Ingleside across Corpus Christi Bay as the home port for battleship USS *Wisconsin*, and Corpus Christi voters approved a half-cent sales tax to fund a regional bus service. A new $4 million Corpus Christi Public Library opened

INSIDERS' TIP

Corpus Christi's founder, Henry L. Kinney, advertised for colonists in Europe, touting the city as the "Naples on the Gulf."

Photo: Daniel Fielder

Miradores line Corpus Christi's seawall and give visitors glimpses of local history.

in 1986, and in 1988 the twin towers known as One Shoreline Plaza opened on the downtown bayfront. Other improvements included a new six-story City Hall and, at the Bayfront Arts and Science Park, the $2.38 million Watergarden, a dancing water sculpture that serves as the park's centerpiece.

The 1990s

By 1990 the population had grown to 257,453. Tourism, the port and the military continued to be the major legs on which the economy stood. Investors bet that greyhound racing would become a popular attraction and, under a recent state law allowing it, opened the Corpus Christi Greyhound Race Track. In that same year the Texas State Aquarium opened to large crowds with exhibits of fish and other marine life indigenous to the Gulf of Mexico. Coastal Bend military installations were threatened by federal budget cuts, and Navy officials said they doubted Naval Station Ingleside would ever become a homeport for the USS *Wisconsin*. A reprieve came in 1991 when it was announced that several mine-sweeping vessels would be stationed at Ingleside, and in 1992 when the Atlantic Fleet designated Naval Station Ingleside as its mine warfare command headquarters. See our Military chapter for more information.

Several tourist-related attractions came to Corpus Christi in the 1990s, including the decommissioned USS *Lexington* aircraft carrier. The Lexington now serves as a museum on the north side of the city in an area known as Corpus Christi Beach. The Spanish-made replicas of the three ships — the *Niña*, the *Pinta* and the *Santa María* — Columbus used to sail to the New World were purchased by the city from the Spanish government in 1993 and are now a part of the Corpus Christi Museum of Science and History.

The international spotlight hit Corpus Christi on March 31, 1995, when Tejano music singer Selena Quintanilla-Perez was fatally shot at a Corpus Christi hotel by the founder of her fan club. The city built a memorial statue in her honor along the bayfront and renamed the city's auditorium after her. For more information, see our Close-up on Selena in the Attractions chapter.

In 1997 the city began work on the Gateway Project to add a parkway and landscaping to the city's entrance. The first phase created a 6-acre greenbelt from the old Nueces County Courthouse to Shoreline Boulevard, where a new $22 million federal courthouse will be built. But the City Council later abandoned plans to create a bayfront park adjacent to the seawall when citizens protested.

Henry L. Kinney wouldn't recognize the trading post he founded 159 years ago or the Coastal Bend cities that have grown up throughout the years. But many of the qualities that attracted him to the area — warm weather, blue-green water and a laid-back lifestyle — continue to attract people here today.

With its glistening waters, plentiful beaches and year-round warmth, the sun-blessed Coastal Bend has long been a favorite playground for Texans.

Area Overview

In the vast expanse that is the state of Texas, the Coastal Bend perches on the water's edge, curved like the inner chamber of a seashell. With its glistening waters, plentiful beaches and year-round warmth, this sun-blessed region has long been a favorite playground for Texans.

And no wonder. Natural wonders include coastal flats and saltwater marshes, wildlife sanctuaries and parks, epic ranches and a colorful history. Camping, swimming, sailing, beach combing, birding, fishing and hunting are among the myriad recreational activities that await visitors.

To help orient you to this region, let's consider the state as a whole.

Texas has 18 million people, with the humans only slightly outnumbering the state's 15 million cattle. Texas was the 28th state to join the union, and is the only state that was an independent nation (the Republic of Texas) before accepting statehood. The state's flag is red, white and blue, like the U.S. flag. It features a single white star on a solitary blue, vertical stripe — thus earning Texas the nickname "Lone Star State" — and two wide horizontal stripes of red and white. As with the U.S. flag, the red stands for bravery, the white for strength and the blue for loyalty.

Texas is larger than all of New England, New York, Pennsylvania, Ohio and Illinois combined — stretching 801 miles from north to south and 773 miles east to west. The state bird is the mockingbird, the state flower is the bluebonnet, and the state tree is the pecan. Texas is known for ranching, farming and oil and gas industry, as well as fishing, hunting and beaches.

The Coastal Bend is a small, southern loop in the vast area of Texas, along a slight bend in the state's coastline, just a few hours from the Mexican border. The area has a semitropical climate with an average mean temperature of 71 degrees. The infrequent cold weather usually occurs in December and January, but seldom does it freeze. Summers can be hot, with July and August the hottest months of the year — and the temperatures have been known to exceed 100 degrees. However, breezes off the Gulf of Mexico generally keep even the hottest days from being too oppressive (see our Natural World chapter).

It takes about 2½ hours to drive from the north end of the Coastal Bend, beginning at the Aransas National Wildlife Refuge, to the southern tip of our region, ending below Kingsville along U.S. Highway 77.

Texans are known for their warmth, hospitality, ferocious pride and independence. And in the Coastal Bend, residents are also known for their relaxed, no-fuss attitude and their friendliness.

When you drive along the coast, you'll encounter many communities, each varying from one another as much in size as in personality. Some towns are small, with a historical flavor; others are more industrial, developed because of the arrival of a petrochemical plant or the military. Some towns have been here for more than a century, while others are bedroom communities whose residents commute to their jobs in other cities. Some communities depend heavily on the waterfront for their livelihood — either in fishing, shrimping or tourism. Others are largely agricultural communities, dependent on the vagaries of land and weather.

Corpus Christi, with a population of 257,453, is the region's largest city and serves as an economic and industrial hub for the rest of the area. Corpus Christi is also where many of the region's residents go to shop, dine out or take in entertainment. But there's also plenty for tourists to see and do in surrounding communities.

In fact, tourism plays an increasingly large part in the region's economic fortunes. While Texans have always known about the Coastal Bend's vacation charms, the area now draws many out-of-state visitors — lured here by the magnetic combination of salt air and gentle surf, sunshine and nature, fishing or boating and fresh seafood.

Nonetheless, the Texas coast doesn't get nearly the publicity of the East and West coasts, which may be one of its charms. The Third Coast, as it is known, remains relatively undiscovered. The region offers miles of sandy stretches that rarely see human beings but that create a mecca for wildlife, including bird species rarely seen in other parts of the country.

In this chapter, we describe the communities in the Texas Coastal Bend for you, telling you a little about the present and the past of each. To make it easy for you to locate these towns on a map, we've arranged the communities into four categories: the North Bay area, which extends from the Aransas National Wildlife Refuge at the north to Portland at the south; Corpus Christi, the region's largest city, and surrounding communities; Port Aransas to Padre Island, which covers the beachfront; and the Kingsville area, including the mammoth King Ranch and surrounding small towns. Within each category, our descriptions of the towns move from north to south.

North Bay

Austwell

Just eight miles south of Aransas National Wildlife Refuge, Austwell is a small, tight-knit community on Hynes Bay. Founded in the late 1870s, its approximately 190 residents are surrounded by cotton fields and the bay waters. Once bustling with business, the town suffered bad harvests and devastation during the 1919 hurricane. Today, the main recreational activity is fishing for redfish and flounder in Hynes Bay or hunting.

Lamar

Continuing south on Texas Highway 35, you'll arrive at the town of Lamar. Named for Mirabeau B. Lamar, who in 1938 succeeded Sam Houston as president of the Republic of Texas, this community failed to develop into the bustling city that its settlers intended. In 1856, Samuel Colt and his brother, James L. Colt, known for their invention of the Colt revolver, purchased 14,000 acres here and planned a large-scale land promotion that never materialized.

To make matters worse, the city was shelled twice during the Civil War and was hit hard by the 1919 hurricane. In 1915, the post office closed and remained so for 30 years.

Today, the community contains several sites of interest to tourists. There's Goose Island State Park with the ancient live oak known as Big Tree, estimated to be about 2,000 years old. There's also the historic Lamar cemetery, Stella Maris Chapel, Schoenstatt Shrine and the scenic drive along St. Charles Bay. Anglers and birders will find much to their liking here.

Fulton

This tiny coastal town with 812 residents is known for its wind-sculpted live oak trees and its fishing. Founded in 1866 and named for George Ware Fulton Sr., who built a house on Aransas Bay in the 1870s, it sits side-by-side with the larger town of Rockport. In recent decades, Fulton residents have resisted annexation attempts by Rockport but have lost jurisdiction over some of their landmarks, including the Fulton Mansion, named after the town's first prominent citizen and operated today by the Texas Parks and Wildlife Department.

The town is populated mostly by long-

Photo: Rockport-Fulton Area Chamber of Commerce

Rockport-Fulton is home to many retirees, artists, boaters and fishermen — anyone who wants a peaceful, relaxing place to call home.

time residents and a few newcomers. It's less of a tourist destination than neighboring Rockport because it's less well-known. Be sure to drive along lovely Fulton Beach Road, where you can watch shorebirds on the water and marvel at the beautiful trees shaped by the coastal winds.

✓ Rockport

Known as a "sportsman's paradise," this city of 4,800 attracts those interested in fishing, birding or waterfront living. A popular retirement home for many visitors and winter Texans, Rockport is a place where many residents have their own boats. It's also an artists' colony and has a sizeable Vietnamese population.

Founded in the late 1800s, Rockport began as a port for cattle slaughter. Boat building and fishing emerged as important industries in the 1880s, and tourism became increasingly important as anglers came here to fish. The 1919 hurricane demolished many buildings, but the town rebuilt and the shrimping industry became a major enterprise. Today, shrimping and tourism, particularly birding tourism, are Rockport's largest industries.

Visitors come to see shorebirds and native birds as well as the hummingbirds that winter here and the endangered whooping cranes that spend the winter at the nearby Aransas National Wildlife Refuge.

The town has 11 art galleries and studios and is home to an estimated 100 artists. It was named for a rock ledge that underlies Rockport's shore.

✓ Aransas Pass

Aransas Pass calls itself "the shrimping capital of Texas," because its livelihood is based on that small crustacean. It is home to several hundred shrimp trawlers, the largest fleet on the Gulf coast. It's also home to numerous shrimp processing plants and marinas, bait and tackle shops and public boat ramps.

The city is named for the entrance pass to Corpus Christi Bay that separates Mustang and San Jose islands, 6 miles south. Its name, Aransas, has been traced to Spanish explorers who named the city after a shrine in Spain called Nuestra Señora de Aranzazu (Our Lady of Aranzazu).

The city got its start in 1909 with what some believe to be the largest and last land lottery in the United States. Tickets were sold for $100 apiece for 12,000 acres on Red Fish Bay that included the townsite of Aransas Pass. It was a lottery that no one could lose: 6,000 tickets were sold for 6,000 lots, with the only gamble being that you didn't know where your lot would be located. Interest was high in the lottery, because the U.S. government was about to finance the dredging of a port and everyone assumed it would be here, the closest outlet to the Gulf of Mexico.

However, the government chose Corpus Christi as the site for its port, not Aransas Pass — to the great disappointment of those who had bought the land lottery tickets. Nonetheless, the 7,600 current residents are ferociously proud of their community, particularly because Aransas Pass has always been confused with the larger, better-known and nearby town of Port Aransas. But this town shouldn't worry; it has its own distinct personality. Long a favorite with winter Texans, this town often attracts retirees who want to settle in for peaceful coastal living.

Birders, too, are attracted here. The city bird is the brown pelican, and plenty of migrating species come through the area.

Ingleside

Developed as a resort area in the late 1800s, this community's early settlers grew grapes and bottled wines sent worldwide. Today, its main industries are major manufacturing plants such as Reynolds Aluminum, DuPont, OxyChem and Aker Gulf Marine. The military is another mainstay of the town's economic growth. Naval Station Ingleside began with a groundbreaking in 1988, with government officials planning to develop the site as a homeport for battleships. Planners chose Ingleside as the location for the new base because of its quick access to the deep waters of the Gulf of Mexico, the well-protected waters inside the barrier islands, the existence of plenty of land for expansion and the area's potential for growth.

In 1991, military officials changed the base's focus to that of a headquarters for the Navy's mine warfare fleet and equipment. Most of the 25 ships to be ported at Ingleside have already arrived, and the town's population has swelled from 5,696 in the last census to an estimated 8,500. Today, the base is the town's largest employer, with 3,600 employees.

Nonetheless, Ingleside remains a small town, where everyone knows each other and the Dairy Queen is the local gathering spot. And although a number of apartment complexes and new houses have been built, the town still experiences an occasional housing shortage for military newcomers and other residents, some of whom choose to live in neighboring communities or in Corpus Christi, a half-hour's drive away.

Corpus Christi Area

Gregory

Founded as a turnoff point on the railroad line to Corpus Christi, this town claims a population of about 2,500 people. Most of the residents are longtime citizens, retirees, refinery workers and employees of the school district it shares with neighboring Portland. Many of the town's businesses were devastated by Hurricane Celia in August 1970.

The town was named after U.S. Attorney General Thomas Watt Gregory when it was established in 1886.

Portland

Situated on U.S. Highway 181 just 12 miles from Corpus Christi, Portland is a bedroom community of about 13,800. One of the town's passions is high school sports at Gregory-Portland High School, which has established a good reputation for its size.

The town was established by a land development firm from Wichita, Kansas, in 1891. Interest in the area dwindled until 1911, when the Coleman-Fulton Pasture Company constructed a wharf and railroad facilities to handle the emerging cotton business. The community prospered until it was hit by hurricanes in 1916 and 1919, but it rallied and continued to grow. Incorporated in 1949, Portland is known today for strong schools and churches — and it's one of the only local communities in which liquor by the glass is banned.

Corpus Christi

Just two hours from the Mexican border, the Coastal Bend's largest city is imbued with the influence of its southern neighbor — from its name, which means "body of Christ" in Spanish, to its Mexican restaurants and festivals.

The seventh-largest city in Texas, with a population of more than a quarter of a million, Corpus Christi is also South Texas's regional center for banking, retailing, healthcare and business. It's an informal city, with a semitropical lifestyle that includes year-round access to golf, sailing, fishing, tennis and sailboarding.

One of the city's most distinctive features is the seawall that lines the bayfront, starting in the downtown area. The seawall, which has steps that descend into the water, serves as a gathering place for visitors, strollers, joggers, bikers and others. When city officials built the seawall, they also created the wide street known as Shoreline Boulevard at its northern end and as Ocean Drive as it progresses through the more residential section of the city. This lovely, scenic thoroughfare is one of the city's main attractions and has ensured that visitors have an expansive and unfettered view of the sparkling bay waters that have earned the city its nickname, "Sparkling City by the Sea."

Many residents take advantage of the natural amenities by making their homes on the waterfront — such as the showcase mansions that line the city's Ocean Drive — or on Padre Island, where you're likely to see fishing piers and boats in folks' backyards.

The bay was discovered by Spanish explorer Alonso Álvarez de Piñeda (see our History chapter) on the religious feast day of Corpus Christi in 1519, hence its name. The city eventually took on the same name. Three centuries later, colonists set up a frontier trading post near what is now downtown, and a community slowly developed. The city became a shipping point for Texas cattle and crops, but its greatest growth occurred when the U.S. government chose to turn the city into what is still the deepest port on the Texas coast. That, in turn, attracted the petrochemical and other industries, which are on the ship channel west of the city's downtown area.

For decades, the Coastal Bend's main sources of revenue were oil and gas, shipping from its port, agriculture and ranching, and the military bases here. When the oil bust came in the 1980s, this region — like many others in the Lone Star State — had to reassess. Today, while oil and gas remain an important element of industry here, tourism plays an increasingly significant role.

Among attractions here are the Texas State Aquarium, the Lexington Museum on the Bay, Corpus Christi Botanical Gardens and the Columbus ships, copies of the vessels that Christopher Columbus used to discover the New World (see our Attractions chapter). The area also offers a wide variety of activities for those interested in the outdoors, from windsurfing and sailing to hunting and fishing, as well as miles of beaches to explore.

The military presence remains strong (see our Military chapter), with Naval Air Station Corpus Christi and the Corpus Christi Army Depot. The Naval Air Station is where the Navy trains student pilots to fly turboprop aircraft, many of whom then go on to fighter jet training in nearby Kingsville or at another Navy base in Meridian, Mississippi.

The Corpus Christi Army Depot is the largest tenant at the Navy base, and it's one of the world's largest helicopter repair facilities.

Violet

Continuing west on Texas Highway 44 past the airport, you'll soon arrive at the community of Violet. This is a tiny town, with an estimated population of about 160, established in the early 1900s by immigrant farm-

King Ranch Chicken Casserole

One of Texas' most beloved and frequently served casseroles, King Ranch Chicken is a mixture of chicken, cheese, onion, corn tortillas and a chili-based creamy sauce. Baked until hot and fragrant, it is popular in homes as well as in many restaurants.

However, mystery surrounds its origins and its name. The famous 825,000-acre King Ranch, known for its quarter horses and beef cattle, has never raised chicken. And King Ranch officials say that while this casserole is occasionally featured on the menu at the main house, it did not originate in their kitchens.

In fact, the King Ranch's cookbook — available for sale at the ranch headquarters or its saddle shop in Kingsville — doesn't even have a recipe for this dish on the menu. And ranch officials say they've had so many requests, they intend to include a recipe in their next printing.

Here's a recipe, courtesy of the King Ranch, for this Texas dish. You might experiment with your own variations on this recipe. We like to saute the onion with a chopped green pepper before adding it to our casserole. And instead of the avocados as garnish, you might try sprinkling sliced green olives atop the casserole before baking. Enjoy!

King Ranch Chicken Casserole

(Serves 8 to 10)
1 3½- to 4-pound chicken, poached, boned and cut into bite-size pieces
1 large onion, chopped
1 8-ounce package corn tortillas, cut into quarters
1 cup grated cheddar cheese
1 can cream of mushroom soup
1 can cream of chicken soup

— continued on next page

Photo: Vivienne Heines

King Ranch cowboys and volunteers keep pans of scrambled eggs and beans warm before the annual visitor's breakfast.

1 can Ro-Tel tomatoes with peppers
1½ teaspoon chili powder
Sliced avocados for garnish

Preheat oven to 350 degrees.
Dip tortilla pieces in hot chicken broth long enough to soften them. In a 3-quart casserole dish that has been sprayed with cooking oil, place the following layers: the softened tortilla pieces, chicken, onion and cheddar cheese. Alternate layers until all ingredients have been used. In a saucepan, combine and heat the mushroom soup, chicken soup, tomatoes and chili powder. Spoon the sauce over the layered chicken mixture.
Bake for one hour, sprinkle with more cheese and put back into oven until cheese melts. Remove from oven and arrange sliced avocados on top before serving.

ers of German descent. The town's population has gradually decreased as the community has been slowly swallowed up by the widening of the highway. Residents hold an annual Germanfest and Oktoberfest that draw visitors hungry for a taste of culture and history (see our Annual Events and Festivals chapter).

The town also contains the Violet Museum, built in 1910 and listed on state and national historic registers, inside the old St. Anthony's Catholic Church. Check it out to see candelabras, priests' vestments and rosaries that date to the late 1800s. Named after the first storekeeper's wife, Violet Fister, the town is about 12 miles west of Corpus Christi.

Robstown

This farming community sits at the crossroads of two large highways, U.S. Highway 77 and Texas Highway 44 — a stopping point for those headed to the Rio Grande Valley, Corpus Christi, Houston or even Laredo. Established in 1907, it has about 13,000 residents and a high school baseball team, the Robstown Cotton Pickers, that's a source of fierce pride.

Many visitors may know Robstown for a famed barbecue restaurant, Joe Cotten's, which attracts folks from around the state. Celebrity patrons have included Lyndon Johnson, the Dallas Cowboys, Willie Nelson and Robstown's own Olympic boxer, Lefty Barrera. (See our Restaurants chapter.)

Others may know the town as a political hotbed where the city council is constantly sparring and recall elections are commonplace. The area's U.S. representative, the county judge, a county commissioner and a district judge are all from this small, dusty town.

Port Aransas to Padre Island

Port Aransas

Known mostly as the "spring break capital" for thousands of college students, this island town of 2,268 residents has long played host to young vacationers. Its 18 miles of beaches have also long attracted surfers, beachcombers, anglers and artists.

Sitting at the northern tip of Mustang Island, Port Aransas (rhymes with Kansas) is known to locals by the shortened name of "Port A." You can get here over the JFK Causeway from Corpus Christi or by the more scenic free ferry boat, which operates 24 hours a day.

Mustang Island was first called Wild Horse Island because of the wild horses called Mestenos that roamed its sandy shores. The horses were brought here by the Spaniards in the 1800s.

Settled in 1855, the town was first called Tarpon and Ropesville before townsfolk settled on the name Port Aransas. Aransas comes from the Spanish word "aranzazu," which means "a place of thorny bushes." Apparently early explorers had to struggle across the dense brush on the island.

President Franklin Roosevelt fished here for tarpon, and thousands of others have hauled in trophy catches. Deep-sea fishing is big business, and there are lots of fishing tournaments (see our Fishing and Hunting chapter).

The atmosphere here is laid-back, as befitting a beachfront community, and you're likely to see residents dressed in shorts and sandals throughout most of the year. Surfing, not football, is the passion of students at the local high school — in fact, in this state where high school football is practically a religion, Port Aransas High School has no football team and doesn't want one.

Longtime residents include professors and graduate students at the University of Texas Marine Science Institute, a research and education facility. Some of the dwellings here are luxurious waterfront condos, while others are simple houses on pilings to prevent flood damage from a hurricane.

Plan to take the ferry across the Corpus Christi Ship Channel and visit some of the beach shops or seafood restaurants. Expect to wait in line at the ferry during the busiest summer months.

Kingsville Area

Bishop

Positioned along U.S. Highway 77 south of Corpus Christi, this coastal prairie community is named for founder Frances Zion Bishop, an ambitious insurance agent. Established in 1910 as an agricultural town, the community has since added a strong industrial base.

In 1945, Celanese Corporation of America opened a plant in Bishop. Now known as Hoechst-Celanese, it produces chemicals, plastics, polymers and pharmaceuticals. It also

employs 1,100 full-time and 500 contract workers — nearly half the community's 3,337 residents. The plant also provides one of the town's two private swimming pools.

The community has a birding trail and a city park. The city-owned Bishop Airport has a paved, lighted, 3,200-foot runway.

The town's claim to fame is Ronnie Bull, a 1958 graduate of Bishop High School, who played football at Baylor University, then went on to the Chicago Bears. He was named Rookie of the Year in 1963 and played professional ball for about a dozen years.

Driscoll

Surrounded by maize and cotton fields, this community sits on U.S. Highway 77 about 30 miles south of Corpus Christi. Driscoll has about 700 residents, most of them farmers and workers at the Denton Petroleum Company. Those who live here tend to go to nearby Kingsville or to Corpus Christi for entertainment and shopping. Driscoll's claim to fame is native son and tennis champion Steve Denton, a two-time finalist at the Australian Open who was known for his powerful serve. His 139-mph serve still is listed in the *Guinness Book of World Records*. He played on the men's tour for 11 years, ranked No. 2 in doubles and No. 11 in singles in 1982.

Kingsville

Established by the bequest of ranch owner Henrietta King, this city boasts long ties with the state's cowboy heritage. The area was once known as the Wild Horse Desert and now serves as main entrance to the 825,000-acre King Ranch.

The ranch, itself a National Historic Landmark, is recognized as the birthplace of the American ranching industry. Its history is worth telling. When steamboat captain Richard King founded his ranch, he went looking for workers. He rode down to Mexico and into a small village, where he told the assembled residents that he would clothe, feed and house anyone who came back with him. He returned with the entire village, and the people who lived on the King Ranch became known as *kiñenos*, or King's Men. Today, you can find third- and fourth-generation kiñenos still living and working on the ranch.

Kingsville was created because King Ranch officials saw the need for a railroad terminal near the ranch. Today officials celebrate the day the first passenger stepped off the St. Louis, Brownsville and Mexico Railway (July 4, 1904) as the town's birthday. The town incorporated in 1911, and its first businesses were also established by the King Ranch, including a hotel, an ice plant, a waterworks, a cotton gin and a weekly newspaper.

Today, with approximately 26,000 residents, the town has a diverse economy based on manufacturing, ranching, tourism, aircraft maintenance, military and education. Historic mission-style buildings often sit beside newly built retail super centers. The town gained a little national infamy a few years ago when a resident began a campaign to get people to greet each other with the word "Heaven-o" instead of "Hello." He didn't like using the word "hell" so much. Thank heaven, the campaign fizzled.

The city also is home to Texas A&M University-Kingsville, a university that has long been known for producing some of the state's best teachers and engineers.

Yet another major source of income is the military. Kingsville is the proud home of the Navy's advanced jet training base, Naval Air Station Kingsville. This is where student pilots learn to fly fighter jets.

There's a quieter side to Kingsville, including its renovated downtown historic district and its plentiful parks. Birders flock here, particularly to see the green jay (the official city bird), which can be seen from Kingsville through South America.

Ricardo

This community began its life as a flag stop on the railway route from Riviera to Kingsville. In 1908, King Ranch officials laid out a town site christened Ricardo that was complete with a little park surrounding a flowing well. Its original park and well no longer exist, but it has its own school district, churches and cotton gin.

The farmer's co-op is the main industry, but it's also a bedroom community for people who work in Kingsville. The community's estimated population is about 800.

Riviera

This agricultural town is the next stop when you travel south from Kingsville. This community also has its own school district, post office and telephone company, and there is even a small business district with a Dairy Queen restaurant. Although the town is unincorporated, the post office estimates that Riviera has about 600 residents.

Founded in 1907, the town received its name from a German developer who hoped it would equal its namesake on the Mediterranean. However, even the pronunciation didn't last — it's pronounced Ree-VAIR-a. And instead of becoming a watering hole for the wealthy, Riviera became a community too small to incorporate but too strong-willed to disappear. Landowners tried to promote the area as a travel destination, but their plans fell through, and hurricanes wiped out the biggest hotel. Today, Riviera is mostly popular with winter Texans and retirees, who bring their mobile homes here.

The area offers excellent fishing and hunting, as well as a high school baseball team that won three state titles in the past 20 years. The best-known place in town is the King's Inn, a seafood restaurant that numbers patrons from around the globe, some of whom arrive in airplanes or helicopters. Famous guests include Gov. George W. Bush, former Gov. Ann Richards and country-and-western singer George Strait. The restaurant, on Baffin Bay, was established in 1935 as a hamburger stand on the waterfront near the pier. Today, it specializes in excellent fried shrimp, fish, onion rings and salads (see our Restaurants chapter).

Many Insiders like the area's out-of-the-way location and low population. So do the thousands of tourists who visit each year.

Getting Here, Getting Around

The Texas Coastal Bend isn't exactly at the center of the universe. Come to think of it, the Coastal Bend isn't at the center of anything. Many Corpus Christi residents will tell you the city is located at the end of the earth. That's not true. It's actually at the end of Interstate Highway 37, which stops when it gets to Corpus Christi Bay. Because no interstate runs *through* the area, the only people who come here are those who planned to in the first place.

This is not necessarily a bad thing. Many Insiders like the area's out-of-the-way location and sparse population. So do the thousands of tourists who visit each year. And despite the increase in tourism during the past decade, the area remains relatively uncrowded and undeveloped. Tired of crowded beaches and overdeveloped vacation spots? Then you'll love the Coastal Bend, where you can still find secluded beaches and a restaurant or two where you won't have to wait for a table.

Most people will arrive here by car or aircraft. Some will arrive by private boat. Others will fly their private planes to the area. No matter what your form of transportation, you'll find helpful information in this chapter on getting to the area. You'll also find out how to get around once you've arrived. Some things to consider before you arrive:

• The roads that bring you here are generally flat and straight, and the scenery is, well, repetitive. The stretch of road between San Antonio and Corpus Christi should be bottled as a cure for insomnia. You'll travel the entire 140-mile stretch of road without encountering a single city, although you will see several convenience stores and ranch and farmland. On a more positive note, Texans love to drive,

so for the most part you'll find the highways wide and in good condition.

• Don't misinterpret the finger wave. In many parts of the country a single uplifted finger is grounds for a fist fight. Texans rarely get angry enough to make rude gestures to a fellow driver, especially motorists in the Coastal Bend. The finger-wave as it is used here is a single finger (usually the index finger) lifted from the steering wheel in acknowledgment of the passengers in an approaching car. Think of it as a nonverbal way of saying "Howdy." You're most likely to encounter the finger-wave on rural two-lane roads.

• Driving on the shoulders is OK in Texas when you're letting someone pass, provided it's an improved shoulder and isn't posted with signs prohibiting it. Someone crowding your bumper as you speed along the highway? Don't dig in your heels and make them pass in the oncoming traffic lane. Drive friendly, the Texas way, and move over to the shoulder. The motorist (or motorists) behind you will pass you with a friendly wave as their way of saying thanks. It's considered polite to say "you're welcome" with a finger-wave.

• Trucks, trucks and more trucks. If you're from the Northeast or Midwest you'll see more trucks on a trip to Texas than you've seen in your entire life. Watch out for Suburbans, too, dubbed by *Texas Monthly Magazine* as "The National Car of Texas."

• Public transportation is rare in Texas. The only public transportation of note in the Coastal Bend is the bus system based in Corpus Christi, which we discuss in the Getting Around section of this chapter. If you don't have a car, you'll find it hard to get around in the Coastal

Bend. But if you do, you'll find it amazingly easy to navigate the uncrowded roadways.

• All front-seat passengers of cars and light trucks must wear auto safety belts.

• Texas law makes it illegal for drivers to have an open container of alcohol in the cab of an automobile, and Corpus Christi law forbids anyone in the vehicle from having an open container of alcohol.

• Don't Mess With Texas: You can be fined as much as $1,000 for littering.

• The speed limit in Texas is 70 miles per hour on many rural roadways.

Getting Here

Major Roadways

Interstate Highway 37 connects Corpus Christi and San Antonio, a distance of 140 miles. In San Antonio IH-37 connects with Interstate Highway 10 to Houston and West Texas and Interstate Highway 35 to Austin, Dallas and Fort Worth.

In Corpus Christi IH-37 connects the Calallen, Five Points and Tuloso-Midway neighborhoods on the city's northwest side with the rest of the city. U.S. Highway 77 connects Kingsville and Corpus Christi and is the most direct route to and from the Rio Grande Valley on the Mexican border. It stretches as far south as Brownsville and as far north as Dallas, where it joins with IH-35. When traveling to the Rio Grande Valley, expect to stop at the Sarita checkpoint south of Kingsville. The purpose of the checkpoint, operated by the U.S. Border Patrol, is to stem the flow of illegal drugs and immigrants into the United States.

Another route to the border is Texas Highway 44 W. connecting with U.S. Highway 59 to Laredo. U.S. Highway 181 runs north from IH-37 near the Corpus Christi bayfront. It crosses the Harbor Bridge, Corpus Christi Beach and the Nueces Bay Causeway on its way to Portland. After passing through Portland, it veers northwest through several small towns until it reaches San Antonio, but this is not the preferred route to San Antonio. The quickest, most direct route to San Antonio is along IH-37, although, as we mentioned earlier, the scenery leaves much to be desired.

Texas Highway 35 runs from U.S. 181 north of Portland to Aransas Pass and Rockport. There are two Texas 35s: Business 35 runs north from Aransas Pass along the water to Rockport, and the second bypasses Aransas Pass on its way to Rockport.

Texas Highway 361 runs east from Texas 35 to Ingleside, Aransas Pass, Harbor Island and the north ferry landing to Port Aransas. Some maps show Texas 361 continuing from the south ferry landing, through Port Aransas and down Mustang Island to the southern edge of Corpus Christi. Other maps designate the road as Old Park Road 53 beginning at the Port Aransas ferry landing. Park Road 53 runs along most of Mustang Island from Port Aransas to the southern edge of Corpus Christi, where it intersects with Park Road 22. Park Road 22 begins at the southeastern end of Texas Highway 358, known locally as South Padre Island Drive, and continues to the entrance to Padre Island National Seashore.

Texas 358 runs from west of the Crosstown Expressway (Texas 286) to Naval Air Station Corpus Christi on the city's southeast side. The section of Texas 358 west of The Crosstown Expressway is referred to as North Padre Island Drive, while the section to the east is referred to as South Padre Island Drive, or SPID for short. The Crosstown Expressway connects IH-37 with South Padre Island Drive (also known as Texas 358) on a mostly north-to-south basis. The Crosstown Expressway is officially designated as Texas Highway 286, but if you ask for it by that name locals won't know what you're talking about.

Ocean Drive/Shoreline Boulevard runs along the Corpus Christi bayfront from north of Interstate 37 to Naval Air Station Corpus Christi. Shoreline Boulevard starts at the South Texas Institute for the Arts to the north and ends at the Furman Street intersection, where it becomes Ocean Drive.

Some visitors will be perplexed by the letters "F.M." seen on many rural road signs. The F.M. stands for Farm-to-Market, as in

Farm-to-Market Road 3512. A Farm-to-Market road is simply a rural roadway originally constructed to help farmers and ranchers deliver their goods to nearby markets.

Bus Lines

Greyhound Bus Lines
702 N. Chaparral St., Corpus Christi
• **(512) 882-2516, (800) 231-2222**

Greyhound Bus Lines operates several buses per day from Corpus Christi to San Antonio, Houston and other points throughout the state and nation. It also provides bus service to Kingsville. For information in Spanish call (800) 531-5332.

Tickets may be purchased by phone with a credit card, but you must allow seven to 10 days for delivery. To receive tickets more quickly you must buy them at a Greyhound terminal.

Valley Transit Company
702 N. Chaparral St., Corpus Christi
• **(512) 882-2516, (800) 580-4710**
219 North A St., Harlingen
• **(956) 423-4710**

This company connects the Rio Grande Valley to Corpus Christi, San Antonio, Austin, Houston and points in between. Valley Transit buses stop in the Coastal Bend towns of Kingsville, Corpus Christi, Aransas Pass and Rockport. For route and fare information call the above numbers.

Airports

Corpus Christi International Airport
1000 International Dr., Corpus Christi
• **(512) 289-0171**

There's good news and bad news when it comes to flying into Corpus Christi International Airport. The good news is the airport is small and easy to get around in. The bad news? Getting here may mean you'll have to fly on a bumpy, noisy turboprop airplane. Five airlines serve Corpus Christi International Airport, which opened in 1958, but only one uses jets on a full-time basis. Another uses a mixture of jets and turboprops, and the others use turboprops exclusively.

The airport is located south of Texas Highway 44 on the west side of town. You can get there from just about anywhere in town in 15 to 20 minutes. From downtown take Interstate 37 toward San Antonio and head south on Texas 44. From the southside of town, take South Padre Island Drive (Texas 358) past the Crosstown Expressway (Texas 286) and veer to the east on Texas 44. Follow the signs and you won't get lost. The airport terminal runs east-to-west. The entrance is on the northern side of the building. You approach it via a parkway running from Texas 44.

Long-term parking is situated farthest from the terminal; hourly parking is closest. Airport parking lots are open from 5 AM to 1 AM daily. The daily parking fee is 75¢ per hour, with a maximum of $5 per 24 hours; the charge is $5 per day if you lose your ticket. The fee for hourly parking is 75¢ per half-hour, with a maximum of $10 per 24 hours and a $10-per-day charge for lost tickets.

When you arrive you'll probably see all sorts of construction going on. The airport is undergoing a $12 million face-lift to expand and renovate existing facilities. Construction began in 1996 and is scheduled to be completed in late 1999. Planned improvements include a new food court, lounge and baggage claim area; renovations to the front of the building; and new restrooms, signs and carpeting. The improvements are needed to keep local travelers from taking their business elsewhere. In 1996 the airport had just over a million passengers, down 21,682 from the previous year. Airlines often charge a higher fare to fly from Corpus Christi than they do from other cities, because of its remote location, which prompts many travelers to drive to Houston or San Antonio to catch a plane.

The five airlines serving Corpus Christi provide a variety of arrival and departure options:
•American Eagle/American Airlines, (800) 433-7300, offers 10 arrivals and departures each day to and from Dallas-Fort Worth International Airport via turboprop. Passengers board and unload at Gate 16.
•Aspen Mountain Air, (800) 877-3932, has four arrivals and departures Monday through Friday to and from Austin via turboprop. On weekends it offers three arrivals and two departures. Passengers board and unload at Gate 12.

•Continental/Continental Express, (512) 883-3554 or (800) 525-0280, provides 10 arrivals and departures each day to and from Houston Intercontinental Airport via turboprop and jet. Passengers board and unload at Gates 14 and 15.

•Atlantic Southeast Airlines/Delta, (512) 289-6893 or (800) 282-3424, which provides connecting flights to Delta Airlines, offers five arrivals and departures each day to and from Dallas-Fort Worth International Airport via turboprops. Passengers board and unload at Gate 11.

•Southwest Airlines, (800) 435-9792, offers eight arrivals and departures per day to and from Houston's Hobby Airport via jets. Passengers board and unload at Gate 5.

Gates 1-10 are on the east side of the terminal. Southwest's gate is at the far end of that side. The other airlines are in the west side of the terminal. The single baggage claim area is in the middle of the terminal next to the rental car agencies.

Airline ticket counters are just inside the terminal entrance on the west side. Arrivals and departures are listed on the wall behind each airline's counter. Smoking is prohibited in all public areas. Inside the terminal you'll find the usual amenities — restrooms, courtesy phones, gift shop, lounge and snack bar — and Riviera Reds, a seafood market where you can have local seafood packaged to take with you or shipped to an address.

Rental car agencies with facilities at the airport include the following: Avis Rent-A-Car, (512) 289-0073; Budget Rent A Car, (512) 289-0434; Dollar Rent A Car, (512) 289-2886; Hertz Rent A Car, (512) 289-0777; and National Car Rental, (512) 289-0515.

You'll find taxicabs, limousines and shuttles through the doors opposite the baggage-claim carousel and between the rental car booths. You'll generally find several taxis and a limousine waiting to take passengers to their hotels. Cab rates are $1.50 a mile with a minimum fare of $1.50. Flat rates are available for trips from the airport to surrounding communities. The Limousine Company offers rides in a stretch limousine for a flat fee based on zones. For information call The Limousine Company at 814-5466.

Several hotels in the area provide free transportation. They include: Holiday Inn Airport, (512) 289-5100 or (800) 465-4329; Embassy Suites, (512) 853-7899 or (800) 362-2779; Drury Inn Airport, (512) 289-8200 or (800) 325-8300; Best Western Sandy Shores, (512) 883-7456 or (800) 528-1234; Omni Bayfront, (512) 887-1600 or (800) 843-6664; and Ramada Inn Bayfront, (512) 882-8100 or (800) 272-6232.

Military personnel requiring transportation to Naval Station Ingleside may contact their commands by using the following numbers: SIMA, (800) 701-7462; MINRON 1,2,3 and ships afloat, (800) 626-6463; and Naval Station and others, (800) 577-6289. Staff and students reporting to the Mine Warfare Training Center may call (800) 675-6982.

Corpus Christi International Airport is a controlled airport with two runways. One is 7,500 feet long and 150 feet wide; the other is 6,080 feet long and 150 feet wide. Jet fuel and low-lead fuel are available for private pilots. Tie-downs, hangar space, courtesy cars, pilots' lounge and aircraft maintenance are available. For further information call Mercury Air Center at (512) 289-1881 or Signature Flight Support at (512) 289-0585.

Aransas County Airport
Texas Hwy. 35, Rockport
• (512) 790-0141

This uncontrolled airport north of town straddles the Fulton city limits on the west side of Texas 35. The airport, which serves private and Navy airplanes only, has two runways: one 5,600 feet long and 150 feet wide, and the other 4,500 feet long and 150 feet wide. Jet A and 100 low-lead fuel is available.

The airport has a rotating beacon, automatic dusk-to-dawn lighting, lighted wind

---

INSIDERS' TIP

The ferry that carries automobiles to Port Aransas across the Corpus Christi Ship Channel is operated by the state highway department. There is no charge.

Photo: Daniel Fielder

Visitors can travel on the Flagship for fun, panoramic tours of Corpus Christi Bay.

cone, tie-down area, pilots' lounge and rental cars. There are no landing or tie-down fees, and there's a waiting list for hangar space. Pilots should watch out for Navy T-34 traffic and note that these aircraft use UHF frequencies. Student pilots practice touch-and-goes weekdays from 10 AM to 5 PM. The airport's unicom call number is 122.8. A maintenance facility is located at the airport but is often closed.

T.P. McCampbell Airport
F.M. Rd. 3512, north of Ingleside
• (512) 758-9910

This airport owned and operated by San Patricio County is located south of Texas Highway 35, 3 miles west of Aransas Pass and 2 miles north of Ingleside. The airport has a 75-foot-by-5,000-foot runway with a full-length 40-foot taxiway capable of handling aircraft weighing as much as 30,000 pounds. The facility can handle single- and twin-engine aircraft and a limited number of business jets.

Other features include a rotating beacon, lighted wind cone and a lighting system that must be keyed on at 123.0. Jet A and 100 low-lead fuel are available, but there is neither a maintenance facility nor hangar space. The unicom call number is 122.7. A paved tie-down area is available; there are no landing or tie-down fees. Amenities include a pilots' lounge (open from 8 AM to 5 PM), a pay phone and rental cars from nearby Aransas Pass.

Mustang Beach Airport
Piper Blvd. and U.S. Hwy. 361, Port
Aransas • (512) 749-4111

The runway at this uncontrolled airport 2.5 miles south of Port Aransas is 3,500 feet long and 75 feet wide. The facility has automatic dusk-to-dawn lighting and a rotating beacon but no fuel or maintenance facilities. Amenities are limited to a pay phone and a room where pilots can plan their trips. Rental and courtesy cars are not available, but a free shuttle comes by every 50 minutes from 10 AM to 5:30 PM every day. The telephone number for a local taxicab company can be found on the door to the pilots' room. Tie-down fees are $5 a day on the tarmac and $4 a day on grass. Hangar space is not available. The unicom call number is 122.9.

Kleberg County Airport
Texas Hwy. 141, 9 miles west of
Kingsville • (512) 595-8540

The runway at this uncontrolled airport is 5,999 feet long and 75 feet wide. It's equipped with automatic dawn-to-dusk lights as well as slope-indicator and runway-end lights that pilots can turn on with three, five or seven clicks of their microphones. Jet A and 100 low-lead fuel are available. Maintenance and pilots' lessons also are available. Facilities include a pilots' lounge but no courtesy or rental cars, although a rental car can be obtained in Kingsville, 10 to 15 minutes away.

Tie-downs are available, as is some hangar space. There are no landing fees. Hangar space goes for $10 a night for single-engine planes and $25 a night for twin-engine. You pay no tie-down fee if you buy fuel; otherwise, the tie-down fee is $3 a night. The unicom call number is 122.7.

Marinas

Rockport Harbor
Downtown Rockport • (512) 729-6661
From the Intracoastal Waterway head west at Marker 49 and go straight in along the marked channel. Rockport Harbor fronts the downtown area near the Texas Maritime Museum and the Rockport Center for the Arts (see our Attractions and Arts chapters). Restaurants, shops and a grocery store are within walking distance. The marina has docking facilities for 28- to 50-foot vessels for $12 a day without electricity or $15 a day with. Fuel is not available but can be purchased nearby.

Dennis Dreyer Municipal Harbor
North of the south ferry landing, Port Aransas • (512) 749-5429
Boaters arriving from the north should follow the Intracoastal Waterway to Port Aransas, while those coming from the south should follow the Corpus Christi Ship Channel. The city harbor is just north of the south ferry landing and adjacent to Roberts Point Park (see our Parks chapter).

The marina has 20 spaces available for larger boats and six for smaller ones. Slip fees range from $8 to $30 a day, depending on the size of the boat. Showers, restrooms and laundry facilities are available. Fuel, groceries and maintenance are available nearby.

San Patricio County Navigation District Marina
1 mile southwest of Dale Miller Bridge, Aransas Pass • (512) 758-1890
Boaters arriving from the north along the Intracoastal Waterway should sail past Conn Brown Harbor and under the Dale Miller Bridge. Go about a mile, look to your right and you'll see the navigation district marina adjacent to public boat ramps and a public fishing pier. Boaters coming from the south will pass the Aransas Pass Community Park (see our Parks chapter) and a wastewater treatment plant.

Boat slips are available for $18 a day with electricity and water or $15 a day for slips without electricity. Large slips can accommodate boats from 38 to 50 feet long and 15 feet wide. Slips without electricity designed for smaller boats are available for $13 a day. Ice, fuel, bait, tackle and snacks can be purchased nearby. Boat maintenance is available in Aransas Pass.

Corpus Christi Municipal Marina
Corpus Christi Bayfront across from downtown Corpus Christi
• (512) 882-7333
The Corpus Christi Marina is one of the more eye-pleasing sites in the Texas Coastal Bend. White-washed sailboats with colorful rigging cluster along the perimeter of the T-shaped and L-shaped land masses jutting from the Corpus Christi Seawall. You can drive, bike or walk down these man-made peninsulas or fish from the rock jetties forming a semicircle around the marina.

Boaters arriving via the Intracoastal Waterway should head west along the Corpus Christi Ship Channel toward the Harbor Bridge. From there you have two choices: cut across the bay and take the eastern entrance to the marina or continue farther along the ship channel before turning to port and enter via the northern entrance. Deeper draft vessels will prefer the northern entrance.

INSIDERS' TIP

Bus passes can be purchased at the RTA office, Sunrise Mall and many H.E.B. Food Stores.

On the Peoples Street T-Head, to the north, you'll find shrimping boats, a seafood restaurant, paddleboat rentals and tour boats. On the Lawrence Street T-Head, you'll find another seafood restaurant, the Bay Yacht Club, air-conditioned restrooms, showers and laundry facilities, sanitary pumpout and the marina offices. The Cooper's Alley L-Head is home to the Corpus Christi Yacht Club, a bait shop, public boat ramp, yacht sales, a boat repair facility, a sailing school, charter services, boat storage and a fuel station with diesel and gasoline.

More than 500 wet slips are available for pleasure or commercial vessels. The marina staff monitors the Coast Guard VHF Channel 16 and provides 24-hour patrols. Leasing rates are available on a visiting and long-term basis. Rates for visiting vessels are based on the length overall (LOA) of a vessel plus a minimum $2 per night utility fee. Electricity charges in metered slips will be calculated on a kilowatt-hour basis. See the gray box for visiting vessel rates.

Dockage Rates

Wet slips (minimums in parentheses):
Daily, $.50/linear foot +$2 ($17/day)
Weekly, $3/linear foot +$14 ($104/week)
Monthly, $6/linear foot +$60 ($240/month)
Trailer/Boat Storage (no minimums):

Daily	**$5**
Weekly	**$20**
Monthly	**$60**

Long-term slip lease rates are for a minimum of six months. The first and last month's rent is due when the lease is executed. Gate keys and security passes are issued to boat owners; a refundable $12 per key deposit is required on gate and restroom keys.

Floating and fixed piers are available. Monthly lease rates are based on the overall length of a vessel or slip, whichever is greater, plus electrical rates based on a vessel's overall length. Lease rates are $2.81 per linear foot for pleasure crafts and $4.40 per linear foot for commercial crafts.

Monthly electrical rates are charged according to the type and length of boat. For commercial boats, the rates are $7 up to 20 feet, $9.50 from 20.1 to 30 feet, $14.50 from 30.1 to 40 feet and $23 for 40.1 feet and longer. Pleasure crafts pay $3 for up to 20 feet, $5.50 for 20.1 to 30 feet, $10.50 for 30.1 to 40 feet and $19 for 40.1 feet and longer.

Drinking water is available at each slip at no additional charge. Gear boxes rent for $3 to $4 a month, or a personal gear box may be installed with Marina Office approval. A flat rate of $43 a month is the fee for trailered boat storage, limited to boats 26 feet long or shorter. A flat rate of $11 a month for upper racks or $14 a month for lower racks is charged for board boat storage.

The marina offices are open from 8 AM to 5 PM every day.

Getting Around

As we mentioned previously, getting around in the Texas Coastal Bend is fairly easy, unless you're without a car. Roads are generally well cared for, and traffic is light except during rush hour and the Christmas shopping season.

Many downtown and uptown streets are one way, so pay attention to signs. Streets here also are somewhat narrower than in many parts of town, so RV drivers may want to avoid these areas.

Driving is allowed on most area beaches. The speed limit is 15 miles per hour, and Texas motor vehicle laws are enforced. For more information see our Beaches and Watersports chapter.

Public Transportation

The Regional Transportation Authority (RTA) in Corpus Christi operates the only public bus system in the Coastal Bend. "The B," as the system is known, covers about 800 square miles from Port Aransas to far west Nueces County, carrying more than 18,000 people on an average day. The majority of its riders live in Corpus Christi, where the RTA provides 21 regular weekday and Saturday routes and nine Sunday routes. Sunday service covers nine routes connecting the west and north sides with the southside shopping district. It also provides links to the city from Robstown and the Calallen and Flour Bluff neighborhoods.

The B operates a reduced level of service or no service on certain holidays. Hours range from as early as 5 AM to as late as 10:30 PM. Check individual routes for times. Schedules for all routes are available at H.E.B. Food Stores, or you can call the B RideLine at (512) 289-2600 to have one mailed to you. System maps outlining every bus route offered by the RTA also are available.

One of the best services the RTA provides is help in planning a trip. Let's say you need to get from your hotel to the Texas State Aquarium but have no idea which bus or buses to take. Simply call the B RideLine at (512) 289-2600 and they'll tell you how to get there and back.

To ride the B, look for a sign with red, blue and orange stripes and a large B on the top with the words "Bus Stop" below. The system has more than 15,000 bus stops. Buses are white with the same red, blue and orange stripes trailing from the B logo. Route numbers and names appear above buses' windshields. The RTA offers the following tips: Be at your stop at least five minutes before the scheduled departure time; have correct change; stay seated until the bus comes to a complete stop; and exit through the rear door.

Fares on weekdays are 50¢ for adults and 25¢ for seniors and the disabled (with a B I.D. or Medicare card) during peak hours (6 to 9 AM and 3 to 6 PM) and 10¢ during non-peak hours and 25¢ for students (with I.D.). Saturday fares are 25¢ per boarding for adults; children younger than 6 ride free. Fares on Sundays are 50¢ for adults and 25¢ for students, seniors, disabled and those on Medicare. Fares on Park & Ride routes are 75¢ to $1. Park and Ride routes are designed for commuters going to and coming from the Corpus Christi Army Depot and Naval Air Station Corpus Christi. Transfers (good for unlimited transfers for two hours after issue) are free. If you board after 7 PM, your transfer slip will be good for the rest of the night.

Care-B/Paratransit service is public transportation designed for persons whose disabilities prevent them from using regular RTA buses. Care-B is a curb-to-curb service for certified riders. You must call 24 hours in advance to schedule a trip. Care-B services are available Monday through Saturday from 5 AM to 10 PM and Sunday from 11 AM to 7 PM. Fares are 50¢ per boarding.

Don't want to mess with change and transfers? Then try a B Bus Pass for unlimited rides. A weekly pass is $5; monthly passes (also good for Care-B) are $20. Monthly discount passes for a fixed route for disabled, senior citizens and students are $11 with proper I.D. An additional fare is required if used on Care-B. Commuter Cards for 11 rides on appropriate Park & Ride shuttles are $11 and can be purchased from a morning B driver or at the RTA office at 1812 S. Alameda Street, where you also can get an I.D. card. Photo I.D. cards are free to seniors and the disabled. Students pay $3. Replacement I.D. cards are $3 for seniors and the disabled and $5 for students.

During the summer months (late May through early September) the RTA offers a number of services for tourists. These include two free rides: Scenic Trail (No. 73), a bus designed to look like an old-time trolley, takes riders to Corpus Christi's historic sights; and Corpus Christi Beach Shuttle (No. 76) takes you to Corpus Christi Beach and the many attractions there.

For a $1 fare per boarding, Water Taxi (No. 77) ferries passengers from downtown Corpus Christi to Corpus Christi Beach and back via the ship channel.

Tourists will also be interested in the Port Aransas Shuttle (No. 94), a free ride offered daily from 10 AM to 5:30 PM in Port Aransas. It passes many, if not most, of the city's hot spots, including Roberts Point Park, University of Texas Marine Science Institute, Nueces County Park, Horace Caldwell Pier, the post office, Mustang Beach Airport, the public library, city hall, chamber of commerce and the offices of the Port Aransas police, EMS and county constable.

Taxis and Limousines

This is not New York City. You can't just step outside your hotel and hail a cab. Try it and you'll stand there so long that you could get arrested for loitering. The only place you'll find unoccupied cabs is at the Corpus Christi International Airport. Otherwise you have to call for your cab. Rates are $1.50 a mile with a minimum of $1.50 per trip.

Limousine service is available for $75 to $90 an hour depending on the size of the car. Flat rates are charged for trips from the airport to surrounding communities.

Coastal Bend taxicab and limousine services include the following:

In Rockport, Arrow Airport Taxi Service, (512) 729-8294; Doug's Taxi, (512) 729-0025; Limo-Van Services, (512) 790-8294; and Rockport Fulton Taxi, (512) 729-8294.

In Aransas Pass, AAA 790-7900; and City Airport vice, (512) 758-5858.

In Corpus Christi, CC ited, (512) 884-5466; City Ca King's Cab Company, (512) 004-9463; Liberty Taxi Service, (512) 882-7654; Limousines AAA, (512) 882-3922; Pinkie's Taxi, (512) 881-5250; Star Cab Company, (512) 884-9451; The Limousine Company, (512) 814-5466; and Yellow Checker Cab, (512) 884-3211 or (800) 944-4983.

In Port Aransas, American Cab Company, (512) 749-5589; and Island Taxi, Port Aransas, (512) 749-5589 or (800) 874-0025

In Kingsville, Joe's Limousine Service, (512) 592-2644; and Yellow Cab, (512) 592-3311.

The Texas Coastal Bend retains much of its unfettered natural beauty, thanks to measures taken to preserve wildlife for future generations.

The Natural World

The Texas Coastal Bend stretches out along a graceful curve of the Gulf of Mexico, its flora and fauna nurtured by the very remoteness that ironically attracts thousands of visitors each summer. However, despite this annual influx of sun worshipers and nature lovers, the area retains much of its unfettered natural beauty, thanks to measures taken to preserve wildlife for future generations. The area is home to the Aransas National Wildlife Refuge — winter nesting grounds of the endangered whooping crane — and the Padre Island National Seashore. See our Parks chapter for more information on both areas.

The North Bay alone has three major areas where the public can view the local flora and fauna in a mostly natural state: Goose Island State Park north of Rockport, described in our Parks chapter; the Fennessey Ranch, 40 miles northwest of Corpus Christi (see our Attractions chapter); and the Rob and Bessie Welder Wildlife Refuge north of Sinton (see our Attractions chapter). You can even get a close-up view of bottle-nosed dolphins with the Dolphin Connection tours based in Ingleside (see our Attractions chapter).

In Corpus Christi you'll find nature hasn't been forgotten. Hans Suter Park on the city's southside and Blucher Park near downtown are popular birding sites, and Hazel Bazemore Park west of town is a popular site for migratory hawks. The King Ranch has 825,000 acres where both cattle and wildlife thrive, and, like many ranches in the area, offers guided tours of native flora and fauna (see our Attractions chapter).

The Coastal Bend has several sites on the Great Texas Coastal Birding Trail. Each year thousands of people travel to the area in hopes of spotting many of the more than 500 species of native and migratory birds that can be seen here. Birding is such a popular attraction here that we've devoted a separate chapter to it. For information on everything else — weather, plants, animals and insects — read on.

Weather

Whatever lasting impressions of Coastal Bend weather you take with you will depend in large part on when you visit. And although that's true no matter where you visit, it seems especially so when speaking of Coastal Bend weather. Arrive in the winter or spring and you'll leave dreaming of a tropical paradise where the temperature rarely dips to uncomfortable levels and a cool, dry wind soothes your body on even the sunniest of days. But plan your trip for summer or early fall and you'll quickly learn why local residents refer to air-conditioning as "life-support." There's no way to sugarcoat it: It's hot and humid down here between late May or early June until late October or early November. The first cool front that arrives each fall is cause for celebration, allowing residents to venture outdoors again. Don't misunderstand: You can enjoy the outdoors in the early morning and late evening without succumbing to heat stroke, but exercising or even taking a short walk in the middle of the day is masochistic. Thank heaven for the beach, swimming pools and water sprinklers.

The Coastal Bend has an average mean temperature of 71.2 degrees and an annual rainfall of 27.5 inches. That sounds quite pleasant until you consider that the temperature is often well above 71.2 degrees. July and August are the warmest months, with mean temperatures between 85 and 86 degrees and highs in the low to mid 90s. In an average year Corpus Christi has 106 days with temperatures of 90 degrees or above and no days with temperatures of zero or below. January is the coldest month of the year, with a mean temperature of 55.2 degrees. The mercury rarely dips below freezing, and then only for a day or so. It almost never snows, occurring for a few hours every seven or eight years, and the chances of seeing snow where you live or stay is remote. It's not unusual to encounter shorts-and-T-shirt weather even in the dead of winter.

Monthly mean temperatures and average monthly rainfall show the seasonal variations: January 55.2 degrees, 1.60 inches; February 58.0 degrees, 2.02 inches; March, 63.5 degrees, 1.36 inches; April, 71.0 degrees, 1.91 inches; May 76.3 degrees, 3.13 inches; June 81.0 degrees, 2.88 inches; July 85.7 degrees, 1.93 inches; August 85.9 degrees, 2.34 inches; September 81.1 degrees, 4.82 inches; October 72.9 degrees, 2.59 inches; November 65.3 degrees, 1.81 inches; and December 58.4 degrees, 1.68 inches.

Gulf breezes are constant here. Humidity is almost always present, too, making summer and fall temperatures seem even hotter. There's a saying down here that goes: "It's not the heat, it's the humidity." Texans do not consider 95 degrees particularly hot for the middle of a summer day. At that temperature — and with a mild breeze — you should be able to sit in the shade without breaking a sweat. But when the humidity reaches 50 percent or more, you can't walk from your house to your car without feeling like you're walking through a sauna. The heat index chart is to Coastal Bend residents what the wind/chill factor is to Minnesota residents. Combine the temperature with the relative humidity and you come up with a number for how hot it *feels*. For instance, when the temperature is 90 degrees and the relative humidity is 70 percent, it feels like 106 degrees.

Hurricanes

Hurricanes are as much a part of the Texas Coastal Bend as sea gulls and shrimp boats. Its proximity to warm Gulf waters makes the area vulnerable to these great storms, and the region's history is replete with hurricanes that have killed hundreds and caused millions of dollars in damage. Hurricane season begins June 1 and runs through November 30. August and September are the most active months, with the peak coming September 10. September has seen more major hurricanes than all other months combined.

Several major hurricanes have made landfall along the Texas Coastal Bend, and many that have landed elsewhere along the coast have caused major flooding and wind damage here. Atlantic hurricanes are born off the African coast and move toward the United States along east-west trade winds. As they gain strength they grow into tropical depressions, then tropical storms and finally into hurricanes. Atlantic hurricanes occur when storm cells migrate over warm tropical waters. If the water is warm enough it will feed the storm cells, causing them to release heat into the atmosphere and form a tropical depression. As the trade winds blow the system westward, barometric pressure begins to drop in the vortex of the storm and winds begin to rotate counterclockwise around it.

When the wind speed reaches 38 mph, the system becomes a tropical storm, with spiral bands of rain clouds extending for more than 100 miles. When the storm's wind speed reaches 74 mph, it becomes a hurricane. Many turn north and either dissipate in the Atlantic or slam into the Atlantic Coast. Others hit Florida, the Caribbean Islands or Mexico's Yucatán Peninsula. Some move into the Gulf of Mexico, where they often gather strength before making landfall. Tropical storms with winds in excess of 39 mph are given names.

Hurricanes are classified into five categories based on strength:

•Category 1 — Winds of 74 to 95 mph with a storm surge of 4 to 5 feet. Damage is minimal with signs, tree branches and power lines blown down.

•Category 2 — Winds of 96 to 110 mph with a storm surge of 6 to 8 feet. Damage is moderate with larger signs and tree branches blown down.

•Category 3 — Winds of 111 to 130 mph with a storm surge of 9 to 12 feet. Damage is extensive. Minor damage to buildings, and trees are blown down.

•Category 4 — Winds of 131 to 155 mph with a storm surge of 13 to 18 feet. Damage is extreme with almost total destruction of doors and windows.

•Category 5 — Winds of more than 155 mph with a storm surge higher than 18 feet. Damage is catastrophic. Buildings, roofs and structures are destroyed.

Hurricanes have struck the Texas Coastal Bend throughout history. The first recorded hurricane to make landfall here slammed into Padre Island in 1791, flooding it and killing an estimated 50,000 cattle. The cattle were believed to have belonged to José de la Garza Falcon, whose family established Santa Petronila Ranch 15 miles southwest of the Nueces River. There were no human casualties. Another major hurricane struck Corpus Christi on August 18 and 19, 1916, killing 20 people and causing $1.6 million in damage. Winds reached 130 mph, and wind and rising tides destroyed many boats and every pier in the city.

On September 14, 1919, another unnamed hurricane hit south of Corpus Christi, killing nearly 300 residents and causing $20.3 million in damage. Winds reached 110 mph, and water ran 10 feet deep on downtown streets. Nueces Bay, north of Corpus Christi, was littered with bodies. Initial estimates placed the death toll as high as 600, but only 287 bodies were recovered. The Corpus Christi seawall, which extends 2 miles along the bayfront, was built as a result of this hurricane.

In more recent history, hurricane Celia came ashore between Corpus Christi and Aransas Pass on August 3, 1970, killing 11

Photo: Greater Kingsville Economic Development Council

Axis deer are sometimes seen on many Coastal Bend ranches.

and causing $453.7 million in damage. Wind gusts reached 184 mph, damaging 66,000 homes. Almost 4,000 people crowded into shelters around the city. Hurricane Allen was the last hurricane to come ashore in the area. It hit near the King Ranch on August 9 and 10, 1980, before moving north to Corpus Christi. Although winds diminished to 90 mph by the time it arrived, the storm surge that hit Corpus Christi Beach killed two people. Fifteen thousand homes lost power, and 3,000 residents lost telephone service.

A hurricane watch is issued for a coastal area when there is a threat of hurricane conditions within 24 to 36 hours. A warning is issued when the threat of hurricane conditions will exist within 24 hours or less.

•When a hurricane watch is issued, you should take action on a number of fronts. First, listen to NOAA Weather Radio or local radio or TV stations for the latest on storm information.

•Prepare to bring indoors any lawn furniture, decorations, trash cans, hanging plants

INSIDERS' TIP

Be careful where you throw your trash or pour out liquids. Many storm drains empty directly into nearby bays.

Kemp's Ridley Sea Turtles

Watching an endangered species struggle to survive isn't on most vacation itineraries — unless your travel plans take you to the Texas Coastal Bend at the right time of year. Each summer, biologists at the Padre Island National Seashore release endangered Kemp's ridley sea turtle hatchlings into the Gulf of Mexico in an effort to expand their nesting grounds, thereby increasing their chance of survival. The public is usually notified of the releases, giving those who attend the rare opportunity to watch science help one of nature's imperiled creatures.

Virtually the entire Kemp's ridley population now nests on a 14-mile stretch of beach near the village of Rancho Nuevo, Tamaulipas, Mexico. Biologists hope to establish a second nesting site on Padre Island as insurance against an environmental or human catastrophe at the Mexico site. In 1997 fewer than 1,500 females nested near Rancho Nuevo, a decrease from an estimated 40,000 in 1947.

Legislation has slowed the killing of turtles — the total adult turtle population is estimated at around 3,000 — and shrimpers now use devices on their nets to prevent the creatures from becoming entangled and drowning. Recently a bi-national effort to save the species from extinction has begun to show promising results.

The Kemp's Ridley Sea Turtle Restoration and Enhancement Project formed in 1978 to establish a secondary breeding population at Padre Island. Participants include the Instituto Nacional de Pesca of Mexico, U.S. Fish and Wildlife Service, National Marine Fisheries, National Park Service and Texas Parks and Wildlife Department. They chose the national seashore because Kemp's ridleys had been known to nest there and because its remote location would provide some protection to the species.

— continued on next page

Photo: Greater Corpus Christi Business Alliance

Each year endangered Kemp's ridley sea turtle hatchlings are released into the wild at the Padre Island National Seashore. Biologists are trying to establish a second breeding colony on the uninhabited barrier island.

Each summer from 1978 to 1988, biologists collected about 2,000 eggs at Rancho Nuevo and sent them to Padre Island National Seashore. Once they hatched, the tiny turtles were released on the beach and allowed to enter the surf before being recaptured with aquarium dip nets. During those 10 years almost 16,000 recaptured hatchlings were transported to the National Marine Fisheries laboratory in Galveston, Texas, where they were allowed to grow for a year until they were large enough to avoid most predators.

About 13,450 survived and were tagged and released, primarily offshore from Padre Island. Biologists hoped the released females eventually would return to Padre Island to lay their eggs. Beach patrols (including many volunteers) for nesting turtles began in 1986, with a number of nests found. Increasing numbers of Kemp's ridley nests have been found along the Texas coast in the past three years. Four were found in 1995, six in 1996 and nine (containing 970 eggs) in 1997, the most ever recorded in the program's 20 years. The greatest reward came in 1996 when two females that hatched on Padre Island in 1983 and 1986 returned to nest.

National seashore officials collect eggs laid each year to protect them from predators. They place the eggs in boxes of sand and monitor them for 48 to 53 days until they hatch. When the hatchlings are deemed strong enough, they're released on the beach and guided into the surf.

Baby Kemp's ridleys measure 1 to 1½ inches in length and are black on top and bottom. Adult Kemp's' ridleys, which take 10 to 15 years to mature, weigh 80 to 100 pounds and reach lengths of 2½ feet. The age at which Kemp's ridleys mature is unknown, but estimates range from eight to 15 years. When mature they are olive green on top and white on the bottom.

Biologists don't know how sea turtles find their way back to the beaches where they were born. One theory is that they remember the smell or texture of the nesting sand; another theory suggests the Earth's magnetic field guides them.

Efforts to educate the public about the Kemp's ridleys continue. Padre Island visitors often help with reporting turtles, and some get the chance to see them released into the wild. There, scientists hope they will begin their long, perilous journey back from the brink of extinction.

and anything else that can be picked up by the wind.

• Prepare to cover all windows. If shutters have not been installed, use precut plywood. Apply long strips of masking tape to exposed glass to keep it from shattering; draw drapes across windows and doors for protection against flying glass.

• Fill your car's gas tank.

• Check batteries and stock up on canned food, first-aid supplies, drinking water and medications. These are the first items to disappear from store shelves when a hurricane threatens, so don't wait until the last minute to replenish your supply.

• Plan an escape route early. Check with emergency management personnel for low points and flooding history of your route. The best road on which to leave Corpus Christi is Interstate Highway 37.

• Tune to 1440 KEYS/KZFM 95.5 or 620 AM as you leave Corpus Christi, then change to WOAI 1200 AM as you near San Antonio.

• Put irreplaceable documents in waterproof containers and store in the highest possible spot. If you evacuate, take them with you.

Flora

The Coastal Bend is home to a wide variety of plant life, ranging from the scattered, low-lying vegetation found on sand dunes to densely wooded thickets in the North Bay. Plants that grow in the Mustang and Padre islands sand dunes play an important role in slowing dune erosion by providing a buffer against high winds. Plants that thrive here not only are wind resistant but tolerant to shifting sand and salt spray. They survive by spreading their roots over wide areas, retrieving nutrients and water from the sand. Among the more notable plants found here are sea oats grass, fiddleleaf and beach morning glories, cattails, prickly pear, beach evening primrose and sunflowers.

The tall, wispy strands of sea oats grass act as windbreaks, slowing breezes and forcing the wind to release its load of sand onto the dunes. Fiddleleaf and beach morning glories are flowering plants that cling to the dunes and send runners across the surface of the sand. Their brightly colored blooms offer a splash of color to the white sand. The fiddleleaf blooms are pink, funnel-shaped flowers, while beach morning glories are white with yellow-tinted centers. The prickly pear grows on both the dunes and the flats between and behind the dunes. It produces large, colorful flowers of yellow, orange or red, along with a red or purple berry. The beach evening primrose is common throughout the summer, but its yellow blooms appear only between the early evening and the late morning.

Grasslands cover the central, flat part of Mustang and Padre islands behind the dunes, an area known as the barrier flats. Here you'll find a greater variety of grasses than those found on the dunes, including seacoast bluestem, Gulf cordgrass, Indiangrass and windmill grass. Various types of rushes and sedges — grasslike plants that are often confused with grasses — also inhabit the barrier flats. The white-topped umbrella sedge (so named because of the white flower that grows atop its slender stem) and goldenrods also are common.

The Coastal Bend's wooded area will never be confused with America's Great Northwest timber region. The trees that grow here are shorter and less abundant than those found in the Northwest or most other wooded areas. They have adapted to this dry, wind-swept region by hunkering close to the ground and developing a tenacious spirit that refuses to succumb to the elements. Goose Island State Park offers a good example of this with its dense forest of live oaks and mesquites, interspersed with paths of coastal prairie grass.

Drive along Fulton Beach Road in Rockport/Fulton and you'll see live oak trees that have adapted to the elements. Buffeted by constant breezes from Aransas Bay, they lean in the opposite direction, their branches bowing to the wind's superiority.

The live oak tree can grow as high as 65 feet and spread its branches as wide as 70 feet. It is a wide-crowned, evergreen species of oak native to the southeastern United States and northern parts of South America. It has a short trunk and leathery leaves and produces acorns. Its branches often are covered with Spanish moss. Live oaks are widely cultivated as shade trees in coastal regions.

The Corpus Christi landscape and that of other area cities has been changed by the availability of water to irrigate lawns and other plants not native to the area. Here you'll find plants popular in other parts of the country, native plants and exotics such as bougainvillea and towering palm trees. Among the native plants you'll find here and throughout the Coastal Bend is the mesquite, an attractive, shade-producing tree found in many yards. Its light, airy appearance produces dappled shade, allowing lawns to grow right to the tree's base, which makes it an attractive choice for landscaping. It has deep and far-reaching roots, and its numerous crooked limbs grow close to the ground. The mesquite is common in pasture and rangeland, growing in such density that measures have to be taken to control it. It reaches a height of about 30 to 35 feet and produces a yellowish-green flower and a shiny brown legume that is eaten by horses, cattle, goats, white-tailed deer and javelina (a pig-like animal that inhabits the area).

Another popular landscaping fixture here is the century plant, which stands as high as 6 feet tall with several long, thick gray leaves shooting up from the ground and fanning outward. It is also known as the agave or American aloe, a type of plant native to desert regions of the western hemisphere. The end of each leaf is tipped with a sharp spine that can produce painful jabs if you get too close. It lives for 10 to 25 years before flowering once and then dying. Before it flowers, a long stalk grows quickly upward to a height of 40 feet. It has large, thick and fleshy leaves that store large amounts of water.

THE GOOSE ISLAND OAK
(Live oak)
Quercus virginiana Mill.

For centuries these gnarled limbs have stood in their silent vigil of man's passing. Estimated to be in excess of 1000 years old, this mighty oak was already a giant when Cabeza de Vaca and Sieur de la Salle explored the Texas coast during the 1500's and 1600's.

The occasionally used name of "Lamar Oak" probably stems from the small village of Lamar. Established here in 1838 by a group of Irishmen, the village received its name in honor of Mirabeau Lamar, the second president of the Republic of Texas. Later, with the Civil War at hand, the "Big Tree" was witness to the burning of most of Lamar.

In 1966 the Texas Forest Service recognized this weathered veteran as the state champion live oak. As you pass in review before this grand old oak, consider those who have gone before you and those who may follow.

CIRCUMFERENCE	421-3/4 inches
CROWN SPREAD	89 feet
HEIGHT	44 feet

This oak tree at Goose Island State Park is believed to be the oldest tree in the state.

The fruit of the Texas prickly pear cactus, aside from being a favorite javelina meal, may be eaten raw or made into a preserve, and the cactus leaves (nopalitos) may be cooked and served with a peppery dressing when young and tender. During droughts farmers burn off the spines so that hungry cattle can graze on the whole cactus plant. Javelina, white-tailed deer and other species of wildlife eat the leaves and fruit. They serve as both a food source and water reservoir for wild animals.

The pecan tree is the Texas state tree, and although it's more abundant in other parts of the state, you will find it represented here. The pecan is a large tree that grows as tall as 150 feet. The trunk is often large. The tree flowers in the spring and produces fruit (the pecan) in the fall. It is widely cultivated for its fruit, and many forms of wildlife depend on it as a part of their diet.

The Texas palm, which reaches a height of 50 feet, has a large trunk and fan-shaped leaves that form a rounded crown. As the leaves die, they fall toward the trunk, where they cling unless trimmed away. Texas palms, also called Texas palmetto, are often used in residential landscaping in coastal communities.

Visitors who arrive in Texas in the spring may be surprised by the large number of wildflowers they see along roadways. Texas is more than the cactus and sagebrush often depicted in the movies. Almost 400 wildflowers are known to bloom in Texas. Many can be found in the Texas Coastal Bend, including the bluebonnet (the official state flower), phlox, Indian paintbrush, Indian blanket, winecup, evening primrose, spiderwort, flax, brown-eyed Susan, common sunflower, lazy daisy and Queen Ann's lace.

In recent years Texans have taken it upon themselves to promote the planting of wildflowers along public roads. With the help of former First Lady Ladybird Johnson, Texans founded the National Wildflower Research Center in Austin. Wildflowers bloom mostly between February and May, and the display varies depending on environmental conditions during the spring and fall. Many wildflowers reproduce by seed and require freeze-thaw, wet-dry cycles or passage through an animal's digestive system before they can germinate and grow.

Each year, the Texas Department of Transportation, (512) 886-6000, extension 7468, operates a wildflower line telling motorists where to find the best display of wildflowers in a 10-county area. The Texas Wildflower Hotline, (800) 452-9292, provides statewide wildflower information in case you're planning a trip during the spring display.

Fauna

The sea holds the most abundant variety of creatures. Blue crabs, stone crabs, ghost crabs, and ghost shrimp populate the intertidal zone along the beach and oysters, and shrimp live in local waters in large numbers. Redfish, speckled seatrout, flounder and red and black drum attract anglers to the Gulf and bays, where stingrays, nurse sharks, groupers, sea turtles and barracuda also reside. Other fish common to Gulf of Mexico waters include sheepshead, Atlantic spadefish, tarpon, ladyfish, snook, yellowtailed snapper, amberjack, Bermuda chub, sandtiger shark, pork fish, cobia and trigger fish.

Among the animals you can spot in the area are white-tailed deer, javelinas, raccoons, wild turkeys, armadillos, opossums, bobwhite (quail), ducks, geese, squirrels and hundreds of bird species. The back dunes on the barrier islands are home to picket gophers, ground squirrels, lizards, snakes and coyotes, among other creatures. Mustang Island State Park is home to grasshopper mice, rice rats, cotton rats, cottontail rabbits, jackrabbits, skunks, snakes and lizards. Take the Grasslands Nature Trail, south of the entrance to Padre Island National Seashore, and you might be lucky enough to spot a Padre Island kangaroo rat, a tiny long-tailed mammal found only on Padre and Mustang islands. And it's the rare visitor who gets the chance to see a nesting Kemp's ridley sea turtle scramble ashore to lay her eggs in the sand. Efforts have been under way for 20 years to help the endangered species establish a second nesting ground on the island (see the Close-up in this chapter).

You're more likely to catch a glimpse of the unusual-looking javelinas native to the area. The javelina, not to be confused with the feral hogs that also can be found here, is a nocturnal wild pig also known as the collared peccary. These squat little creatures with bristly hair roam in groups of two to 50, feeding on insects, roots, fruit and reptiles. A favorite food is prickly pear cactus, although many have taken to accepting handouts from picnickers at the Aransas National Wildlife Refuge (much to the displeasure of park rangers).

You can often spot bottle-nosed dolphins from Roberts Point Park in Port Aransas or from the ferry that shuttles people and cars across the Corpus Christi Ship Channel. A favorite dolphin pastime is to swim in the bow wave created by huge oil tankers and barges. On rare occasions they have even been spotted inside the breakwater along the Corpus Christi bayfront.

Alligators and western diamondback rattlesnakes inhabit the area. Alligators can be found in wetlands like those at the Aransas National Wildlife Refuge, while rattlesnakes make their homes in dry places such as sand dunes and the South Texas brush country.

Insects

Insects enjoy the warm Coastal Bend weather as much as the people who live and visit here do. Why, the bugs even love it during the dog days of summer. Flies, moths, butterflies, roaches, spiders, crickets and all manner of caterpillars crawl, fly and hop here.

The most pesky insect to inhabit the region is the mosquito, whose bloodsucking propensities can ruin a picnic or camping trip. Mosquitoes can do more than leave a tiny red mark that makes you itch. They can also spread viruses like dengue fever and St. Louis encephalitis, although such occurrences are rare. The best way to deal with mosquitoes is to prevent them from breeding. Remove or empty all containers with stagnant water so that mosquitoes cannot lay their eggs there. Puddles, leaky pipes, potted plants and blocked gutters are common culprits. Insect repellent, bug zappers and citronella candles will deter some mosquitoes, although nothing is 100 percent effective. Visitors to the Aransas National Wildlife Refuge will want to take special precautions. The refuge's marshlike setting makes it a stellar insect breeding ground. Visitors are advised to wear protective clothing such as long pants, long-sleeved shirts, hats and boots.

Fifty to 60 types of mosquitoes live in the Coastal Bend. Some can be found in fresh water, others in salt water. Some live in holes in trees, and others can be found in holes that crabs make at the beach. Mosquitoes can fly 20 miles in search of blood. Their eggs can lie dormant in dry fields for as long as a year, and once covered with water can hatch in 10 minutes. It takes seven to 10 days for the mosquito larva to mature.

Another common pest — and one that may surprise, fascinate and gross you out — is a species of giant roach that lives here. Most people just call them "giant roaches." Others call them "tree roaches." Whatever the name, they are big. Really big. We're talking 2 to 3 inches in length and an inch or so wide. Step on one and you'll hear a loud "snap." They appear in warm weather and disappear when it turns cold. You'll most likely run into them outside, although they do venture indoors through cracks and holes. They're also fairly swift and will skitter to safety before you can say "rolled-up newspaper."

Other insects you may encounter on a trip here include the June bug, so named because it appears around the month of June. These round, dark brown bugs don't stay long or appear in great numbers, but their lack of flying ability makes them genuine pests while they're here. June bugs are horrible pilots, flying helter-skelter and into everything and everyone in their vicinity. And, like many other insects, they seem to congregate near porch lights.

And that loud buzzing noise you hear during spring and summer is produced by cicadas.

The Coastal Bend has experienced remarkable growth in its tourist industry during the past decade, including the addition of several accommodations.

Hotels and Motels

Finding a place to stay in the Texas Coastal Bend shouldn't be difficult, especially if you reserve your room in advance. In our Hotels and Motels chapter you'll find a variety of both types of lodgings divided into our four geographic areas: North Bay area, Corpus Christi, Port Aransas to Padre Island and Kingsville area. Tourists and business travelers alike will find plenty to choose from among our listings.

The Coastal Bend has experienced remarkable growth in its tourist industry during the past decade, including the addition of several accommodations. You'll find many of the major hotel/motel chains represented here, along with a few locally owned establishments. We've tried to offer you choices in a variety of locations, styles and price ranges. Those of you planning to stay for more than a few days, or anyone who prefers to stay in a condominium, will want to turn to our Weekly and Long-Term Rentals chapter. There you'll find information on several condominium complexes that cater to guests needing long-term rentals, along with those who plan stays of as short as a day.

Hotels and motels in the Texas Coastal Bend generally fall into four categories based on their surroundings and the people who visit. In the North Bay, fishing is a huge draw, luring anglers from all over Texas and the nation for some of the best fishing in the state. Accordingly, accommodations in that area sometimes skimp on creature comforts in exchange for accessibility to the water and the fish who live there. Fish-cleaning stations are common in the North Bay area but less so in other areas. This is not to say that the North Bay area is lacking in luxurious accommodations: Homes for rent in Rockport's Key Allegro subdivision rival many found along Corpus Christi's prestigious Ocean Drive, and several leasing agencies rent medium- to high-end condos and homes in the North Bay area.

The Corpus Christi lodging scene caters to both business people and tourists with a healthy mix of accommodations along Corpus Christi Bay as well as the industrial corridors of Interstate Highway 37 and Padre Island Drive. Lodgings here range from the very basic to luxurious, with a good number of medium-priced accommodations available. You'll have to clean your fish elsewhere, but you'll most likely enjoy more amenities here than you would if you stayed in the North Bay motels and cottages.

The Port Aransas to Padre Island section caters to tourists whose main reason for staying in the area is its proximity to the beach. This is a good area for people who want to swim in the Gulf of Mexico, walk on the beach, lounge around the pool and enjoy recreational activities not found in urban lodgings.

Kingsville's motels and lodges generally cater to hunters and anglers. Hunters are drawn to the wide-open spaces to bag deer, quail or dove, while anglers come to hook a redfish or speckled trout.

The least expensive lodgings can be found in Kingsville, but choices there are limited. North Bay area prices are slightly higher, topped by rates in Corpus Christi and Port Aransas to Padre Island. Summer (late May through early September) is the high season for the area, with some accommodations also charging high rates in March,

---

INSIDERS' TIP

No matter where you choose to stay while in the Coastal Bend, the beach is nearby. Several bed and breakfast inn owners provide beach towels and folding beach chairs for guests' use.

when the area is inundated with high school and college students on spring break. You can expect higher rates on weekends, holidays and on dates that coincide with special events. Other seasons are the regular season (roughly September, October, early November, April and part of May) and the winter season (mid-November to the end of March), with winter the least expensive. Winter rates can be less than half of summer rates, with regular season rates somewhere in the middle. Weekends, holidays and special-event dates will generally run you an additional $10 to $30 a night.

The closer you are to the water the more you will pay; and the better your view of the water the higher your rates will be. Discounts are available for active military, seniors, groups and for extended stays. Daily, weekly and monthly rates are available at many places; most, if not all, accommodations in the area are open year round.

The listings are arranged alphabetically in the Corpus Christi section and north to south by city in all other sections.

You can assume that all accommodations have televisions, telephones and maid service unless otherwise mentioned. You can also assume that a lodging accepts major credit cards unless otherwise noted. Pet policies vary. Some accept them, some don't. Some charge a fee. Smoking and nonsmoking rooms are available in most places, as are handicapped-accessible rooms. Check before making reservations.

Price Code

Prices are for high season, double occupancy per night for one-bedroom units or the smallest unit available. Some offer a variety of rooms for two adults and the range in prices is reflected in our listing.

$	$50 or less
$$	$50 to $75
$$$	$75 to $100
$$$$	$100 to $150
$$$$$	$150 or more

North Bay Area

Best Western Inn by The Bay
$$ • 3902 Texas Hwy. 35 N., Fulton
• (512) 729-8351, (800) 235-6076

Nestled among shady live oak trees, this 72-room Best Western offers quiet accommodations just east of Texas Highway 35 and a half mile west of Aransas Bay. It looks more like a quiet apartment complex than a motel. Live oak trees mute traffic noise, and the rooms are divided into two buildings separated by a courtyard with gazebo, benches and picnic tables.

Amenities include a free full breakfast, screened recreation patio, swimming pool, guest laundry, television with HBO, free boat hookups, fish-cleaning station and fax and copy service. Guests can choose from a room with two double beds or one king-size bed. The hotel has facilities for bus tours, banquets, meetings and conferences of fewer than 100 people. The hotel does not have its own restaurant, but eating establishments are close by. The Best Western's Seahorse Recreational Vehicle and Motor Home Park is next door.

Days Inn, Rockport
$$-$$$ • 1212 Laurel St., Rockport
• (512) 729-6379, (800) 329-7466

This three-story motel at the corner of Laurel Street and Texas Highway 35 looks out over the Texas Maritime Museum and the Rockport Marina. Downtown shopping and restaurants and the beautiful Key Allegro neighborhood are a short drive away. The grounds and swimming pool area are beautifully landscaped, and the white stucco exterior gives the hotel a tropical look appropriate to the warm climate.

Rooms come with a surprising number of decorator touches such as ceiling fans, sofas, fireplaces in some rooms and mirrored walls. You can choose a room with two queen-size beds or one king.

Holiday Inn Express
$$ • 901 Texas Hwy. 35 N., Rockport
• (512) 727-0283, (800) 465-4329

This motel opened its doors in the summer of 1997. The 50 rooms have peach walls; hardwood floors and crown molding add elegant touches to the lobby. The motel is across Texas Highway 35 from Rockport Beach Park; the Texas Maritime Museum and Rockport Marina are nearby. Amenities include cable with HBO and a free continental breakfast. Children 19 and younger stay free. Meeting rooms can accommodate as many as 50 people.

Kontiki Beach Resort Motel Suites
$$-$$$ • 2292 N. Fulton Beach Rd., Fulton • (512) 729-4975, (800) 242-3407

You can't get much farther away from civilization and remain in the Rockport/Fulton area than in this three-story, blue-and-white motel. These two-room suites overlooking Aransas Bay are at the end of Fulton Beach Road. Boaters and anglers will love the proximity to Aransas Bay fishing and the canal behind the motel where they can moor their boats for the night.

Amenities include a boat launch, a tennis court, recreation room, 485-foot lighted fishing pier and swimming pool. Each suites comes with a separate bedroom with a king-size bed, a complete kitchen with dishwasher and microwave, living area with sofa sleeper and cable television.

Laguna Reef Hotel
$$$-$$$$ • 1021 Water St., Rockport • (512) 749-1742, (800) 248-1057

The Laguna Reef Hotel offers a great view and a convenient location two blocks south of downtown overlooking Aransas Bay. This modern four-story complex offers one- and two-bedroom suites and hotel guest rooms. All suites come with fully equipped kitchens, queen-size beds and double sofa beds. Two-bedroom suites come in small and large floor plans, and the second bedrooms are furnished with two twin beds. Hotel guest rooms come with one king-size bed, one queen-size bed or_ two double beds. Some rooms are on the bay side, while others overlook the parking lot. Hotel amenities include balconies, cable television, meeting rooms, a swimming pool, a 1,000-foot lighted fishing pier, free continental breakfast, picnic and barbecue area and a putting green.

Sandollar Resort
$-$$ • 918 N. Fulton Beach Rd., Fulton • (512) 729-2381

The Sandollar Resort combines a motel with a 76-space recreational vehicle-park set amid windswept oak trees between Texas Highway 35 and Fulton Beach Road. The RV spaces are on the highway side; the motel faces Fulton Beach Road and Aransas Bay. Motel rooms come in two sizes: The smaller size is a regular motel room with two double beds and a bath; larger rooms come with two double beds and kitchenettes equipped with a small dinettes, refrigerators and stoves. Children 6 and younger stay free.

Outside you'll find two swimming pools, shuffleboard, horseshoes, volleyball court and a fishing pier and marina. Across the street the Sandollar Pavilion serves burgers, steaks and seafood.

Days Inn Suites
$$$-$$$$ • 410 Goodnight Ave., Aransas Pass • (512) 758-7375, (800) 325-2525

The 32-unit Days Inn Suites in Aransas Pass is only a few years old but the rooms are already being remodeled to keep the place looking sharp. The hotels' white walls and red-tile roof echo South Texas' Spanish heritage, and its location in the middle of town along Texas Highway 361 places it close to local attractions. The old-fashioned downtown shopping district is just down the street, and Conn Brown Harbor, where the shrimp boats dock, is a short distance away. Port Aransas, Ingleside and Rockport are within driving distance.

The hotel offers a choice of a single room with two queen-size beds or a suite with a king-size bed and a queen-size sofa sleeper in the living area. Each suite comes with two cable televisions (with HBO and Cinemax), two telephones, a hairdryer, microwave and refrigerator. Other features include a swimming pool, exercise room and conference rooms for as many as 40 people.

Super 8 Motel, Aransas Pass
$$ • 500 E. Goodnight Ave., Aransas Pass • (512) 758-7888, (800) 800-8000

This tan-and-white, 49-room motel near the Days Inn Suites is a recent addition to Aransas

Tarpon Inn

The Tarpon Inn in Port Aransas is as much a lesson in history as it is a place to stay. This 24-room hotel at 200 E. Cotter Avenue is a throwback to an era when anglers came from all over the country to fish for tarpon in the Gulf of Mexico.

The more than 7,000 autographed tarpon scales tacked onto the lobby's walls

testify to the former abundance of this coveted trophy fish, which is now scarce in local waters. For decades anglers left a record of their catch by writing their name, home city, the size of the catch and the date on a 2- to 3-inch tarpon scale that was then attached to the walls.

So prized was the tarpon that celebrities the world over came to Port Aransas, and many stayed at the Tarpon Inn. Movie star Heddy Lamarr stayed there. So did evangelist Aimee Semple McPherson, aviator Douglas "Wrong Way" Corrigan and gourmet Duncan Hines, who was married at the hotel.

During his visit to Port Aransas in May 1937, President Franklin D. Roosevelt opted for his private yacht rather than the Tarpon Inn's small rooms. But a souvenir of his visit can be found on the hotel's back wall, where his framed, autographed tarpon scale is displayed prominently behind protective glass.

— continued on next page

Photo: Greater Corpus Christi Business Alliance

The Tarpon Inn in Port Aransas is listed on the National Register of Historic Places. Its lobby walls are covered with autographed tarpon scales, including one signed by Franklin Delano Roosevelt.

The inn's ties to history have landed it on the National Register of Historic Places and designation as a Texas Landmark. Frank Stephenson, a boat pilot and assistant lighthouse keeper, built the hotel in 1886 from lumber taken from Civil War barracks on nearby San Jose Island.

During the next 100-plus years, the inn endured fire, hurricanes and several changes in ownership. In 1991 Houston-area businesswoman Priscilla Conoley bought it with plans to restore it.

Work included painting the building, installing new wallboard and rebuilding the bathrooms, railings and supports. Conoley had the 200-foot-long porch overlooking Cotter Avenue rebuilt, and refurbished the rooms by ripping up carpeting, refinishing the hardwood floors beneath them and decorating the rooms with area rugs and antiques.

Beulah's Restaurant, behind the Tarpon Inn, is one of the Coastal Bend's finest restaurants, serving international cuisine with an island flair. Take a seat inside or dine on the porch overlooking the Tarpon Inn courtyard.

The Tarpon Inn's rooms are small and lack many amenities found at other lodgings (the rooms have no telephones nor televisions), but you won't find a hotel in the Coastal Bend with more charm — or history — than this 19th-century inn. For more information see our Hotels and Motels chapter.

Pass and still has that new sparkle to it. A small but clean heated swimming pool is on the east side of the motel in front of a covered, lighted picnic area for motel guests. Amenities include two whirlpool suites, guest laundry, free coffee and toast in the morning and cable television with HBO.

The Super 8 is a short walk from Aransas Pass' downtown shopping district and is just around the corner from Conn Brown Harbor. Port Aransas, Ingleside and Rockport are a short drive away.

Days Inn
$$-$$$ • 2025 Texas Hwy. 361, Ingleside • (512) 776-2767

This beige-and-plum, two-story motel is popular among the military and laborers brought in to work on ships stationed at Naval Station Ingleside. Tourists are more common in summer months. Each of its 34 rooms comes with one king- or two queen-sized beds, a microwave oven and a refrigerator. A free continental breakfast is served every morning in the enclosed breakfast area next to the lobby.

Comfort Inn
$$-$$$ • 1703 Texas Hwy. 181 N., Portland • (512) 643-2222

If you don't mind driving a few minutes, this moderately priced hotel on Portland's main thoroughfare may be the place you're looking for. Only 10 minutes from downtown Corpus Christi, this recent apricot-and-seafoam-colored addition to Portland is convenient to both Corpus Christi, Port Aransas and much of the North Bay area.

Each single room comes with one king-size or two queen-size beds, a microwave, refrigerator and cable television. Other amenities include a swimming pool and VCR and movie rentals. A VCR and one movie can be rented for $6.99 a day; a VCR and unlimited movies are available for $9.99 a day. Guests also receive a free continental breakfast.

Corpus Christi

Best Western Sandy Shores
$$$-$$$$ • 3200 Surfside Blvd., Corpus Christi • (512) 883-7456, (800) 528-1234

You won't find a hotel more convenient to Corpus Christi's major tourist attractions than the Best Western Sandy Shores on Corpus Christi Beach. This 250-room hotel is within walking distance of the Texas State Aquarium and the Lexington Museum on the Bay (a decommissioned aircraft carrier). It's also a five-minute drive across the Harbor Bridge to downtown Corpus Christi, the South Texas Institute for the Arts, The Museum of Oriental Cultures, The Corpus Christi Museum of Arts and Sciences and several other attractions (see our Attractions chapter).

Hotel amenities include basketball, shuffleboard, swimming pool, whirlpool, cable television and HBO. All you have to do is step outside the Best Western's doors to see the sun and surf on Corpus Christi Beach or the Corpus Christi skyline to the southeast.

You'll find three restaurants inside the Sandy Shores. Espresso is a coffee shop offering casual meals; The Pantry is a full-service snack bar serving burgers, chicken and other fast food; Calypso, a multilevel restaurant and bar, serves dinner and touts its Monfort corn-fed steaks. More than 6,000 square feet of meeting space is available.

Drury Inn Airport
$$ • 2021 N. Padre Island Dr., Corpus Christi • (512) 289-8200, (800) 325-8300

Chief among the Drury Inn's main selling points is its proximity to the airport, the Port of Corpus Christi, the city's industrial district and Corpus Christi Greyhound Racetrack. Corpus Christi International Airport is a mere five minutes away from this 15-year-old, four-story motel. Amenities include a free continental breakfast served in an area adjacent to the lobby, free evening cocktails and snacks from 5:30 to 7 PM Monday through Thursday, a swimming pool, cable television with HBO and The Disney Channel, free fax service and almost 1,000 square feet of meeting space.

The lobby is cozy and well-lighted thanks to the four-story glass wall on the room's eastern side. Cushy armchairs and sofas abound. Rooms come in several sizes. The single deluxe has a living area with love seat, armchair, microwave, refrigerator and coffee maker. The main drawback? There aren't any eateries within walking distance, but the price keeps business travelers and summer tourists coming back.

Embassy Suites
$$$-$$$$ • 4337 S. Padre Island Dr., Corpus Christi • (512) 853-7899, (800) 362-2779

Embassy Suites has the biggest lobby in the Coastal Bend. Rooms in this three-story hotel open onto the cavernous lobby where you can lounge in a sofa or armchair or have a bite at the hotel snack bar. Keep walking and you'll come across the hotel lounge and, beyond that, the swimming pool. Each two-room suite has a separate living room with a sofa bed, coffee maker, refrigerator, microwave, wet bar, two telephones with voice mail and modem capabilities, two televisions and an iron and full-size ironing board. Each room is furnished with either a king-size bed or two double beds.

Amenities include a free newspaper every weekday morning, a free shuttle to the airport and to anywhere within 5 miles of the hotel, a free continental breakfast, free evening beverages and snacks, indoor heated swimming pool, whirlpool, sauna and exercise facilities. The hotel also has a full-service restaurant, the Oasis Fare.

Holiday Inn Emerald Beach
$$$$ • 1102 S. Shoreline Blvd., Corpus Christi • (512) 883-5731, (800) 465-4329

The Holiday Inn Emerald Beach has two things that no other Shoreline Boulevard hotel can claim: a site right on the water and a beach. This 600-foot public beach is outside its back doors, at the end of the seawall a half-mile south of the city marina. Many of its 368 rooms have bay views; others open onto the indoor recreation area that's outfitted with a swimming pool, sauna, whirlpool, Ping-Pong tables and a children's Playport similar to those found at Discovery Zone or McDonald's restaurants. Other amenities include cable television with Showtime, coffee makers, a fitness center and more than 10,000 square feet of meeting space.

The hotel has a full-service restaurant, a grill serving a breakfast buffet and sandwiches and a bar. Children younger than 12 eat free if dining with an adult.

Holiday Inn Padre Island Drive
$$ • 5549 Leopard St., Corpus Christi • (512) 289-5100, (800) 465-4329

The Holiday Inn Padre Island Drive is only 3 miles from Corpus Christi International Airport and five minutes — via Interstate Highway 37 — from downtown and the bayfront. Its proximity to Padre Island Drive also makes it fairly convenient to Padre and Mustang islands, which on a good traffic day (and in Corpus Christi most days are good traffic days) is only a 20-minute drive.

This 247-room hotel offers free airport transportation 24 hours a day, six two-room suites with oversize whirlpool baths, coffee makers, an indoor heated swimming pool, whirlpool, dry saunas, sun deck, exercise facility, gift shop and 11 meeting rooms for as many as 700 people. An in-house sports bar offers nightly specials and appetizers and the Atrium Cafe serves breakfast, lunch and dinner. There's also a multilevel lounge with a fountain that's decorated with greenery.

Koronado Motel
$$ • 3615 Timon Blvd., Corpus Christi • (512) 883-4411, (800) 883-0424

The Koronado Motel can't match the luxury found in the Coastal Bend's more expensive hotels, but you can tell by the way the place is kept that the owners take pride in their establishment. Located one block from Corpus Christi Beach, the hotel features attractive and well maintained grounds. Rooms come with full-size kitchens, private balconies (some with bay views) and cable television. Outdoor amenities include a swimming pool, grills, volleyball, swings and shuffleboard. Suites are available.

La Quinta Inn South
$$$ • 6225 S. Padre Island Dr., Corpus Christi • (512) 991-5730, (800) 531-5900

La Quinta Inn's rooms have been upgraded in recent years to "Gold Medal" status, which means they're a lot nicer than they used to be and a good value as well. Included in the 129 rooms are crown molding, built-in closets and wood furniture. The bathrooms have been enlarged and decorated with ceramic tile floors, designer vanities, angled mirrors and better lighting. Each room has a work area and dataport phones for visitors needing to use a laptop computer.

The inn is near Corpus Christi's main shopping area. Two malls and several shopping centers are within a few miles. Amenities include a free continental breakfast, first-run movies, video games, messaging and fax service, same-day laundry and dry cleaning, a swimming pool and a meeting room for 25 to 30 people. Children younger than 18 stay free in their parents' room.

Marriott Residence Inn
$$$ • 5229 Blanche Moore St., Corpus Christi • (512) 985-1113, (800)331-3131

Shopaholics will love the location of the Marriott Residence Inn. It sits smack dab in the middle of the Blanche Moore Shopping Center and across the highway from Corpus Christi's two malls. It's a block from the city's main thoroughfare, South Padre Island Drive (SPID), and right behind Barnes and Noble Booksellers, a favorite hangout for those who love books and Italian coffee.

Inside this traditional-style brick building

you'll find a heated indoor swimming pool and spa, exercise room, breakfast area and guest laundry facilities. What you won't find is a restaurant, but that's no problem because several fine restaurants are along SPID. Amenities include a free continental breakfast, HBO, a social hour Monday through Thursday with free food and drinks, fax and copy services and a sports court where you can play basketball, tennis or badminton.

Omni Bayfront Hotel

$$$-$$$$ • 900 N. Shoreline Blvd., Corpus Christi • (512) 887-1600, (800) 843-6664

The Omni Bayfront Hotel may well be the finest hotel in the Coastal Bend. It boasts a good location as well. The hotel, as its name suggests, overlooks Corpus Christi Bay and the seawall where tourists and locals walk, jog and glide along on in-line skates. Its 474 guest rooms, including 28 suites, are nicely furnished and come with bayfront views. The Private Executive Level features deluxe rooms and upgraded amenities.

Amenities for all guests include free airport shuttle, health club, sauna, indoor/outdoor heated swimming pool, more than 30,000 square feet of meeting and banquet space and two restaurants. The Glass Pavilion on the second floor offers casual dining for breakfast, lunch or dinner, while the multilevel Republic of Texas Bar and Grill on the 20th floor features prime beef and seafood and a great view of the bay.

Omni Marina Hotel

$$$$ • 707 N. Shoreline Blvd., Corpus Christi • (512) 882-1700, (800) 843-6664

The Omni Marina is two doors down from the Omni Bayfront and shares something with its sister hotel: Both provide excellent rooms and service at reasonable prices. They're so popular with tourists, one concierge told us, that they don't have to charge more for their rooms. They make up for it with volume. The outside of this high-rise hotel is brown brick

with teal accents on top of the first-floor lobby, lounge and restaurant. Its 346 guest rooms, including 19 suites, come with private balconies and bayfront views. The view from the swimming pool, on the roof above the lobby, is spectacular.

The Corpus Christi Marina is just across the street and the rest of the bayfront stretches out to the north and south. Amenities include a complete health club with dry sauna and whirlpool, indoor/outdoor heated swimming pool, meeting rooms and conference space. The Omni Marina has a lounge and a cafe serving breakfast, lunch and dinner.

Ramada Inn Bayfront

$$$ • 601 N. Water St., Corpus Christi • (512) 882-8100, (800) 272-6232

Call the Ramada Inn Bayfront as soon as you've picked your travel dates and ask for a room facing the bay. This 200-room hotel is one block from the Corpus Christi bayfront with several rooms that face due east toward the rising sun and the ever-changing waters of Corpus Christi Bay. You'll not only be close to the water and popular tourist attractions (the Texas State Aquarium and Lexington Museum on the Bay are just across the Harbor Bridge), you'll also be close to downtown restaurants and shops. Rooms come with a seating area, work desk, coffee maker and cable television with in-room movies.

The Atrium Lounge offers live entertainment, drink specials and free hors d'oeuvres. The Sports Page Bar serves up a sports motif with drinks, and the Palms Restaurant serves American, seafood and homemade soup for breakfast, lunch and dinner.

Amenities include a swimming pool, fax and copy center, gift shop, free airport transportation, car rental, a gourmet coffee bar and an on-site beauty salon. The Ramada Inn Bayfront has about 14,000 square feet of meeting space, including the 10th floor La Vista Room that offers a panoramic view of Corpus Christi Bay.

INSIDERS' TIP

Most places charge a fee, typically $5, for each extra person who stays in the room.

Photo: Daniel Fielder

The Omni Bayfront is the largest hotel on Corpus Christi's Shoreline Drive.

Port Aransas to Mustang Island

Tarpon Inn
$-$$$ • 200 E. Cotter Ave., Port Aransas
• (512) 749-5555, (800) 365-6784

Named for the abundant trophy fish in the nearby Gulf of Mexico, the Tarpon Inn is one of only two accommodations in the Coastal Bend to be listed on the National Register of Historic Places. Built in 1886 by Frank Stephenson, a boat pilot and assistant lighthouse keeper, the Tarpon Inn has survived fire, hurricane and tidal wave to become one of the Coastal Bend's most interesting lodgings.

Many famous people have stayed here in the more than a century since the founding of the Tarpon Inn, near the Port Aransas wharf. Franklin D. Roosevelt, who disdained the inn in favor of his private yacht, left behind an autographed tarpon scale that is now framed and displayed prominently in the motel lobby along with 7,000 others caught by former guests.

The Tarpon Inn offers 24 small guest rooms filled with an eclectic blend of antiques. All rooms open onto a shady porch where you can rock the day away while watching traffic roll by when you're not busy enjoying the ambiance of the town. Rooms do not have telephones. Beulah's, one of the best restaurants in the Coastal Bend, is in back of the Tarpon Inn (see our Restaurants chapter). Eat inside or on the porch overlooking the Tarpon Inn courtyard. The beach is less than a mile away. For more on the Tarpon Inn, see the Close-up in this chapter.

Alister Square Inn
$$$ • 122 S. Alister St., Port Aransas
• (512) 749-3000, (888) 749-3003

If you like your rooms to have that new-motel cachet, you might want to check out the Alister Square Inn on Port Aransas' main drag, also known as Texas 361. Only a mile from the beach (and just about everything else in town), this recent addition to the Port Aransas lodging scene offers space-efficient rooms with queen-size beds, microwaves, refrigerators and cable televisions. Rooms with kitchenettes are available.

Amenities include a swimming pool, voice mail, computer outlet jacks, fax service and a meeting room for as many as 150 people. A free trolley service is available for city and beach travel and for transportation to and from the Island Moorings Airport. The motel's second-story rear balcony is a great place to catch the sunset.

Holiday Inn Sunspree Resort
$$$$-$$$$$ • 15202 Windward Dr., Padre Island • (512) 949-8041, (888) 949-8041

The Holiday Inn is the only full-service hotel directly on the Gulf of Mexico. Step into the lobby and you'll know you're near the Gulf: The walls have been painted with vistas of undersea life (complete with dolphins, sharks and other sea creatures), and marine aquariums encircle the front desk.

Amenities include a fully equipped exercise room including a sauna, an athletic swimming pool equipped for water volleyball and water basketball, an outdoor swimming pool for sun lovers, a hot tub, playgrounds, shuffleboard, bike rental and golf and tennis at the nearby Padre Isles Country Club. Meeting rooms can accommodate as many as 200 people.

Each room comes with a microwave, refrigerator, coffee maker, in-room safe, hair dryer and fax/modem capabilities. The nautical motif is evident here, too, in the starfish that decorate bedspreads and window accents.

Kingsville Area

Days Inn Suites
$$ • 715 S. U.S. Hwy. 77, Bishop
• (512) 584-4444, (800) 329-7466

The Days Inn in Bishop, a few miles north of Kingsville, offers 40 suites on two floors. Located on U.S. Highway 77 (the main thoroughfare through town), this spartan pink-and-blue motel features single rooms, each of which has one king-size bed, or double rooms, each with two queen-size beds. Suites with a separate living area come with refrigerators, microwaves and small desks. Jacuzzi suites also are available. Amenities include a swimming pool, hot tub and free continental breakfast.

Holiday Inn Kingsville

$$ • 3430 U.S. Hwy. 77 S., Kingsville
• (512) 595-5753, (800) 465-4329

You won't forget you're in South Texas if you stay at the Holiday Inn Kingsville. Its red-tile roof and Spanish-mission look invites you to contemplate the strong influence of Mexican culture on the region. Amenities include a swimming pool, lounge and — for those of you driving an 18-wheeler — adjacent convenience store and truck stop.

Each room comes with one king-size bed or two full-size beds. A large meeting room can hold as many as 75 people; a smaller room can accommodate as many as 25. A suite with kitchenette, bar, living area and fireplace also is available.

Best Western Kingsville Inn

$$ • 2402 E. King Ave., Kingsville
• (512) 595-5656, (800) 528-1234

The Best Western's peach walls and teal trim lend a definite tropical flavor to this 50-room motel at the intersection of King Avenue and U.S. Highway 77. You'll also find a few palm trees and brightly colored flowers decorating the grounds of this highly regarded lodging. Each room comes with one king-size bed or two queen-size and cable television with HBO. Amenities include a swimming pool with hot tub and a free continental breakfast.

Quality Inn

$ • 221 U.S. Hwy. 77 S., Kingsville
• (512) 592-5251, (800) 424-4777

This beige-and-forest-green, two-story motel is at the intersection of U.S. Highway 77 and King Avenue, a five-minute drive from downtown Kingsville. The Quality Inn offers newly remodeled rooms, each of which has one king-size bed or two queen-size beds. Some rooms come with microwaves and refrigerators. Other amenities include cable television with HBO, a free continental breakfast and complimentary evening cocktails.

Some bed and breakfasts, especially those in the towns surrounding Corpus Christi, offer special interest features such as birding information or hunting trips. Others simply offer the combination of intimacy and luxury that many travelers have come to expect.

Bed and Breakfast Inns

From a graceful antique-filled guest room to a woodsy primitive cottage, visitors to the Coastal Bend will discover a wide-ranging assortment of bed and breakfast inns.

In this longtime resort region along the Gulf coast, the bed and breakfast inn is a relatively new phenomenon that caters to a select but growing population, according to Pat Hirsbrunner, owner of Sand Dollar Hospitality, a company that handles reservations for more than a dozen of the facilities in the area.

Hirsbrunner's company began handling reservations for bed and breakfasts in 1983, and she has since marveled at the robust health of the local industry. One of the first facilities was Anthony's, which had its start in Corpus Christi and is today doing business in the nearby town of Rockport.

"I'm pleased to say there are more midweek guests than ever before. Business people are discovering the charm of bed and breakfasts," she said.

Today, an estimated 500 to 1,000 Coastal Bend visitors a year choose to stay in local bed and breakfast inns. Some are weekend travelers, while others may be corporate executives who remain in town for months.

During our journeys around the region, we've been charmed by the assortment and beauty of the area's bed and breakfast inns.

Finding these little jewels — each unique and attractive in a distinctive way — is like exploring for hidden treasure. With a good set of directions, you too will be able to discover these gems — tucked behind a grove of oak trees, hidden inside a 100-year-old mansion or ensconced on a restful island cove.

Some bed and breakfasts, especially those in the towns surrounding Corpus Christi, offer special-interest features such as birding information or hunting trips. Others simply offer the combination of intimacy and luxury that many travelers have come to expect from this type of accommodation.

Some inns have a two-night minimum and require a deposit; if you cancel, make sure to do so at least 48 hours in advance to get a refund on your deposit.

Rates at Coastal Bend bed and breakfasts range from $65 to $125 per night. You can expect to see a 12 to 13 percent hotel-motel tax added to the price tag.

In general, most of the bed and breakfast inns listed below do not allow small children or pets. As a rule, then, we'll only make a note if youngsters or pets *are* permitted. However, you should always check with the innkeepers before you make reservations.

Price Code

As elsewhere in this book, we've created a price structure intended to provide a general overview of the cost of staying here. The prices listed are for one night, double occupancy; tax is not included in our price estimate.

$	$75 or less
$$	$76 to $95
$$$	$95 to $125

North Bay

Anthony's by the Sea
$-$$ • 732 Pearl St., Rockport
• (512) 729-6100, (512) 853-1222,
(800) 460-2557

With a tree-shaded front lawn that opens onto a small city park, this longtime bed and breakfast inn has unique and unpretentious charm. Owners Denis Barsness and Anthony Borghi pride themselves on their community involvement, their friendliness and their eclectic furnishings, which include some real finds from local antique dealers, such as ironwork chandeliers (bought for $20 apiece) that hang on the covered patio and an 1848 bedspread (a gift from a guest).

Breakfast is just as varied and accommodating — your choice could include poached eggs on toast, eggs Benedict, or Grand Marnier strawberry French toast.

There are three rooms in the main house, including a honeymoon suite complete with velvet furniture and a wet bar; and two smaller rooms with a shared bath. A guest house across the patio has two double beds, a sleeper sofa and a kitchen. The inn also offers the Spanish room with stone floors, a living suite and old family photos along the wall.

Children and pets are allowed and the owners' resident schnauzer, Miho, keeps an eye on visitors — an estimated 6,500 during the past five years. An outdoor pool, covered patio, and hot tub (as well as an abundance of hummingbirds) are among the outdoor attractions.

Blue Heron Inn
$$-$$$ • 801 Patton St., Rockport
• (512) 729-7526

This 100-year-old yellow-brick house has been a bed and breakfast since 1994, offering guests a view of Aransas Bay and access to Rockport beaches. The Federal-style house was built in 1890 by an Oklahoma developer. It was sold and renovated in the early 1900s, and it withstood the hurricane of 1919 but suffered much damage.

Its antiques, crystal chandeliers and picturesque waterfront views provide gracious accommodations for visitors. The four rooms are decorated in inviting pastel colors. The two upstairs share a bath. Breakfast includes coffee, juice, fresh fruit, a meat or egg dish, muffins and toast.

With its bricked patio and large tree-shaded yard, this inn has been the setting for many weddings and parties. The grounds are well-tended, accented with bougainvillea blooms and palm trees. The inn will happily provide picnic lunches, bicycles, beach towels and information about area daytrips.

Cayman House
$$, no credit cards • 5030 Texas Hwy. 35
N. , Rockport • (512) 790-8884,
(888) 660-BIRD

Billed as "the birder's bed and breakfast," this graceful wooded inn features a main house with two guest rooms, a guest cottage with two full beds, a hummingbird garden and sea kayaks or bicycles for rent.

Owners Donna Knox and Michael Marsden are lifelong birders who moved to the Coastal Bend from the Cayman Islands — hence the name. Their inn is in a wooded corridor that's frequented by migratory birds coming through the area. Eighteen species of warblers were sighted here one October weekend in 1996. In addition, Cayman House is headquarters for Coastal Bend Birders, which offers full- and half-day birding tours of the area. Marsden, a guide himself, provides assistance in locating and identifying rare birds, as well as an extensive collection of field guides, videos and sound recordings. See our Birding chapter for more about Marsden's tours.

---

www.insiders.com
See this and many other **Insiders' Guide®** destinations online — in their entirety.
Visit us today!

INSIDERS' TIP

Even if you're not staying at the historic Chandler House B&B, you may want to stop by for lunch in the tearoom.

Breakfast includes a fresh fruit plate, juices, homemade nut breads, muffins and home-made jams, and a hot entree of an egg dish, waffles or buttermilk pancakes, and a choice of tea or coffee. Complimentary sack lunches are available for those birders heading out for a day in the field.

Chandler House

$$-$$$ • 801 Church St., Rockport
• (512) 729-2285, (512) 853-1222,
(800) 843-1808

Built in 1874, this two-story gray-and-cream house retains much of the authentic flavor of its past. Built of long leaf pine, its walls are unvarnished wood. Lace curtains line the windows, and doilies sit atop the antique furniture.

Owners Mary Burney and Michelle Barnes also operate a tea room out of this home, which serves soup, salad, sandwiches and desserts at lunch.

There are three huge rooms for guests: The Anchorage Room has its own fireplace and a king-size bed, television and private bath. The Leeward and Windward rooms, both of which have two queen-size beds, share a bath. Guests can use the large great room, with fireplace and parlor games, a spacious formal dining room, and outdoor verandas upstairs and downstairs.

Breakfasts include fruit, rolls, biscuits, an egg casserole or a specialty such as apple pancakes, or Belgian waffles.

Cygnet

$, no credit cards • 1450 Weeping Willow St., Rockport • (512) 729-7009, (512) 790-7992, (512) 853-1222, (800) 528-7782

Owners Analisa and Steven Kennedy have created a country-style cottage in a secluded area that's sure to enchant those looking to escape life's stresses. The cottage features American primitive decor and is on 16 acres near Rockport. It features a double bed, a queen-size sleeper sofa, kitchenette and — perhaps most unusual of all — an outdoor hot tub in an old cattle tank.

The Kennedys provision the cottage with fixings for breakfast, including farm-fresh eggs, a loaf of homemade bread, cereal, milk, juice,

Photo: Knolle Farm & Ranch

The Knolle Farm & Ranch Bed, Barn and Breakfast in Sandia gives visitors a charming old-fashioned view of the Coastal Bend.

fresh fruit and whatever else the season inspires them to include.

Hoopes' House

$$$ • 417 N. Broadway St.
• (512) 729-8424, (800) 924-1008

Built in the 1890s, this graceful yellow mansion is listed in the National Register of Historic Places. Its history of serving guests dates back nearly a century as well: Carefully preserved historic documents indicate that Mrs. Jim Hoopes ran a boarding house here as early as 1906. Today, Hoopes' House is one of the more enchanting inns available, with polished hardwood floors, intricately carved fireplaces, and fine art decorations such as Audubon prints, antiques and Oriental rugs.

Breakfast is likely to include fresh fruit, an egg casserole or French toast, or blueberry pancakes.

The main house contains four guest rooms with private baths, each furnished in a different theme and color. A newly added wing has four additional guest houses, including one with handicapped access. The manicured grounds feature seasonal plants such as bright hibiscus flowers around a sparkling swimming pool, hot tub and shady gazebo.

Knolle Farm and Ranch, Bed, Barn and Breakfast
$-$$$ • F.M. Rd. 70, Sandia
• (512) 547-2546, (512) 853-1222,
(800) 528-7782

Many of the city's older residents remember school field trips to this longtime dairy operation among towering oak trees in the Nueces River Valley. The Knolle family has have since swapped Jerseys for Texas beef cattle, and have turned part of their lovely ranch into a unique inn.

Billed as a "bed, barn and breakfast," the Knolles also offer accommodations for guests' horses: eight stalls in the barn, two riding arenas and acres of trails to ride. It costs an extra $25 per night to stable your horse here.

As for the more traditional bed and breakfast services, guests can choose from three rooms with different prices, all furnished in French country style with antiques and down comforters. The main quarters offer accommodations for six to eight, including a king-size bed, four twin beds, a foldout sofa, kitchen and laundry room. A smaller hunting cabin has two twin beds, a foldout sofa, kitchen and bathroom, while the smallest room — called "The Dog House" — has a double bed and private bath.

Nonriders are welcome, too — activities include fishing, canoeing, birding and relaxing. A continental breakfast consisting of pastry, cereal, fresh fruit and beverages is provided. In addition, guests can arrange picnic baskets (at an extra charge); gourmet dinners; private hunting for dove, duck and goose; riding instruction; and participation in a cattle roundup. Children are welcome.

Corpus Christi

Bay Breeze Bed and Breakfast
$-$$ • 201 Louisiana Ave., Corpus Christi • (512) 882-4123, (512) 853-1222, (800) 528-7782

Step into Perry and Frank Tompkins' charming bayside mansion for a touch of yesteryear's elegance. The couple turned their family home into a bed and breakfast after their children went to college and, by doing so, utilized a astonishing wealth of family antiques. Perry Tompkins says her mother never threw anything away and the results are impressive — from her grandmother's crocheted lace tablecloth to her great-grandfather's christening gown and Perry's own handmade wooden dollhouse (a gift from her grandparents).

The two guest rooms in the main house are airy and bright, filled with fresh flowers. There is also "the nook," a neat little cranny separated from the main house, furnished with southwestern accents including a rough-hewn bookcase. But our favorite is the treehouse, a second-story hideaway with a private sun deck, a queen bed, fireplace, shower bath and small kitchen. On the day we visited, hummingbirds were hovering around the bright yellow buds on the rain tree and the view of the bay was spectacular.

Perry serves a formal sit-down breakfast that includes seasonal fresh fruit, juice, coffee, and various entrees from an artichoke omelet to French toast.

Colley House
$, no credit cards • 211 Indiana Ave., Corpus Christi • (512) 887-7514, (512) 853-1222, (800) 528-7782

This lovely older home sits a block from the bayfront and offers old-fashioned charm and easy hospitality. Owners Evelyn and Tom Bookout once ran a bed and breakfast in Newark, New Jersey, and they've turned this home into a quaint and restful paradise.

Two rooms for guests include gleaming hardwood floors, crown molding, floral rugs, antique dressers and old framed black-and-white photographs. The two bedrooms are separated by a charming living area that has double French doors, saltillo tile floors, sofa, television, VCR and refrigerator. It opens onto a shady wooden deck and a peaceful garden — a popular place for guests to breakfast.

Evelyn, who teaches business technology at a local college, and Tom, a retired naval officer, make breakfast a creative culinary experience: Recent offerings have included spinach omelet and banana bread, oatmeal pancakes with Cointreau sauce, or migas (Mexi-

At Padre Island's Fortuna Bay Bed & Breakfast, guests have a
great view of the area's canals.

can-style eggs scrambled with corn chips, onions and more) with cinnamon rolls.

La Maison du Soleil
$, no credit cards • Buckingham Estates, Corpus Christi • (512) 992-0115, (512) 853-1222, (800) 528-7782

The owners of this tasteful, art-filled residence on the city's south side have been hosting visitors for more than three years. The Braswells' love of all things French is clearly visible in many aspects of their elegant home, from its name to the furnishings and menu, which may include homemade French madeleines. A collection of dainty glass statues fills a china cabinet, while French paintings and framed posters hang on the walls. The guest room is painted a romantic pale pink and decorated with antiques, a double bed, a swag of French fabric over the headboard, and bouquets of fresh roses. There is a

swimming pool, access to tennis courts and a wonderfully inviting library for visitors' use.

Breakfast is served in the formal dining room and can include such gourmet delicacies as iced or hot cappuccino, gingerbread pancakes with lemon sauce or individual ham-and-cheese souffles served with raspberry mini-muffins.

Manitou Cottage
$$$, no credit cards • Near Corpus Christi Bayfront, Corpus Christi • (512) 853-1222, (800) 528-7782

This New England-style cottage offers an intimate, cozy retreat that's perfect for honeymooners or couples celebrating their anniversary — and it's just three blocks from the bayfront. It's nestled in a quiet residential neighborhood, behind the main house, and contains a full-size antique brass bed, pine floors and walls, bathroom with shower, television, VCR, microwave, refrigerator and coffee maker. Nifty antiques include an old barber's chair, an old-fashioned wooden telephone and Americana quilt. The fridge is stocked with soft drinks, bottled water and yogurt; guests are given homemade cookies, fresh fruit and wine when they arrive.

The cottage also opens up to a patio with deck chairs and swimming pool. Guests are also offered the use of bicycles for exploring the area. A full hot breakfast is delivered to the door and can include eggs Benedict, blueberry pancakes, homemade biscuits and fresh fruit.

Smith Place
$$ • Lamar Park, Corpus Christi • (512) 853-1222, (800) 528-7782

Two cozy guest cottages are tucked inside the glorious backyard of this home about four blocks from the bayfront in one of the city's loveliest neighborhoods. Cissy and Sid Smith opened their bed and breakfast two years ago, with admirable results. The cottages are small, but comfortable with a television, VCR, telephone, refrigerator, microwave, private bath, toaster and coffeemaker. Cissy treats her guests like valued relatives — she'll bring you lemonade and snacks while you sit poolside; offers use of her huge pool, outdoor deck, spacious yard and even her son's basketball hoop and treehouse; and supplies you with beach towels, coolers and beach chairs.

Breakfast is casual and Cissy says most of her guests prefer to eat by themselves, so she supplies bounteous fruit baskets, bagels and muffins, and she also stocks guests' fridges with soft drinks, yogurt, jams and wine. She clears and washes the breakfast dishes and replaces them in the cabinet, restocking any food items that may be running low.

Children and pets are allowed but she says most of her guests are corporate visitors, who tend to stay for months and end up becoming friends with the Smiths. This place keeps a low profile — it's homey, cozy, warm and very welcoming.

Port Aransas to Padre Island

Harbor View B&B
$$$ • 340 W. Cotter Ave., Port Aransas • (512) 749-4294, (512) 853-1222, (800) 561-8180

This three-story, Mediterranean-style townhouse contains three large bedrooms and two baths as well as a master suite. Located on one of the main streets in Port Aransas, the house is near the Port Aransas ferry landing.

A wooden deck behind the house features potted plants, deck chairs and a pier. Overlooking the Port Aransas Municipal Harbor, guests have easy access to swimming, beachcombing and boat charters. Guests can also moor their own boats but need to make reservations well in advance of arrival.

Owner Marlene Urban serves an elegant breakfast that includes seasonal fresh fruit, juices, blueberry muffins, pancakes or waffles and egg-and-meat casseroles, depending on guests' preferences.

Fortuna Bay B&B
$$$, no credit cards • 15405 Fortuna Bay Dr., Corpus Christi • (512) 387-5666

You can fish for trout from the wooden deck of this condominium-turned-bed and breakfast, take a leisurely swim in the pool or head out for a day at the beach. Owner John Fisher has turned two of the 10 condos on his three-story, red-tile roofed property into bed and breakfast places. Each has a living room with couch and chairs, television, kitchen with all the amenities, bedroom with queen-size bed, large bathroom and a washing machine and dryer (a real plus at the beach!)

INSIDERS' TIP

Walking and jogging are favorite activities for locals and visitors, and a good way to get a better look at the neighborhood while you're staying here. In the summer, take your stroll in the morning or evening to avoid the midday heat.

As an added attraction, John provides guests with an hour-long boat tour of the area that usually includes sightings of pelicans, roseate spoonbills and blue herons. Because John belongs to the nearby country club, guests also have golfing, swimming and tennis privileges.

A continental breakfast is provided in each condo; it includes coffee, juice, fresh grapefruit or cantaloupe, strawberries, bananas, homemade pigs-in-blankets and cinnamon rolls or apple fritters. He even has fishing rods available for guests' use. Children younger than 2 can stay here free, but no teenagers or pets are allowed.

Kingsville Area

B Bar B Ranch
$-$$ • County Rd. 2215, Kingsville
• (512) 296-3331

Originally part of the historic King Ranch, the B Bar B is an old ranch house that has been restored and turned into an inn by owners Patti and Luther Young.

There is a rustic, relaxed atmosphere at this inn, which is nestled beneath a mesquite grove, 8 miles south of Kingsville. Surrounded by a 220-acre working ranch, the B Bar B is a favorite for hunters (for dove, quail, turkey or nilgai, an exotic antelope-like animal) and people needing a weekend getaway. Furnishings are reminiscent of a luxury hunting lodge — a stone fireplace, high ceilings with wooden beams, mounted trophy heads, overstuffed furniture and old West artwork. There are six bedrooms with private baths, two hot tubs, a swimming pool, a gazebo and a picnic area. In addition, the Youngs have a cottage by the pool with four additional beds.

The breakfast menu varies, but usually includes fresh fruit and an entree such as French pancakes, biscuits and gravy with nilgai sausage, or a breakfast taco buffet.

Pets are not allowed indoors, but there are 98 kennels for boarding. There is an additional cost for boarding your dog.

Most long-term rental properties in the Texas Coastal Bend are near the beaches from Port Aransas to Padre Island and in the Rockport/ Fulton area.

Weekly and Long-Term Rentals

If you prefer staying somewhere that more closely resembles a vacation home than a hotel, then the accommodations listed in this chapter are for you. The lodgings listed here — most of which are condominiums — are designed with long-term renters in mind. Most, if not all, come with full kitchens, housewares, washers and dryers and more space than your average hotel room or suite.

Most long-term rental properties in the Texas Coastal Bend are near the beaches from Port Aransas to Padre Island and in the Rockport/Fulton area. This is not to imply that you cannot stay as long as you want at area hotels and motels (you can stay as long as your money holds out), or that brief stays are not allowed at the lodgings mentioned in this chapter. But the accommodations we include here generally deal with people planning to stay more than a couple of nights. You're more likely to run into vacationers or winter Texans in these types of places, whereas business travelers will more likely be found at the establishments listed in our Hotels and Motels chapter.

Many visitors to the Coastal Bend stay a week, several weeks or even months at a time. Summer is the high season (late May through early September), with some accommodations charging high-season rates in March, traditionally colleges' spring break. Other seasons are the regular season (roughly September, October, early November, April and early May)

and the winter season (mid-November to the end of March), with winter the least expensive. Winter rates can be less than half of summer rates, with regular-season rates somewhere in the middle. Expect to pay $10 to $30 more per night on weekends, holidays and dates that coincide with special events.

The closer you are to the water, the more you will pay; and the better your view of the water, the higher your rates will be.

Discounts are available for active military, seniors and groups and for extended stays. Daily, weekly and monthly rates are available at many places, and most, if not all, accommodations are open year round.

Most properties mentioned here require a two-night minimum stay most of the time and three nights during major holidays. Reduced monthly rates are available at some places after the summer season is over.

Maximum occupancy rules are strictly enforced, including those for children of all ages. Vehicles must be registered at the front desk or risk being towed at owners' expense. Many properties require an advanced deposit of one night's rent for all reservations, and some require you to pay the balance due upon check-in. The accommodations listed in this chapter accept major credit cards unless otherwise indicated. Most do not accept personal checks.

You can assume that all accommodations have televisions, telephones and maid service unless otherwise mentioned. Pet policies vary. Some accept them, some don't. Others charge a fee (nonrefundable). Smoking and nonsmoking rooms are available in most places, as are handicapped-accessible rooms. Check before making reservations.

Our listings are divided into our four geographical areas: North Bay, Corpus Christi, Port Aransas to Padre Island and Kingsville. The listings are arranged alphabetically in the Corpus Christi section and north to south by city in all other sections.

Price Code

Prices indicated by the dollar-sign code are for high season, double occupancy per night for one-bedroom units or the smallest unit available. Some places offer a variety of rooms for two adults, and the range in prices is reflected in our listing.

$	$50 or less
$$	$50 to $75
$$$	$75 to $100
$$$$	$100 to $150
$$$$$	$150 or more

North Bay Area

Bayfront Cottages
$ • 309 Fulton Beach Rd., Fulton
• (512) 729-6693

These small, salmon-colored cottages next to the fully restored 19th-century Fulton Mansion run west from Aransas Bay on 2 acres of well-kept grounds. Each one- and two-room unit comes with a kitchenette, and most come with queen-size beds. The waterfront unit has a king-size bed and most two-room units come with sofa sleepers in the living room.

Amenities include a boat launch and docking facilities for vessels as long as 25 feet, cable television, a lighted 660-foot fishing pier, swimming pool, RV hookups, guest laundry, shuffleboard and banquet facilities.

Calm Harbor Rentals
$$$$ • 3805 Texas Hwy. 35, Rockport
• (512) 729-1367

Calm Harbor Rentals handles medium-priced homes and condominiums on canals mostly in areas south of Rockport. The company handles both medium- and long-term rentals for properties in City By The Sea, Bahia Bay and Palm Harbor. A minimum two-night stay is required.

Key Allegro Rentals
$$$$-$$$$$ • 1798 Bayshore Dr., Rockport • (512) 729-2333, (800) 348-1627

Key Allegro Rentals handles more expensive rentals primarily in waterfront areas. Most locations are either right on the water or have a view of it. Its rentals are concentrated in Key Allegro and the Rockport Country Club, with some in Copano Ridge, Lamar and City By The Sea. Key Allegro requires a two-night minimum stay.

Security Real Estate Rentals
$$$$ • 1329 Broadway, Rockport
• (512) 729-2256, (800) 221-5028

Security Real Estate handles mostly short-term condo rentals in the Rockport/Fulton area. It manages more than 100 properties in the medium price range. A minimum two-night stay is required.

Sun Harbour
$$ • 1141 N. Fulton Beach Rd., Fulton
• (512) 729-2073

These 13 small cottages on Fulton Beach Road lie nestled between twisting live oak trees and towering palms on a hill running west from Aransas Bay. Cottages are laid out on either side of a driveway divided by a small greenbelt. Hammocks hang from the many trees that dot the landscape. Amenities include laundry room, swimming pool, hot tub, 440-foot lighted pier, barbecue area, picnic tables and bait stand.

One-bedroom and studio cottages also are available. All cottages come with fully equipped kitchens. A two-bedroom cottage overlooking the bayfront has a screened-in porch and large private deck. A two-story townhouse comes with one full bath, two half-baths and a balcony overlooking the swimming pool and bay.

Corpus Christi

Christy Estates Executive Suites and Apartments
$$$-$$$$ • 3942 Holly Rd., Corpus Christi • (512) 854-1091, (800) 678-4836

The executive suites at Christy Estates just might make staying several miles from the bay worth it. These 16 one- or two-bedroom suites, which the company refers to as mini-spas, feature freshwater, European-style, individually controlled Whirlijet Spas. Apartments come with newly redecorated living rooms, dining rooms and full kitchens with new appliances (refrigerator, oven, stove, microwave and dishwasher).

Christy Estates Suites provides maid service, housewares and satellite television with The Movie Channel. Outdoors you'll find two swimming pools and an Italian-tile in-ground hot tub.

Villa Del Sol
$$$$ • 3938 Surfside Blvd., Corpus Christi • (512) 883-9748, (800) 242-3291

You won't find a better view than the one from a room facing southeast in this Corpus Christi Beach condominium project. Step out on the balcony and take in the view of Corpus Christi Bay and the Lexington Museum on the Bay set amid the backdrop of downtown Corpus Christi and the bayfront. If that's not pleasing enough to the eye, check out the villa's award-winning gardens replete with red and orange oleander and bougainvillea, palm trees, pastel lilies and purple and pink petunias.

One-bedroom condominiums come with a small kitchen, stereo, in-room movies and a full bath. Some come with a queen-size bed, a sofa sleeper and two bunks in the hallway that children find irresistible. Other amenities include laundry facilities, two swimming pools, three hot tub/spas, barbecue pits, meeting rooms and an adjacent playground.

Port Aransas to Mustang Island

The Dunes
$$$$ • 1000 Lantana St., Port Aransas • (512) 749-5155, (800) 288-3863

At The Dunes condominiums you get the best of both worlds: a first-class condominium right on the beach and proximity to Port Aransas shops and restaurants. The Dunes is one of the few properties that isn't separated from the beach by sand dunes. The beach comes right up to the back door. It's also positioned in such a way that many guests have views of the beach, the Gulf of Mexico and sunsets behind the Corpus Christi skyline.

The Dunes offers 85 furnished one-, two-, and three-bedroom suites with balconies measuring more than 200 square feet. Amenities include a fitness center with weight equipment, power treadmills and exercise bikes, a heated, heart-shaped swimming pool, and a spa ringed with tropical flora, tennis courts and a lighted, concrete fishing pie

Sand & Surf Condos
$$-$$$ • 1418 S. 11th St., Port Aransas • (512) 749-6001

This may be the only vacation spot that brags about what it doesn't have. It doesn't have a swimming pool or tennis courts or a Jacuzzi or boccie ball courts. What it does have are 20 one-bedroom units a short walk from the water. Each unit has a separate living room area, fully equipped kitchen. Some come with two televisions and a washer and dryer. Daily and weekly rentals are on the second floor and have a beach view.

Sea Sands Condominiums
$$ • 1421 S. 11th St., Port Aransas • (512) 749-6246

The Sea Sands Condominiums are less than a block from the Gulf of Mexico in Port Aransas proper. The buildings are white brick

---

INSIDERS' TIP

Many lodgings require a two- or three-night stay, especially on weekends and holidays.

with a red-tile roofs, and the layout resembles an apartment complex's. Efficiency, one-, two- and three-bedroom units are available. A swimming pool is on the complex.

Sandcastle Fine Luxury Resort Condominium

$$$$-$$$$$ • 800 Sandcastle Dr., Port Aransas • (512) 749-6201, (800) 727-6201

The name isn't a marketing gimmick. This place is nice — very nice. Begin with the fact that each of its 180 rooms overlooks the Gulf of Mexico, add an eye-pleasing and unusually shaped swimming pool and finish it off with attractive, wicker furniture. What you end up with is a well-planned, well-kept high-rise resort that's ideal for a beach vacation.

Efficiencies, one-, two-, and three-bedroom condominiums come with cable television, complete kitchens and linens. Some balconies not only look out on the Gulf of Mexico, but overlook the swimming pool and sunbathing area as well. Among the many amenities you'll find here are tennis courts, a boardwalk to the beach, a fish-cleaning building, separate sun deck area and a protected beach area.

Executive Keys

$$ • 820 Access Rd. 1-A, Port Aransas • (512) 749-6272

Comfort and function are the selling points at this condominium complex, not luxury and eye-popping decor. Amenities include a private balcony or patio, swimming pool, recreation room, laundry facilities, volleyball, shuffleboard and picnic areas. Condominiums in this three-story complex are privately owned and leased to the public part of the year. Efficiency, two-bedroom, three-bedroom and two-story townhouses are available. The Executive Keys is on the beach.

Aransas Princess

$$$$$, no credit cards • 720 Beach Access Rd. 1-A, Port Aransas • (512) 749-5118, (800) 532-9225

Sand and saltwater get you down? Then hang out around the swimming pool and enjoy the beach without all the mess. The Aransas Princess has the best pool-side view: The

swimming pool overlooks the Gulf of Mexico. Or, if the beach and waves beckon, take the short stroll down the boardwalk and you'll be ready to build sandcastles or go for a swim in the surf.

Amenities in this nine-story, beautifully landscaped complex include fully equipped kitchens with microwaves, trash compactors and dishwashers, wet bars with built-in ice makers, full-size washers and dryers, large bathrooms and closets and private balconies facing the Gulf. A second swimming pool, shuffleboard, lighted tennis courts, heated outdoor Jacuzzi and dry sauna with dressing rooms and showers are available. Two-bedroom, two-bedroom with den and three-bedroom residences are available, as is a penthouse.

Although the Aransas Princess doesn't accept credit cards as payment, you'll need one to make reservations and at check-in time.

Port Royal Resort Condominiums

$$$$$ • 6317 Texas Hwy. 361, Port Aransas • (512) 749-5011, (800) 242-1034

They say everything is big in Texas, and Port Royal proves it with its 500-foot-long, four-tiered swimming pool, heralded as the state's largest. With a swim-up bar and grill and a mountain slide, the swimming pool is the centerpiece of this U-shaped, 210-unit complex overlooking the Gulf of Mexico. Only a 30-minute drive from Corpus Christi International Airport, this gated community on Mustang Island is a world away from city life.

A five-minute stroll across a boardwalk takes you over rolling sand dunes to the sparsely populated beach, where you can hunt for seashells or swim in warm gulf waters.

Units come with one, two or three bedrooms, a complete kitchen with full-size appliances, dining area, living room with built-in stereo system, washer and dryer, cable television, wet bar and master suite with whirlpool tubs. Three-bedroom units have full gulf views and built-in spas on the balconies. Other amenities include 7,000 square feet of meeting space, water and sand volleyball, lighted tennis courts and shuffleboard courts. The third-floor restaurant, The Atrium, serves seafood, hamburgers and sandwiches and overlooks the swimming pool and gulf.

Sandpiper Condominiums

$$$$-$$$$$ • 6745 Texas Hwy. 361, Port Aransas • (512) 749-6251, (800) 789-2898

You'll find the 12-story Sandpiper Condominiums situated on the Mustang Island beach 7 miles from Port Aransas and 17 miles from Corpus Christi. Each of its 107 units overlooks the beach and the Gulf of Mexico. Large balconies off the living areas of all condos offer great views and enough space for outdoor furniture. Condos come in a two-bedroom plan or two three-bedroom plans. All come with full kitchens, living rooms, dining rooms and two bathrooms. Amenities include a swimming pool with whirlpool spa, sun decks, tennis courts and meeting and activity rooms.

The Sandpiper is particularly proud of its spacious and comfortable lobbies (they have two). The largest is the Gulf Front Lobby, where you'll always find a full pot of coffee. Guests can relax and talk in wicker chairs with plum-colored cushions. The Gulf Front Lobby's smaller neighbor, the Sunken Reading Lobby, beckons those looking for a cool and quiet place to curl up with a favorite book or chat with a close friend.

Mayan Princess

$$$$-$$$$$ • 7537 Texas Hwy. 361, Port Aransas • (512) 749-5183, (800) 662-8907

The oversized Jacuzzi hot tub in the master bedroom is one reason visitors return to the Mayan Princess year after year. Others include its three-lagoon swimming pool with swim-up bar and hot tub, its two tennis courts, its location on the Gulf of Mexico and its luxurious one-, two- and three-bedroom units. All condos come with complete kitchens, living areas, dining areas, washers and dryers and basic cable. You can rent a VCR and movies in the lobby of this five-story complex. All rooms face the beach; guests on the second floor and higher have a view of the water.

El Constante Beachfront Condominiums

$$$$ • 14802 Windward Dr., Padre Island • (512) 949-7088

You won't find many places to stay on Pa-

An exotic plumeria shows its brillance.

---

dre Island that are right on the beach, so El Constante has a leg up over many condominiums in the area by virtue of its location on North Padre Island, although not all units face the beach.

Condos here come with one or two bedrooms. One-bedroom units will sleep four people. Two-bedroom condos are two stories tall with two full bathrooms upstairs and a half-bath downstairs; they sleep six. Amenities include a swimming pool, heated Jacuzzi and fully equipped kitchens.

Gulfstream

$$$$-$$$$$ • 14810 Windward Dr., Padre Island • (512) 949-8061, (800) 542-7368

Next door to El Constante you'll find The Gulfstream, a six-story condominium project on North Padre Island's beach and seawall. Many of the Gulfstream's 131 units overlook the Gulf of Mexico and the beach between J.P. Luby Park and Bob Hall Pier. All units overlook a heated, fan-shaped swimming pool.

Amenities include cable television, all-electric kitchens including microwave and dishwasher, hot tub, shuffleboard, laundry facilities and a recreation, party and game room. All units come with two bedrooms, two baths and fully equipped kitchens with dining and living areas. Guests have access to nearby Padre Island Country Club, including golf, tennis, and club and bar facilities.

Photo: C.C. Botanical Gardens/MaryJane Crull

You'll find an RV park in almost every Coastal Bend town and at least one that's miles from the nearest town. The area also has several campgrounds.

Campgrounds and RV Parks

Each fall the population of the Coastal Bend swells by the thousands as RV owners from the Midwest and other northern points head south for the winter. To accommodate them, RV parks have cropped up throughout the Coastal Bend, especially in the Rockport area, which boasts more than 20 RV parks in a city of 6,500 people.

You'll find an RV park in almost every Coastal Bend town and at least one that's miles from the nearest town. Some are big, fancy professionally run facilities that resemble miniature cities, while others are mom-and-pop operations where solitude and peace are favored.

The Coastal Bend also has several campgrounds. As you might expect they tend to be far from populated areas. Many allow RVs, and many RV parks allow tents. The best time for tent camping (unless your tent is air-conditioned) is between late November and early May when the temperature and humidity are relatively low. A word of warning: Hot, sticky conditions are possible year round, although these tropical spells are generally shorter and less severe than in the summer. The high season for RV camping is between October and March. You'll need to make reservations for that time period several months in advance.

Campsites and RV parks are listed together in this chapter. They're divided into four sections — North Bay, Corpus Christi, Port Aransas to Padre Island and the Kingsville area — and are listed from north to south within each category. You may be surprised by the low number of RV parks in Corpus Christi. For several years, economic development proponents have lamented the lack of a major RV park in the city. Maybe that's because the neighboring communities have done such a good job of catering to the RV market, or perhaps its because RVers prefer to settle in more remote areas.

Each listing gives you a general description of the site's location and appearance as well as a list of amenities. You can assume that each site is well-maintained, has a good reputation and would be a good place to spend a week, a month or longer. Each listing includes daily rates for two adults, including sales tax where applicable. Utilities are included in the price unless otherwise noted, and all parks offer more economical weekly and monthly rates. In most parks, electricity is charged separately when you pay by the month. Major credit cards are accepted unless otherwise indicated.

Other miscellaneous tips:

• Some parks have cable television at every site; others have it at only a few sites. Some include the cost of cable in their daily rates; others charge extra for it.

• Propane gas can be purchased at all sites, either from the proprietor or from a delivery truck that visits regularly.

• Discounts are available at most parks. They include discounts for stays of two days or longer, groups of more than a certain number and members of the Good Sam Club, an RV organization whose members receive a 10 percent discount from participating parks.

• Cancellation policies vary. Many parks require a 48-hour notice to receive a full refund.

• Generally there are no maximum or minimum stays. Stay a day or a lifetime.

• Wheelchair-accessible sites are available at some parks.

• Most parks allow pets and children.

• Public consumption of alcohol or the display of an open container in Texas state parks is prohibited.

• Overnight visitors pay a daily fee, and the number of occupants allowed at each site often is limited.

• Most campgrounds and RV parks observe a quiet time, which generally falls between 10 PM and 8 AM.

North Bay

Goose Island State Park
Park Rd. 13, Lamar • (512) 729-2858

You can camp in the woods or at the beach when you pitch your tent or park your RV at Goose Island State Park. This 314-acre facility overlooking Aransas Bay stretches inland for a mile to dense brush and abundant live oak and mesquite trees. This state-run facility is about 6 miles north of Rockport in an unincorporated area known as Lamar. From Texas Highway 35 head east for 1.4 miles down tree-lined Park Road 13. On your way visit a Catholic shrine and the ancient Stella Maris Chapel. When you come to a four-way stop, hang a right (you'll still be on Park Road 13) and drive south for 1.2 miles to the park entrance.

All 127 sites come with water; 102 come with electricity. Sites with electricity (30-amp electrical service) can accommodate either an RV or a tent, but sites without electricity are a tight fit for RVs. Reservations are accepted. Amenities include a recreation hall, dump station, toilets, showers, grills, a lighted (and extremely long) fishing pier, boat ramp and playgrounds.

Rates are $11 per night plus an entry fee of $2 per person per day for anyone age 13 to 65. Sites without electricity are $8 per night

plus entry fees. See our Parks chapter for more information.

Rockport Gulf Resort
5451 Texas 35 N., Rockport
• (512) 729-1334, (888) 729-7317

You won't find a more scenic RV park in the Coastal Bend than this facility a few miles north of Rockport. It's laid out around a beautiful freshwater lake, and the grounds are covered with shady live oak trees. You'll find plenty to do right outside your door at this 200-site park. Amenities include two swimming pools (one adults-only), two hot tubs (one adults-only), volleyball court, shuffleboard, horseshoes, table tennis, video games, children's play area, pavilion, two fishing piers, miniature golf, clubhouse, organized activities and a sports court. You'll also find a general store, pay phones, laundry facilities, restrooms, showers, an RV and vehicle washing area, dump station and RV storage lot.

RV sites with full hookups (30- and 50-amp electrical service) are available for $20 a day. Six to eight tent sites also are available. A tent site without utilities is $15 a day; one with water and electricity costs $20 a day.

Rockport 35 RV Park
No credit cards • 4851 Texas 35 N., Rockport • (512) 729-2307, (800) 392-2930

White concrete streets and pads give this 178-site RV park that clean, well-maintained look that makes you want to stay awhile. It's like walking into a hotel room and finding the carpet has just been vacuumed. Shady sites are limited here, but the lack of development on the surrounding land and the park's proximity to Rockport and other local attractions make it an appealing spot to park your rig. Amenities abound at this 11-year-

---

INSIDERS' TIP

Camping at the Padre Island National Seashore can be a lesson in protecting endangered species: Each year park biologists release endangered Kemp's ridley sea turtle hatchlings into the wild in an effort to establish a nesting spot on Padre Island.

Orchids bloom in the tropical wing of the Exhibit House at
Corpus Christi Botanical Gardens.

old RV park. They include showers, phone hookups, cable television, on-site resident managers, security, laundry facilities, enclosed hot tub, 4,000-square-foot recreation room, exercise room, horseshoes, picnic tables, portable barbecue pits and a fish-cleaning table. Sites come with full hookups (30- and 50-amp electrical service).

Rates are between $18.50 and $20.50 a day depending on the size of your vehicle.

Circle W RV Ranch
No credit cards • 1401 Smokehouse Rd., Rockport • (512) 729-1542

This 244-site park is at the end of Smokehouse Road a few miles south of Rockport and about a mile west of Aransas Bay. It's laid out around several small ponds, a clubhouse and an indoor pool and hot tub. Amenities at this retirement-oriented RV ranch include restrooms, showers, paved streets, exercise room, mail room, pool room, barbecue shack, laundry facilities, pay phones, cable television, planned activities and a recreation room. The manager lives on the ranch, which has a main clubhouse and two smaller ones. Planned activities include exercise classes, line dancing, bingo, bridge, cribbage and occasional live music.

Rates for sites, which have full hookups (30- and 50-amp electrical service), are $20 a day.

Sea Breeze RV Park
1026 Seabreeze Ln., Portland
• (512) 643-0744, (888) 212-7541

Tucked away on the southwest end of Portland, this 99-site RV park provides a secluded spot overlooking Nueces Bay. This is a destination park with a creek running through tree-studded grounds. Only a few sites actually overlook the water, and most of those do not have trees. Spots farther inland are surrounded by shade trees. Sites come with complete hookups (30- and 50-amp electrical service) and phone hookups. Amenities include a clubhouse, showers, cable television, laundry facilities, picnic tables, barbecue pits, RV storage, dump station and a spa with sun deck. Corpus Christi's major tourist attractions are a 10-minute drive away.

Rates are $18 to $20 a day.

Corpus Christi

Puerto del Sol RV Park
5100 Timon Blvd., Corpus Christi
• (512) 882-5373

Water lovers will adore this 53-site park

d on the northern tip of Corpus Christi ach. Just a stone's throw from U.S. Highway 181, this small RV park overlooks Corpus Christi Bay. Two popular Corpus Christi tourist attractions are nearby: The Texas State Aquarium and the Lexington Museum on the Bay (a decommissioned aircraft carrier). See our Attractions chapter for more about these sites. Downtown Corpus Christi and the scenic Corpus Christi bayfront are a five-minute drive away. Amenities include picnic tables, ice, recreation room, game room, RV supplies, planned activities, full hookups (30- and 50-amp electrical service), laundry facilities, showers, dump station and eight sites with telephone hookups.

Rates range from $16 to $19 a day depending on how close you are to the water. Tent sites are not available.

Colonia del Rey
1717 Waldron Rd., Corpus Christi
• **(512) 937-2435, (800) 580-2435**

Colonia del Rey is a perfect compromise for those who can't decide whether they would rather be close to the beach or to Corpus Christi's shopping and restaurants. This 180-site RV park is in Flour Bluff, a Corpus Christi neighborhood on the city's south side. Padre Island is a 10-minute drive south, and Corpus Christi's main shopping and restaurant district is an equal distance in the opposite direction. You'll find Flour Bluff less crowded and more rural than most Corpus Christi neighborhoods. Folks here have their own school district, and many think of themselves as Flour Bluff residents first and Corpus Christi residents second.

Sites come with full hookups (30- and 50-amp electrical service). Amenities include a dump station, cable television and telephone hookups, restrooms, showers, laundry facilities, swimming pool, picnic tables, seasonal recreation hall, game room, planned activities, general store with RV supplies and a pay phone.

Rates are $19.50 to $21.50 a day. Tent sites are available for the same price.

Port Aransas to Padre Island

Island RV Resort
700 Sixth St., Port Aransas
• **(512) 749-5600**

This 199-site RV park made our list because of its reputation for good service. It's in the middle of Port Aransas, less than a mile from the beach and about the same distance from local restaurants and shopping. A few newer sites are paved, the rest are grass. Amenities include a dump station, vehicle wash area, bathhouse, ice, RV supplies, pool, spa, shower, public telephone, recreation hall, organized activities, laundry facilities, playground, patios and cable television.

Rates range from $16 to $18 a day depending on whether you want a new site or an older one. Electricity is extra. Tent sites are available at $16 a day plus electricity.

Nueces County Park
No credit cards • East end of Cotter Ave., Port Aransas • (512) 749-6117

Head east on Cotter Avenue from the ferry landing in Port Aransas. Wend your way through a residential area and continue past the University of Texas Marine Science Institute on your left. When you get to the beach, you've arrived at the Nueces County Park in Port Aransas. The park has 75 sites with electricity and water and allows primitive camping on the beach. Amenities include a dump station, flushing toilets, showers, bathhouse, picnic shelters and the Horace Caldwell Pier, a 1,245-foot lighted pier. On the pier you'll find a snack bar/convenience store where you can buy ice and basic groceries and rent fishing

INSIDERS' TIP

Most RV parks in the Coastal Bend allow pets on a leash. But many prohibit certain breeds of dogs (such as Doberman pinschers and pit bull terriers), and others approve or reject pets on a case-by-case basis.

tackle. Pier operators charge a $1 admission fee. Park rangers are on duty 24 hours a day.

Rates are $15 a day for sites with electricity and water. The fee for primitive camping is $6 a day. There is a 14-day limit on all stays. See our Parks chapter for more information.

On The Beach RV Park
907 Beach Access Rd. 1A, Port Aransas
• (512) 749-4909, (800) 932-6337

The name sums up the major appeal of this 60-site RV park in Port Aransas. You'll be a short stroll from the Gulf of Mexico and a brief car ride from local restaurants and shops. On The Beach has full hookups, a fish-cleaning station, restrooms, hot showers, laundry, recreation room, horseshoe pit, public telephone and cable television.

Rates are $18 to $20 depending on how close you are to the water. Tent sites are not available.

Pioneer RV Resort
120 Gulfwind Dr., Port Aransas
• (512) 749-6248, (888) 480-3246

Pioneer RV Resort is a recent addition to the family of RV parks that populate the Coastal Bend. Pioneer is so new it almost sparkles compared with many of its older competitors. Concrete streets and pads gleam under the South Texas sun, and the grounds are freshly landscaped. This 14-acre park on the beach side of Texas Highway 361 has 211 full hookup sites with 50-amp electrical service. It also features a recreation meeting hall with kitchen, swimming pool, climate-controlled bathhouse, fish-cleaning station, laundry facilities, general store, dump station, cable television, telephone service and playground equipment. Guests may take part in organized activities — the resort has a seasonal activity director — and a manager is on-site.

Rates are $17.50 to $19.50. Cable is extra. Tent sites are not available.

Mustang Island State Park
Texas Hwy. 361, Port Aransas
• (512) 749-5246, (800) 792-1112

The state of Texas runs this 48-site RV park and campground, and what it lacks in amenities it more than makes up for with good, solid service. You won't find a swimming pool or recreation center here, but the grounds are clean and well-maintained and you'll feel safe knowing that park rangers are keeping an eye on the place. Upon arriving you'll pay an entrance fee of $3 per person older than 12. The park is on the beach of Mustang Island, 14 miles south of Port Aransas. Paved RV sites (also available for tent camping) come with water and electricity. Hot showers are nearby. Primitive and freshwater tent sites are available along the beach. Amenities include restrooms, recycling bins, pay phones, picnic shelters, a dump station and a Texas State Parks Store where you can buy ice and souvenirs.

Rates are $12 a day for paved sites and $7 a day for unpaved beach sites. See our Parks chapter for more information.

Nueces County Padre Balli Park
15820 Park Rd. 22 • (512) 949-8121

You'll find this county park north of the Padre Island National Seashore, just south of the Corpus Christi city limit. It has 66 RV sites and 12 tent sites with water and electricity (bring a 50-foot extension cord) and an unspecified number of primitive camping sites along the beach. Amenities include a dump station, restrooms, hot showers, concession stand, picnic shelters, laundry facilities, first-aid station and a lighted fishing pier. Park rangers are on duty 24 hours a day. Each person will pay $1 to enter the pier and a $1 fee per fishing pole.

Camping rates are $15 a day for RV and tent sites with utilities and $6 a day for primitive camping. There is a 14-day limit for both RV and tent campers. See our Parks chapter for more information.

Padre Island National Seashore
9405 S. Padre Island Dr., Corpus Christi
• (512) 949-8068

Whether camping in a tent or parking your RV, you won't find more primitive conditions than those at Padre Island National Seashore. The trade-off? Pristine beaches, an abundance of wildlife and a location far removed from civilization. The national park has slabs without hookups for more than 40 RVs and tents and unlimited primitive camping along the 65-mile-long barrier island's beaches. The

Photo: Greater Corpus Christi Business Alliance

The national windsurfing championships are held each year along Corpus Christi's Bayfront.

first 5 miles of beach are accessible by two-wheel-drive vehicles; the next 60 miles are accessible via four-wheel-drive vehicles only. Your stay is limited to 14 days. The park has a dump station, toilets, cold showers at the visitors center, summer interpretive programs and nature trails.

The park charges a $10 entrance fee good for seven days; an annual pass is available for $20. An additional $5 fee is charged for anyone wishing to visit the popular windsurfing site known as Bird Island Basin; an annual pass sells for $10. Sites with slabs go for $8 a night; camping on the beach is free. Discount passes for senior citizens and the people in wheelchairs are available. See our Parks chapter for more information.

Kingsville Area

Oasis RV and Mobile Home Park
2415 E. Santa Gertrudis, Kingsville
• (512) 592-0764

This RV and mobile home park at the intersection of Santa Gertrudis and U.S. Highway 77 in Kingsville is an ideal spot for those who want to be close to local attractions. Naval Air Station Kingsville is 2 miles east, and downtown Kingsville and Texas A&M University-Kingsville are fewer than 2 miles to the west. Oasis is a 147-site park on 24 enclosed acres. Amenities include a playground, recreation hall, mail boxes, laundry facilities, showers and a nearby driving range.

Rates are $13 a night.

Country Estates Mobile Ranch Inc.
No credit cards • F.M. Rd. 1717,
Kingsville • (512) 592-4659

Take a nice drive in the country past mesquite trees and farmland to Country Estates, a 125-site RV and mobile home park 1.5 miles south of Kingsville. Watch the Navy training

jets take to the air as they practice takeoffs and landings at nearby Naval Air Station Kingsville. Amenities include a recreation building, swimming pool, laundry facilities, showers and restrooms. The park offers full hookups and 30- and 50-amp electrical service.

Rates are $18 a day.

Kaufer-Hubert Memorial Park and SeaWind Resort
F.M. Rd. 628, Loyola Beach
• (512) 297-5738

When developers announced plans to build a 134-site RV park east of Loyola Beach at the end of a country road way out in the middle of nowhere, more than a few people shook their heads and wondered how anyone could come up with such a crazy idea. But it turns out a lot of people like living far from civilization, especially when they can do it in an RV park packed with amenities and situated on a beautiful South Texas waterway.

The SeaWind Resort overlooks the Cayo del Grullo, which leads to the popular fishing spots of Baffin Bay and the Laguna Madre. Anglers and bird watchers will love this park laid out near two freshwater lakes. Amenities include a beach, group picnic shelters, single picnic tables with grills, restrooms, a two-story observation tower overlooking the bay, a 500-foot lighted fishing pier and four-lane boat ramp. You'll also find a parking area, birding overlook, 1-mile walking/jogging trail with 12-station senior fitness course, playground, horseshoe pits, soccer fields and softball fields. The resort offers laundry facilities, a recreation center, restrooms, showers, a meeting room, post office boxes and planned activities. Sites come with full hookups (30- and 50-amp electrical service), and telephone service is available.

Rates are $16 a night. Tent sites are available at $10 a night.

Be sure to try some of
our regional specialties,
which represent the
culinary influences that
converge in South
Texas: Mexican, Texan
and coastal.

Restaurants

South Texas' hospitality is never more evident as in the kitchen and dining room. There is a wide-ranging assortment of restaurants to visit throughout the region, from small-town family diners to national franchises.

The local restaurant selection has expanded greatly in recent years, particularly in Corpus Christi. It seems that every major national restaurant chain has arrived in this city, and residents of neighboring towns frequently drive to the big city of Corpus Christi to dine out. You can see these restaurants when you drive along S. Padre Island Drive, which has earned the nickname "Restaurant Row" among locals.

But please don't limit your culinary experimentation to those franchises while you're here. There are also a number of excellent locally owned restaurants that may offer you a more authentic taste of Corpus Christi. We've selected the best of the local hangouts for inclusion in this chapter, trying to lead you to some of South Texas' best eating. Because you already know what to expect from the chains, we're not going to include them in here.

We're also pleased to relate that there are definitely some restaurants worth visiting here — Beulah's in Port Aransas, the King's Inn near Kingsville, Joe Cotten's Barbecue in Robstown, Water Street Seafood and the Yardarm in Corpus Christi. All offer cuisine that would compare favorably in much larger metropolitan areas.

Be sure to try some of our regional specialties, which represent the culinary influences that converge in South Texas: Mexican, Texan and coastal. Grilled fresh seafood is always a good choice, as is fried shrimp. The range of Tex-Mex fare, including enchiladas, tacos, chalupas, homemade tortillas and chile rellenos, is very popular. Chicken fried steak is a Texas specialty that makes ordinary beef — in this case, tenderized round steak dredged in flour and fried in hot oil — into a dish that's tasty, filling and altogether delicious. And beef barbecue, that mainstay of Texans' midday meal, is also worth sampling — slow-cooked over glowing coals for hours until it's fork tender and sure to please anyone's palate.

As for dress, South Texas is a casual kind of place, particularly in the summertime. We don't know of any restaurants that require the men to wear ties to dinner. Men can usually get by with jeans and khakis — remember that for cowboys, a freshly pressed pair of jeans and a starched white shirt equals fancy dress. Women wear shorts, slacks or sundresses to most of the restaurants, and sandals seem to be the favorite year-round footwear. Of course, there are always those special occasions when you're a little more gussied up than usual, and that's fine, too. But don't feel you have to dress to the nines for any of these restaurants.

As in other chapters, the restaurants are grouped by area, then listed alphabetically under the name of each city or town. The areas include North Bay, which encompasses the towns from the Aransas National Wildlife Refuge through Portland; Corpus Christi; Port Aransas to Padre Island; and the Kingsville area. So if you wanted to find a restaurant in Aransas Pass, you would look in the North Bay Area section then under the heading for Aransas Pass.

Prices can range widely, from incredibly inexpensive Mexican meals to pricier steak dinners. Unless otherwise noted, you can assume that the restaurants accept major credit cards.

While we hope that we've included your favorite eatery in this chapter, we know it's possible that we may have missed a few places worth mentioning. If you have a suggestion for a restaurant that you would like to see included in a revised edition of this book, please contact us at Insiders' Publishing, P.O. Box 2057, Manteo, NC 27954.

Price Code

The dollar-sign code in each restaurant listing serves as a guide to give you an idea of the cost for an average dinner for two, excluding cocktails and wine, appetizers and desserts, tax and tip.

$	Less than $10
$$	$10 to $20
$$$	$20 to $40
$$$$	More than $40

So loosen your belt and enjoy!

North Bay Area

Aransas Pass

Julie's Backyard Bistro
$$-$$$, no credit cards • 2212 A-1 Hill Rd., Aransas Pass • (512) 758-7895

Billed as "a gourmet haven in the middle of nowhere," this place certainly is as advertised. It takes a little doing to find it, tucked between Aransas Pass and Rockport off the Texas Highway 35 bypass. But the food is worth the trouble — elaborate seafood and steak dishes prepared lavishly and served in an elegant outdoor patio. You have to drive past bass boats and chain-link fences to get to this little bistro, and then cross a Japanese footbridge over a dancing brook.

Each night's innovative nouvelle cuisine is chalked on a board. Among the entrees we've sampled or heard praised by friends are snapper Florentine, in a crunchy breading topped with green chile sauce; crab cakes and adobe mayonnaise; and stuffed shrimp. Desserts can range from cappuccino bread pudding to truffle chocolate torte. Only open for dinner Wednesday through Saturday, it's best to make reservations because the dining area is rather small.

Mac's Pit Barbecue
$$ • 1933 W. Wheeler Ave., Aransas Pass • (512) 758-0641

For more than two decades, the Martinez family has been serving slow-cooked beef brisket, pork ribs, beef ribs, chicken, polish sausage and ham to customers in the Coastal Bend. This is the most recent arrival of three area restaurants run by the family; other locations are Texas Highway 35 in Gregory and 815 Market Street in Rockport. The restaurant also caters.

Fulton

The Boiling Pot
$$$ • 201 S. Fulton Beach Rd., Fulton • (512) 729-6972

Informal is the word for this restaurant. Wear your old clothes and prepare to get your hands messy feasting on the kind of Gulf Coast fare you'd be served at a typical Louisiana-style crab boil. The food is tossed into a big kettle and boiled with peppery spices, then literally dumped onto your butcher-paper covered table. Diners don bibs and take mallet in hand to crack open a steaming pile of boiled crabs. Also served with the crabs are shrimp, crawfish, spicy sausage, potato chunks and corn on the cob.

Rockport

Back 40
$-$$ • 1101 Texas Hwy. 35 N., Rockport • (512) 729-3478

Stop here for a hearty breakfast before heading for the water. Known for its home-style cooking and the colorful wall murals, this restaurant offers a variety of family-pleasing meals for breakfast, lunch and dinner. You can get eggs, bacon and biscuits in the morning, or steaks, chicken and seafood at lunch and dinner.

The Big Fisherman Seafood Restaurant
$-$$ • 519 Texas Hwy. 188, Rockport • (512) 729-1997

This longtime family-owned restaurant specializes in big appetites, offering an assortment of all-you-can-eat deals on steak, seafood, and chicken. The Texas Boil features two pounds of assorted crab legs, crab claws and boiled shrimp for $21.95 — enough to feed at least four. You'll also find great prices on lunch specials, including steak and fried shrimp with a baked potato, salad or gumbo — all for $5.95. There's also an oyster bar and lounge.

Chandler House Tearoom
$$ • 801 S. Church St., Rockport
• (512) 729-2285

Treat yourself to an elegant lunch in this historic home, which has been renovated and turned into a bed and breakfast inn (see our Bed and Breakfast Inns chapter). Owners Michelle Barnes and Mary Burney serve light lunches, including chicken salad with celery, apple, nuts and grapes, fruit salads with poppy-seed dressing and pasta salad with muffins, as well as a variety of sandwiches, soups, homemade desserts and gourmet coffee and tea.

Charlotte Plummer's
$$ • 202 N. Fulton Beach Rd., Fulton
• (512) 729-1185

This is a longtime local favorite dining spot, serving fresh seafood and grilled steaks overlooking the peaceful waters of the Fulton Harbor. Try the whole stuffed flounder, or the chargrilled shrimp. You can also get seafood salads, steaks, homemade desserts and more. With its traditional seafood fare, pleasant atmosphere and variety, this is a good place to take a group or a large family.

Copano Provisioning Co.
$-$$ • 6619 Texas Hwy. 35 N., Holiday Beach • (512) 729-1703

This Italian deli beside a gas station north of Rockport serves spaghetti, spicy muffalettas and crunchy cannolis. We like the calzone stuffed with ham, salami, provolone and tomato, and the Italian salads. The food is served on paper plates, which seems incongruous with the fare — but the kitchen makes it all worthwhile.

Crab-N
$$ • City by the Sea, Texas Hwy. 35 S.
• (512) 758-2371

This casual, waterfront restaurant between Rockport and Aransas Pass specializes in fresh seafood and unique combinations — such as a pecan-crusted flounder with crab relish, or shrimp grilled with mango chile sauce. They also offer chicken, heavy beef and blackened prime rib. You can also bring your own ready-to-cook catch and the kitchen will fix it how you like — blackened, sautéed, broiled or fried. For dessert, try the homemade key lime pie.

Duck Inn
$$ • 701 Broadway St., Rockport
• (512) 729-6663

Established in 1946, this venerable restaurant specializes in breakfast specials, steaks and fresh seafood. Try the homemade deviled crab, golden fried shrimp or baked flounder and crispy fried onion rings. Across from Rockport Beach Park, it also offers daily lunch specials, senior citizens' and children's menus. Stop on your way out for a day of fishing.

Portland

Country Cajun
$-$$ • 100 Fifth St., Portland
• (512) 643-1181

Louisiana-style cuisine and down-home hospitality are merged in this restaurant, including a cement alligator that peers at visitors near the front door. For hearty eaters, try the Acadiana — catfish smothered in crawfish etouffee, served with coleslaw, and a cheesy, Cajun-spiced stuffed potato. We are particularly fond of the Cajun fried shrimp salad, which features tiny fried popcorn shrimp on a bed of lettuce, tomato, mushrooms, cheese and bacon. The combination of crunchy and smooth textures will delight your taste buds. We also like the rich seafood gumbo, with its hearty portion of shrimp, oysters and fish, and the small skillets of buttery cornbread that are set promptly upon each table. For dessert, try the New Orleans bread pudding.

Elm Street Cafe
$$ • 900 Elm St., Portland
• (512) 643-5350

This cheery blue-and-white cafe serves home-style cooking of the sort you might find in your grandmother's kitchen. We've sampled a tasty beef stew here, thick with chunks of potato, carrots and onion, and topped with two flaky biscuits. They also make an excellent chicken-fried steak.

Corpus Christi

Bamboo Garden
$$ • 1220 Airline Rd., Corpus Christi • (512) 993-7993

Sneak into this quiet, peaceful Chinese restaurant when you're tired of shopping at the nearby malls and strip centers. House specialties include a spicy beef in brown sauce with baby corn and mushrooms, fresh shrimp and scallops in a delicate garlic sauce, and Peking duck.

www.insiders.com

See this and many other Insiders' Guide® destinations online — in their entirety.

Visit us today!

Bar B Q Man
$$ • 4931 IH-37 S., Corpus Christi • (512) 888-4248

This barbecue restaurant has been catering to generations of professionals and laborers alike with its no-nonsense emphasis on tender beef brisket, pork ribs, sausage, chicken and ham. You go through a cafeteria-style line and tell the servers what you want from the steaming platters, then take your heaping plate to a table in the large dining area. Plates come with barbecue sauce, beans, salad and bread. As the menu says, "A sandwich here is a meal — plenty of meat." You can also get orders to go, meat by the pound, smoked whole hams or turkeys and quarts of side dishes.

Bayou Grill
$-$$ • 3741 S. Alameda St., Corpus Christi • (512) 854-8626

With fishing nets hanging from the walls and wooden signs, you get the feeling that you're inside a Louisiana camp house. And the food is just as authentic, from the hefty portions to the flavoring. We've had the catfish po'boy, and red beans and rice, served with a large and tasty sausage. On another visit, we had tender broiled Gulf snapper with bonne sauce (cream gravy with crawfish tails), accompanied by creamed spinach and French-fried corn on the cob (interesting). The

Bayourita (a frozen Margarita boasting 14 percent alcohol) comes from an old family recipe.

Bee's Bar-B-Que
$, no credit cards • 4301 S. Alameda St., Corpus Christi • (512) 991-3364

This tiny, family-owned barbecue eatery is easy to miss. But owner Beatrice Moore has been serving succulent beef brisket and finger-lickin' pork ribs since 1978. The furnishings are basic, but everything is neat and clean. And don't expect a waiter — order from the counter and then go sit at one of the tables and wait for your name to be called. But do expect great chopped beef sandwiches and tender barbecued chicken.

Bel-Aire Drugs
$ • 2741 S. Staples St., Corpus Christi • (512) 853-0396

We have friends who swear that this 1950s-style pharmacy lunch counter makes the best hamburgers in town. And they may be right — the burgers are grilled and juicy, with just the right amount of greasiness. If you're going to lunch here, be sure and arrive a little before noon because seating is limited. You may have to wait among the aisles, where you can browse the selection of shampoo and greeting cards.

Blue Swan Delicatessen
$-$$ • 319 Lawrence St., Corpus Christi • (512) 882-1370

One of the city's most popular delis, this chic and eccentric little shop serves wonderful sandwiches served on fabulous home-baked rolls. Our favorite is the turkey and Swiss on wheat, which may sound bland but is anything but — meat and cheese heaped on a roll that is crusty on the outside, soft and almost creamy inside. Sandwiches come with an oniony potato salad and a slice of dill pickle. You can pick one up to go if you're in a hurry, or even have one delivered. We also like the way each day's copy of USA Today is tacked to the wall so customers can catch up on world events while they're munching.

Photo: Greater Corpus Christi Business Alliance

Diners can feast on scrumptious seafood while admiring
the beautiful Corpus Christi Bayfront.

B&J's Pizza
**$$ • 6335 S. Padre Island Dr., Corpus
Christi • (512) 992-6671**

This place will spoil you forever for eating
ordinary pizza. We should know — it's awfully
difficult to settle for anything less now that
we've come to know and love their version of
the Italian dinner pie. All the ingredients are
fresh, and the crust is thin and crispy and alto-
gether perfect. Plus, there are literally hun-
dreds of beverage selections here: domestic
and imported beers, non-alcoholic beers, soft
drinks, iced tea and more. Among favorite piz-
zas to try here are the Polynesian with Cana-
dian bacon, pineapple and mushrooms; Jack's
Special with fresh garlic, onions, Italian sau-
sage and pepperoni; and the vegetarian gar-
den pizza, with fresh tomatoes, green pep-
pers, broccoli, fresh garlic and herbs. Sand-
wiches are served here, too. A game room/
bar is adjacent.

Catfish Charlie's
**$$ • 5830 McArdle Rd., Corpus Christi
• (512) 993-0363**

The name says it all — the best thing to
get here is the fried catfish, which is crisp
and buttery tasting, served with coleslaw,
jalapeno-flecked hush puppies, peppery
Cajun red beans and thick fries. There are
also frog legs, shrimp, chicken-fried steak,
gumbo and SOB's (shrimp stuffed with oys-

INSIDERS' TIP

Here's a Texas bumper sticker that pays homage to the state's
love of red meat: "Support beef — run over a chicken."

Whataburger

In Texas' Coastal Bend, the fast-food battlefield contains a uniquely Texan contender — and one that's headquartered in Corpus Christi.

Alongside the ubiquitous golden arches and burger monarchy found in all major — nay, even many minor — communities, you'll see something just as distinctive to South Texans and equally enticing. It's the orange-and-white striped roof of a Whataburger restaurant.

Whataburger (pronounced exactly the way it's spelled) is a burger joint with a Texan flavor. You can get jalapenos on those hearty quarter-pound hamburgers. Or you can order chicken fajitas for lunch or sausage-and-egg taquitos for breakfast.

Close-up

And while it's classified as fast food, Whataburger's specialty is made-to-order burgers, so it's not quite as quick as the other Mc-chains. To some eaters, that's a disadvantage; to others, it's a plus. We figure it depends on your preference.

Harmon A. Dobson, a Corpus Christi entrepreneur whose dream was to "provide the public with the ultimate burger — the Whataburger" — founded Whataburger in 1950. The chain's slogan was: "It's not just a hamburger — it's a Whataburger." And the philosophy was to allow the customer to dictate what would be on the burger, including fresh lettuce, tomatoes, pickles, onions, salad dressing, ketchup or mustard.

Dobson's first restaurants served the signature Whataburger, cold drinks and potato chips from large wooden boxes, 10-feet-by-23-feet.

The now-familiar structure of the restaurants was designed in 1961, featuring the orange-and-white striped roof on an A-frame building. Other additions since then have included drive-through facilities.

Dobson died in an airplane accident in 1967, and his wife, Grace, took over the corporation.

— continued on next page

Photo: Whataburger

Whataburger restaurants have a distinctive orange-and-white striped roof and a South Texas flavor.

The company has expanded mightily. Whataburgers can now be found throughout the Sunbelt, in Texas, Alabama, Arizona, Florida, Louisiana, New Mexico and Oklahoma. There are approximately 525 Whataburger restaurants in the southern United States and Mexico, with 80 percent of them in Texas.

Still, the basic foundation of the franchise remains the same: a grilled, quarter-pound 100-percent beef patty on a 5-inch bun with a sprinkling of lettuce, three slices of tomato, four slices of dill pickle, chopped onion, mustard, salad dressing or ketchup. Whataburger added chicken sandwiches and chicken strips in 1988 and began accepting credit cards in 1989. The company opened its 500th site in 1995.

As for us, we like Whataburger's juicy burgers and fried chicken strips, crispy french fries and fountain drinks. We find the fare fresher tasting and more flavorful than at the other fast-food restaurants.

On the other hand, we know of folks who can't stand Whataburger and would much prefer to pick up a burger at McDonald's or Burger King. Late-night debates sometimes focus on the pros and cons of Whataburger's offerings and speculation about whether there are some innate reasons why some people love 'em and others hate 'em. Could it be a regional thing? Are native Texans more likely to prefer the more full-bodied, home-cooked flavor of these burgers?

You'll have to open wide and let your taste buds decide for you.

---

ters, wrapped in bacon and grilled). Rustic surroundings, friendly atmosphere and quick service make this a good place to take the family.

Che Bello
$-$$ • 320-C William St., Corpus Christi • (512) 882-8832

Check out the wall display of local artistic talent when you stop here for something sweet or an espresso. We like the vegetarian sandwich of sliced tomato, avocado, sprouts, green onion and cream cheese on a flaky croissant, or the chunky chicken salad. But we tend to gravitate toward the display of lovely pastries, including cream-filled horns, bagels, cheesecake and gelato — an Italian version of sherbet that is richly colored and flavored. Great cappuccino and coffee are available, and you can sit at the tiny outdoor patio in good weather.

Coffee Cove Cafe
$-$$ • 5838 S. Staples St., Corpus Christi • (512) 993-1911

Specializing in giant country breakfasts, this is a great place to stoke up for a hard day's work or play. For $6, you can get coffee or tea, a country omelet, six-ounce rib eye, biscuits and gravy and hash browns.

The atmosphere is friendly and inviting, with red-and-white checked tablecloths and floral curtains in the windows. We recommend the homemade pastries — flaky pastries bursting with fat cherries, streusel-topped blueberry muffins and crumbly sugar cookies. Lunch and dinner is also served, featuring an assortment of American and Mexican standards such as chicken-fried steak, fried chicken, enchiladas and fajitas.

The County Line Barbecue
$$ • 6102 Ocean Dr., Corpus Christi • (512) 991-7427

With an entire wall of windows, this restaurant provides a spectacular view of the bayfront. And the food is pretty good, too. As at other restaurants in this chain, you can get slow-cooked ribs, chicken, brisket and sausage, along with an excellent potato salad and coleslaw. There's also homemade bread, all served in a rather elegant, nostalgic atmosphere (be sure to check out the old advertising posters at the entrance and in the restrooms).

Crystal's
$$ • 4119 S. Staples St., Corpus Christi • (512) 857-8081

An eclectic menu and a pleasant atmosphere make this a popular dining spot. You can get anything from Tex-Mex to baby-back ribs or dinner salads at this restaurant. We recommend the chicken-stuffed chile relleno, which is topped with pecans, raisins and sour cream. Appetizers are also tasty — nachos, fried potato skins and fried mozzarella cheese sticks.

Dentoni's Pizza
$$ • 415 William St., Corpus Christi
• (512) 881-9886

With its sleek decor and late-night hours, this chic pizzeria caters to the club crowd and the hip business workers. There are 12 varieties of pre-made pizza, but the staff will also customize for you — and you can get a single slice or a whole pie. The crust is homemade and yeasty, the spicy tomato sauce is laced with oregano, and the toppings range from traditional to unusual. We like the white pizza (topped with olive oil, mozzarella cheese and oregano), the spinach Florentine (spinach, tomatoes, red onion and mushrooms) and the Southwest version (pesto sauce, mozzarella cheese and grilled chicken). Salads are good too, particularly an antipasto salad that features different types of greens, salami and pepperoni slices, black olives, green pepper, tomatoes, cucumbers and anchovies.

Edelweiss
$$ • 1209 Airline Rd., Corpus Christi
• (512) 993-1901

This hospitable house-turned-restaurant serves traditional German dishes, hearty soups and thick sandwiches. We like the lean, juicy Weiner schnitzel served with warm sauerkraut and potato salad. With your meal, try one of the creamy soups and a slice of fresh pumpernickel bread. We also recommend the chicken salad with pineapple, grapes, almonds and light mayonnaise. For dessert, try the delicious apple strudel with raisins and almonds. Service is good, but it does take time to create these meals so don't be in a hurry. The blue-checked tablecloths and the flowers on each table offer a cheerful, homey touch.

Elva's
$, no credit cards • 3511 S. Staples St.,
Corpus Christi • (512) 851-9931

This unpretentious diner features some of the best Tex-Mex deals in town. For less than

$5, you can get a Mexican platter of enchiladas swathed in beef gravy, a crispy beef taco, a bean and cheese chalupa and fresh flour tortillas. Meals come with a basket of fresh fried tortilla chips, thin, salty and slight greasy — just as they should be.

Executive Surf Club
$-$$ • 309 N. Water St., Corpus Christi
• (512) 884-SURF

Surfboards jutting from the walls serve as tabletops at this casual eatery, which serves assorted burgers, batter-dipped french fries, nachos, gumbo and salads. We recommend the surf burger — a hamburger topped with refried beans, corn chips, onions, cheese and salsa. For lighter appetites, try the grilled chicken salad — tender slices of chicken atop lettuce, served with cheese, tomato and the fabulous house creamy walnut dressing. There's also live music most nights. Order at the bar, then wait for your number to be called to pick up your food hot from the grill. You can eat indoors or outside on the patio, which makes it a great place to take restless children.

Frank's Spaghetti House
$$ • 2724 Leopard St., Corpus Christi
• (512) 882-0075

As one restaurant reviewer put it, this Italian eatery was launched long before noodles became known as pasta. This renovated house is cozy and intimate, with red-checked tablecloths and traditional Italian favorites. Try the meaty lasagna, or the chicken piccata.

Frenchy's Crab House
$$ • 13309 S. Padre Island Dr., Corpus Christi • (512) 949-8201

This is one of two seafood restaurants side-by-side underneath the causeway bridge to Padre Island on the Laguna Madre. Both Frenchy's and Snoopy's are casual restaurants that specialize in fried seafood and hamburgers, and are favorite stopping places for beach goers. You can sit outside on the deck and down fried shrimp, fried fish, french fries, coleslaw and hush puppies — washed down with a soft drink or beer. The view is great, the atmosphere is relaxing, and the prices are good.

Gallagher's
$$-$$$ • 5013 Everhart Rd., Corpus Christi • (512) 853-9953

Prime rib and steak are the offerings of choice at this restaurant, which is decorated like an Irish hunting lodge. The meat is thick and juicy and the salad bar has an excellent assortment of vegetables and garnishes. For side dishes, try the O'Brien potatoes, which are diced and mixed with cheddar cheese, bacon and seasonings, then baked. We also like the sautéed mushrooms, cooked in garlic butter and red wine.

Golden Crown Chinese Restaurant
$$-$$$ • 6601 Everhart Rd., Corpus Christi • (512) 854-5506

Classy Cantonese-style fare is served in this elegant south side restaurant. Lunch is a good bet, with an assortment of daily specials such as chicken and asparagus. Garnishes include storks and cranes carved from sweet potatoes.

Hofbrau Steaks and Bar
$$ • 1214 N. Chaparral St., Corpus Christi • (512) 881-8722

Texas flags, neon beer signs and bargain lunch specials are the hallmarks of this rugged steakhouse. Regulars know that the Wednesday lunch special is chicken-fried steak, and they plan their day accordingly. We've also enjoyed a chopped sirloin topped with cheese and jalapeño sauce, served with thick steak fries and a salad.

Jeron's Tea Room
$-$$ • 5830 McArdle St., Corpus Christi • (512) 980-1939

This graceful tearoom serves salads, sandwiches, quiches and more in an antique-laden renovated house. We recommend the house lasagna, which is rich and creamy and satisfying. We also love the cheesy broccoli quiche, with its flaky crust and generous portion (even a real man could fill up on this quiche!). The entrees come with generous green salads and miniature corn muffins that have a delightful hint of sweetness. For vegetarians, try the garden sandwich of fresh avocado, cucumber and mushrooms on honey-wheat bread. Lemon cake and apple crisp are among the daily dessert offerings. Owner Bette Hoelscher also provides teas for special occasions and private receptions.

Jezebelles
$$, no credit cards • 100 Shoreline Blvd., Corpus Christi • (512) 887-7403

Inventive sandwiches and salads are served in this soothing restaurant in the Art Center of Corpus Christi. You can browse the center's gift shops and art displays after you finish your meal, or you can get your art-gazing in while eating — paintings on the restaurant's walls are by local artists and are changed monthly. A wall of windows facing the bay provides patrons with a great view. As for the food, we like the chicken salad flavored with chopped grapes, walnuts and chutney, as well as the roast beef with melted Monterey Jack cheese, sautéed onions and mushrooms. Desserts are also worth trying — the kitchen usually has several sinfully sweet offerings each day. This restaurant is open for lunch only and is closed on Sunday and Monday.

Kiko's
$-$$ • 5514 Everhart Rd., Corpus Christi • (512) 991-1211

A perennial favorite for standard Tex-Mex food, this restaurant serves massive portions of favorites. Fresh, hot tortillas accompany enchiladas, tacos, tamales and rice and beans. We also like the beef and chicken fajitas, served on a sizzling skillet and accompanied by Spanish rice, refried beans, guacamole and fresh flour tortillas. Service is quick, and the food is good. It can be crowded so you may have to wait for a table on a weekend night. Breakfast is also a popular choice here, with taquitos, omelets and more.

La Bahia
$ • 224 Mesquite St., Corpus Christi • (512) 888-6555

This is where locals come for breakfast and lunch, taking sustenance for their business day from the hearty fare served quickly and at extremely low prices. You can get a plate of huevos rancheros (eggs with salsa) and refried beans, tortillas, bacon and coffee for under $5. However, we prefer to visit here at lunchtime to fill up on cheesy enchiladas, tacos, nachos, rice and refried beans. This is near the police station, so you're sure to see plenty of cops inside. County and city officials also tend to frequent this amiable place.

The Lighthouse and the Landing
$$ • Lawrence St. T-Head, Corpus Christi • (512) 883-3982, 883-5263

Gaze at the bayfront while you dine on South Texas seafood at these adjoining restaurants — the Lighthouse is upstairs and the Landing is its more casual companion restaurant downstairs. Many people like to come here for drinks and appetizers, while others prefer to make an evening of it. The menu includes shrimp fajitas, grilled swordfish steak and crab cakes.

Longhorn Steak and Ale
$$ • 4307 Avalon St., Corpus Christi • (512) 992-7731

Steaks, seafood, chicken and southwestern favorites are the specialty of this comfortable restaurant near a row of antique shops. You can get a rib eye, fried chicken, stuffed flounder or a chicken-avocado salad here. There are also daily blackboard specials and a children's menu.

Mamma Mia's
$$-$$$, no credit cards • 128 N. Mesquite St., Corpus Christi • (512) 883-3773

The atmosphere, from Italian arias in the background to the odor of fresh-baked bread and garlic, is great at this downtown restaurant. And the food is fabulous. Favorites include red snapper linguine in a cream sauce with capers and artichoke hearts to pasta pesto alla marino, which features basil, pine nuts and olive oil with broccoli and mushrooms. Owner Marino Delzotto, with pipe in mouth, goes from table to table, greeting customers and making sure all is well. Assorted slices of thick, warm homemade breads arrive rapidly

on your table, for dipping in a plate of olive oil, balsamic vinegar or both. If you order wine, they'll set the jug on your table and rely on you to count your own glasses. If you have room for dessert, try the zabaglione, strawberries in a sauce of marsala, egg and sugar. This is one of the city's most popular Italian restaurants, so it can get a bit crowded. Its popularity is largely by word of mouth because they don't advertise.

Mao Tai
$$ • 4601 S. Padre Island Dr., Corpus Christi • (512) 852-8877

Easily one of the city's best Asian restaurants, there are more than 80 items on the extensive menu. Among the favorites are spicy General Tso's chicken and the Hunan-style combination of beef, scallops and shrimp.

Marbella's
$$-$$$ • 1002 Chaparral St., Corpus Christi • (512) 883-8087

A sophisticated, eclectic menu is the hallmark of this downtown restaurant in a cavernous warehouse-like building. Patrons tend to be more enthusiastic about the dinner menu than the lunches. Among the recommendations are the pecan-crusted redfish, which is served with a cilantro beurre blanc sauce and surrounded by chunks of tomato and avocado.

Marco's
$$-$$$ • 3812 S. Alameda St., Corpus Christi • (512) 853-2000

Great pasta and fresh seafood prepared by a consummate Italian chef are worth the high price tag. During a recent visit, we began our meal with hot, homemade bread and a pureed tomato-and-basil spread. Next we had fettuccine Alfredo with chicken, which was creamy and rich, studded with morsels of tender chicken breast. A friend had the linguini alla vongole, fresh clams in the shell steamed with oil, garlic, white wine and tomato sauce.

INSIDERS' TIP

If you're going to barbecue your own meat while visiting here, check out Moody's Meat Market, 4703 S. Alameda Street, (512) 992-6512, for the city's best selection of steaks, ribs, roasts, chicken and German-style sausage.

Photo: Daniel Fielder

The Yardarm is a favorite with locals for fresh seafood and a quaint atmosphere.

We also like the red-pepper pasta stuffed with sausage and broccoli, served with walnuts, black olives and a creamy tomato sauce. Dessert was a sinfully rich slice of dark chocolate cake flavored with amaretto, layered with marzipan and glazed with dark chocolate.

Ninfa's

$$ • 4551 S. Padre Island Dr., Corpus Christi • (512) 853-9895

This restaurant is among several in Texas established by owner Ninfa Laurenzo, whose eateries have gained fame for hearty Tex-Mex fare and colorful cantina-style decor. The house specialty is sizzling, juicy fajitas. We also recommend the tender baby-back ribs, the crispy chicken flautas, and the flavorful chile rellenos. For dessert, try the sopapillas — light, flaky fried bread dusted with powdered sugar and cinnamon, and served with honey — yummy!

Old Mexico

$$ • 3329 Leopard St., Corpus Christi • (512) 883-6461

For many longtime residents, a visit to this Mexican restaurant is a time-honored tradition. All the new culinary arrivals in town have thinned the crowds, but this place continues to serve dependable Tex-Mex fare. We par-

ticularly like the puffy tacos — fried to a delicate, air-filled fluffiness, then topped with cheese or guacamole. Enchiladas are good, rice is fluffy and the tortillas are freshly made and hot. A pecan praline or bowl of sherbet comes with each meal.

Origami

$$-$$$ • 1220 Airline Rd., Corpus Christi • (512) 993-3966

If you like sushi, you'll like this neat Japanese eatery. There are more than 50 varieties with ingredients ranging from raw tuna and cucumber to cooked shrimp and smoked eel. Entrees include shrimp tempura and teriyaki chicken.

Price's Chef

$ • 1800 S. Alameda St., Corpus Christi • (512) 883-2786

At this venerable and old-fashioned coffee shop, you can linger over a steaming cup of java and a plateful of scrambled eggs and toast, while reading the daily newspaper. Our favorite breakfast item is the pecan waffle, which is fluffy and thick and altogether a sweet wake-up call for your taste buds. Lunch is just as satisfying with home-style Southern culinary delights such as meatloaf, ham steak or chicken with dumplings. The entrees vary daily, and are served with vegetables and a dessert. Long a tradition with many locals, this coffee shop fills up quickly at lunchtime and after church on Sundays. Waitresses are friendly and easy-going, and they're likely to remember your preferences when you've been here several times.

Republic of Texas Bar and Grill

$$$-$$$$ • 900 N. Shoreline Blvd., Corpus Christi • (512) 886-3515

On the 20th floor of the Corpus Christi Marriott Bayfront, this restaurant offers a spectacular view of the waterfront and equally spectacular food. Its lush, opulent surroundings harken to Texas' oil-boom era, and its unabashed emphasis on quality beef reflect a time when steak was the first choice of those dining out. The restaurant also typically serves wild game each evening, including exotics such as ostrich and wild boar. This is a great place for celebrating an anniversary or other special occasion, or for a romantic escape. Service is excellent. Try to get here around sunset for a front-row seat at nature's nightly drama. It's also a good place for drinks and appetizers.

Rosita's

$-$$ • 2319 Morgan St., Corpus Christi • (512) 883-8363

Start your day with an order of breakfast taquitos — that's eggs and a filling such as potato, cheese, bacon or sausage, wrapped in a fresh flour tortilla — and you may have to skip lunch. For lunch try the enchilada platters, cheesy, chili-sauced enchiladas with refried beans and rice. Owners Johnny and Rosie Rodela have been offering their brand of traditional Mexican cooking to an appreciative clientele in this bustling westside restaurant for decades. Furnishings are basic Tex-Mex, from the posters featuring Tejano stars and the calendar with the picture of the Virgin of Guadalupe. Servers can be a bit brusque, but the food is great.

Rusty's

$-$$ • 1645 Airline Rd., Corpus Christi • (512) 993-5000

Hamburgers, chicken sandwiches, rib-eye steak sandwiches and Bohemian sausage are the purview of this unpretentious restaurant. Order your food at the front counter, where you can check out the thick, fresh hamburger patties. The bread is homemade, and there is a nice selection of domestic and imported beer and wine (by the glass).

Saigon Vietnam Restaurant

$$ • 5505 Saratoga Blvd., Corpus Christi • (512) 991-1122

One of the area's best Vietnamese restaurants, this place features an extensive menu of longtime favorites as well as house specialties. Try the spring rolls, or the ga nuong banh hoi (grilled chicken with vermicelli and homegrown herbs). Fried bananas make an interesting dessert.

Santa Fe Deli

$, no credit cards • 1124 Ayers St., Corpus Christi • (512) 882-3354

Sandwiches or daily hot entrees, including cabbage rolls and moussaka, are available at this unassuming deli. The menu includes traditional offerings such as pastrami, roast beef and ham and cheese, as well as more unusual items including the Power Veggie sandwich, with cream cheese, sprouts, white onion, tomato, avocado and tabouli.

Small Planet Delicatessen and Bakery

$$ • 42 Lamar Park Ctr., Corpus Christi • (512) 855-1892

We can't resist the crumbly, buttery scones (preferably washed down with a nice big cup of cafe mocha) at this supernaturally delicious deli. Its wide-ranging clientele, from the young and hip to the older and upscale, converge in the mornings and at lunchtime to partake of gigantic sweet rolls, cappuccino,

INSIDERS' TIP

The fiery pepper called the jalapeño is much beloved by South Texas cooks. It actually originated in Jalapa (or Xalapa), the capital of the Mexican state of Veracruz.

fruit salad, vegetarian lasagna, pesto pizza and the like. The cakes, pies and tarts are displayed with artistic grace under glass. The food almost looks too good to eat. Almost, we said. Look for the blackboard specials on daily hot entrees or try one of the specialty sandwiches, such as the Mediterranean, which features spinach, onion, feta cheese and fresh dill in flaky filo pastry. The furnishings are equally celestial, and the staff is personable and attentive.

Snoopy's Pier

$$, no credit cards • 13313 S. Padre Island Dr., Corpus Christi • (512) 949-8815

This is our favorite of the eateries beneath the JFK Causeway. It features traditional fried shrimp, juicy hamburgers and broiled fish. As befits a waterfront restaurant, the atmosphere is casual and rustic, with an outdoor deck that fills up quickly during warm spring and summer evenings. Order at the front of the restaurant, then come to pick up your food when your name is called. During the occasional cool days, the fireplace in the front room lends a cozy atmosphere.

Sonja's

$$ • 424 N. Chaparral St., Corpus Christi • (512) 884-7774

With veal marsala and baked brie, this cafe-and-bakery brings a touch of European dining to downtown Corpus Christi. Try the French onion soup or the roasted pork loin in a cognac-apple glaze. And don't forget to leave room for some of the sumptuous homemade pastries for dessert.

Taqueria Acapulco

$-$$ • 1133 Airline Rd., Corpus Christi • (512) 994-7274

You'll find good, hearty Tex-Mex food at bargain-basement prices here. As an added bonus, the kitchen does some intriguing combinations that go a bit beyond ordinary Tex-Mex such as the aguacate gordita, a thick corn tortilla split open and stuffed with avocado, refried beans and pico de gallo. Even the tacos are better than average, featuring finely cubed beef in a soft corn tortilla. The fresh fruit milkshakes, available in strawberry and banana, are also worth tasting.

Taqueria Jalisco

$-$$ • 902 S. Port Ave., Corpus Christi • (512) 881-8739

With nine locations in Corpus Christi and surrounding towns, this locally owned restaurant chain is a longtime crowd pleaser. This is the original with an open view of the kitchen with the rich fragrance of chili, posole and pepper. Expect traditional Mexican food, from breakfast taquitos to rich carne guisada.

Tien Tan

$-$$ • 5898 Everhart Rd., Corpus Christi • (512) 980-0748

Sleek black and purple decor, ceiling fans and sconces adorn this nifty Oriental restaurant. We recommend the lunch buffet, where you can sample a range of dishes including crab rangoon — fried wonton stuffed with crabmeat and cream cheese — beef with broccoli, lo mein noodles, sesame chicken, and fresh green beans sautéed with pork.

Tokyo Den

$$ • 5625-B S. Padre Island Dr., Corpus Christi • (512) 992-9611

Tucked into a strip center near the local Chuck-E-Cheese, this small Japanese restaurant is a soothing retreat from shopping stress and traffic jams. The menu includes Korean and Japanese specialties, and an array of sushi prepared by an expert chef. For a real treat, ask for bulgogi (beef) or Kaibi (short rib) to be grilled at your table.

The Torch

$$-$$$ • 4425 S. Alameda St., Corpus Christi • (512) 992-7491

Steaks are the specialty at this family-owned Greek restaurant, which is reminiscent of the small, intimate restaurants that abounded in the 1950s and 1960s — before franchises took hold. The best night to visit is Wednesday, Greek night, when you can select from seven Greek entrees, including one that offers "a little bit of everything." The moussaka is a wonderful casserole of thinly sliced potatoes and eggplant with meat sauce and bechamel sauce atop. While you're dining, you're likely to see owners Telly and Linda Gialouris circulating to chat with customers.

Town and Country Cafe

$-$$ • 4228 S. Alameda St., Corpus Christi • (512) 992-0360

For down-home cooking like Mama used to make, head for this homey cafe. Regulars hit this place for coffee, omelets and blueberry pancakes every morning. Others head over at noon to have the daily specials, which recently included beef tips and noodles, salmon patties and liver and onions. The cooked vegetables (which can include anything from broccoli, carrots, fried okra, turnip greens to mashed potatoes) are excellent here, and you can get a plate with a choice of four vegetables plus cornbread — a healthy and satisfying meal.

Vietnam

$$ • 4501 S. Padre Island Dr., Corpus Christi • (512) 853-2682

This family-owned restaurant specializes in fresh, attractively presented food. Appetizers include deep-fried crab rolls and shrimp rolls wrapped in rice paper; try the Vietnamese crepe cake stuffed with shrimp, bean sprouts and chicken.

Wallbangers

$$ • 4100 S. Staples St., Corpus Christi • (512) 855-8007

Remember that old commercial where they keep asking, "Where's the beef?" Well, this is where the beef is — unabashed, monster servings of ground beef. With unfinished wood floors, neon beef signs, high-backed wooden booths and quick service, this caters mostly to families and young people. In addition to the half-pounder, the pounder, and the junior burger (a third of a pound of meat), you can also order something known as "The Big Banger," a three-pound burger and two pounds of french fries. It supposedly feeds six people. Diners place their orders at a counter, and wait for their names to be called. Chicken sandwiches and baked potatoes are also available.

Water Street Oyster Bar and Water Street Seafood Co.

$$-$$$ • 309 N. Water St., Corpus Christi • (512) 881-9448, (512) 882-8684

These sister restaurants, with the same owner and same location, offer great fresh seafood in a classy atmosphere. This is the hands-down choice for locals who want to entertain out-of-town visitors. A nautical motif, complete with trophy fish hanging from the walls, adorns the Seafood Co., while an interesting rendition of Botticelli's *The Birth of Venus* is featured in the Oyster Bar. Our favorite entrees are the skewered, bacon-wrapped shrimp, and the grilled snapper in a crawfish Nueces sauce, but there is always an array of blackboard specials featuring fresh seafood. Although this restaurant serves a decent gumbo, the soup to get is the caldo xochitl (a fragrant chicken-and-rice soup served with slices of fresh avocado); and the house salad with creamy walnut-laced dressing.

Yardarm

$$$-$$$$ • 4310 Ocean Dr., Corpus Christi • (512) 855-8157

Hidden inside this cheery yellow house on the bayfront is some of the area's best and most elegant cuisine. The atmosphere is straight out of Nantucket, complete with thick bowls of creamy chowder and a pierside view. The tables are cozy and close together, which lends an intimate and rather romantic feel to this restaurant. Start your meal with the oysters Rockefeller, which are hot and fragrant, bursting with flavor. The house salad, with red onion, black olives, lettuce and clove-marinated carrot coins, is wonderful. As for entrees, among those we've had and loved are pompano en papillote (cooked in a paper bag) and sole cooked in white wine, draped in spinach and topped with Hollandaise sauce. This is a great place for a romantic dinner or anniversary celebration. Expect a leisurely meal here — servers are attentive but this is fare meant to be savored, not gulped down.

INSIDERS' TIP

The mesquite tree that dots the South Texas landscape actually provided a beverage for some of the more destitute early settlers, who reportedly dried and roasted the tree's beans to make a bitter sort of coffee.

Corpus Christi's Lighthouse Restaurant, which is located on the end of the Lawrence Street T-head, offers a fabulous view of the bayfront.

Robstown

Cotten's Bar-B-Que
$$-$$$, no credit cards • U.S. Hwy. 77, Robstown • (512) 767-9973

State governors and out-of-state dignitaries have been known to fly into this tiny community — even landing helicopters on the grassy median along the interstate — in order to partake of the beloved barbecue served in this wooden structure. Founder Joe Cotten, who died in 1992, established his reputation by slow-cooking corn-fed beef over mesquite wood all night. Family members who inherited the restaurant have continued his tradition. This place is simple, straightforward and unpretentious. There is no menu — customers select sliced pork, beef brisket, ribs or sausage. It arrives at the table on sheets of butcher paper. Served with it are the basic accompaniments of pinto beans in rich broth, sliced bread, tangy barbecue sauce and thick slices of raw onion, radishes, pickle and jalapeño. If you want seconds, summon the waiter to your table. Truly a South Texas tradition, many longtime customers eat here at least once a week, if not more often. And among the celebrities who have frequented Cotten's are Lyndon Johnson, Willie Nelson, Roger Staubach and many of the Dallas Cowboys.

Port Aransas to Padre Island

Beulah's at Tarpon Inn
$$$ • 200 E. Cotter Ave., Port Aransas • (512) 749-4888

Chef-owner Guy Carathan's kitchen produces fabulous and creative dishes that entice locals and visitors to this graceful restaurant in the historic Tarpon Inn (see our Accommodations chapter). This is a place to go and make an evening out of the dining experience, so you can savor dishes like bacon-wrapped fresh tuna, roasted garlic mashed potatoes, a salad of greens in a dressing of toasted pecans, blue cheese, and soy balsamic vinaigrette. Patrons can sit indoors or on the breezy open veranda. The menu always includes fresh fish, steak and rack of lamb. The restaurant is open for dinner Wednesday through Sunday and for Sunday brunch. Note: It closes from Thanksgiving until right after Christmas.

Crazy Cajun

$$ • 303 Beach St. at Station St., Port
Aransas • (512) 749-5069

This is a casual, down-home eatery that
serves Cajun-style seafood. The boiled dinner
of crab legs, shrimp and crawfish comes to
your butcher-paper-covered table for every-
one to dig in. There's also live entertainment,
including local bands.

Marcel's

$$$ • 905 Alister Rd., Port Aransas
• (512) 749-5577

A romantic dinner for two at this cozy gourmet restaurant might feature grilled salmon
with crushed black peppercorns and garlic
herb-butter sauce, or venison scallopini with
shiitake mushroom sauce, cranberry-apple
relish and homemade spaetzle (German egg
noodles). Or what about sautéed flounder with
Hollandaise sauce and capers, served with
new potatoes. Chef Marcel Althauser pairs Gulf
Coast seafood with hearty Germanic flavors
for a winsome combination. There are always
several daily specials on the blackboard, as
well as the menu standbys of fresh seafood
and fresh-cut steaks. It's open for dinner only.

Seafood and Spaghetti Works

$$ • Alister Rd. at Ave. G, Port Aransas
• (512) 749-5666

This funky geodesic dome seems an un-
likely place to dine, but don't be put off by the
odd-looking exterior. The kitchen has been pro-
ducing a unique mixture of seafood, steaks and
Italian food for years. Be sure to check out the
homemade desserts. It's open for dinner only.

Pelican's Landing

$$-$$$ • 337 N. Alister Rd., Port Aransas
• (512) 749-6405

Serving locally caught fish and aged beef-
steaks, this restaurant offers quality dining in
an island-inspired atmosphere. Decor includes
palm trees in the front and an outdoor cov-
ered deck that's open for lunch and rustic fur-
nishings. In business for more than two de-
cades, it is known for the freshness of its sea-
food and its island specialties, including the
popular shrimp Port Aransas (sautéed giant
shrimp in a garlic butter sauce with mushrooms
and tomatoes, served over fettuccine noodles.

Shell's Pasta Seafood Restaurant

$$ • Ave. G and 11th Sts., Port Aransas
• (512) 749-7621

A relative newcomer to the island restaurant scene, this bistro has rapidly gained a following with its pasta dishes, seafood entrees
and fresh baked breads. The luncheon blackboard specials on a recent winter day included:
linguine with hickory smoked fennel sausage,
baby corn, roasted peppers and herbs; spinach fettuccine with apple-smoked bacon, diced
tomatoes and broccoli in a cream sauce; a fish
sandwich on focaccia bread with baby mixed
greens; capellini with seafood, roasted tomatoes, green onion and cilantro; and a Caesar
salad with marinated grilled chicken. All the
breads and desserts are homemade.

Venetian Hot Plate

$$-$$$ • 232 Beach St., Port Aransas
• (512) 749-7617

Paintings of gondolas and Italian scenery
set the tone at this cozy little restaurant. The
entrees are delicious, from classics such as
spaghetti carbonara to more creative items
like a filet mignon with a gorgonzola sauce.
Other offerings include pasta, veal, steak, and
fresh croissants.

Kingsville Area

Black Diamond Oyster Bar

$-$$ • 503 E. Corral St., Kingsville
• (512) 592-6051

This restaurant is an institution for many
longtime residents, serving fried shrimp and
fish in an unpretentious setting.

El Jardin

$$ • 330 E. Henrietta Ave., Kingsville
• (512) 595-5955

Indulge in a hearty platter of grilled beef
with fresh flour tortillas, seasoned pinto beans
and Spanish rice at this family-owned cantina.
Servings are generous, and the service is
friendly and courteous.

Harrell's Kingsville Pharmacy

$ • 204 E. Kleberg Ave., Kingsville
• (512) 592-3355

Hop on a stool and order a double-meat

home-style burger with a fountain cherry Coke. Nick Harrell III is the third-generation owner of this longtime drugstore and soda fountain. He has a keen sense of the business's place in local history. Service is friendly and warm. We also like browsing among the sundry items in the drugstore after our meal.

King's Inn
$$$ • F.M. Rd. 628, Riviera • (512) 297-5265

This seafood restaurant that sits on the edge of Baffin Bay is one of the area's best — as attested to by the legion of loyal customers who routinely make the 90-mile trek from Corpus Christi to dine here. For decades, the Ware family has been dishing up golden fried shrimp in a beer-batter crust and crunchy fried oysters in cornmeal breading. Your meal comes with french fries, but don't waste time filling up on those — instead, try the thick, juicy sliced tomatoes in the house tartar sauce. As for that tartar sauce, it bears no resemblance whatsoever to the usual gooey mixture that comes in a jar. Its ingredients are a closely guarded secret. The sliced avocado salad and the Bombay salad — mashed avocados with a touch of curry — are heavenly. Food is served family-style, and it is plentiful. The atmosphere is waterfront casual, with linoleum floors, fake wood paneling and old family photos on the walls, offset by crisp white table linens and excellent service.

Young's Pizza
$-$$, no credit cards • 625 W. Santa Gertrudis Ave., Kingsville • (512) 592-9179

A classic college-area hangout, this has an eclectic atmosphere and menu. The house specialty sandwiches and baked potatoes have monikers that are as creative as the ingredients. Patooties are Young's accompaniment-laden potatoes, such as the Aw Rootie, with avocado, cheddar and Parmesan cheeses, tomato, onion, salt, pepper, butter and the mysterious Aw Rootie Sauce. Our hands-down favorite sandwich is the Texicali, which features tender sliced beef, sautéed onion and mushrooms, melted cheese, sliced jalapeños and mayonnaise on a soft, fresh-baked bun. And even though we're willing to mention it here, we've not yet gathered up our nerve to taste the shrimp and sauerkraut pizzas.

Wild Olive
$$ • Seller's Market, 205 E. Kleberg Ave., Kingsville • (512) 595-4992

This tearoom attracts shoppers and visitors alike and you can browse among the handcrafted wares after you finish lunch. There are sandwiches, soups, quiche and desserts available. It's open for lunch Wednesday through Friday.

Since the first cowboys
crooned to their cattle
under the starry skies,
there has always been
night music in
South Texas.

Nightlife

Since the first cowboys crooned to their cattle under the starry skies, there has always been night music in South Texas. The many-splendored styles of music favored by South Texans keep the mood lively at a variety of clubs throughout the region, from boot-stompin' country-and-western tunes to the mournful jazz and blues and the lively rhythms of rock 'n' roll.

Many clubs have decades of history in this region, while others are relative newcomers. Corpus Christi has experienced an explosion of new nightclubs, particularly in the downtown area, that cater to a varied and diverse clientele — from a luxurious cigar-and-martini lounge to a Tejano dance club.

Remember that the drinking age here is 21, and although 18- to-21-year-olds are allowed into some bars, they usually pay a higher cover charge and aren't permitted to drink alcohol.

If bars aren't your scene, you'll find plenty of other nighttime activities in the Coastal Bend including outdoor events as well as romantic waterfront cruises. Movie theaters abound, as do video stores for rental of films to watch at home or your hotel room. Some of our favorite haunts are the local bookstore-coffee bars, great places to meet folks, visit and even listen to live music. We would also urge you to spend at least one evening simply walking along the bayfront in the moonlight. Particularly in the summertime, when the cooling breezes temper the heat, it may be the best time of day to be outdoors.

Most of these clubs are open seven days a week unless otherwise indicated.

As in most of our other chapters, we've grouped our nightlife offerings into categories, then further broken them down by geographical area. So you can look for live music in Corpus Christi or Kingsville, or movie theaters in the North Bay area.

The geographic groupings begin at the northernmost tip of our coverage area and proceed southward along the coastline. Of course, the preponderance of nightlife is available in the larger cities, such as Corpus Christi and Kingsville, but you'll discover a few clubs worth visiting in the smaller towns as well. Check the Corpus Christi newspaper's "Weekend" section on Friday for a listing of all the live bands appearing over the weekend; the newspaper also lists weekend events and activities as well as those for the coming week.

Live Music

North Bay Area

Boiling Pot
Fulton Beach Rd., Rockport
• (512) 729-6972
This restaurant hosts a house band on select evenings; call first to see if there will be live music, which includes blues and country. Open jam sessions are scheduled on Sundays during the summer. For more information about the food served, see our Restaurants chapter.

Rudder's Bar and Grill
415 S. Austin St., Rockport
• (512) 790-7245
Rudders, a longtime restaurant and bar in downtown Rockport, features live blues and folk music on Tuesday nights, with an open mike jam session starting at 8 PM. There is no cover charge. The atmosphere is casual, and the food is eclectic, ranging from hamburgers and nachos to seafood and steaks.

Sandollar Pavilion
Fulton Beach Rd., Rockport
• (512) 729-8909
Steaks, seafood and live music, including everything from rock to country, on weekends

make this a good nightspot to try. An outdoor bar offers a view of the bayfront and the boats, while pool tables and a large-screen television offer activities indoors.

Port Aransas to Padre Island

Sharky's
730 Trout St., Port Aransas
• **(512) 749-4254**

You can hear classic rock to country-and-western tunes in this casual, nautical atmosphere. In addition to music and dancing, you'll find pool tables and other games.

Temerario's
445 W. Cotter Ave., Port Aransas
• **(512) 749-5599**

This Mexican restaurant and cantina offers a variety of music, ranging from South Texas grassroots to bluegrass to big band. There's usually no cover charge, but call first. Check out the Monday night football in the TV room. Temerario's also has a play area for the youngsters.

www.insiders.com
See this and many other Insiders' Guide® destinations online — in their entirety.
Visit us today!

Trout Street Bar and Grill
104 W. Cotter Ave., Port Aransas
• **(512) 749-7800**

Come to this harbor side seafood restaurant and bar to hear recorded reggae, Caribbean and Jimmy Buffet tunes. Or, if you prefer, you can catch sporting events on the big-screen television or pick up some tips from the how-to fishing videos.

Corpus Christi

Buckets
227 N. Water St., Corpus Christi
• **(512) 883-7776**

This sports bar and grill offers munchies and drinks in an athletic-inspired atmosphere. It's a great place for watching the Monday night football game or televised boxing

matches, as well as for shooting pool. A variety of live music is featured on the outdoor patio. The kitchen serves munchies including chicken strips, hamburgers and salads.

Chelsea Street Pub and Grill
5858 S. Padre Island Dr., Corpus Christi
• **(512) 993-3322**

This eatery at Sunrise Mall features live music, usually rock 'n' roll, Monday through Saturday. Cover charge is $1 on Friday and Saturday.

Club La Playa and Starz
407 Schatzell St., Corpus Christi
• **(512) 882-2664**

Two venues for the price of one provide variety at this dance club. Club La Playa offers recorded Tejano music and dancing, with occasional live bands. At the adjoining Starz club, you'll find dance music and retro and international music — and you can enter both clubs for one price. Customers 18 and older pay a cover charge Wednesday through Saturday, and the price varies depending on which day of the week you're there.

Club UBU and Frenz
511 Starr St., Corpus Christi
• **(512) 882-9693**

This downtown bar caters mostly to the gay crowd, but also attracts a hip straight clientele. The club has two sides: Frenz, which plays mostly jukebox music, and UBU, which features underground or top-40 music and occasional live bands. Regular drink specials include dollar drinks on Thursdays and 50¢ draft beer on weekends. The cover charge ranges from $1 to $3 for adults and is slightly higher for minors.

Dr. Rockit's
709 N. Chaparral St., Corpus Christi
• **(512) 884-7634**

Open since the mid-1980s, Dr. Rockit's is one of the city's oldest venues for live music. It features an impressive lineup of noted musicians who play everything from reggae to blues and jazz, seven nights a week. All the standards from the Austin music scene play here, including the Killer Bees and Omar and the Howlers. Other performers have included Clarence Gatemouth Brown, Canned Heat, Charlie Musselwhite, Lou Ann Barton and Marcia Ball. The crowd here tends to be a bit older and more into the music than the social scene, unlike some of the other downtown haunts. The music is free Sunday through Thursday, and the cover charge on Friday and Saturday night can range from $3 to $10, depending on the musician featured.

Executive Surf Club
309 N. Water St., Corpus Christi
• (512) 884-7873
Owned by the same folks who operate the Water Street Seafood Co. restaurants next door, this perennially popular nightspot is a gathering place for the after-work crowd. Great munchies include nachos, batter-dipped fries and burgers. And the outdoor patio makes for a fun place to listen to live music, which usually includes folk, country or rock. Among performers who've been here recently are Robert Earl Keen and Johnny Lang. The mike is open for amateurs on Wednesdays, and you'll find 30 different beers on tap. There can be a cover charge, depending on the artist. For more information about the food served, see our Restaurants chapter.

Tom Foolery's Chill and Grill
301 N. Chaparral St., Corpus Christi
• (512) 887-0029
The laid-back ambiance at this bar and restaurant attracts mostly a young crowd, with top-40 and alternative music. Refreshments include burgers and sandwiches, and the drink of choice is likely to be beer or kamikazes. Three wide-screen television sets, as well as 20 smaller TV screens, are ideal for the sports fanatic. Karaoke music is the big draw on Tues-

days, and live music, mostly rock, and dancing are featured on Friday and Saturday. Attire here is very casual — usually jeans or shorts and T-shirts. There is sometimes a cover charge here.

Yellow Rose
2001 Saratoga Blvd., Corpus Christi
• (512) 855-6616
Yellow Rose is the major local site to hear live Tejano music, which is featured nearly every weekend. It serves as the major Latin music center for most of the area, drawing big-name bands such as Intocable, La Mafia and Ramon Ayala y Sus Bravos Del Norte.

Zero's Hard Rock Club
6327 McArdle Rd., Corpus Christi
• (512) 991-6042
This is one of the only places where you can hear live, head-banging, heavy metal music, so it's worth a mention. The place itself is rather unprepossessing, but our sources tell us that the rock 'n' roll is authentic, loud and satisfying.

Kingsville Area

Country Luau Saloon
115 University St. at W. King St., Kingsville • (512) 595-4331
Welders and cowboys rub elbows at this casual saloon deep in the heart of South Texas. You can hear live country-and-western music on weekends. It's also especially popular with university students.

Cutter D's
817 W. King St., Kingsville
• (512) 516-1114
This club features live Tejano music on weekends, including the sounds of local groups such as Jennifer y Los Jetz, La Sombra and Increible. There can be a cover charge.

INSIDERS' TIP

Be sure to appoint a designated driver if you're planning a night out on the town. Many clubs serve nonalcoholic drinks, such as Sharps and O'Doul's beers, in addition to the regular beers and wines.

Gin Mill Saloon
1020 S. Sixth St., Kingsville
• **(512) 592-8835**

This large, informal facility is a casual place especially popular with the city's young professionals, who stop in after work to unwind. Karaoke music is featured on Tuesday, Thursday and Saturday.

Other Bars and Nightclubs

Port Aransas to Padre Island

Moby Dick's
517 S. Alister St., Port Aransas
• **(512) 749-5769**

This colorful nautical haunt offers a little bit of everything: pool tables, video games, a jukebox, burgers, fries, beer and wine.

Corpus Christi Area

B&J's Back Room
6331 S. Padre Island Dr., Corpus Christi
• **(512) 993-8773**

Pool tables, large-screen television screens and great munchies make this a popular place to host going-away parties, reunions and bachelor parties. The atmosphere is basic pool hall (dark, neon beer signs, etc.), but the adjoining pizza parlor has what many consider the area's best pizza, as well as an incredibly diverse array of foreign and domestic brews. See our Restaurants chapter for more information.

Dragon Lounge
326 N. Chaparral St., Corpus Christi
• **(512) 885-0465**

Modeled after a Prohibition-style pub, this dimly lit cigar-and-martini bar is glamorous in an old-fashioned kind of way. Sit on Victorian sofas and sip single-malt scotches while listening to Frank Sinatra tunes. The lounge also has a private smoking room and sells an assortment of gourmet cigars. The attire is a little

dressier here, and the crowd's age ranges from 21 to 60. It's closed Sundays.

Santa Fe Cantina
1011 Santa Fe St., Corpus Christi
• **(512) 888-8769**

This longtime local bar and restaurant serves lunch and drinks in a casual atmosphere. There are pool tables, a jukebox and a covered patio with a Ping-Pong table. The menu includes hamburgers, shrimp baskets and salads.

Scoots
208 N. Water St., Corpus Christi
• **(512) 888-8767**

Inside this club's country-rustic atmosphere, you can dance or listen to your favorite country-and-western tunes. This is the only downtown place to hear country music, so it draws a good crowd.

Stetson's
5831 Weber Rd., Corpus Christi
• **(512) 855-4886**

Put on your cowboy boots and hat when you head out to this country-and-western club, which has a disc jockey and dance floor. It draws a diverse range of ages and is open Wednesday through Sunday.

Vernon's Bar-B-Que
1030 Third St., Corpus Christi
• **(512) 884-6552**

A fixture on the local scene, this dark and unpretentious nightspot has been serving beers to blue collar workers as well as professionals for many years. Barbecue is served during the noon hour and free peanuts in the evenings.

Movie Theaters

North Bay Area

This area is served by **Cinema 4**, (512) 729-4448, on Texas Highway 35 N. in Rockport.

Corpus Christi

Corpus Christi's movie houses include the following: **Cine 6**, (512) 992-7821, 4700 S.

Staples Street; **Discount Cinemas**, (512) 993-6965 or (512) 993-6966, Sunrise Mall, 5858 S. Padre Island Drive; **Silver Cinemas**, (512) 242-9121, 4147 Five Points Road; **The Movies**, (512) 993-8500, Padre Staples Mall, 5488 S. Padre Island Drive; and **Tinseltown 16**, (512) 814-3100, S. Padre Island Drive at Greenwood Drive.

Kingsville

In Kingsville, you can catch a flick at the following cinemas: **Cine I and II**, (512) 592-0641, 2001 Brahma Boulevard; and **Rio VII Cinemas**, (512) 516-1303, 1601 S. U.S. Highway 77.

Dinner Cruises

Corpus Christi Sailing Center Inc.
200 S. Shoreline Blvd., Corpus Christi
• (512) 881-8503

Sail aboard a yacht to Landry's Seafood House for a four-course dinner, then back on board for a two-hour cruise into the setting sun. The cost is $55 for adults and teens, $25 for children ages 6 to 12 and $10 for children younger than 6.

Coffee Houses

Corpus Christi

Café Calypso
Inside Half-Price Books, Moore Plaza, Corpus Christi • (512) 993-5282

Folk music, bluegrass, classic rock and jazz are among the offerings at this coffee bar inside a bookstore. Coffee drinks and pastries are served. Seating can be a bit tight, but tables are available outdoors too. Moore Plaza is at 5425 S. Padre Island Drive.

Carousel Café and Bakery
1821 S. Alameda St., Corpus Christi
• (512) 882-5921

This is kind of a young-artist hangout, with sculptures and paintings by local talent, belly dancers and an open mike for amateur performers — musicians, poets, writers or dreamers — on Thursday nights. On Friday, there's live music and Saturday is open mike or bands. This bakery also hosts meetings for study groups and other organizations, including a computer group. Cover charge for open mike nights is $1 per person.

Barnes & Noble Cafe
5129 Blanche Moore St. at Moore Plaza, Corpus Christi • (512) 992-1339

Students, scholars and book lovers gather at this coffee shop in the middle of this massive bookstore, where they can read or chat while sipping Starbucks coffee, espressos and specialty drinks. The cafe also serves soup, pastries and cookies. Live music is featured several times a month, usually on a Saturday. The cafe is open daily until 11 PM.

Planetariums and Observatories

King High School
5225 Gollihar Rd., Corpus Christi
• (512) 994-6917

View a program detailing the items of interest in the local night skies at this high school planetarium, which offers public shows on Tuesday evenings. The show changes with the seasons and costs $2 per person.

Texas A&M University-Kingsville Observatory
Lon C. Hill Hall, 955 W. University St., Kingsville • (512) 593-2699

Watch the starry skies of South Texas through the telescopes at this university observatory, which is used for astronomy classes taught by the physics department. The observatory is open to the public periodically for special events and is also available for group tours. For information call Dr. Julian Schreur.

The Coastal Bend offers some interesting attractions for shoppers, especially in renovated downtown historic districts and seaside souvenir shops.

Shopping

Although the Coastal Bend has its share of unique shops and buyers' enticements, let it be said from the start that shopping is not the primary reason most people visit this region. The Coastal Bend has only a few malls, and they are more likely to contain typical department and specialty stores than to offer buyers a unique retail experience.

Let it also be said that strip centers have been booming, and those enormous, warehouse-like discount stores abound. You can find at least one Wal-Mart or Kmart in nearly every community — in Corpus Christi, the two sit side by side in at least one location. "Discount" is often the operative word here, because the low per capita income in South Texas probably tends to deter many of the nation's more upscale retailers from locating here. Weekend garage sales are especially popular; check the newspaper classified ads for locations and hours.

Nonetheless, the Coastal Bend offers attractions to shoppers. Several communities have renovated their downtown business districts to spotlight historical or unique attributes. And if you're looking for something fancy, you'll discover several posh shopping districts that specialize in designer clothing and jewelry, or artwork and antiques.

Keep in mind that the majority of stores and the greatest variety will be found in the area's largest city, Corpus Christi. The stores and malls in Corpus Christi tend to draw shoppers from the surrounding, more rural, communities as well as from over the border in Mexico.

On the plus side, friends from Houston and Dallas say they find better bargains here than in their own malls. Our out-of-town friends also like the less-crowded atmosphere at the shops and malls here. On the other hand, we can't deny that you'd find a wider selection of merchandise in more sophisticated and larger cities, including Dallas, Houston and San Antonio.

As for food sales, it's worth noting that the primary grocery retailer in the Coastal Bend is H.E.B. Foods Inc., headquartered in San Antonio. Corpus Christi has three Albertson's supermarkets (a big chain in Texas) and numerous smaller grocery stores. Diversity is sorely lacking here — we have but a smattering of health-food stores and none of the upscale gourmet markets that more metropolitan areas may have. The good news, though, is that groceries seem to be competitively priced, and fresh fruit and vegetables are particularly attractive year round.

Roadside vendors can also be a good source for fresh produce, particularly during peak growing seasons. You'll see pecans for sale in the fall and winter, ruby red grapefruit in the winter and assorted vegetables during the spring. We enjoy stopping and checking out the produce at these stands, and recommend it to visitors. The produce is often fresh from the field and bursting with flavor, and the prices are more than reasonable.

We'd be remiss if we failed to mention the shrimpers that sell their catch right off the boat. The T-heads in downtown Corpus Christi and Conn Brown Harbor in Aransas Pass are where the boats moor for the evening, and they definitely have the freshest shrimp around — those crustaceans were happily swimming in the water a few hours earlier. We've bought from them and find the prices reasonable, but some

INSIDERS' TIP

During the winter months, you can get wonderful grapefruit from the roadside vendors. Oranges and grapefruits are grown in the Rio Grande Valley in far South Texas.

buyers are a little more wary of such independent vendors. As always, use common sense when purchasing seafood — it should look fresh, feel firm and not have an overly pungent odor.

Here's a quick rundown of the area's largest retail centers and the more intriguing small venues. This is by no means an all-inclusive list, but we do want to provide visitors and newcomers with a good starting point to find what they need.

We'll start with the area's malls, including two in Corpus Christi and one in Kingsville, and large shopping centers. We'll then wend our way through the area's shopping districts, antiques, thrift and consignment stores, farmer's markets, bookstores, music stores and Western wear and souvenir shops.

Malls and Shopping Centers

Corpus Christi

Moore Plaza Shopping Center
5425 S. Padre Island Dr., Corpus Christi • (512) 993-4100

The newest, fastest-growing retail center in the city, this strip center opened in 1989. Its major tenants include H.E.B. Food Stores, Target, PetsMart, Old Navy Store, Barnes and Noble Booksellers and Pier 1. The choices of stores here provide everything from dining to coffee bars, and home furnishings to beauty supplies and clothing.

Among the restaurants at this center and nearby are EZ's, which specializes in burgers and pizza; Blimpie's sandwiches; Sirloin Stockade for steaks; Taco Cabana for Mexican fare; and Taiwan Restaurant. A number of other restaurants, many part of national chains, line the expressway that leads to this strip center.

For the bargain-minded, there's a Half-Price Books, which contains a nice cappuccino bar and live music on weekends (see our Nightlife chapter); Once Upon A Child, a re-

sale shop specializing in children's items; and Hit or Miss, a discount clothing retailer.

Look here also for dry cleaners, auto parts, tuxedo rentals, haircuts, beauty supplies, electronics, video stores and office supplies.

Padre Staples Mall
S. Padre Island Dr. at S. Staples St., Corpus Christi • (512) 991-5718

This 25-year-old, two-story mall is anchored by major department stores including Dillard's, JCPenney, Foley's, Bealls and Palais Royal. With more than 100 tenants, this mall has everything from shops to restaurants and a movie theater. Popular clothing chains include The Limited, The Gap, Gapkids, Benjamin's and Victoria's Secret. Among the more regional offerings are Smith's Guns and Texan Hats Inc. and Trader Rick's Gem's and Gold, selling just what their names imply.

At the center of the mall is a beautiful merry-go-round, with old-fashioned brightly painted horses on two revolving levels. This is a favorite for kids of all ages, and it can provide a fun break from shopping.

To quench your post-buying thirst and appetite, the mall has a food court near the movie theater entrance with such tenants as BBQ International, Chao Praya (Chinese fare), Dairy Queen, Famous Corn Dog, the Original Cookie Company, Texas Hot Dog, Tropical Treats and Villa Pizza. Other restaurants in the mall include Casa Olé, Chick-Fil-A, Harvest House Restaurant, Luby's Cafeteria and My Favorite Muffin. A number of restaurants are also on the outskirts of the mall, including the Olive Garden, Chili's and McDonald's.

The mall also has covered parking, stroller rentals and wheelchairs (free with a refundable deposit).

Sunrise Mall
S. Padre Island Dr. at Airline Rd. • (512) 993-2900

Just a block away from Corpus Christi's other mall (why do they all congregate in the same area?) is Sunrise Mall, which contains more than 100 shops, restaurants and business offices. The anchor tenants at this two-story mall are Mervyn's, Sears, Montgomery Ward, Stein Mart and Burlington Coat Factory. This complex seems to cater to a slightly more youthful shopper, with clothing shops such as Contempo Casuals, Foxmoor, Rock 'n Roll Plus and Melrose, as well as athletic stores like FootAction, Foot Locker, Lady Foot Locker and Oshman's Supersports USA.

A food court includes restaurants such as Anna's Ice Cream and Deli, Chick-Fil-A, Corn Dog 7, Famous Corn Dog, Fitzsimmons Gourmet Fries, Great American Cookie Company, Las Palmas Express, Orange Julius, Oriental Express, Treats N' Sweets and Wendy's. Sitdown restaurants include Chelsea Street Pub and Joe's Mexican Restaurant.

In addition, a military recruiting center and a hospital program for senior citizens is housed here, as is a branch of the Corpus Christi Police Department.

As at the city's other mall, you can rent strollers, borrow wheelchairs and take advantage of a free escort to your car.

Kingsville Area

Kingsville Mall
1724 S. Brahma Blvd., Kingsville
• (512) 595-5741

A half-mile north of Southgate Mall (see next entry) is this shopping center anchored by Sears Roebuck Co., which is also the only retail outlet here. This mall contains mostly professional services, including La Paloma Adult Day Care, and a home-healthcare service and rehabilitation center for nearby Spohn Hospital.

Southgate Mall
2331 S. Brahma Blvd., Kingsville
• (512) 595-5741

This is the larger, more established of two small malls in this town. Anchor stores are Bealls (a department store) and Eckerd Drugs. Other tenants include a video arcade, barber shop, Radio Shack, On-Cue Music and Books, Texas State Optical, Payless Shoe Source and Regis Hair Stylists.

Shopping Districts

North Bay Area

Austin Street
Downtown Rockport

This downtown shopping district in the middle of Rockport offers a nice grouping of local and specialty shops, all within walking distance and near the waterfront.

In the Austin Street General Store, 502 S. Austin Street, you'll find fragrances, collectibles, linens and seaside sculptures.

Belles & Bows, 203 S. Austin Street, offers decorative accessories that range from antiques and teddy bears to music tapes and CDs.

Bent Tree Gallery, 504 S. Austin Street, sells 18th- and 19th-century antiques such as furniture, silver, crystal, pocket watches and Oriental rugs.

At Connections, 209 S. Austin Street, the merchandise includes unique jewelry, clothes, candles, CDs and tapes.

Dojiggers Crafts and Gifts, 211 S. Austin Street, sells handmade crafts and gifts including Rockport T-shirts and country signs.

There's also the Estelle Stair Gallery, 406 S. Austin Street, with art, sculpture, furniture, jewelry and tables made from cypress taken from an offshore oil rig buried since 1910.

Quilters will be in heaven at Golden Needles and Quilts, 701 Allen Place, which has fabric, patterns, supplies, books, kits and — of course— needles. Instruction is available, and machine quilting services are provided.

Hidden Treasures, 207 N. Austin Street, has casual resort wear and a collection of Brighton purses, belts and wallets.

Moby Dan's, 415 S. Austin Street, is for sailors and dreamers, with World War I British-issue sextants and compasses, an 1850 telescope, brass divers' helmets, lighthouses, carved coastal bird statues, T-shirts and educational toys.

For the artist in everyone, visit the Rockport Artist's Gallery, 414 S. Austin Street. It has a large collection of coastal and seascape artwork, antique crosses, pottery, sand animals and glass sculptures.

Seaside Brass and Wood, 508 S. Austin Street, features art and gifts from around the world.

Sweet Peas, 205 S. Austin Street, sells jewelry, frames, cards, antiques, gift items, Appalachian music, cappuccino, gourmet coffee and kids' books and stuffed animals.

Tejas Gallery, 415 S. Austin Street, offers an assortment of Lone Star State memorabilia, from artwork to canned rattlesnake and wildflower seeds. Be sure to check out the Hummingbird Room.

Victoria's Gold and Gems, 415 S. Austin Street, sells jewelry with a nautical theme, from sterling silver to diamonds.

Galley Gadgets, 193 S. Austin Street, has cooking equipment, cookbooks and entertainment accessories, from place mats to paper goods.

Kaelin's Closet, 105 N. Austin Street, is billed as "Grandma's favorite place to shop." And we can see why, with its large selection of lovely christening gowns, toys, books and children's clothing. There are also consignments, kites and baby gifts.

The Niche Artglass Gallery, 415 S. Austin Street, is a working studio and gallery that showcases stained glass, antiques and hanging redfish and shorebirds.

Corpus Christi

Crossroads Shopping Village
Airline at McArdle, Corpus Christi

Unique gifts in a quaint atmosphere is the hallmark of this tidy little shopping village. Among the retailers and restaurants here are Gruene Outfitters, where you can find an assortment of outdoor gear from kayaks and fly-fishing rods to Birkenstocks and Patagonia outdoor wear; Salon Salon, which provides hair care, massage, facials, pedicures and manicures; Benjamin's, a youth-oriented clothing store that deals in Southern California-style fashions; and Goosefeathers, with clothing and furniture in soft, earthy hues and natural fabrics.

When you get hungry, you can stop at Jeron's Tea Room and Cafe for lunch, dinner or afternoon tea; Edelweiss for German-style cuisine; or Catfish Charlie's for fried fish and shrimp.

You'll also find The Needle Nook for knitting supplies and needlework; Phillip Randolph Jewelers, which offers designer jewelry from watches to rings, pearls to platinum; Nature's Bird Center, with a nice supply of items for birders and bird-lovers; and Disc Go Round for music needs.

Across the street is The Promenade shopping center, anchored by the perennially popular Toys R Us. Other stores and eateries in this center include Cavender's Boot City, for Western wear; Bamboo Garden Oriental Restaurant and Origami Japanese Cuisine; Arrow Parcel and Post; Payless Shoe Source; Tobacco World for cigars, pipes and tobacco; One-Hour Photo; and several other businesses.

Lamar Park
Doddridge St. at Alameda St., Corpus Christi

This little shopping village just three blocks from the bayfront is full of interesting and pricey stores. You can dine at several restaurants within this complex, and more shops and services are nearby, including a post office branch.

One of the most fun stores to visit here is Pilar's, 32 Lamar Park Center, which carries unusual items that fall into the category of colorful, creative or folk art. The selection includes carved candlesticks and furniture, Mexican-style crucifixes and wooden toys, exotic jewelry and one-of-a-kind clothing. We also like the bags, belts and artwork.

Nearby is Small Planet Deli, 42 Lamar Park Center, which serves food that is as artistic as it is delicious. Stop by for a mocha cappuccino or slice of three-layer carrot cake. Italian-food fans can also check out Marco's Restaurant, 3812 S. Alameda Street, which serves great pasta for lunch and dinner.

Madeline's Before and After, 11 Lamar Park Center, offers beautiful maternity clothes and exquisite infant and children's items, from lace gowns to fun animal-print toddler clothes.

Talbots, 3812 S. Alameda Street, carries high-quality, classic women's clothing.

At Gift and Gourmet Co., 3812 S. Alameda Street, you can find just about anything you want for your kitchen, from pasta makers to imported chocolates and gourmet coffees.

Craftsmen at the King Ranch Saddle Shop make saddles and other high-quality leather products such as boots and purses.

Leon's, 3850 S. Alameda Street, has fashionable women's shoes and handbags. Three upscale women's clothing shops — Franceska's at 3844 S. Alameda Street, Margaret's at 3842 S. Alameda Street, and Julian Gold Inc., 3840 S. Alameda Street — sit side-by-side here. And you can stop at Goldsmith's Jewelers for the crowning touch to your new outfit.

Leslie, 425 Doddridge, offers fun and casual fashions and jewelry.

Water Street Market
309 N. Water St., Corpus Christi
• (512) 881-9322

About a dozen specialty shops and restaurants surround a courtyard downtown that draws residents and visitors alike. The anchors are the Water Street Seafood and Water Street Oyster Bar restaurants, as well as the more casual Executive Surf Club (see our Restaurants chapter). But you can also buy souvenirs and other items at an array of shops.

For all things from the Lone Star State, visit Totally Texas, which offers T-shirts, gourmet foods, gift baskets and other items.

Water Street Beach Club is a great place to pick up beachwear, towels, sand buckets and souvenirs.

Nomadic Creations has an exotic assortment of imported clothing and jewelry.

Gifts by the Sea has all the souvenir items you might want.

The Cat House is a store for feline fanciers, with cat cards, clothing, books and even gifts for your own pet cat.

You can look for interesting items at Antiquity, which offers antiques including furniture, dolls, jewelry and Oriental rugs.

The Victorian Lady, around the corner, specializes in American antiques from the late 1700s through the 1940s, including nautical items, furniture, cut crystal, art pottery, estate jewelry, first-edition books and collectible glassware.

The Gold Bug specializes in jewelry, including antique pieces.

CMR Art Gallery and Frame Shop showcases the work of local artists and artisans and offers framing services. It also carries jewelry and beads and offers instruction in jewelry-making.

Kingsville

Historic Downtown Kingsville

Start your shopping in this renovated downtown area with a visit to the King Ranch Saddle Shop, 201 E. Kleberg Avenue. This luxury shop contains leather goods, of course, including saddles, as well as women's and men's clothing, gifts and luggage. It's a bit pricey, but you might be able to spring for a top-grain leather wallet embossed with the King Ranch's distinctive cattle brand.

Two Hands in Clay, 300 E. Kleberg Avenue, features pottery creations by local artist Mark Dykes, who specializes in functional stoneware.

For vintage items, check out the crystal goblets, lace cloths, furniture, jewelry and art glass at Cynthia's Antiques, 214 E. Kleberg Avenue. More antiques can be found at Josiebelle's Antiques and Gifts, 225-227 E. Kleberg Avenue, which carries richly hand-painted furniture with an antique flair.

La Potpourri of Gifts and Things, 219 E. Kleberg Avenue, offers a sampling of South Texas such as jellies, salsas, pottery and picture frames. Upstairs in the same building (which housed the city's first newspaper and first City Hall) is Glenda's Attic, full of antiques, collectibles and Christmas decorations.

The Pineapple Shop at Allen Furniture, Sixth and King streets, is a complete gift and bridal store, offering crystal, pottery, wood and pewter items.

Roy's Hobbies and Electronics, 217 E. Kleberg Avenue, has art and crafts supplies, cellular phones and pagers, model trains and coins.

Seller's Market, 205 E. Kleberg Avenue, is a creative marketplace where a variety of vendors sell handmade crafts, paintings and jewelry. The historic building that houses this art center has been renovated as part of a downtown revitalization. Items for sale often include quilts, homemade desserts, paintings, jewelry, clothing and notecards.

Other notable shops here include Kingsville Jewelry and Watch Repair, 228 E. Kleberg Avenue, which specializes in custom jewelry, and Oliver's Distinctive Jewelry, 220 E. Kleberg Avenue, with a large selection of fine jewelry and gifts.

The best place to satisfy your appetite from shopping is at Harrel's Kingsville Pharmacy, 204 E. Kleberg Avenue, which has an ample selection of cards and gifts and an old-fashioned soda fountain that serves up memorable milkshakes and burgers.

Another place to eat is the Wild Olive, a tea room in the Seller's Market, which serves great sandwiches and desserts.

You can sip cappuccino while browsing literature by Southwestern authors or perusing children's books at Heritage Bookstore, 211 E. Kleberg Avenue, which has its own coffeehouse.

Antiques

Here's a list devoted to some of the best antique shops int he Coastal Bend. Don't miss the ones we've already mentioned in the previous Shopping Districts section, though.

North Bay Area

Bent Tree Galleries
504 Austin St., Rockport
• **(512) 729-4822**

Named for the area's windswept oak trees, this gallery is set in a historic downtown build-

The King Ranch Saddle Shop in Kingsville is a mecca for cowboy-loving tourists who want to take home a touch of South Texas.

ing where you can find crystal, china, silver and furniture from decades past.

Harcrow's Bluebonnet Mall
Hwy. 188, a half-mile from Texas Hwy. 35 S. between Rockport and Aransas Pass • (512) 729-1724

Furniture, jewelry, gifts, memorabilia, glassware and fishing gear can be found in the 20 booths that fill this shopping area. This place is for the serious bargain hunter or the adventurous shopper.

Mary Ann's Antiques
1005 Main St., Rockport • (512) 729-1945

From porcelain dolls to handmade quilts, this shop features unique items from yesteryear. Furniture, pottery, jewelry, collectibles and Steiff animals comprise its inventory.

Moore Than Feed
902 W. Market St., Rockport • (512) 729-4909

Yes, you can get tack, feed and animal healthcare products in this old-fashioned country store. The shop also offers frontier antiques and a great selection of salt and pepper shakers.

Corpus Christi

Antiquity Ltd.
318 N. Chaparral St., Corpus Christi • (512) 882-2424

You can find furniture, dolls, jewelry and Oriental rugs here.

Betty's Trash to Treasures
3301 Ayers St., Corpus Christi • (512) 882-9144
4315 S. Alameda St., Corpus Christi • (512) 882-9144

Antiques, collectibles, primitives, household items and used furniture are among the collections of a variety of dealers here. Expect to spend some time browsing — the variety can be overwhelming.

Country Peddlers
317 N. Chaparral St., Corpus Christi • (512) 887-6618
4337 S. Alameda St., Corpus Christi • (512) 993-7237

A splendid selection of antiques and gifts is on display at these two shops, the first situated downtown and the other in the central part of the city's "Antique Lane," Alameda Street.

Edlin's Auction
210 N. Alameda St., Corpus Christi
• (512) 882-7253

Antiques and other items can be had — sometimes for a song — at the twice-weekly auctions held here. The auctions begin at 7 PM every Friday and Saturday, with estate items and consignments that come from as far away as England and France.

Emma's Arbor
4309 S. Alameda St., Corpus Christi
• (512) 985-8309

What they call "gently used" furniture is offered at this pleasant shop, which also sells glassware, vintage jewelry and collectibles.

Expressions of Love
1005 Airline Rd., Corpus Christi
• (512) 992-2707

You'll discover handmade items, collectible porcelain dolls and antique furniture in this cozy store.

Gene's Antiques
4331 S. Alameda St., Corpus Christi
• (512) 994-0440

This dealer offers the best of American and European antiques and furniture, as well as matches sterling silver pieces.

Home Sweet Home
4333 S. Alameda St., Corpus Christi
• (512) 991-4001

Furniture, jewelry, glassware and books are displayed through this store. The owners also do refinishing and repair of antiques.

Remarkable Consignments
525 Everhart Rd., Corpus Christi
• (512) 992-2283

This shop specializes in previously owned fine furniture and accessories, so you can find many exquisite items here. Prices can be high because this store specializes in luxury items.

Second-Hand Rose Antiques
4343 S. Alameda St., Corpus Christi
• (512) 993-9626

In addition to antique furniture, you can pick up collectible dolls and teddy bears here.

Sister Sue's Antique Market
4323-B S. Alameda St., Corpus Christi
• (512) 992-5300

Everything in here has been restored to its original luster, and the quality is excellent. Lovely antique furniture, delicate lacework, clothes and gifts can be found here.

Through the Garden Gate
1001 Airline Rd., Corpus Christi
• (512) 994-7204

Antiques, gifts, dried floral arrangements, candles and gourmet foods can be found in this quaint garden cottage.

Two J's Antiques
613 Everhart Rd., Corpus Christi
• (512) 994-0788

Look here for quality antique furniture, collectibles and consignments. Estate liquidation services are also provided.

Victorian Lady
315 N. Chaparral St., Corpus Christi
• (512) 883-1051

Fine furniture, dolls, collectibles, cut glass, pottery and estate jewelry are available at this downtown store.

Yours and Mine
1021 Airline Rd., Corpus Christi
• (512) 980-8188

We like the mix of new and old at this store, where you can buy Fossil handbags and belts, rustic antique furniture, fine Talavera art from Mexico and women's clothing.

INSIDERS' TIP

Many of the malls stay open late during the Christmas season, and the stores are often less crowded during those evening hours.

Port Aransas to Padre Island

Finders Keepers
354 S. Commercial St., Aransas Pass
• (512) 758-8001

Antique furniture, primitive art, jewelry, toys, fishing lures and pottery are among the items offered in this shop.

Kingsville Area

Cynthia's Antiques
214 E. Kleberg Ave., Kingsville
• (512) 592-0855

Crystal goblets, great-grandmother's lace and art glass can be found at this downtown shop.

Glenda's Attic
219 E. Kleberg Ave., Kingsville
• (512) 592-7035

Antique furniture, collectibles and Christmas decorations are for sale in this upstairs shop, in a historic building.

Josiebelle's Antiques and Gifts
225 E. Kleberg Ave., Kingsville
• (512) 592-3701

Look for hand-painted furniture, antique items and other gifts here.

Farmers' Markets

North Bay Area

Jimmy Woods Produce
Texas Hwy. 35 N., Fulton
• (512) 729-6856

Open-air bins are filled with seasonal fresh produce, including juicy oranges and grapefruit, squash, avocados, melons, sweet potatoes, grapes, lettuce, apples and more. The enticing arrangement of fruits and vegetables makes it hard to pass this place by. You can also purchase hot sauces and local honey here.

Bookstores

North Bay Area

The Bookshelf
1005 Concho St., Rockport
• (512) 729-9801

The Bookshelf sells used paperbacks for every age and taste, from thriller and mysteries to self-help books and science fiction. You can buy or barter (trade your own books for something else) at this store.

The Western Warehouse
3801 Hwy. 35 N., Rockport
• (512) 729-0437

This self-described "ugly yellow building" is home to thousands of used paperbacks, all for sale or trade. You can also purchase new Western wear here, from jeans to boots.

The Bookworm
3014 Hwy. 35 N., Ste. B, Rockport
• (512) 790-8399

Buy new or used books, get books appraised or locate hard-to-find volumes here.

Pat's Place
415 S. Austin St., Rockport
• (512) 729-8453

Pick up a copy of the latest bestseller or delve into a bit of Texana in this neat little shop. You can also place special orders, buy greeting cards or stationery, keep the kids amused with puzzles and games or explore local history. A good selection of birding books can be found here.

Corpus Christi

Barnes & Noble Booksellers
5129 Blanche Moore St., Corpus Christi
• (512) 992-1339

This massive and tastefully appointed bookstore often seems almost like a library, with its comfortable reading chairs, hushed atmosphere and wide selection of literary material. Bring the kids to storytime or let them explore the book selection in the children's section while you browse through the many aisles. You can pick up soup, sandwiches or sweets and gourmet coffee at the little cafe on the store's center island.

Books Plus
2211 Ayers St., Corpus Christi
• (512) 884-0797
This shop deals in used books, records and tapes. You can even swap your just-finished paperback for one you haven't yet read. There is also a large supply of old magazines.

Half-Price Books, Records and Magazines
5425 S. Padre Island Dr., Corpus Christi
• (512) 991-4494
Buy, sell or trade your used reading material at this friendly store. New and used books are for sale here, as are albums, tapes and magazines. There's also a good selection of calendars and a coffee bar with live music.

Rainbow Books and Learning Center
4252-D Town and Country Center, Corpus Christi • (512) 992-0590
This is the best place in town to buy children's books. Not only is the selection great, but the employees are knowledgeable about children's authors and tastes. Gifts and educational materials are also available.

Waldenbooks
Padre Staples Mall, Corpus Christi
• (512) 991-8034
When you get tired of looking for that perfect outfit, stop here to refresh your mind with something a little more intellectual. You'll find a large selection of the latest bestsellers, and there's always a sale rack near the front for browsing.

Kingsville

Heritage Bookstore
211 E. Kleberg Ave., Kingsville
• (512) 516-0233
Bestsellers, magazines, children's books and literature by Southwestern authors are among the wide range of reading material this downtown bookstore offers. There's also

a Cappuccino Coffee House here, which offers specialty coffees, soups, sandwiches and desserts.

On-Cue Music, Books and Movies
Southgate Mall, Kingsville
• (512) 516-1210
This store sells new books, cassette tapes, videotapes and CDs, and it also buys used CDs. Both adult and children's literature are featured.

Western Wear

North Bay Area

The Western Warehouse
Texas Hwy. 35 N., Rockport
• (512) 729-0437
Pick up a pair of jeans, a shirt or some boots at this store — and then grab some reading material. In addition to selling new clothing, this store carries an inventory of 80,000 used books.

Corpus Christi

Boots-n-Britches Western Wear
4938 S. Staples St., Corpus Christi
• (512) 992-3501
Whether you're an urban cowboy or a real cowboy, you'll find plenty of variety at this store. Dress boots, work boots, jeans, fashion accessories, belts and buckles are available.

Cavender's Boot City
1220 Airline Rd., Corpus Christi
• (512) 992-9225
Name-brand Western wear and boots can be found in this huge store. Staff people are friendly, ready to explain the differences in types of boots and to help you find the right fit. Cavender's also sells jewelry and other accessories.

Texan Hats Etc.
Padre Staples Mall, Corpus Christi
• (512) 991-4482
Get yourself a real Western hat at this

Artisans at Two Hands in Clay in Kingsville create one-of-a-kind pottery treasures.

store, where the hardest decision will be selecting the style you want. Belts, buckles, Indian jewelry, boots and moccasins are also available.

Kingsville Area

King Ranch Saddle Shop
201 E. Kleberg Ave., Kingsville
• (512) 595-5761

Here's a truly authentic Western store, where the King Ranch saddles are made — and tourists can buy quality leather goods that range from purses to belts. Clothing, hats and other souvenirs, many embossed with the ranch's famous brand, are also available.

Variety Markets

Corpus Christi

Corpus Christi Trade Center
2833 S. Padre Island Dr., Corpus Christi
• (512) 854-4943

There are more than 150 different merchants here selling their wares in 70,000 square feet of space. Items include everything from Mexican dresses and ponchos to electronics and toys. Prices are generally reasonable, and most buyers are looking for a bargain. The trade center is open Friday, Saturday and Sunday.

Beachwear and Souvenirs

North Bay Area

Gulf Breeze Gifts and Resale
201 Texas Hwy. 35 S., Rockport
• **(512) 790-8987**
The front end of this place is a gift shop with Rockport T-shirts, sunglasses, hats and Texas jams and jellies. In the back is a re-sale shop with household items such as pots, pans, baby strollers and lawn equipment.

Maritime Museum Store
Texas Maritime Museum, 1202 Navigation Cir., Rockport
• **(512) 729-1271**
This shop in the museum lobby carries seafaring gifts that include reproductions of maritime artifacts, brass ship's bells, bosun's whistles, postcards and educational toys.

Port Aransas to Padre Island

Absolutely Everything Gifts
314 Ave. G, Port Aransas
• **(512) 749-4738**
You can eat a hamburger, buy T-shirts or shorts, or play a round of miniature golf at this interesting little gift shop. It's a great place to visit when you're tired of the surf and sun.

Bo Jon's Surf and Gifts
100 E. Cotter Ave., Port Aransas
• **(512) 749-5365**
Get a hat, sunglasses, T-shirts and other beachwear at this shop. It's hard to miss — a yellow VW bus protrudes from the shop's roof.

Cool Breeze Gift Shop
319 Church St., Port Aransas
• **(512) 749-6609**
This quaint and fun shop sells T-shirts, swimsuits, inflatable rafts, seashells and sun-

glasses. You can also rent, buy or sell surf-boards. Easily recognized by the large toothy shark that hangs over the front door, the old fishing nets and other nautical items.

Fly It!
Ave. G and 10th St., Port Aransas
• **(512) 749-4190**
A splendid selection of windsocks, color-ful kites, gifts and toys make this a fun place to visit. This kite shop offers great opportuni-ties for recreation or nice souvenirs.

Islander
Alister Rd. at Ave. G, Port Aransas
• **(512) 749-5408**
A wide assortment of beach parapherna-lia can be found here, including hats, beach chairs, inflatable rafts, suntan lotion, windsocks, umbrellas and beach towels.

Moby Dick's
317 S. Alister Rd., Port Aransas
• **(512) 749-5769**
Local color abounds here, from the big blue marlin in the front window to the risque signs that play on this shop's name. You can rent surfboards or buy T-shirts, shells, jewelry and sunglasses — or pick up a burger at the adjoining snack bar.

Pat Magee's
101 Ave. G, Port Aransas
• **(512) 749-4177**
Bathing suits, shorts, T-shirts and sandals can be found at this popular beachwear shop. Open since 1969, it's one of the more well-known places to buy surfing gear.

Silver Fox Trading Co.
221 Beach St., Port Aransas
• **(512) 749-4899**
Owner Pat Stone offers a large collection of hand-crafted jewelry, including Indian jewelry, ethnic and silver beads, crosses and charms. The store also carries clothing and accessories.

Souvenir City
100 E. White St., Port Aransas
• **(512) 749-5564**
In addition to buying shells, souvenirs and plastic crabs, you can mail letters and pack-

ages at this shop, which also serves as a branch of the U.S. Postal Service.

Corpus Christi

Island Sports
S. Padre Island Dr., Corpus Christi
• (512) 949-7443
115 E. Ave. G, Port Aransas
• (512) 749-5369

Each Island Sports location is marked by a gigantic pink octopus — one of those beachfront landmarks that kids just love. You can get swimsuits and more here.

Ocean Treasures and Gifts
14049 S. Padre Island Dr., Corpus Christi
• (512) 949-7558

A giant conch shell marks the front entrance to this beachwear shop on the road to Padre Island National Seashore. You'll find plenty of swimsuits, sandals, T-shirts, shells and inflatable rafts.

Padre Islander
14514 S. Padre Island Dr., Corpus Christi
• (512) 949-8809

This large store contains shells, floats, jewelry, T-shirts and other souvenirs related to sun and surf.

Sea Treasures
2902 Surfside Blvd., Corpus Christi
• (512) 882-5160
10513 S. Padre Island Dr., Corpus Christi
• (512) 937-6341

Swimwear, T-shirts, floats and seashells are available at this store. You can also rent Boogie Boards for the beach.

Treasures on the Beach
2618 Surfside Blvd., Corpus Christi
• (512) 881-9883

T-shirts, toys, shells and other items are available at this shop near the Texas State Aquarium and the aircraft carrier-turned-museum, Lexington Museum on the Bay.

The Texas Coastal Bend
offers visitors a lively
mix of traditional tourist
attractions and unique
wildlife access sights.

Attractions

You may be surprised upon reading this chapter to find several wildlife preserves listed among Texas Coastal Bend attractions. But residents and frequent visitors will tell you that wildlife is one of the main reasons to visit the area. While there is no shortage of more traditional tourist attractions in the area, it's the abundant wildlife and access to it that sets the Texas Coastal Bend apart.

Talk to any avid bird-watcher and chances are they've either visited or wanted to visit the area to see the large variety of migratory and resident birds here. The Coastal Bend is situated along the Central Flyway, the route many birds take on their annual migration north-south migration. The most-watched bird to inhabit the area is undoubtedly the endangered whooping crane, which spends its winters at the Aransas National Wildlife Refuge. For more information on this and other birds see our Birding chapter.

You'll find several wildlife preserves and nature tours listed in this chapter. But you'll also find museums, the state's largest aquarium, a decommissioned aircraft carrier and smaller attractions, too. This chapter doesn't mention two of the most popular attractions in the area: beaches and fishing. That's because they've been given chapters of their own (see our Beaches and Watersports and Fishing and Hunting chapters).

We've divided attractions into our four geographical areas: North Bay, Corpus Christi, Port Aransas to Padre Island, and Kingsville. Attractions in the North Bay area are listed north to south. Those in the other areas are listed alphabetically.

North Bay Area

Aransas National Wildlife Refuge
F.M. Rd. 2040, Austwell • (512) 286-3559
This 70,504-acre wildlife refuge 35 miles north of Rockport is the winter home of the endangered whooping crane, which, in the past 50 years, has made a comeback from the verge of extinction. The federal government created the refuge in 1937 to protect the whooping crane and other threatened coastal wildlife. Several boat tours to view the cranes are available (see our Birding chapter). The refuge also is home to alligators, deer, javelina, coyote, bobcat, raccoon and feral hogs.

Thousands of migratory birds are attracted to the refuge on their journey between North America and Central America. As many as 392 species of birds have been spotted here.

The refuge is open between sunrise and sunset. Public facilities include a 16-mile paved tour road, Wildlife Interpretive Center, 40-foot observation tower, several miles of walking trails and a picnic area. The Wildlife Interpretive Center is open daily from 8:30 AM to 4:30 PM. There's an entrance fee of $5 per carload or $3 if you're visiting the refuge alone. For more information see our Parks chapter. The refuge is 7 miles south of Austwell.

The Big Tree of Lamar
2 mi. west of Park Rd. 13, Lamar
• (512) 729-2858
This giant live oak is a charter member of the Live Oak Society of America and a former subject of one of *Ripley's Believe It or Not* cartoons. It stands 44 feet tall, measures 35 feet around and has a crown 89 feet in circumference. The Texas Forest Service estimates its age at more than 1,000 years. This state-champion live oak is said to have been a council tree for the Carancahua Indians and for the white men who came after them. It's in Goose Island State Park. To get there take Texas Highway 35 N. out of Rockport across the Copano Bay Causeway. Turn right on Park Road 13 a half-mile north of the causeway bridge. Drive 2 miles until you come to a four-way stop. Turn left on Palmetto Street and follow the signs to Big Tree.

Lamar Cemetery

Bois D'Arc St., Lamar • (512) 729-9952, (800) 242-0071

The Lamar Cemetery lies on a 1-acre tract in the Lamar Community, 10 miles north of Rockport near Goose Island State Park. The cemetery was established in 1838 when James W. Byrne and associates bought a league of land on Lookout Point and laid out the Lamar townsite, named after Mirabeau B. Lamar, president of the Republic of Texas.

The oldest grave marker is that of Patrick O'Connor (1822-1854), the New Orleans bookkeeper employed by James Byrne who married Byrne's niece, Jane Gregory. O'Connor had traveled west in the hopes of improving his poor health, but died a few hours after arriving in Lamar. The earliest known soldier buried here is John Fagan (1820-1860), a survivor of the battles of Lipantitlan and Goliad (see our History chapter). He and his 16-year-old daughter, Mary, both died of pneumonia in May 1860. Four sea captains are buried here, along with other prominent figures in Lamar's and Aransas County's history.

When the railroad passed Lamar by and the post office closed in 1915, the town dwindled and almost died. Vegetation overtook the cemetery, which became known as "Lost Lamar Cemetery." Few knew its location. An association formed in the 1940s raised money to clear and restore the cemetery. In 1968 the Lamar Women's Club sponsored the reorganization of the Lamar Cemetery Association and obtained a historical marker for the site. In May 1986 the oldest structure in Aransas County — Stella Maris (Star of the Sea) Chapel — was moved to a spot across from the cemetery.

The history of Lamar Cemetery and biographies of the people buried here are available at the Aransas County Library in Rockport, (512) 790-0153, 701 E. Mimosa Street. To get to the cemetery, take Texas Highway 35 N. from Rockport, cross the Copano Bay Causeway and turn right on Park Road 13. Take a left on Bois D'Arc Street. Lamar Cemetery is at the end of the street.

Stella Maris Chapel

Bois D'Arc St., Lamar • (512) 729-6445

Stella Maris (Our Lady of the Sea) Chapel in Lamar is reported to be the first church and oldest building in Aransas County. A French architect with the last name of D'Alsure, who also supervised construction of several homes in Lamar, designed the Catholic church. It was built by Moses Ballou in 1858, with the townspeople (and their slaves) making shellcrete bricks used in the construction.

The chapel survived two shellings during the Civil War. But a hurricane that hit the area in 1919 almost destroyed it, and it was nailed shut and abandoned. In 1931 Bishop Ledvinna of the Diocese of Corpus Christi rebuilt the structure, adding sleeping quarters and a porch. He, other priests, and seminarians used the church as a vacation and recreation center until the Sisters of Schoenstatt acquired it. After the sisters built a chapel of their own, they allowed Lamar residents to use the old church as a nondenominational church until another one was built in the area. Without a congregation, the church soon began to deteriorate. In 1972, Rockport resident Dennis O'Connor, who in 1920 had visited the church with his mother, Kathryn, sent a $10,000 donation from the Kathryn O'Connor Foundation to repair and maintain Our Lady of the Sea Chapel. In 1986 the chapel was moved to its present location near Lamar Cemetery, and the Aransas County Historical Society raised $50,000 to restore and preserve it.

The interior and its contents are virtually unchanged since the early 1930s. Today the Knights of Columbus, a Catholic fraternal organization, operates Stella Maris Chapel, maintaining it through donations. It's available for special services of any denomination, and arrangements may be made for tour groups. It's open from 1 to 4 PM every Sunday. Admission is free. To get there, take Texas Highway 35 N. from Rockport, cross the Copano Bay Causeway and turn right on Park Road 13. Take a left on Bois D'Arc Street. The chapel is at the end of the street.

Photo: Greater Corpus Christi Business Alliance

The Harbor Bridge offers a stunning backdrop for the Water Gardens at the Corpus Christi Arts and Sciences Park.

Schoenstatt Lamar
100 Front St., Lamar • (512) 729-2019, (512) 729-2771

This small Catholic shrine is an exact replica of the original shrine in Schoenstatt, Germany, which is the center and "power station" of a Catholic religious movement of renewal known as the Schoenstatt Sisters of Mary. The Schoenstatt Movement, which is rooted in the shrine and strives to continue the mission of Mary, was founded by Father Joseph Kentenich (1885-1968), who believed an oncoming crisis in the church and world was imminent. In 1958 the Schoenstatt Sisters of Mary acquired the former Diocese of Corpus Christi property on which to build their motherhouse and shrine.

The small shrine, on a tree-shrouded hill overlooking Copano Bay, offers pilgrims a quiet spot in which to pray, meditate and reflect. In the Schoenstatt Movement Center — built in 1974 to meet the needs of the growing Schoenstatt Movement — you can visit the Founder Memorial Room, which bears a similarity to the Founder Chapel in Schoenstatt, Germany, where Father Kentenich was laid to rest in a sarcophagus. The shrine and Movement Center are open from 6 AM to 9 PM. Admission is free.

Copano Bay State Fishing Pier
Rockport • (512) 729-8519, (512) 729-7762

This fishing pier began as a causeway across Copano Bay, but when a wider, stronger causeway was built the old one was closed to traffic and turned into a pier. Because taller boats are able to pass under the new causeway, the middle section of the old one was removed. That left two sections, one of which stretches 6,190 feet from the north side, while the other extends 2,500 feet from the south side. You can't miss this pier. Just head north on Texas Highway 35 from Rockport. When you get to the Copano Bay Causeway look to your left. The pier runs alongside it. Anglers can catch redfish, flounder, speckled trout, drum, sheepshead and other species.

Open year round, this lighted pier has a public boat ramp on the south side, fish cleaning tables, concessions and restrooms. Admission is $1.75 per fishing pole. Hours are 7 AM to 11 PM every day during the colder part of the year (October or November through February). Warm-weather hours are 6:30 AM to midnight Sunday through Thursday and 24 hours Friday and Saturday.

Fennessey Ranch
F.M. Rd. 2678 10 mi. north of Bayside
• (512) 529-6600

In recent years the 169-year-old Fennessey Ranch opened its doors to tourism for the first time, offering birding trips, hay rides, wildlife photography workshops, wetland educational tours, hiking, and trips along the Mission River. In September and October, the ranch sponsors hummingbird and hawk expeditions along the river as thousands of birds rest in the trees on their way south. All tours are guided by naturalists.

The ranch is part of a 750,000-acre Spanish land grant bestowed upon Irish immigrant Tom O'Conner in 1834. It covers several thousand acres adjacent to the Mission River, 40 miles northwest of Corpus Christi. Habitats on the ranch include wetlands, natural lakes, meadows, woodlands, miles of river and associated uplands. An environmental management plan calls for enlargement and enhancement of existing wetlands along with a wildlife management and rotational grazing program designed to maximize the diversity of species found there. Birders have spotted more than 400 species here, including green jays, woodstorks and masked ducks. Sixteen plant communities exist here, along with 50 species of amphibians and reptiles and 70 types of moths and butterflies.

Admission fees per person are as follows: a half-day birding expedition, $17.50; a full-day birding expedition, including lunch, a river trip and hiking, $87.50; a one-day wildlife photography workshop, $75; and a two-day wildlife photography workshop, $150. Reservations are required for all events.

To get to the Fennessey Ranch from Corpus Christi, take U.S. Highway 181 across the Harbor Bridge. Drive through Portland and take Texas Highway 35 N. when you reach Gregory. Turn left on Farm-to-Market Road 136 and follow it for 13 miles until you reach Bayside. In Bayside the road becomes Farm-to-Market Road 2678. Follow it for 10 miles until you reach the Fennessey Ranch entrance on the west side of the road.

Paws and Taws Convention Center
402 Fulton Beach Rd., Fulton
• (512) 729-2388

A trip to this rustic building overlooking Aransas Bay is worth it just so you can gaze at the gleaming hardwood floor where square dancers face off from 8 to 10 PM every Wednesday night. Rockport-Fulton residents' love of square dancing led to construction of this building in 1965. Along with the regular Wednesday night dances, it hosts square dancing weekends several times a year and line dancing from 10 AM to noon Monday, Wednesday and Friday. The "Paws and Taws" name comes from square dancing terms: Male dancers are called "Paws," and females are their "Taws." Along with square and line dancing, the center hosts a variety of community activities and private functions.

The center's office is open 9 AM to noon and 1 to 4 PM Monday through Friday. Drop by and take a look inside. The office is closed weekends, but the center is usually open for community or private functions. Admission is free.

Fulton Mansion State Historical Park
317 Fulton Beach Rd., Fulton
• (512) 729-0386

George and Harriet Fulton spared no expense when they built their Victorian mansion in 1874. With its ornate trimwork and Victorian-era furnishings, this stately mansion dwarfed its nearest neighbors. Along with the eye-pleasing flourishes evident to passersby, this 6,200-square-foot home was built with all the modern conveniences, including running water, flush toilets, central heat, a gas lighting system, a water cooling system to preserve perishable food and a simple clothes dryer. Finishing touches included walnut and cypress woodwork, chandeliers, fine rugs and ornate furniture.

Fulton came to Texas in 1837 to fight in the war for Texas's independence, but he arrived too late to participate. After working at

INSIDERS' TIP

Hours at many Coastal Bend attractions change from season to season, so we recommend you call ahead.

several jobs, Fulton took over his wife's inheritance when her father died, establishing an extensive cattle-ranching business. Business was good, and in 1874 the Fultons began constructing their home. Most materials and construction equipment were shipped in from New Orleans and the East Coast at considerable expense.

This three-story, French Second Empire-style home is on a 2.3-acre lot overlooking Aransas Bay at the corner of Fulton Beach Road and Henderson Street. Guided tours are held year round Wednesday through Sunday at 9, 10 and 11 AM and 1, 2 and 3 PM. Admission is $4 for adults and teens and $2 for children 7 and older. Children 6 and younger get in free. Wear soft-soled shoes to protect the mansion's floors and rugs. Picnicking is allowed on the mansion's grounds.

The mansion is the setting for special events throughout the year, including "Christmas at Mansion," a two-day event every December that celebrates a traditional 1880s Christmas, and "All Hallow Even," a two-day event held each October to celebrate Halloween and to explore the mansion's alleged history of hauntings.

Connie Hagar Cottage Sanctuary
Church and First Sts., Rockport
• **(512) 729-9952, (800) 242-0071**
Named after renowned Texas bird-watcher Connie Hagar, this wildlife sanctuary in Rockport provides a viewing platform and trails that lead to areas where you may spot resident and neotropical migrant birds. The sanctuary is open sunrise to sunset. Admission is free. For more information about Connie Hagar, see our Birding chapter.

The Texas Maritime Museum
1202 Navigation Cir., Rockport
• **(512) 729-1271, (512) 729-6644**
Inside the modern-looking Texas Maritime Museum next to Rockport Harbor you'll find exhibits and artifacts dedicated to the museum's mission to preserve and interpret the rich maritime heritage of Texas. Exhibits cover everything from the early days of French and Spanish exploration to the modern search for offshore oil and gas. Inside you'll be able to stand on a life-size ship's bridge and let

your children board a concrete boat known as *The Pirate's Ship*. The museum also houses a lifeboat from an oil tanker and a hands-on knot-typing exhibit, where you can learn to tie nautical knots. Several videos related to Texas maritime history run continuously. And look for "The Allure of Fishing," an exhibit chronicling the history of Aransas Bay fishing from 1900 to 1960. Most of the artifacts were donated by a Fort Worth billionaire, whose family owns nearby San José Island.

While you're there, check out the Museum Store for gifts and collectibles. You'll find books, caps, T-shirts, jewelry, model boats, note cards and toys, all with a nautical theme.

Museum hours are 10 AM to 4 PM Tuesday through Saturday and 1 to 4 PM Sunday. Admission is $4 for adults and teens and $2 for children ages 5 to 12. Children 4 and younger get in free.

Rockport Center for the Arts
901 Broadway, Rockport
• **(512) 729-5519**
The Rockport Art Association calls this Victorian-style building at Rockport Harbor its home. Inside you'll find artwork by local and regional artists. The house contains 5,000 square feet of gallery, classroom, lecture and library space. The center's gallery presents work by local artists on a rotating basis, and hosts classes for adults and children. The center is open from 10 AM to 4 PM Tuesday through Saturday and 1 PM to 4 PM Sunday. Admission is free. For more information see our Arts chapter.

Rob and Bessie Welder Wildlife Foundation
U.S. Hwy. 77, Sinton • (512) 364-2643
Robert H. Welder founded this wildlife refuge through a device in his will. It occupies 7,800 acres, a small portion of a large ranch that has been in the Welder family for more than 150 years, having come to them through a land grant from the king of Spain. The refuge, which opened in April 1961, is dedicated to wildlife research and education and is funded through private means, having no official connection with state or federal agencies. The foundation provides fellowships for graduate students in wildlife ecology and manage-

ment and related subjects. The foundation also publishes scientific papers and offers lectures to scientific, civic and conservation groups.

The refuge, which lies 7.4 miles northeast of Sinton, operates as a working cattle ranch and oil field. Sixteen plant communities exist on the refuge, including about 1,400 species of native plants. More than 380 species of birds, 55 species of mammals and 55 species of reptiles and amphibians have been recorded on the refuge. About 1,000 deer live on the refuge along with javelinas, Río Grande wild turkeys, Northern bobwhites and several species of ducks and geese.

Free guided tours are given at 3 PM every Thursday except on holidays. The gates are locked at all other times. Tours take about two hours and include a visit to the foundation headquarters and museum in addition to a 10-mile bus tour of the refuge. While you're on the tour you'll learn about foundation objectives and current research.

Organizations wishing to schedule tours at times other than Thursday afternoon should contact Conservation Education, Welder Wildlife Foundation, P.O. Box 1400, Sinton, TX 78387. Special tour groups are limited to a minimum of 15 and a maximum of 50 people. Tours will not be booked on Sundays. Cameras are allowed; pets are not. Water fountains and restrooms are available; food and other beverages are not. Picnicking and camping are not allowed. Admission is free.

Naval Station Ingleside
1455 Ticonderoga St., Ingleside
• (512) 776-4206

On the northern side of Corpus Christi Bay, Naval Station Ingleside is home to the Navy's mine warfare fleet, which so far amounts to 22 ships. The USS *Inchon*, the Navy's first command-and-control ship, is included in that figure, along with 12 Avenger-class mine countermeasures ships and nine Osprey-class coastal mine hunters. The base features a 4,600-foot waterfront, with an 1,100-foot double-deck pier.

The base is open to the public at all times, and free tours are available every Tuesday at 1:30 PM. Once a month, usually on a Saturday, a ship is designated for free public visits. Pre-arranged ship tours also are available for

groups. For more information see our Military chapter.

Dolphin Connection
Ingleside • (512) 882-4126

Since 1985, Erv and Sonja Strong have made it their business to befriend dolphins living in Corpus Christi Bay. Sonja Strong says she knows 65 dolphins by name and recognizes about 200 others by their dorsal fins. On your one-hour Dolphin Connection boat trip you will meet several pods of dolphins swimming just out of reach and occasionally coming close enough to touch. Tickets are $17 for adults and teens and $12 for children 12 and younger. Reservations are required. You'll receive directions to the launch site when you book your trip.

Corpus Christi

Asian Cultures Museum & Educational Center
1809 N. Chaparral St., Corpus Christi
• (512) 882-2641

The museum features Japanese and other Oriental art, sculpture, furniture, paintings, scale models of famous pagodas, shrines and temples, and the largest U.S. collection of hand-crafted Hakata dolls.

The museum is open from 10 AM to 5 PM Tuesday through Saturday. Admission is $4 for adults, $3.50 for senior citizens and military, $2.50 for youths ages 6 to 15 and free for children 5 and younger. For more information see our Arts chapter.

Captain Clark's Flagship
Peoples Street T-Head, Corpus Christi
• (512) 884-1693, (512) 884-8306

Set sail for a narrated tour of the Corpus Christi bayfront and the Port of Corpus Christi aboard an air-conditioned, 400-passenger paddlewheeler or the 250-passenger *Gulf Clipper*. Board the *Captain Clark* on the Peoples Street T-Head and sit inside or out. Your port tour will take you past the *Lexington* Museum on the Bay, the Texas State Aquarium and the Columbus Fleet. Sunset cruises into Corpus Christi Bay also are available.

Four types of tours are available between

Memorial Day weekend and Labor Day. A daytrip — a one-hour tour of the port leaving at 11 AM and 1 and 3 PM daily — costs $7 for adults and teens, $4 for children ages 4 to 11 and free for children 3 and younger. A sunset cruise, a 90-minute tour of the port and bay, leaves at 7:30 PM Sunday through Friday; tickets are $8 for adults and teens, $4.50 for children ages 4 to 11 and free for children 3 and younger. If you prefer a livelier outing, take the sunset cruise with entertainment, a 90-minute harbor and bay tour leaving at 7:30 PM Saturday; tickets are $9 for adults and teens, $5 for children ages 4 to 11 and free for children 3 and younger. The party cruise with entertainment is a two-hour bay tour leaving at 9:30 PM Saturday; tickets are $10 for adults and teens, $5 for children ages 4 to 11 and free for children 3 and younger.

At all other times of the year, one-hour tours begin daily at 3 PM and Saturday and Sunday at 1 and 3 PM. A 90-minute tour also leaves at 7:30 PM Saturday. There are no tours on Tuesday.

Centennial House
411 N. Upper Broadway, Corpus Christi
• (512) 992-6003

The city's oldest existing structure sits on a bluff overlooking downtown Corpus Christi and Corpus Christi Bay. Known by many as the pink house on the hill, Centennial House sits next to the Corpus Christi Cathedral.

This Classic Revival home furnished in American Empire furniture offers a glimpse into the lives of a wealthy Corpus Christi family of the 1850s. Centennial House was originally home to Capt. Forbes Britton and family. It later served as a hospital for Confederate and, after 1862, Union soldiers, and for victims of the yellow fever epidemic of 1867. Several prominent Corpus Christi residents resided here over the years until 1937 when Southern Minerals purchased it for offices. The Corpus Christi Area Heritage Society bought the structure in 1965 and repaired it.

The house is open for tours from 2 to 5 PM every Wednesday when the Texas and U.S. flags are displayed. Tours on other days for groups of 10 or more may be arranged a week in advance. Admission is $ for students and children.

Corpus Christi Botanic
8545 S. Staples St., Corpus
• (512) 852-2100

You'll find more than a thousand native plants at the 180-acre Corpus Christi Botanical Gardens, on the southern end of the city near new residential neighborhoods and the Kings Crossing Golf & Country Club. Nature trails wend their way along Oso Creek. You'll find mesquite trees, wetlands and plenty of flowers. The Orchid House is home to the Larkin Orchid Collection, one of the largest collections in the Southwest with some 2,100 varieties. In the exhibit house you'll see bromeliads, cycads, fern and plumeria surrounding a center courtyard and fountain. The shaded bird and butterfly trail will lead you to the birding tower overlooking Gator Lake. There you're likely to spot roseate spoonbills, egrets, white pelicans and ducks.

The visitors center hosts a rotating gallery of exhibits and a gift shop, where you can purchase botanical mementos made by volunteers. The gardens are open 9 AM to 5 PM Tuesday through Sunday. They're closed on Monday. Admission is $2 for adults and teens, $1.50 for seniors 65 and older, $1 for children ages 5 to 12 and free for children younger than 5.

Corpus Christi Cathedral
505 N. Upper Broadway, Corpus Christi
• (512) 883-4213

The Corpus Christi Cathedral may be the most architecturally impressive building in the Texas Coastal Bend. Built in the 1940s at a cost of $425,000, the cathedral was built to meet the demands of the city's growing Catholic population. It sits on a bluff overlooking downtown Corpus Christi and Corpus Christi Bay, and although much taller buildings have been added to the city's skyline, none stands taller in the hearts of the city's Catholic community.

The cathedral's architecture is described as late Spanish Colonial revival, with glazed terra cotta-roofed domes, rosette wrought-iron grillwork, spiral-turned stone columns, cop-

Selena Quintanilla-Perez

Raised on Corpus Christi's Westside, Selena Quintanilla-Perez quickly rose to the top of the Tejano music scene with her spirited style and melodic voice. But on March 31, 1995, her starry life came to a end when her fan club president gunned her down at a Corpus Christi motel.

Her death at age 23 inspired a Hollywood movie in 1997 starring Jennifer Lopez and Edward James Olmos. Her killer, Yolanda Saldivar, was convicted of murder and is serving a life sentence in a Texas prison.

Even in death, Selena has continued to draw fans to Corpus Christi, where they can visit several landmarks of her life and tragic death. While brochures and highlighted maps aren't provided for visitors, local cab drivers and tourist officials know the route for the tour of Selena sites.

Stops include her house on Bloomington Street, her clothing boutique on Everhart Road, her recording studio on Leopard Street and her grave at Seaside Memorial Park. Fans also go to the Days Inn, 901 Navigation Boulevard, where Selena was shot. The motel has discouraged fans from visiting by putting new room numbers on every door. The number of the room where Selena was shot is not displayed, but fans continue to try to seek out the room and take photographs where they think the crime occurred.

— continued on next page

Photo: George Gongora

Selena Quintanilla-Perez, who grew up in Corpus Christi, rose to the top of the Tejano music scene before the president of her fan club shot her to death at a Corpus Christi motel.

The city also has paid homage to Selena by naming a public auditorium after her. More picturesque and photogenic is the Mirador de la Flor, a $600,000 pavilion in honor of the late singer. The pavilion, at the entrance of the Peoples Street T-Head on the city's bayfront, features a bronze statue of Selena facing the water.

The memorial was developed and funded by the Devary Durrill Foundation and individual contributions. The sculpture was designed and made by local sculptor H.W. "Buddy" Tatum.

In addition to the memorial, there are a number of wooden boards where fans can inscribe messages. Adjacent to the pavilion is the Paseo de la Flor, or Walk of the Flower, a tile mural along the bayfront walkway below and behind the Mirador de la Flor. More than 500 children from South Texas towns created the mural featuring white roses.

Next to the sculpture of Selena is a single white, sculpted rose with an inscription that reads: "Her stage is now silent. Yet, her persona enriched the lives of those she touched and her music lives on

---

per doors, stone urns on dome bases, a red-clay tile roof and two open belltowers. Builders used the beige brick in many area buildings in the period when the cathedral was built. The taller of the two towers contains a 32-bell carillon and a clock on each of the four walls; the shorter tower holds the three original bells, which hung in the former cathedral building. On the front of the cathedral are two rondels which encircle the episcopal crests of Bishop Emmanuel B. Ledvina and Coadjutor Bishop Mariano S. Garriga, who oversaw the Cathedral's construction.

The pipe organs, which originally had 38 ranks, were renovated between 1978 and 1984 to bring the number of ranks to 97. It is one of the largest pipe organs in South Texas and the largest of any Catholic church in the state. The cathedral houses the Emmanuel Chapel (in the basement on the south side of the building), which includes a crypt for the burial of as many as 24 bishops of Corpus Christi. Four are buried there now. On the west side of the cathedral is the chancery of the Diocese of Corpus Christi, and to the north is the building housing parish offices and religious education.

Daily masses are held in Emmanuel Chapel at 7:05 AM Monday through Friday and 12:05 PM Monday through Saturday. Sunday masses are held in the cathedral at 7:30 AM, 9:30 AM and noon.

You can visit the cathedral complex at any time. The cathedral itself is open from 8:30 AM to 4:45 PM Monday through Friday, 8:30 AM to 7 PM Saturday, and from 7:30 AM to noon Sunday. If you plan to visit the cathedral when a mass is not being held, enter through the courtyard door.

Corpus Christi Greyhound Racetrack
IH-37 at Navigation Blvd., Corpus Christi • (512) 289-9333, (800) 580-7223

Open at 11 AM year round seven days a week, the Corpus Christi Greyhound Racetrack offers live greyhound racing and wagering, along with simulcast greyhound and horse racing via live satellite. Races from Dallas, Houston, San Antonio, Arizona, Arkansas, Florida and Massachusetts are broadcast seven nights a week and every afternoon. You can see live greyhound racing Wednesday through Saturday nights beginning at 7:30 PM, and Wednesday, Saturday and Sunday afternoons beginning at 1:30 PM. Grandstand seating is completely enclosed and air-conditioned. The track has a food court.

Grandstand admission is $1, clubhouse admission (with monitors at your table) is $2, and parking is $1. Senior citizens get in free at all matinees.

Corpus Christi Museum of Science and History
1900 N. Chaparral St., Corpus Christi • (512) 882-1232

Visitors pay one price to see life-size replicas of two of Christopher Columbus' discovery ships and tour the adjacent Corpus Christi Museum of Science and History. Visit a working shipyard from the 15th century as the master shipwright and his journeymen restore the *Pinta* and the *Santa María* to their original state. The ships, built by the Spanish government to commemorate the 500th anniversary of Columbus' discovery of the New World, were damaged when a barge collided with them. Climb aboard the tiny ships and venture below decks for a glimpse of an ancient sailor's life.

Inside the museum learn about Columbus's voyages and their impact on the New World in "Seeds of Change," a Smithsonian Institute exhibit on permanent display. Plans call for the Niña, docked on the Corpus Christi bayfront, eventually to be opened for tours. The museum also houses artifacts from three Spanish galleons that wrecked on Padre Island in 1554.

The kids will enjoy the Children's Wharf, designed for ages 3 to 7. The Children's Wharf has hands-on activities for small children, including a kid-size shrimp boat, playhouse and magnet tables.

The museum is open 10 AM to 6 PM Monday through Saturday between Memorial Day and Labor Day, 10 AM to 5 PM Monday through Saturday the rest of the year, and noon to 5 PM on Sundays year round. Admission is $8 for adults, $6.50 for senior citizens, $7 for youths ages 13 to 17, $4 for children ages 5 to 12, and free for children 4 and younger.

H.R. Brunner Telephone Pioneer Museum
4605 Kostoryz Rd., Corpus Christi • (512) 853-9997

This museum inside the Southwestern Bell central office building chronicles the technological changes that have occurred in telephony during the past century. Exhibits include phones from before the turn of the century, a working cordboard that allows visitors to patch calls to and from phones in the museum, a coin-operated telephone from 1896, several hand-crank telephones, a display on the advent of dial telephones and displays of different types of cable used throughout the years.

The museum is open from 10 AM to noon every Thursday or by appointment. Admission is free.

Heritage Park
1600 block of N. Chaparral St., Corpus Christi • (512) 883-0639

Tour several beautifully restored homes representative of the Coastal Bend's diverse heritage at this unusual park on the city's northern end. Several nonprofit organizations in Corpus Christi had nine historic local homes brought to this area along N. Chaparral Street between Fitzgerald and Hughes streets. Each organization has restored one home for historical and educational purposes.

The Galvan House, the large yellow house in the center of the park, serves as the Multicultural Center, and features changing art exhibits depicting the city's heritage. It's open from 10 AM to 5 PM Monday through Thursday and 9 AM to 2 PM Friday and Saturday.

Guided tours of the park and six of the nine houses are offered at 10:30 AM on Wednesday and Thursday and 10:30 AM and 12:45 PM on Friday and Saturday. Tours are $3 for adults and teens, $2 for seniors 55 and older and $1 for children. Bring a picnic and lunch on the park's beautiful grounds or enjoy lunch at Sally's Cafe, (512) 887-9043.

International Kite Museum
3200 Surfside Blvd., Corpus Christi • (512) 883-7456

Corpus Christi is a fitting place for a kite museum. Gulf breezes cool the city year round, offering kite lovers plenty of chances to test their skills. The museum, inside the Best Western Sandy Shores Resort, traces the history of kites from their origin in the Orient until the present time. Learn how famous people like Alexander Graham Bell, Benjamin Franklin, and Orville and Wilbur Wright used kites to benefit mankind. At the Kite Shoppe you can buy a kite, then step outside on Corpus Christi beach and give it a test flight.

Hours are 10 AM to 5 PM every day. Admission is free.

Pirates of the Gulf
2901 W. Surfside Blvd., Corpus Christi
• (512) 884-4774

This 18-hole miniature golf course is laid out around a small mountain and includes two waterfalls, a cave and a dungeon. Some holes are makeable in two, while others are par 3. The course is in the Corpus Christi Beach area, north of the Harbor Bridge. The cost is $5 for adults and teens and $4 for children ages 4 to 12. Children 3 and younger play for free. Summer hours are 11 AM to 11 PM daily. Winter hours are 4 to 8 PM Friday, 11 AM to 8 PM Saturday, and noon to 6 PM Sunday.

Port of Corpus Christi and Harbor Bridge
1305 N. Shoreline Blvd., Corpus Christi
• (512) 882-2080

One of the most spectacular sights you'll see during your visit to the Coastal Bend is a mammoth oil tanker cruising into port. With tiny and powerful tugboats leading the way, these enormous ships pass a few feet away from your vantage point beneath the Harbor Bridge, which arches 235 feet above the water. As one of the nation's busiest ports, Corpus Christi is visited by ships from nearly every country in the world, moving grain, farm products, oil and chemicals. Viewing spots are available near the Harbormaster's office.

While you're there check out the James C. Storm Pavilion, formerly known as Cargo Dock One. Or drive across the Harbor Bridge and watch from the three-story observation tower. A pedestrian walkway on the bridge offers a great view of the port and city. To find out when ships will be arriving at or departing from the port, check Page B-2 of the *Corpus Christi Caller-Times*. This is a free attraction.

Putt-Putt Golf & Games
8306 S. Padre Island Dr., Corpus Christi
• (512) 991-0830

Chances are you're familiar with the Putt-Putt Golf & Games concept. The Corpus Christi

version has two 18-hole courses, a redemption game room, and batting cages. Golf is $4 per person ($1 for children 4 and younger). Daily specials, including $6 a person for unlimited golf on Saturdays, are available. Game tokens cost $1 for four. At the batting cages you get 16 pitches for $1 or 96 for $5.

It's open from 10 AM to 8 PM Monday through Thursday, 10 AM to 9 PM Friday and Saturday, and noon to 6 PM Sunday.

South Texas Institute for the Arts
1902 N. Shoreline Blvd., Corpus Christi
• (512) 980-3500

Designed by renowned architect Philip Johnson, the institute for the arts, formerly known as the Art Museum of South Texas, overlooks the bay and the Corpus Christi Ship Channel. Inside you'll find traveling exhibits of painting, sculpture and photography. The permanent collection of photographs includes works by Ansel Adams and Victoria Livingston. The museum also has a children's area and gift shop.

The museum is open Tuesday, Wednesday, Friday and Saturday from 10 AM to 5 PM, Thursday from 10 AM to 9 PM, and Sunday from 1 to 5 PM. The museum is closed on Monday. Admission is $3 for adults and teens; $2 for students, military and senior citizens; $1 for children ages 2 to 12; and free for children younger than 2.

Texas State Aquarium
2710 N. Shoreline Blvd., Corpus Christi
• (512) 881-1200, (800) 477-4853

The Texas State Aquarium looks right at home perched on the tip of Corpus Christi Beach on the city's north end. The blue-and-white, four-story building overlooks Corpus Christi Bay, the city's bayfront and the entrance to the Port of Corpus Christi, the seventh-largest port in the United States.

The aquarium, dedicated to the study of plants and animals native to the Gulf of Mexico, opened in 1990, more than two decades after it was first proposed. The $31.6 million facility (funded entirely by private donations) opened to more than 100,000 visitors in its first month. Each year, between 400,000 and 500,000 people visit the aquarium, the first large public facility to focus exclusively on the Gulf of

Mexico. Exhibits feature sand and nurse sharks, moray eels, barracudas, tarpons, and tropical fish.

The facility also boasts a seabirds and shorebirds exhibit and a touch tank where visitors can hold hermit crabs and other harmless sea creatures. Tourists stroll by dozens of small tanks in addition to a 132,000-gallon aquarium featuring a reproduction of an offshore oil rig and a smaller, although more colorful, tank with a coral reef similar to one found in the Gulf of Mexico. Other attractions include a 2,250-square-foot sea-turtle exhibit, a pool where visitors can pet a shark or a stingray, North American river otters and The Octopus' Garden, a kid-friendly playground with a giant purple octopus as its centerpiece.

In addition to its many fish and other sea creatures, the aquarium offers a full day of educational programs at no extra charge. Visitors can get a close look at animals like baby alligators or birds of prey and watch scuba divers feed fish by hand.

Summer hours (from Memorial Day to Labor Day) are 9 AM to 6 PM Monday through Saturday, 10 AM to 6 PM on Sundays, and extended hours to 8 PM on Tuesdays. Hours the rest of the year are 9 AM to 5 PM Monday through Saturday and 10 AM to 5 PM on Sundays. The aquarium is closed Christmas Day.

Admission is $8 for adults, $6.75 for senior citizens, active-duty military and for ages 12 to 17, $4.50 for children ages 4 to 11 and free for children 3 and younger.

Lexington Museum on the Bay
2914 N. Shoreline Blvd. Corpus Christi
• (512) 888-4873, (800) 523-9539

You can tour World War II's most decorated aircraft carrier without having to worry about being shelled by enemy planes. The former USS *Lexington*, now decommissioned and converted into a floating museum, sits in shallow water off Corpus Christi Beach, a short distance from the Texas State Aquarium and downtown Corpus Christi.

Commissioned in 1943, the USS *Lexington* CV-16 served longer and set more records than any carrier in the history of the U.S. Navy. During World War II Tokyo Rose dubbed her the "Blue Ghost" after repeatedly defying reports that she had been sunk. She was the first U.S. carrier to enter Tokyo Bay after the treaty was signed with Japan in 1945.

Several historic planes are on display on the ship's flight deck, including a jet flown by the Blue Angels and an F-14, the Navy's premier fighter plane. Visit the flight deck, hangar deck, captain's quarters, admiral's quarters, navigation and flag bridge, sick bay and the engine room. The ship also has a store and cafe on board.

While you're here, see what it's like to fly a jet fighter in the *Lexington's* flight simulator.

The *Lexington* is open 9 AM to 5 PM every day except Christmas. Admission is $8 for adults and teens, $6 for seniors 60 and older and active or retired military, $4 for children ages 4 to 12 and free for children younger than 4.

Port Aransas to Padre Island

Absolutely Everything
405 E. Ave. G, Port Aransas
• (512) 749-4738

This 18-hole miniature golf course is four blocks from the beach. The holes are wrapped around a boat, sculptures and various odds and ends. You'll find a fast-food restaurant and gift shop adjacent to the course. The cost is $3.50 for people 12 and older and $2.50 for children 11 and younger. It's open 10 AM to 7 PM every day.

Birding Center
Ross Ave. off Cut-Off Rd., Port Aransas
• (512) 749-5919

Local and migratory birds find the Port Aransas wetlands an irresistible spot in which to live or visit. The birding center provides seasoned bird-watchers and novices with plenty to look at. Vegetation is designed to attract hummingbirds as they migrate in the spring and fall. You may also catch a glimpse of a 6-foot alligator who lives here.

A boardwalk takes you over the wetlands to an observation tower, where you can look out over the Corpus Christi Ship Channel. The birding center is open 24 hours a day, and there is no admission fee.

Photo: Greater Corpus Christi Business Alliance

Children of all ages enjoy watching the playful otters at the Texas State Aquarium.

Dolphin Watch
136 W. Cotter Ave., Port Aransas
• (512) 749-5252

Hop aboard the 48-foot *Duke* for a two-hour tour of Port Aransas waters. Search for bottle-nosed dolphin and watch them play in their natural environment. Then watch as the crew pulls a plankton net through the water and empties the contents into an aquarium for you to see. From the bird world, look for egrets, herons, spoonbills, gulls, pelicans, curlews and other species.

You'll also get a chance to examine the contents of a shrimp trawl net pulled through the water and dumped into a sampling bin. The catch is often filled with crabs, shrimp, and fish.

The *Duke* leaves from Woody's Sport Center at 2 PM every day. Tickets are $15 ($10 for children 10 and younger). Call ahead for reservations.

The Jetty Boat
136 W. Cotter Ave., Port Aransas
• (512) 749-5252

Ride the jetty boat to San José Island north of Port Aransas and see what life is like on a privately owned island. Reachable only by boat, San José Island offers beachcombing, shelling, surfing and swimming. Bring your own fishing equipment and fish from the north jetty. You also can go surf fishing, crabbing on the bay side and seining.

The ferry leaves Port Aransas as early as 6:30 AM and as late as 6 PM. The island has no restrooms or other public facilities. Tickets are $8.95 for adults and teens and $4.95 for children.

Tarpon Inn
200 E. Cotter Ave., Port Aransas
• **(512) 749-5555, (800) 365-6784**

The Tarpon Inn's history is the reason we've included it in this chapter as well as in the Hotels and Motels chapter, where you can read our Close-up on the inn. It is one of two accommodations in the Coastal Bend to be listed on the National Register of Historic Places (the Hoopes' House Bed and Breakfast is the other). Inside its lobby you'll find a tarpon scale autographed by the late President Franklin D. Roosevelt. The scale is among more than 7,000 others caught by guests (Roosevelt wasn't one of them) and displayed on the walls of the hotel's lobby. The inn offers 24 small rooms filled with antiques.

The lobby is open from 8 AM to 10 PM every day. Admission is free.

University of Texas Marine Science Institute
750 Channel View Dr., Port Aransas
• **(512) 749-6711**

Learn about Gulf marine life, plants and oceanography at this laboratory and research facility on the northern tip of Mustang Island. The institute is the center for the study of Texas' bays, the Gulf of Mexico and the world's oceans. Through audio/visual technology, faculty can share their expertise with students far from the coast. The institute offers undergraduate courses and provides master's and doctoral students immediate access to a variety of marine habitats.

The visitors' center is open from 8 AM to 5 PM weekdays. Inside you'll find several aquariums featuring sea creatures common to the Gulf of Mexico. Call ahead to find out whether a movie is planned for that day. Additional displays in the main building highlight current and past research projects.

Admission is free. From the ferry go straight down Cotter Avenue and follow the signs. You'll go past a traffic signal and one stop sign. The institute is at the end of the road right before you get to the beach.

Kingsville Area

John E. Conner Museum
Texas A&M University, Kingsville
• **(512) 593-2819**

The John E. Conner Museum is designed to preserve the social, political and natural history of the area and to interpret the bicultural heritage of the borderlands. Exhibits inside the Caesar Kleberg Hall of Natural History explore the ecosystems of the South Texas and Northern Mexico biospheres. Lifelike dioramas, nature's sounds, slide shows and an award-winning video will give you a good idea of what the region is like.

The museum's ranching area features a chuck wagon, branding irons, saddles, barbed wire and small ranching equipment. It also has on display 264 trophy mounts of North American game, including elk, moose, antelope, bighorn sheep, mountain goats, grizzlies and whitetail deer. Exhibits change every four to six weeks. Two per year come from the museum's collections, while others are science exhibits from various sources. Each Tuesday from November until April, informal lunchtime lectures feature area citizens with interesting jobs.

The museum is open from 9 AM to 5 PM Monday through Saturday. Admission is free.

King Ranch Museum
405 N. Sixth St., Kingsville
• **(512) 595-1881**

This museum set in a restored ice house is home to custom-made automobiles, saddles and other memorabilia. Experience life on the King Ranch in the early 1940s through the award-winning photographs of Toni Frissell. See a collection of saddles from around the world, various guns, including a King Ranch commemorative issue Colt Python .357 Magnum pistol. Also on display are antique carriages and vintage cars, including a custom-designed Buick Eight hunting car built in 1949 by General Motors.

The museum is open from 10 AM to 4 PM Monday through Saturday and from 1 to 5 PM Sunday. Admission is $4 for adults and teens, $2.50 for children ages 5 to 12 and free for children younger than 5.

King Ranch
Texas Hwy. 141 W., Kingsville
• (512) 592-8055, (800) 282-5464

At 825,000 acres the King Ranch is larger than Rhode Island and is one of the largest ranches in the world. It's also home to more than 60,000 cattle. Capt. Richard King founded the ranch in 1853. The Santa Gertrudis and King Ranch Santa Cruz breeds of cattle were developed there, along with the first registered American Quarter Horse.

Guided historical and agricultural tours are available daily. During the winter season (roughly November through March), tours leave the visitors center on the hour between 10 AM and 3 PM and 1 to 5 PM Sunday. Tickets, including tax, are $7.45. Tickets are sold on a first-come, first-served basis. Get there 45 minutes early to make sure you get a ticket.

Tours last 90 minutes and cover a 12-mile loop in which you will visit historical buildings and learn about horses and cattle. The following nature tours also are available at various times throughout the year (costs are quoted without tax included):

• Wildlife — This half-day, 26-mile loop through the Santa Gertrudis division of King Ranch introduces participants to common native wildlife. The cost is $17.50 per person.

• Wildlife/cultural Retreat Package—A three-day, two-night wildlife tour through areas of the Santa Gertrudis and Laureles divisions, the package includes a visit to local museums and historical areas. Tour participants stay at a private lodge adjacent to the ranch and get a thorough introduction to common native wildlife species and to King Ranch and South Texas culture. The cost is $350, which includes five meals, lodging, guide, and transportation to and from the Corpus Christi International Airport.

• Bird-watching Day Tour — Designed for the avid bird-watcher, this nine- to 10-hour excursion covers areas of the Norias division of King Ranch. The cost of $99 includes lunch and transportation.

• Bird-watching Retreat Package — Four days and three nights include visits to the Laureles, Norias and Santa Gertrudis divisions, providing avid bird-watchers with a comprehensive cross-section of the species on King Ranch. The cost includes eight meals, lodging at King Ranch cottages, guide and transportation to and from the Harlingen airport. The cost is $550.

Gather up the younger
set for an A-to-Z tour of
fun things to see and do
with kids in the
Coastal Bend.

Kidstuff

We've turned to the ABCs for help in guiding you to the kid-oriented activities in the Coastal Bend. Commercial, organized activities for the little ones are few and far between in this area, but don't let that discourage you. With the nearby beaches and year-round mild weather, the Coastal Bend provides one of the state's best natural playgrounds.

In this chapter we've abandoned our usual geographic divisions in favor of an alphabetical listing of things to see and do throughout the area. Some letters have more than one activity listed under them, and many are mentioned in greater detail in our Attractions chapter. We're sure that once you've visited the Coastal Bend, you'll soon be adding your own favorites to the list.

A is for . . .

aquarium. At the **Texas State Aquarium** in Corpus Christi you'll see all sorts of creatures that make their homes in the Gulf of Mexico. Stare eye-to-eye with an alligator (from behind a thick pane of glass) or watch a stingray glide silently through the water. Let a hermit crab walk across your hand or reach in and pull out another harmless sea creature on display in the aquarium's touch tank. Marvel at the 132,000-gallon tank that recreates the habitat around an offshore drilling platform and gaze at the beautiful Flower Gardens coral reef exhibit. Downstairs you'll laugh at the antics of the frolicsome Texas river otters and squeal as you pet a bamboo shark. Outside you'll find pelicans and great blue herons living in their natural habitat. You'll also find sea turtles, birds of prey and a playground. Children 3 and younger are admitted free. See our Attractions chapter for more information or call (512) 881-1200.

B is for . . .

boats that you can watch or rent along the Corpus Christi bayfront. Every Wednesday local sailors get together to race on **Corpus Christi Bay**. They gather inside the jetty that forms a semicircle around the two T-heads and one L-head (land extensions) protruding from the seawall. Take a seat on the Lawrence Street T-head and watch the boats cross in front of you while they await the starting horn. If you'd rather captain a boat yourself, check out the paddleboats for rent along the Peoples Street T-head. The cost is $10 per half-hour. You'll sail your boat in calm seas in an area free of large boat traffic. There's no number to call, just drop by the T-heads. For more information on sailing, see our Beaches and Watersports chapter.

C is for . . .

Children's Wharf at the Corpus Christi Museum of Science and History, (512) 883-2862, 1900 N. Chaparral Street. The Children's Wharf is in a large, open room that looks out on a circular fountain. Start with the life-size replica of a bay shrimping boat complete with life jackets and a bridge from which to captain the boat. Grab a fishing pole and troll for colorful plastic sharks, shrimp and starfish, or finish building a house with toy bricks. Play with magnets or a miniature car fitted with a sail and propelled by electric fans. Laugh at your reflection in funhouse mirrors or spell your name in giant letters on the museum wall. See our Attractions chapter for more information.

Guess what else C stands for: **Chuck E Cheese's**, (512) 993-8824, 5118 S. Staples Street, Corpus Christi. Chuck E Cheese's is loads of fun. This kid-oriented pizzeria is packed with video games and other games of skill. Win tickets and cash them in for prizes.

D is for . . .

dolphins that swim in the sea. Get up early and visit wild dolphins. You can't feed them, but if they're feeling friendly you might get to pet one. Since 1985 the proprietors of the **Dolphin Connection**, (512) 882-4126, have met and named more than 65 dolphins. Pay attention and you might just learn something. The proprietors are walking encyclopedias of dolphin information. Dolphin Connection tours leave from Ingleside. See our Attractions chapter for more information.

E is for . . .

exploring for seashells at local beaches. The best place to find them is on the Gulf of Mexico beaches, especially on the unpopulated **San Jose Island** north of Port Aransas. A boat takes visitors to and from the island several times a day. Another good place to search is **Padre Island National Seashore**. The farther you get from the visitors center, the greater your chance of finding a seashell or sand dollar. Keep your eyes peeled for hamburger sea beans, too. These marble-size wonders look like miniature hamburgers. Remember, the earlier bird gets the seashell. For information on boats to San Jose Island see our Attractions chapter or call (512) 749-5252.

F is for . . .

feeding sea gulls. You can do this anywhere sea gulls congregate, although it should be noted that many restaurants and other commercial establishments discourage the practice. Buy a cheap loaf of bread — sea gulls are not picky eaters — and head for the water. In Corpus Christi the **T-heads** and **Cole Park** are good places to find hungry sea gulls. The gulls at Cole Park are especially aggressive. Bring a camera and snap a picture with 20 or 30 sea gulls suspended in the air above you. Brave souls should try this: Hold a piece of bread (a large one is preferable) high in the air and wait for a gull to snatch it from your fingers. Don't worry, sea gulls are incredibly accurate. They rarely snatch a finger by mistake.

F also stands for fishing. You can fish all over the Coastal Bend, but one good spot for kids is **Indian Point Park and Pier**, (512) 643-8555, on U.S. Highway 181 in Portland. The fishing is good, and the accommodations are nice. Fish from a 720-foot pier with a 280-foot T-head. For more information see our Fishing and Hunting chapter.

G is for . . .

golf — miniature and disc. You'll find several miniature golf courses in the Coastal Bend. **Putt-Putt Golf & Games**, (512) 991-0830, 8306 S. Padre Island Drive in Corpus Christi, is the most recognized name. Putt-Putt's three courses challenge you with few gimmicks and hold out the possibility of making a hole in one on every hole. **Pirates of the Gulf**, (512) 884-4774, 2901 W. Surfside Boulevard in Corpus Christi, takes a different approach. This 18-hole course is laid out around a miniature mountain and includes two waterfalls, a cave and a dungeon. In Port Aransas you can tee up at **Absolutely Everything**, (512) 749-4222, 405 E. Avenue G.

The Coastal Bend has two disc golf courses. Disc golf is played with a flying disc rather than clubs and a ball. It doesn't cost much to get started, and anyone can play. A nine-hole course is in **Live Oak Park** on Sherry Street, Ingleside. For more information see our Parks chapter or call (512) 776-2517. An 18-hole course is in Corpus Christi's **West Guth**

Park on Up River Road north of Rand Morgan Road. Call the Bay Area Disc Golf Association, (512) 758-6466, for more information.

H is for . . .

horses. You can ride carousel horses at **Padre Staples Mall**, (512) 992-3348, on S. Padre Island Drive in Corpus Christi or real horses at various riding stables throughout the area. Try **Painted Dreams Riding Facility**, (512) 991-3474 or (512) 812-0936, 6201 Bradley Drive, in Corpus Christi. Want to ride on the beach? Then visit **Mustang Island Riding Stables**, (512) 991-7433, on Texas Highway 361 south of Port Aransas. For more information on Mustang Island Riding Stables see our Recreation chapter.

I is for . . .

ice cream. In Corpus Christi try either of the two locations of the **Marble Slab Creamery**, (512) 851-1236, 3133 S. Alameda Street, and 5521 Saratoga Boulevard, (512) 993-2202. They both serve a wide variety of homemade ice cream with all sorts of candy and other yummy treats that can be mixed in.

J is for . . .

jumping on a giant trampoline floating on Corpus Christi Bay. The folks at the **Holiday Inn-Emerald Beach**, (512) 883-5731, 1102 S. Shoreline Boulevard, will let you jump to your heart's content as long as you pay the cabana boy (the cost is $5 per person per day) for the pleasure. During the summer months you'll find the trampoline floating in the shallow water right outside the Holiday Inn's back door.

K is for . . .

kites. You can fly them, study them or both. The Coastal Bend is a great place to fly a kite provided you launch your rig near the shore where you can take advantage of the strong gulf wind. Corpus Christi's **Cole Park** and the **Rockport Beach Park** in Rockport are among the best places to fly kites. You can also learn about kites at the **International Kite Museum**, (512) 883-7456, on the grounds of the Best

Photo: Greater Corpus Christi Business Alliance

KidsPlace in Cole Park is a mega-jungle gym that was built by the Junior League of Corpus Christi.

Western Sandy Shores Beach Hotel, 3200 Surfside Boulevard in Corpus Christi. The museum traces the history of kites and their various uses. For more information see our Attractions chapter.

L is for . . .

libraries. Corpus Christi has several. Aransas Pass, Ingleside, Kingsville, Port Aransas, Portland and Rockport have one each. At Corpus Christi libraries toddlers and preschoolers enjoy weekly storytime sessions performed by the local children's librarian. Each brief session is filled with age-appropriate stories and songs designed to interest children in books. In Corpus Christi, call (512) 880-7020. Or call the Corpus Christi Central Library, (512) 880-7000, 805 Comanche Street, for more information. Although not a library, **Barnes & Noble Booksellers**, (512) 992-1339, 5129 Blanche Moore Street, does have its own storytime sessions every Saturday.

M is for . . .

McDonald's. Really. In the middle of the long hot summer you won't find a better place to run wild than the indoor play area at the **Flour Bluff McDonald's Restaurant**, (512) 939-7907, 1229 Waldron Road. Sometimes it's too hot outside — even for kids — and who wants to melt in the sun when you can sip on a cold beverage in air-conditioned comfort?

M also stands for museums and marine science. In the Kingsville area check out the **John E. Conner Museum**, (512) 595-2819, on the Texas A&M University-Kingsville campus and the **King Ranch Museum**, (512) 595-1881, 405 N. Sixth Street. For more information on marine science in the area, grab the gang and head for the visitors center at the **University of Texas Marine Science Institute**, (512) 749-5919, in Port Aransas. See our Attractions chapter.

N is for . . .

Niña. And *Pinta* and *Santa María*. These replicas of Christopher Columbus' discovery ships can be found at the **Corpus Christi Museum of Science and History**, 1900 N. Chaparral Street, and docked at the **Corpus Christi Marina**. The *Pinta* and *Santa María*, which reside at the museum while undergoing restoration after a recent collision with a barge, are open for tours. Plans call for the *Niña*, docked on the Corpus Christi bayfront, eventually to be opened for tours. For more information see our Attractions chapter or call (512) 882-1232.

O is for . . .

octopus, as in **Octopus' Garden**, a playground at the Texas State Aquarium, (512) 881-1200, featuring a giant purple octopus figure as its centerpiece. Local children came up with the idea for the giant purple octopus, and a local architect turned their imaginings into reality. The playground has equipment for both toddlers and older kids. Swings, monkey bars, slides and a fountain are among its main attractions. Kids will love climbing inside the octopus and looking out on the playground below. For more information see our Attractions chapter.

P is for . . .

playground. Corpus Christi's Cole Park on the bayfront has one of the largest and best playgrounds anywhere. The main attraction is **KidsPlace**, an 18,000-square-foot wooden play area featuring castle turrets, drawbridges, cubbyholes, crawl spaces and conventional playground equipment such as swings and slides. KidsPlace has areas for big and small kids and benches for weary parents. For more information see our Parks chapter.

Q is for . . .

quick cars at the **Crash Carlock Speedway**, (512) 289-8847, 241 Flato Road, Corpus Christi. The speedway holds stock car races every Saturday night around a quarter-mile track. We recommend ear plugs, especially for the kids. Children 12 and younger get in free with a paying adult. For more information see our Spectator Sports chapter.

R is for . . .

roller-skating at **Cityskates**, (512) 993-7456, 8051 S. Padre Island Drive, Corpus Christi. This old-fashioned skating rink has a 14,000-square-foot hardwood (maple) skating area, snack bar and video games. Friday night is teen dance night. Admission and skate rental costs $5.25.

S is for . . .

surreys. During warm months you can rent one of these four-wheeled, pedal-powered carriages along the Corpus Christi bayfront. They hold as many as four people. It's a great way to tour the bayfront while giving mom and dad some badly needed exercise. Take our advice: You'll enjoy it more in the spring and fall when the heat isn't as bad. Look for them along the seawall between the Peoples Street and Lawrence Street T-heads. They rent for about $10 per half-hour.

T is for . . .

taxi. No, not the four-wheeled kind. We're talking about the **water taxi** that travels between the barge dock on the north end of the bayfront to the Texas State Aquarium on the other side of the Corpus Christi Ship Channel. The water taxi runs only during the peak tourist season each summer. For more information see our Getting Here, Getting Around chapter or call (512) 289-2600.

U is for . . .

the former USS *Lexington*. This decommissioned aircraft carrier-turned-museum, Lexington Museum on the Bay, is on Corpus Christi Beach. What kid wouldn't like visiting this World War II-era warship? Commissioned in 1943, the USS *Lexington* served longer and set more records than any carrier in the history of the U.S. Navy. It now serves as a floating museum stocked with aircraft, exhibits and displays. For more information see our Attractions chapter or call (512) 888-4873 or (800) LADY LEX.

V is for . . .

video games. One of the best places to play is **Tilt**, (512) 991-0333, on the upper level at Corpus Christi's Padre Staples Mall. You'll find dozens of video and arcade games for all skill levels and interests.

W is for . . .

welcoming ships into the Port of Corpus Christi. Check for a schedule of incoming and outgoing ships on Page B-2 in the *Corpus Christi Caller-Times* then take Chaparral Street past the Corpus Christi Museum of Science and History and park under the Harbor Bridge. Another good place to watch is from an observation tower on the opposite side of the ship channel near the Texas State Aquarium. Cargo ships and oil tankers are common sights. Call (512) 882-5633 for a schedule of incoming and outgoing vessels.

W also stands for whooping cranes and windsurfing. Take a narrated tour by boat of the whooping cranes' winter habitat. For more information see our Birding chapter or call (512) 729-9952 or (800) 242-0071. To learn to windsurf or to rent equipment, head out to Bird Island Basin at the Padre Island National Seashore. For more information see our Beaches and Watersports chapter or call (512) 937-2621 or (800) 793-7471.

X is for . . .

xeriscaping. The **Corpus Christi Museum of Science and History**, (512) 883-2862, 1900 N. Chaparral Street, has a xeriscape exhibit on the west side of the building featuring plants native to the Coastal Bend. Xeriscaping is a method of landscaping using native plants that thrive under dry conditions. You'll get a good look at Coastal Bend flora without having to trek all over the area to find them.

Y is for . . .

YMCA and YWCA. Both facilities have exercise equipment, gymnasiums, swimming pools and programs for children. The **YMCA**, (512) 882-1741, 417 S. Upper Broadway, has racquetball/handball courts. The **YWCA**, (512) 857-5661, 4601 Corona Street, provides free child care for members. A one-day visitor's pass costs $10 to the YMCA and $6 to the YWCA.

Z is for . . .

zipping down the seawall on in-line skates. This is Corpus Christi's favorite place for in-line skating. Adults and children alike will enjoy the view and the wide-open expanse of the seawall. You can rent skates at **M D Surf & Skate**, (512) 854-7873, 4016 Weber Road, in Corpus Christi. They're also available at **Giggles Skate & Surf**, (512) 882-7554, 403 N. Shoreline Boulevard on the Corpus Christi bayfront. In-line skates rent for about $10 a day for both children and adults, pads included.

It seems that almost any topic can find itself the focus of a celebration — from art and music to ranching and history — and serve as a reason to break out the music and refreshments, and have some fun!

Annual Events and Festivals

Maybe it's the proximity of sand and surf, maybe it's the unquenchable sunshine — all we know is that South Texans love celebrations. Many of these celebrations seem to have been inspired by residents' devotion to the coastal elements. There are festivals devoted to oysters, shrimp, fishing, piracy and the bay itself.

On the other hand, there are also a variety of more offbeat events: a cactus celebration, a hummingbird festival and a bull-riders challenge. It seems that almost any topic can find itself the focus of a celebration — from art and music to ranching and history — and serve as a reason to break out the music and refreshments, and have some fun!

The events we've listed occur across the spectrum of Coastal Bend communities and celebrate everything from the area's coastal industries to the presence of the U.S. Navy.

Besides the annual events listed in this chapter, you'll want to mark your calendars for monthly happenings at a wide-ranging list of locations, particularly in the area's largest city, Corpus Christi. Some examples:

• A children's treasure hunt at the Corpus Christi Museum of Science and History is held every Saturday at 1:30 PM, and live animals are the focus of a program every Saturday at 11 AM. For more information call (512) 883-2862.

• Dive shows and fish feedings attract lots of visitors to the Texas State Aquarium in Corpus Christi. The shows are 10:30 AM and 2:30 PM daily in the Island of Steel Gallery, and 3:30 PM daily in the Outdoor Marsh Exhibit. For more information call (512) 881-1200.

• A waterfront art market in Corpus Christi is open to all artists and crafters, and is held 10 AM to 5 PM the first and third Monday of each month, March through December. For more information call (512) 880-3461.

• In the summer, free Sunday evening pops concerts and Thursday evening "Bay Jammin' Concerts" take place at Cole Park, along Ocean Drive in Corpus Christi. Call (512) 880-3100 for more information.

• Sailors and spectators can check out the Wednesday evening sailboat races at the Corpus Christi Marina. The races start at 5:30 PM and are visible from the T-head and L-heads along the bayfront.

• Monthly guided tours of the mine hunting vessels stationed at Naval Station Ingleside are available; check the local newspaper for times and dates. The base also offers a driving tour at 1:30 PM every Tuesday. For more information call (512) 776-4204.

Check the Friday "Weekend" section of the *Corpus Christi Caller-Times* for entertainment information about the upcoming weekend. Also, don't forget to review our Attractions chapter for information about other sights to see.

In addition, there are always plenty of happenings at local bookstores, playhouses and museums. Please check our Arts and Culture chapter for more information about these places and how to find out about ongoing or traveling exhibits, plays or book readings.

We've listed admission fees when available and tried to give an approximate time of the month for each event. However, please check with organizers for the specifics on these events.

January

Tuff Hedeman Professional Bull Riders Challenge
J.K. Northway Exposition Center, Dick Kleberg Park, U.S. Hwy. 77, Kingsville • (512) 592-8516, (800) 333-5032

A fairly recent addition to the area's event calendar, this professional bull-riding competition began in 1997. The three-day event, held the first weekend in January, attracts professionals from all over the country and is a national final qualifying event.

For those of you who've never been to one, bull riding is every bit as exciting as you've imagined. The cowboys take turns trying to remain seated on the back of a rearing, kicking, bucking bull for the required eight seconds — it sounds like a short period of time to us, but it's probably the longest eight seconds of their day! The park is north of Kingsville. Admission is $10 and $15.

February

Stage Door Canteen
Lexington Museum on the Bay, 2914 N. Shoreline Blvd., Corpus Christi • (512) 888-4873

This musical revue is modeled after the USO shows performed during World War II and now presented aboard this decommissioned aircraft carrier, which has been converted into a museum. The show, held in early February, includes plenty of Big Band-era music, dancing and variety acts. Call for reservations and ticket prices.

A Celebration of Whooping Cranes and Other Birds
710 West Ave. A, Port Aransas Civic Center, Port Aransas • (512) 749-5919, (800) 45-COAST

Three days of workshops, seminars, birding tours, nature tours and bird-related vendors honor the annual visit of a flock of whooping cranes to this coastal community.

These elegant, endangered birds travel 2,500 miles to spend their winters on the Texas Coast. They arrive each October and stay through February or March. A record 159 birds wintered at the Aransas National Wildlife Refuge in 1996, and officials hope to see their numbers continue to increase each year. Naturalists and bird lovers from around the world come to study and monitor the population of these cranes, which are the largest birds native to North America.

The celebration is held during the latter part of February through the beginning of March. Admission to the exhibits is free; tours are $5 per person and seminars are $10.

See our Birding chapter for more about whooping cranes.

March

Fulton Oysterfest
Fulton Harbor on Fulton Beach Rd., Fulton Navigation Park, Fulton • (512) 729-2388, (800) 242-0071

They say it was a brave person who ate the first raw oyster. Well, this festival is for those who pay homage to that courageous soul — an estimated 200,000 raw oysters will be consumed during this three-day salute to the delectable bivalve.

Sponsored by the Fulton Volunteer Fire Department, the event is held the first weekend in March and attracts an estimated 30,000 oyster lovers. Expect outdoor fun, games, entertainment and activities that include oyster-shucking and oyster-eating contests. Last year's winners downed more than 200 raw oysters in five minutes!

There's also a carnival for kids and lots of arts and crafts booths that feature the talents of local artisans. Admission is $2.

South Texas Ranching and Heritage Festival
Conner Museum, various sites at Texas A&M University Kingsville • (512) 592-8516, (800) 333-5032

Ranch craftsmen, artisans and storytellers demonstrate their skills during this three-day event held in honor of the city's ranching heritage. It's usually held the first week of March and is as educational as it is entertaining. Watch cowboys create leather goods for their ranch work, listen to ranchers recite poetry and enjoy a guitar serenade under the mesquite trees. There are booths, crafts, artwork, a chuckwagon cookoff and ranch rodeo. Admission is free.

April

Buccaneer Days and Rodeo
Various locations in Corpus Christi
• (512) 882-3242

Celebrating the 1519 discovery of Corpus Christi Bay, this festival begins each year with a group of "pirate queens" capturing the city's mayor and making him or her walk the plank. That good-humored dunking of the mayor in the bay waters represents the city's surrender to pirate rule for 11 days of entertainment and gaiety. A rodeo is held the week before Buc Days begins.

Other activities include an illuminated night parade through downtown to the bayfront, fireworks, music, sports events, an arts and crafts show and a carnival. The festivities also include tournaments for tennis, golf, racquetball and archery, a bike ride, an airshow for radio-controlled craft and a shoebox parade for youngsters (they build miniature floats out of a shoeboxes). A music competition brings 5,000 to 6,000 students from high school bands and choirs to the city.

All the festivities are usually held the last week of April and the first week of May. Admission varies for the different events.

May

Ingleside Navy Days
Various locations in Ingleside
• (512) 776-2906

Ingleside Navy Days pays homage to the U.S. military presence that has revitalized this small town. Events include a beauty pageant, carnival, dance, entertainment,

Young visitors share an early-morning meal at the King Ranch annual Ranch Hand Breakfast.

parade, 1-mile run, car show, games and refreshments. Admission is free. The festival is usually held in mid-May.

Beach to Bay Relay Marathon
From Padre Island to downtown Corpus Christi • (512) 225-3338

Held on the third Saturday in May (Armed Forces Day), this popular relay marathon has gained a loyal and wide-ranging audience. Since its inception with two dozen teams in 1976, it has grown to include a field of thousands of runners from all over the state, nation and Mexico. Each team of six runners must complete a marathon-length course (26.2 miles), with each of the six runners logging approximately 4.4 miles.

A total of 1,000 teams (or 6,000 runners) compete in the race each year. The course begins on Padre Island Beach at Nueces County Park and winds over the causeway, through the Naval Air Station and down Ocean Drive to Cole Park on Corpus Christi Bay. It concludes with a huge party at the park, where runners eat pizza and fruit, and drink soft drinks and beer while listening to live bands. Early registration is $120 per team.

Texas Whooping Cranes

Avian visitors are always welcome in the Coastal Bend, but few arrivals are more eagerly awaited than the flock of whooping cranes that has wintered here for decades.

These tall, elegant cranes are an endangered species. And the cranes that fly to the Aransas National Wildlife Refuge each fall are the world's only naturally occurring wild flock. That means that they reproduce in the wild, not in captivity, and it makes them objects of immense interest to scientists as well as birders.

Close-up

With their cottony white plumage, black-tipped wings and red foreheads, whooping cranes are striking water-fowl. They are North America's largest birds, with adults standing at 5 feet tall with a wingspan of 7½ feet.

In 1996, a flock of 159 birds came from their nesting grounds in Canada to the Coastal Bend — a flight of 2,500 miles and about 50 days. Officials estimate that there are only about 330 of the birds alive today, with half of them in captivity. The world's population of migrating whooping cranes fell to 14 or 16 in the 1940s. The whoopers that winter at Aransas National Wildlife Refuge, which was established in 1937, are the descendants of that flock.

For many in the Coastal Bend, the arrival of the whoopers is one of the area's more thrilling fall rites. Rangers at the refuge count more than 80,000 registered visitors between November and March, from as far away as Canada and other foreign countries. Visitors can also see the cranes on boat tours that leave from Rockport, Fulton and Port Aransas. Tours generally begin November 1 and continue through March. See our Birding chapter for phone numbers and prices.

In Port Aransas, officials celebrate the bird with a four-day festival that includes seminars, workshops, nature trips, demonstrations and food and crafts booths. It's held annually in late February and early March. See our Annual Events and Festivals chapter for more information. — continued on next page

Photo: Greater Corpus Christi Business Alliance

The endangered whooping cranes spend their winters at the Aransas National Wildlife Refuge north of Rockport.

In Rockport, officials estimate that crane-seeking visitors spend approximately $5 million here each year.

The cranes are known for their size and also their trumpeting call, a distinctive and loud bugle-like sound that can be heard up to two miles away. And like all other cranes, the whooping crane symbolizes long life, fidelity and happiness in many cultures.

One reason visitors so enjoy seeing the cranes is, of course, because the birds are so rare. They can also put on quite a show for their guests. The birds mate for life, and their life span is approximately 25 years in the wild or 40 years in captivity. They perform elaborate dances, bouncing up and down, flapping their wings and bobbing their heads, to attract and keep their mates.

They dine on blue crabs while in Aransas and spend their winters on the marshlands at the refuge. They usually raise one chick per year, which has made their population growth painstakingly slow.

Humans have been the cause of the whooping cranes demise. Development has meant the loss of breeding grounds and made the birds nearly extinct. In addition, the elusive birds and their eggs were prized by hunters.

Many experts believe that knowledge gained from the efforts to save the whoopers has benefited other endangered creatures, including six other species of cranes found around the world. Worldwide, there are 15 species of cranes, but only two are found in the United States: the endangered whooping cranes and the abundant sandhill crane, a smaller, gray crane.

Scientists who've been working to increase the cranes' numbers hope they can be downgraded from their current endangered status to the less-serious threatened status. To be put on the threatened list, there must be at least three self-sustaining wild flocks, with at least 40 nesting pairs in the Texas flock and 25 pairs in the non-migrating Florida flock, as well as an additional 25 pairs in a third flock expected to be started around the year 2000.

To help, officials have collected eggs from wild nests, raised the young in captivity to be released in new flocks and even led cranes on their cross-country migration in aircraft. But the greatest success in helping the cranes population grow has been in protecting the birds' natural habitat — such as the refuge along the Texas coastline.

U.S. Open Windsurfing Regatta, Corpus Christi
Oleander Point at South Cole Park on Ocean Dr., Corpus Christi
• **(512) 985-1555**

Windsurfers and enthusiasts from around the world converge on the city for this annual event, usually held over the Memorial Day weekend. The four-day event, which was started in 1987, attracts windsurfers of national renown as well as spectators and amateurs. The city's bayfront location, with consistent southeast winds of 18 to 20 mph, has made it a premiere site for windsurfers. Winners can receive up to $70,000 worth of prizes during the weeklong competition. Other events include parties, music and kite-flying.

King Ranch Wild Game Lunch and Texas Cactus Festival
Various locations in Kingsville
• **(512) 592-8516, (800) 333-5032**

Taste the "prickly pear" (also known as cactus) in a variety of dishes that range from entrees to beverages. Sponsored in mid-April by the King Ranch, Kingsville Downtown Business Association and the Texas Prickly Pear Council, this event aims at promoting and informing folks about the lowly cactus and its many uses. Symposiums, cooking demonstrations, information about medicinal properties of cactus and research into cactus are scheduled.

Also, there is an annual wild-game luncheon that includes a trail ride, hay wagon ride, musical entertainment and activities for children. Arts and craft booths, games, and shopping are also offered.

Rockport Festival of Wines
Texas Maritime Museum, 1202 Navigation Cir., Rockport
• **(512) 729-1271**

Ten major Texas wineries participate in this festival launched in 1997. The affair offers samples of wine and specialty foods, plus participation by local restaurants and celebrity chefs. Local bands provide live entertainment. Proceeds benefit the museum. Admission is $12 per person, and that includes a commemorative wine glass plus three tickets for wine tasting. You can purchase additional tickets separately.

June

C-101 C-Sculptures
J.P. Luby Surf Park, Old Park Rd. 53, Mustang Island • (512) 289-1000

Held annually on the second Saturday in June, this event is sponsored by local radio station KNCN-FM and was launched in 1977. It pays homage to the artistry, humor and endurance needed to create massive sculptures out of beach sand.

As many as 110,000 people come to watch individuals and teams carve their impressive creations. These are nothing like the sandcastles you built as a kid: They can be as large as 20 square feet and require many hours of painstaking labor. Some entrants begin their work at midnight Friday, contest start time, and continue until judging time at 2 PM Saturday. One amazing recent entry was a beautifully detailed chameleon with its tongue stuck out to catch an unsuspecting fly.

Entry fees are $25 for the solo division and $25 per team, plus $5 for each team member.

First-place winners get $1,000 for their efforts. The fun also includes live music, a volleyball contest, bikini contest and bodybuilding contest. Proceeds benefit Texas Special Olympics.

July

Rockport Art Festival
Festival Grounds, Rockport Harbor, Rockport • (512) 729-5519

This weekend around the Fourth of July is devoted to the display of beautiful, juried fine arts such as pottery, watercolor, acrylics, oils, woodcarving and more. More than 100 booths set up in a colorful tent village on the festival grounds allow artists from throughout the Southwest to display and sell their works. The two-day event, sponsored by the Rockport Art Association, also offers food and music. Admission is $2. The festival grounds are on Texas Highway 35 Business.

Rockport Air Show
Rockport Beach Park, Rockport • (512) 729-5519, (800) 242-0071

Aviation enthusiasts can spend the day at this annual event, held on the Fourth of July. In the morning, there are static displays of aircraft ranging from modern planes to military jets to vintage aircraft. In the afternoon, there's a two-hour air show featuring aerial stunts, aerobatics and military flyovers. There's no admission for the show, but there's a $3 parking fee to get on the beach. The park is on Texas Highway 35 Business.

Fourth of July Big Bang Weekend
Various sites downtown, Corpus Christi • (512) 994-4884

A celebration of Independence Day that includes a children's parade, fireworks along the bayfront, concerts and patriotic ceremonies.

INSIDERS' TIP

Buccaneer Days originated from a celebration first begun in 1917, known as Splash Days, which consisted of a bathing-beauty contest on the beach to signify the start of summer. The event was expanded and modified when residents felt the beauty contest lacked the necessary glamour for the growing city of Corpus Christi.

Photo: Greater Kingsville Economic Development Council

La Posada de Kingsville ... A Celebration in Lights is an annual holiday festival stretching over several weeks that includes parades, a processional and more.

Enjoy food, refreshments and plenty of flag-raising during this Fourth of July weekend.

Stars and Stripes
2914 N. Shoreline Blvd., Lexington Museum on the Bay, Corpus Christi
• (512) 888-4873

This Fourth of July event is held on the flight deck of this aircraft carrier-turned-museum and features a live performance by the Corpus Christi Symphony Orchestra. Musical selections include both popular and traditional patriotic music, and celebrated soprano Flicka Rahn performs as guest artist — a real treat. Dinner is served buffet style, and the evening ends with a fireworks display over the bayfront, choreographed to the symphony's music.

This is the museum's major annual fund-raiser, and the ticket prices reflect that. In previous years, admission has been $75 per couple, $45 per individual and $25 for ages 17 and younger. You can also buy a table for 10 for $750. For current ticket prices, call the *Lexington*.

Deep Sea Roundup and Boat Show
Roberts Point Park and Civic Center, 710 W. Ave. A, Port Aransas • (512) 749-6339

This fishing tournament, hosted by the Port Aransas Boatmen Association, lays claim as the oldest on the Texas coast. First held in 1932 as the Tarpon Rodeo, organizers changed the name when the tarpon ran out years later. Usually held the second weekend in July, champions receive substantial cash prizes and trophies for the largest fish caught in a number of categories.

The weekend's activities begin with registration and a cocktail party Thursday, fishing and a dinner Friday followed by more fishing, a dinner and a dance Saturday. The event closes with a fish fry and awards ceremony on Sunday. Entry fee is $70 in advance and $80 at the door, which includes the weekend's meals. The dance is open to the public at $10 per person.

George Strait Roping Classic and Concert
J.K. Northway Exposition Center, Dick Kleberg Park, U.S. Hwy. 77, Kingsville
• (512) 592-8516, (800) 333-5032

This annual three-day roping event draws thousands of country-and-western fans to Kingsville, where they get to watch superstar George Strait rope cattle by day and croon his country ballads by night. Usually scheduled for June or July, it features Strait and his relatives in competition with roping teams from across the country.

Fifteen years ago, when this event first began, Strait was an up-and-coming performer, but not the superstar he is today; attendance at the roping and concert has grown exponentially with his fame. Many fans consider this the pivotal happening of the country-western calendar. Concert tickets vary in price, but are usually more than $25 per person — and sell out rapidly.

The park is on the south edge of Kingsville between the U.S. 77 business and U.S. 77 bypass.

August

La Feria de las Flores
Downtown, Corpus Christi
• (512) 992-4209

Since 1959, La Feria de las Flores has celebrated the beauty and diversity of Hispanic traditions and crowned the community's young women with college scholarships in a spectacular pageant. Participants wear elaborate traditional costumes and perform regional Mexican dances that are breathtaking to watch. The young women also raise money by selling ads for the festival, providing additional scholarship funds for needy college-bound students. Since 1959, the council has awarded more than $817,000 in scholarship funding. Sponsored by the League of United Latin American Citizens Council No. 1, it is held the second Saturday in August. Admission is generally $5 to $10 per person.

The Miss Corpus Christi Area USA Pageant
Richardson Auditorium, Del Mar College, Baldwin and Ayers Sts., Corpus Christi
• (512) 985-1555

Teens and young women throughout the area vie to be crowned Miss Corpus Christi Area Teen USA and Miss Corpus Christi Area USA during this annual competition. Entrants participate in three categories — personal interview, swimsuit and evening gown — for the chance to win up to $6,000 in cash and prizes. Winners represent the area in the Miss Texas Teen USA and the Miss Texas USA

pageants. Tickets are $10 in advance and $12 at the door.

September

Fiesta En La Playa
Rockport Festival Grounds, Rockport Beach, Rockport • (512) 729-2063, (800) 242-0071

The Spanish name of this event translates literally to Festival on the Beach — and that suits this event that celebrates the community's Hispanic heritage. Held on Labor Day weekend, this fiesta features folklorico dancers, mariachi bands and piñata contests. If you dare, you can participate in the jalapeño-eating contest, the tamale-eating contest and the macho legs contest. Live music features local Tejano bands and country western music. Admission is $2.

Hummer/Bird Celebration
Various locations, Rockport
• (512) 729-6445, (800) 242-0071

Thousands of hummingbirds travel through this town during their annual fall migration, and this festival focuses on the vagaries and beauty of this tiny, fascinating bird. During the three-day festival, there are lectures, workshops, bus and boat field trips and other programs, often presented by nationally renowned birding experts.

Although the hummingbird is the centerpiece here, there are also programs and trips to see many of the more than 500 other species of birds that can be found here including the whooping crane. It's held the second full weekend after Labor Day. Admission is $1 per person.

Zachary Taylor Days
730 S. Pearl St., Zachary Taylor Park, Rockport • (512) 729-6100, (800) 242-0071

Sponsored by the Aransas County History Project and the Rockport-Fulton Area Chamber of Commerce, this three-day weekend focuses on Gen. Zachary Taylor's visit here more than 150 years ago during the war between the United States and Mexico.

Events scheduled include a reenactment

of Taylor's arrival and his placement of the first American flag on Texas soil, a flyover of Navy planes, and recognition of local POW/MIAs. On a lighter note, residents wear period costumes and conduct other historical reenactments, including an old-fashioned street fair with an auction of picnic baskets, a general store, pony rides, food booths, face painting and children's games. Live music, a hand-cranked ice-cream contest, a beard and mustache contest and a pecan-pie bakeoff are other features. Admission is $1, and children younger than 12 are admitted free.

Aransas Pass Shrimporee
Highway 361 at Johnson Ave., Aransas Pass Community Park, Aransas Pass • (512) 758-2750, (800) 633-3028

Touted as "the biggest shrimp celebration in Texas," this event held in mid-September pays tribute to the small, succulent crustacean that this town's economy is based on. There are arts and crafts booths, a shrimp-eating competition, a men's sexy legs contest, a parade, a children's area, a carnival and the Great Outhouse Race (which is exactly what it sounds like). And of course, there's lots of not-to-be-missed seafood — the full culinary range of shrimp — fried shrimp, shrimp gumbo, shrimp Creole, boiled shrimp, Cajun-style shrimp, etc., as well as standard festival fare of cotton candy, candy apples and funnel cakes. Live entertainment usually includes Tejano music, country-and-western and even some rock 'n' roll. Other performers have included jugglers, comedians and acrobats. Admission is $3 for adults, $1 for children and free for youngsters younger than 6.

Bayfest
Shoreline Boulevard and the Bayfront Arts and Sciences Park, Corpus Christi • (512) 887-0868

This fall festival is aimed at families, offering every form of entertainment from carnival rides to arts and craft booths, fireworks, a parade and a veritable smorgasbord of foods. Begun as a bicentennial celebration, this has become one of the major festivals in the area. And it's a boon for the local nonprofit groups, hundreds of which set up booths on the grounds and earn profits from the sale of everything from lemonade and

ice cream to turkey legs and tacos. The children's area is especially worth visiting: It's got entertainment and hands-on creative games for the youngsters. Admission is $5.

Kleberg County Airshow
Kleberg County Airport, Texas Hwy. 141, Kingsville • (512) 595-8540, (800) 333-5032

This festival, held every other year on a Saturday at the end of September, features a spectacular all-day air show with music, food, a carnival, dynamic air performances and the "world's longest line dance" on the runway of the airport. Stunt pilots, naval aviators, vintage airplanes and international performers are usually on hand. There's also a carnival, food booths and refreshments. The day concludes with live music and dancing. The next one is scheduled for 1999. Admission is $7 per carload. The airport is west of Kingsville.

October

Rockport Seafair
Downtown and Rockport Harbor, Rockport • (512) 729-3312, (800) 242-0071

Crab races, a seafood gumbo cookoff, a sailing regatta and a children's fishing tournament are part of this annual Columbus Day festival's homage to the sea. One of the more fun events to watch is the "Anything that Floats But a Boat Race." The semi-seaworthy entries in this wacky race seem to pay homage as much to the creators' senses of humor as to their love of the water. We once saw something that looked like a floating outhouse make its way across the bay!

Expect an abundance of fresh seafood for sampling, including fresh shrimp and oysters. Other highlights include 5- and 10-kilometer runs, live entertainment, dancing, a parade and a carnival. Admission is $2.

Violet Oktoberfest
Old St. Anthony's Catholic Church and Museum • U.S. Hwy. 44, Violet • (512) 387-4434

The legacy of German settlers is recognized during this annual event, held the third

Sunday in October at the historical old Catholic Church and museum. Come see the classic cars on display and enjoy a barbecue beef dinner with beans, potato salad, coffee or tea and dessert. For browsing, there's a country store that sells handcrafted arts and trinkets.

However, the real attraction for most visitors is a tour through the quaint old museum, which contains vintage farm equipment, cooking implements and a display of turn-of-the-century priest's robes. The church, 5 miles west of Corpus Christi, dates back to 1910. There's no admission charge, but donations are requested. The meal costs $6.

Texas Jazz Festival
Corpus Christi Bayfront, Corpus Christi
• (512) 883-4500

The longest running free festival in the country, this celebration of jazz was first held in 1958. Performers and fans from nationwide come to hear their favorite musicians play the sultry and glorious music of the jazz world. Audiences also are treated to blues, salsa, gospel, gunk, reggae, fusion and swing music.

There's also an outdoor jazz Mass held on Sunday morning, informal cutting competitions held each evening, and a two-hour jazz cruise along the bayfront. Admission to the festival, concerts and Mass is free, but there is a $15 charge for the cruise. This festival is usually held the fourth weekend in October.

November

King Ranch Hand Breakfast
Texas Hwy. 141 W., King Ranch,
Kingsville • (512) 592-3250

Come see real cowboys lasso steers and pound horseshoes onto the hooves of their steeds during this widely attended event held in early November. This is a rare glimpse into the operation of the King Ranch, which is one of the world's largest working ranches. For the price of breakfast, you get served by a crew of cowboys and volunteers who ladle

out scrambled eggs, biscuits, sausage, tortillas, refried beans, coffee and orange juice. The event is outdoors, and visitors eat standing up or sitting on bales of hay around the show arena. Wear your cowboy boots and bring a hearty appetite. Admission is $5.

La Posada de Kingsville
Various locations downtown, Kingsville
• (512) 592-3250, (512) 592-8516,
(800) 333-5032

A series of events conducted from late November through mid-December commemorate the community's celebration of Christmas. A reenactment of *la posada* — the trip Mary and Joseph took as they searched for lodging on Christmas Eve in Bethlehem — is a high point of the celebration. Other events include a downtown lighting ceremony, Christmas caroling, breakfast with Santa Claus, a Jingle Bell Walk/Run, a tour of homes and a parade. Admission is free.

December

Holiday Forest at the South Texas Institute for the Arts
1902 N. Shoreline Blvd., Corpus Christi
• (512) 980-3500

Since 1960, the museum's volunteer auxiliary has presented an array of holiday exhibits, each designed by an organization, institution or club in the area, as a Christmas gift to the public. The results are quite dazzling — trees of every shape, size and theme, holiday artistry that runs the gamut from primitive children's art (contributed by schools) to elaborate spiritual renditions from churches or synagogues.

The museum chair chooses the year's theme, and the 50 or 60 invited participants use that as a starting point for their imagination and creativity. This exhibit is definitely worth seeing. It usually opens the Saturday a week after Thanksgiving. Suggested donation is $1 for adults, 25¢ for children.

INSIDERS' TIP

A hat, sunglasses and sunscreen are essential when attending many of the Coastal Bend's summer festivals.

Photo: Greater Corpus Christi Business Alliance

Each year, Corpus Christi hosts the Texas Jazz Festival - the only jazz festival in the nation still free to the public.

Harbor Lights Festival and Boat Parade
Bayfront and various locations in Corpus Christi • (512) 985-1555

The official lighting of the city's 75-foot-tall Christmas tree is the centerpiece of this annual yule celebration. Santa Claus arrives by boat, of course, and the boats along Shoreline Boulevard sport colorful lights for the oc- casion. In fact, the entire downtown area, from office buildings to the Harbor Bridge, wears Christmas lights, which gives the city a beauti- fully festive appearance for the season. Other activities include a children's parade down Shoreline, live entertainment, arts and crafts activities for the children, an illuminated boat parade through the bay waters and fireworks. Admission is free.

The Texas Coastal Bend
has a flourishing and
diverse arts community
that draws, paints and
shares its vision and
creativity at dozens of
area galleries
and studios.

The Arts

Artists have always drawn inspiration from nature, be they painters, sculptors or dancers. And in a coastal region, where climate and conviviality converge, artists have often found both a source of creativity and a welcome haven.

That's certainly true in the Coastal Bend, which has a flourishing and diverse arts community that draws, paints and shares its vision and creativity at dozens of area galleries and studios. And although your best bet for viewing the work of local artists is at the museums and art centers, you can also find plenty of illustration in your everyday travel through the region — from the bayfront sculptures along the waterfront in Corpus Christi to displays at area restaurants.

Corpus Christi is one of several major Texas cities to fund a public art program. Since its inception in 1987, 23 pieces of art have been installed in various locations throughout the city. Forms include pink granite sculptures, bronze sculptures, ceramic tile murals and oil paintings, depicting subjects that range from wildlife to history. The program commissions two to four pieces a year, paying $8,000 to $10,000 per piece. For information or locations of public art in Corpus Christi, call Pamela Gooby at the city's Park & Recreation Department, (512) 880-3461.

Our area boasts many renowned artists. Kent Ullberg is a sculptor whose larger-than-life statue of Jesus Christ adorns the entrance to the First United Methodist Church on Shoreline Boulevard. Jesus Bautista Moroles, a native Corpus Christi sculptor, is known for his work with large-scale granite figures. William Wilhelmi is a studio potter known worldwide. His work is featured in the Smithsonian Institution.

The Rockport region has attracted more than its share of fine artists, and the area has a healthy and active community of artists and studios. Newcomers are welcome, and many studios offer lessons and classes for adults as well as children.

Theater productions and music, too, are available in the Coastal Bend. There is a fine symphony, as well as several university theaters and local playhouses. Increasingly, national productions have made their way down south to Corpus Christi — a welcome and long-awaited development for drama lovers. The Selena Auditorium often hosts traveling exhibits, including Broadway-based theater performances of *Joseph and the Amazing Technicolor Dreamcoat* and *Grease*.

To find out what's playing at local theaters or about upcoming exhibits, your best source is the *Corpus Christi Caller-Times'* "Weekend" section in the Friday newspaper. The section provides up-to-date information about what's going on in the local and area community in the coming week, as well as later in the month. It also usually lists admission fees and telephone numbers to call for reservations.

Galleries

North Bay Area

Rockport

Little Gallery
Cactus and Fourth Sts., Fulton
• **(512) 729-0246**
Artist and owner Chris Ely's gallery has been in this tree-shaded location for 23 years. She displays and sells her sketches and watercolors of local scenes and birds as well as other artists' sketches, paintings and note cards. The gallery is open 1 to 4 PM daily except Wednesday.

Moroles Inc.
408 W. Sixth St., Rockport
• **(512) 729-6747**
Nationally known sculptor Jesus Moroles

works at a studio in Rockport, as well as at his newer exhibition center in New Mexico, to produce granite sculptures that adorn places as diverse as Houston and Albuquerque. Among his best-known pieces are: *Lapstrake,* a 64-ton, 22-foot sculpture for the E.F. Hutton, at CBS Plaza in New York City, across the street from the Museum of Modern Art; a 22-foot sculpture fountain for the Albuquerque Museum of Art in New Mexico; his largest single work, the Houston Police Officers Memorial; and a sculpture plaza created for the Edwin A. Ulrich Museum in Wichita, Kansas.

Born in Corpus Christi, Moroles lives in Rockport. His studio is not open to the public. However, groups can arrange for tours by appointment. In 1996, Moroles also opened his Cerrillos Cultural Center, an exhibition, performance and studio space in Cerrillos, New Mexico. His work has been featured in more than 200 publications, and he lectures regularly about his work and the issue of public sculpture.

Estelle Stair Gallery
406 S. Austin St., Rockport
• (512) 729-2478

This gallery, in a century-old downtown building, features oils, watercolor and sculpture focused on the coast. Displays include carvings, exotic furniture, fountains and jewelry. Art classes and workshops are available. The building itself has an old-fashioned, graceful feel, with high ceilings, wood floors and etched brick walls, as well as a garden in the back. It's open Tuesday through Sunday.

Po Po's Art Studio Inc.
1114 Main St., Rockport
• (512) 790-5104, (512) 790-3736

This gallery and studio showcases the work of local artist Charles "Po Po" Cosby, as well as work by other artists. The collection of coastal and sporting artwork features shore-

birds, lighthouses, hunting, fishing and boating scenes. Classes are taught here, too.

Simon Michael School of Art and Gallery
510 E. King St., Rockport
• (512) 729-6233

This was the first art gallery in the area when it was established in the 1950s. Long-time artist Simon Michael works in all media, including oils, acrylics and watercolors, and features scenes and figure work from his worldwide travels. You can also view Remington and Russell bronzes (part of the artist's private collection) at this downtown gallery, which is open daily.

Rockport Artists' Gallery and Gift Shop
414 S. Austin St., Rockport
• (512) 729-0600

A working gallery, this is a great showcase of affordable art and gifts from the coast. You can find watercolors, oils, prints, jewelry and more at this gallery, including ornamental pottery. The gallery offers classes and sells unpainted canvases.

Rockport Center for the Arts
902 Navigation Cir., Rockport
• (512) 729-5519

The Rockport Art Association is housed in the 1890s Bruhl-O'Connor House, a blue-and-white Victorian-style building on the harbor. Created in 1967, the association was organized to promote work by local and regional artists, both professional and amateur. The building that houses the center was donated in 1983 and moved to the current site on the harbor. The center contains 5,000 square feet of gallery, classroom, lecture and library space and counts more than 15,000 annual attendees at its events. Local artists' work is hung in

www.insiders.com

See this and many other **Insiders' Guide®** destinations online — in their entirety.

Visit us today!

INSIDERS' TIP

Most of the area's art centers offer classes for children and adults. This can be a great way to meet people and explore your creativity.

Photo: Greater Corpus Christi Business Alliance

Mexican-American culture - dance, music and art - plays a large role in the social climate of South Texas.

the gallery on a rotating basis, and classes for adults and children are available.

The Rockport Art Association, which operates this center, sponsors an annual Art Festival each July (see our Annual Events chapter). The center provides tours, classes and in-school workshops for more than 800 Coastal Bend children each year.

Among the better-known professional members of the association are Al Barnes, Herb Booth, John P. Cowan, Jesus Bautista Moroles, Harold Phenix, Steven Russell, E.M. "Buck" Schiwetz and Kent Ullberg.

Admission is free. The center is closed on Monday.

Portland

Dinah Bowman Studio and Gallery
312 Fifth Ave., Portland • (512) 643-4922

Local artist Dinah Bowman is best known for her fish prints, which are meticulous prints of fishes on canvas as well as on T-shirts. She's also an expert at capturing the beauty and detail of other aspects of maritime life. Her gallery also displays work by other artists, mostly with coastal and marine life themes.

Ingleside

Golden Triangle Art Association and Gallery
Texas Hwy. 361, Ingleside
• (512) 776-7583

This art gallery was established in early 1997 and is housed in a historic city building decorated with the official city bird, the blue heron. A nonprofit association, the Golden Triangle offers exhibits and lessons. It's open Tuesday through Saturday and features the work of local artists in a variety of media, including oil and acrylic and pottery.

Corpus Christi

Art Center of Corpus Christi
100 Shoreline Blvd., Corpus Christi
• (512) 884-6406

In this lemon-ice colored building, on the median of Shoreline Boulevard, you will find exhibits that change monthly and a delightful tearoom, Jezebelles (see our Restaurants chapter). Chartered in 1972, the Art Center is committed to the promotion of local and area art and art education. Its membership includes approximately 600 working artists of all ages and skill levels, as well as a number of art patrons. Exhibit and work space for members is available for members, and free exhibits allow the community to view and enjoy the artwork.

The rotating exhibits display the work of individuals as well as 11 member groups from throughout the area. More than 5,000 visitors signed the guest register during 1997. The center also has classes, workshops, demonstrations and gift shops. It's open Tuesday through Sunday.

Corpus Christi Art Connection
3636 S. Alameda Ave., Taylor Center,
Corpus Christi • (512) 854-1057

This gallery features works from local as well as national and international artists. You'll find original artwork and limited-edition prints by varied artists such as Kent Ullberg, Herb Booth, Doug Dawson, Guy Harvey, Lars Johnson, Mike Stidham, Tina Close, Jim Dearman, Lee Holt, Robert Moore and Nico van de Linde. The gallery is open weekdays and by appointment on weekends.

Earth Works Pottery
15851 F.M. Rd. 624, Robstown
• (512) 387-6462

John and Barbara Wisnewski have been potters since 1967, creating distinctive pieces with clean lines and soft pastel glazes. In addition to pottery, their showroom features original work by other artists, including paintings, handmade dolls, cutting boards, jewelry and weavings. The 10,000-square-foot studio and gallery, west of Corpus Christi, is open Monday through Saturday or by appointment.

Guy Morrow Art Studio
817 Airline Rd., Corpus Christi
• (512) 992-2204

Artist Guy Morrow, best known for his work in egg tempera, showcases his own works at this studio. Morrow, who grew up in Corpus Christi, specializes in private commissions. Art enthusiasts in the United States, Mexico and Austria collect his works. His studio is open Monday through Friday.

Joseph A. Cain Memorial Art Gallery
Del Mar College Fine Arts Center,
Baldwin and Ayers Sts., Corpus Christi
• (512) 886-1216

This college gallery hosts visits from major artists such as Jesus Bautista Moroles, James Surles, Peter Selz, Ivan Karp, Luis Jimenez, Fritz Scholder, Marisol, Peter Saul and Melisa Miller. In spring, the gallery holds an annual National Drawing and Small Sculpture Show and hosts a Tri-Group Exhibition by the South Texas Art League. In summer, selections from the Del Mar College Art Department permanent collection are on display.

Oliver's Village Gallery
3847 S. Alameda St., Corpus Christi
• (512) 855-0911

Opened in 1977, this family-owned gallery features paintings and graphics from international and national artists and from prominent galleries such as Meredith Long Gallery in Houston, Gallerie De Tours in Carmel, California; and Wally Findlay Galleries in New York, Paris, Chicago, Los Angeles and Palm Beach. The gallery specializes in stone lithographs, serigraphs, mezzotints, aquatints, etchings,

INSIDERS' TIP

The free concerts offered by the Cathedral Concert Series are quite popular, so plan to arrive early enough to get a good seat.

Photo: Daniel Fielder

The South Texas Institute for the Arts, which was designed by renowned architect Philip Johnson, presents a rotating schedule of diverse exhibitions and showcases work by local and regional artists.

limited-edition prints, woodcarvings, art glass and bronze sculptures.

Ullberg Studios Inc.
3636 S. Alameda St., Corpus Christi • (512) 851-1600

World-renowned wildlife sculptor Kent Ullberg, a native of Sweden, works here in Corpus Christi. Ullberg is perhaps best known for the more than two-dozen large-scale works he has done for museums and municipalities from Washington, D.C., to South Africa. A recent project was the largest bronze casting ever attempted, 36 feet high and 120 feet long, that captures the stages of a sailfish leaping from the water.

Ullberg has received numerous awards, and his work can be found in the private collection of H.R.H. Prince Berhard of the Netherlands as well as in countless museums and corporations worldwide.

In Corpus Christi, his "It is I" statue of Jesus Christ with arms outstretched toward the bayfront adorns the front entrance of the First United Methodist Church on Shoreline Boulevard (see our Close-up in the Worship chapter).

Weil Gallery
Center for the Arts, Texas A&M University Corpus Christi, 6300 Ocean Dr., Corpus Christi • (512) 994-2314

This university gallery features traveling exhibits of paintings, drawings and pottery. It's open daily when the university is in session.

Wilhelmi-Holland Gallery
300 Chaparral St., Corpus Christi • (512) 882-3523

This gallery showcases the work of well-known Corpus Christi potter William Wilhelmi, who is known for his intricate and ornate pottery. It also features artwork and ceramics by a variety of local artists. Ben Holland is gallery director for this downtown studio. Wilhelmi, who came to Corpus Christi in 1969, is known for his landscapes of eucalyptus trees, sunsets, cows and cacti, calla lilies and geometric designs on stoneware. Also popular are his so-called "little monsters," eccentric clay creatures that reflect a baroque style and offbeat wit. Wilhelmi's now-famous porcelain cowboy boots are permanently housed at the Renwick Gallery of the National Museum of Art of the Smithsonian Institution in Washington, D.C.

Port Aransas to Padre Island

Gary Osborne Fine Art
345 N. Alister St., Port Aransas
• (512) 749-6982

This studio offers a wide-ranging collection of art including original works by nationally known artists such as Kent Ullberg, Dalhart Windberg, Raul Gutierrez, Joe Russell, Arlene Morgan, Stephanie Wooley and Sherridan M. "Sam" Smith. In addition to featuring original artwork, this gallery also offers framing services and sells handpainted furniture.

Art Center for the Islands
309 N. Alister St., Port Aransas
• (512) 749-7334

This nonprofit art center for Mustang and Padre Islands is under the auspices of the Island Art Association, created to promote art activities and education. The center, which is staffed by volunteers, features exhibits by Coastal Bend member artists as well as guest artists and students. It also houses a working studio and classroom, workspace and a gathering area for artists and students. Classes offered include painting, pottery, sculpture, writing and music. The center, in the city's old pharmacy building near Pelican's Landing restaurant, is open daily.

Kingsville Area

Ben Bailey Art Gallery
Texas A&M University-Kingsville, University Blvd., Kingsville
• (512) 593-2619

This university art gallery is open daily when the university is in session and features traveling exhibits as well as student art. The exhibits change regularly and admission is free.

Seller's Market
205 E. Kleberg Ave., Kingsville
• (512) 595-4992

This downtown art center features paintings, crafts, jewelry, home-baked goods, quilts, prints and clothing. Housed in a renovated century-old building, Seller's Market is open Tuesday through Saturday.

Museums

North Bay Area

Texas Maritime Museum
Rockport Harbor, Rockport
• (512) 729-1271

Devoted to maritime objects, lore and artwork, this museum is worth a visit for all those who enjoy the sea. Recently, a spectacular traveling exhibit featured a collection of maritime art from the Cigna Museum and Art Collection of Philadelphia, including paintings and other artwork of shipwrecks, epic storms and flames at sea. The museum is open Tuesday through Sunday. Admission is $4 for adults and teens and $2 for children ages 5 to 12. Children ages 4 and younger get in free.

Corpus Christi

Asian Cultures Museum & Educational Center
1809 N. Chaparral St., Corpus Christi
• (512) 882-2641

This museum contains an outstanding collection of Japanese and other Oriental art, collectibles and dioramas. The exhibits rotate periodically. The center is open Tuesday through Saturday. Admission is $4 for adults, $3.50 for senior citizens and military, $2.50 for youths ages 6 to 15 and free for children 5 and younger.

South Texas Institute for the Arts
1902 N. Shoreline Blvd., Corpus Christi
• (512) 980-3500

Even the building is a work of art, by renowned New York architect Philip Johnson. Its lean lines blend gracefully with the coastal landscape. Inside you'll find traveling exhibits of painting, sculpture, photography and folkart. The permanent collection of photographs includes works by Ansel Adams and Victoria Livingston.

Stunning works by sculptor Kent Ullberg line Shoreline Drive in downtown Corpus Christi.

The South Texas Institute for the Arts, formerly the Art Museum of South Texas, is open Tuesday, Wednesday, Friday and Saturday from 10 AM to 5 PM, Thursday from 10 AM to 9 PM, and Sunday from 1 to 5 PM. The museum is closed on Monday. Admission is $3 for adults; $2 for students, military and senior citizens; $1 for children ages 2 to 12; and free for children younger than 2.

Kingsville

John E. Conner Museum
Texas A&M University-Kingsville, 700 University Blvd., Kingsville
• **(512) 595-2819**

The exhibits in this museum, established in 1925, are designed to preserve the social and natural history of the area. Displays include those about the ecosystem and geosciences and lifelike dioramas. The collection spans eras from pre-Colombian through the 1980s, featuring artifacts from machinery and art to arrowheads and deer antlers. One of the more intriguing exhibits is that of a Colombian woolly mammoth approximately 13,000 years old that was excavated a mere 40 miles from the university campus. The museum is open weekday afternoons and by appointment. Admission is free.

King Ranch Museum
405 N. Sixth St., Kingsville
• **(512) 595-1881**

This cowboy-themed museum near downtown contains a permanent exhibit of ranching and cattle-related items from the archives of the massive King Ranch, which is considered the birthplace of the American ranching tradition. The museum also hosts traveling exhibits such as a recent collection of photographs of Texas cowboys by David Stoecklein. It's open daily. Admission is $4 for adults; $2.50 for children ages 5 to 12; and free for children younger than 12.

Music

Corpus Christi Symphony Orchestra
1901 N. Shoreline Blvd., Corpus Christi
• **(512) 882-4091, (512) 883-6683 for tickets**

World-class conductor Cornelius Eberhardt directs this symphony, a select group of almost 100 musicians. Its concert selections range from classics by Mozart, Hadyn and Beethoven, to modern masterpieces by Ibert, Stravinsky and Prokofiev. During its 52-year history, internationally renowned guest artists such as Felipe Entremont, Van Cliburn, Helen Donath, Itzhak Perlman and Leonard Rose have performed with the symphony. Other guest appearances have featured The Canadian Brass, The Romeros, Danny Wright and the national tour production of Gilbert and Sullivan's *The Mikado*.

The symphony performs at annual events such as Bayfest and the Fourth of July celebration aboard the Lexington Museum on the Bay (see our Annual Events chapter).

Recent performances have included The Smothers Brothers, Prokofiev's *Alexander Nevsky*, *Bugs Bunny on Broadway*, the Corpus Christi Youth Symphony and the Side By Side Symphonic Spectacular featuring winners of the Corpus Christi and Kingsville International Young Artists Competition.

Cathedral Concert Series
Corpus Christi Cathedral, 505 N. Upper Broadway, Corpus Christi
• **(512) 888-6520**

With a half-dozen performances a year, this series is designed to offer high-quality cultural presentations for Coastal Bend residents at no charge. Since 1984, the series has featured diverse ensembles including the Vienna Boys Choir, the Roger Wagner Chorale, the King Singers, The Romeros and the Academy of St. Martin-in-the-Fields Chamber Ensemble. Most of the performances are in the historic Cathedral, on the bluff in the heart of downtown Corpus Christi — a church with a wonderful acoustic temperament.

Funding for the performances is provided through corporate and private donations. More than 72,000 people have attended the series during the past decade. Recent performances have featured diverse artists such as Crystal Gayle, the Tommy Dorsey Orchestra, the London Brass and the Texas Boys Choir.

Wolfe Recital Hall
Del Mar College, Baldwin and Ayers Sts., Corpus Christi • (512) 886-1214

The college's orchestra, concert choir and theater singers use this college recital hall. It also is the setting for programs by guest artists. The college performances are free, and the guest artist performances cost $1.

Theater

Port Aransas to Padre Island

Port Aransas Community Theater
(512) 749-6036, (512) 749-5340

Established in 1990, this theater group produces a variety of shows. Recent productions include *Sylvia* and *A Night at the Theatre.* The outdoor stage, at the corner of Alister and White streets, begins its season with a spring cabaret show and continues with productions through August. During the winter, the productions are held indoors at various restaurants and community centers. Productions have included *The Taming of the Shrew*, *Peter Pan*, *Greater Tuna*, *On Golden Pond*, *Mousetrap*, *Little Shop of Horrors*, *The Gin Game*, *The Lion in Winter*,

Nunsense and *The Odd Couple*. The group also hosts a Halloween haunted house and a summer children's play.

Corpus Christi

Neil Tribble Bartlett Theatre
Del Mar College, Baldwin and Ayers Sts., Corpus Christi • (512) 886-1509

In the college's Fine Arts Center, this theater has an annual Shakespeare festival in the summer and a Mime Plus One-Acts each spring. Recent productions included *Macbeth*, *The Musical Comedy Murders of 1940*, *Reckless* and *Sophomore Showcase*. Tickets are $4 for general admission; $3 for senior citizens, faculty and staff; and $1 for students. The Shakespeare Fest tickets are $5.

Harbor Playhouse
1 Bayfront Park, Corpus Christi • (512) 888-7469 box office, (512) 882-5900 business office

Harbor Playhouse is the oldest and most popular venue for theater in Corpus Christi, hosting a variety of plays that range from adult to children's fare. The playhouse traces its history to February 12, 1925, when a group recruited by a newspaper ad did a single performance of Booth Tarkington's *Seventeen* at the old high school on Carancahua Street. Calling itself the Corpus Christi Players, the group averaged four plays a year until the Great Depression; it incorporated as Little Theatre Corpus Christi in 1948 and opened a building on Alameda Street. In 1972, the current theater was built by the city at Bayfront Plaza, near the city's museums, convention center and auditorium. The organization has a mailing list of 12,000 patrons. More than 40,000 subscribers, individual ticket buyers and tourists see productions each year.

The playhouse has a main stage season of six productions, including three musicals and a variety of both modern and classic comedies and dramas. There is also a summer

INSIDERS' TIP

Outdoor productions at the Port Aransas Community Theater are fun to attend, but remember that it can be quite warm — even after dark — in the summer. Dress accordingly.

musical, a one-month miniseason of summer melodramas and a Young People's Theatre program for children ages 5 to 18.

Tickets are $14 for main stage musicals and $8 for non-musicals. Reservations are recommended.

Richardson Auditorium

Del Mar College, Baldwin and Ayers Sts., Corpus Christi • (512) 886-1355

This college auditorium is used for a number of community events, including the Buccaneer Classics Music Festival each April and the Corpus Christi Concert Ballet's production of *The Nutcracker* each December. In addition, the college hosts the Driscoll Foundation/Dr. McIver Furman Del Mar Lectureship in the Health Sciences in February, the International Corpus Christi Young Artists' Competition in February and the Del Mar Jazz Band Concert in the spring.

Recent performances included a reading by novelist and poet Ana Castillo, and a one-act show, *The Witty World of Will Rogers*, a theatrical performance by Gene McFall.

Warren Theater

Texas A&M University-Corpus Christi, 6300 Ocean Dr., Corpus Christi • (512) 994-5800 box office

You can see drama, opera, musicians and musicals at this university theater. In recent years, featured performers during the Distinguished Visitors in the Arts Series have included pianist Gayle Martin Henry, the Haydn Trio Vienna, cello and piano duo Joanne Kong and James Wilson, and pianist Berenice Lipson-Gruzen.

Productions are also presented at the Wilson Studio Theatre. In 1997, the university produced *Jesus Christ Superstar* and *The Passionate Puccini* as well as Neil Simon's *Rumors*.

Kingsville

Jones Auditorium and Little Theatre

Texas A&M University-Kingsville, 700 University Blvd., Kingsville • (512) 593-3401

The university's theater arts and communications department regularly presents productions that range from Shakespearean drama to modern farces. Recent productions included *The Lady from Havana, Sorority Sisters from Hell, King Henry IV, The Dream of Don Juan Gaspar, Aladdin, Day of Absence, Confessions of Women from East L.A.* and *Charley's Aunt*. Admission is $3 per person.

Photo: Greater Corpus Christi Business Alliance

Corpus Christi's Bayfront Arts and Sciences Park includes the South Texas Institute for the Arts, Selena Auditorium, Bayfront Convention Center and Harbor Playhouse.

Dance

Corpus Christi

Ballet Nacional
4411 Gollihar Rd., Corpus Christi
• (512) 854-6528

Founded in 1983, this dance company's goal is to promote and preserve the Latin cultural heritage through music and dance. Under the guidance of artistic director Ricardo Villa, the company of 45 men and women stage two annual productions, including an elaborate and formal show known as *Noche de Gala* each winter, and a more lighthearted show in the summer called *Summer Salsa*.

The winter show in 1998, held in February at the Selena Auditorium, ran the musical gamut from Beethoven's Fifth Symphony to a scene from the Broadway hit *Miss Saigon,* and included Ravel's Bolero and a Tejano rendition of *Charanga*. Guest artists were Efrain Guerrero and mariachi vocalist Mari McLean. Tickets are priced from $6 to $12. The dance group celebrated its 15th anniversary in 1998.

Corpus Christi Ballet
5610 Everhart Rd., Corpus Christi
• (512) 991-8521

Founded in 1974, the Corpus Christi Ballet's first season included *Peter and the Wolf* and *The Nutcracker*. It continues to perform *The Nutcracker* as an annual Christmas production, in addition to numerous other works.

In 1991, Mikhail Baryshnikov's White Oak Project came to Corpus Christi. Other guests companies who have performed here include the Fort Worth Ballet, Stars of the American Ballet, Ballet Stars of Moscow, the Jose Limon Dance Company and the Houston Ballet.

The 1997 season featured performances by the St. Petersburg Ballet, four performances of *The Nutcracker* and two performances of *Cinderella*.

The ballet has also played host to international stars including Damian Woetzel of the New York City Ballet; Paloma Herrera, Guillaume Graffin and Julie Kent of the American Ballet Theatre; and Carlos Acosta and Tiekka Scoffield from the Houston Ballet. The ballet also has an educational outreach program that includes special performances for young children and lectures/demonstrations on school campuses.

Corpus Christi Concert Ballet
3441 S. Alameda St., Corpus Christi
• (512) 854-7969

This 20-member ballet company, under the direction of Nancy Sulik, performs several productions a year. In a recent season, its classical and contemporary ballet productions included *The Nutcracker, Tales of Hans Christian Anderson* and *Tea and Tales*.

As a member group of the Student Performing Arts Series, the company also produces the dance segment each year for 8,000 area students, who attend the educational ballet matinees of *The Nutcracker* and a selected spring gala, both of which feature professional guest artists.

Shows are designed to stimulate student interest in the performing arts and different styles of dance, performed by company members. The ballet company is supported by the Concert Ballet Guild, a volunteer organization that promotes and publicizes the company's activities.

Padre Island National Seashore and Aransas National Wildlife Refuge give visitors a good look at what coastal Texas looked like before Spanish and American settlers began pouring into the area.

Parks

Residents of the Texas Coastal Bend are fortunate to have two national parks within reasonable driving distance. The Padre Island National Seashore is a few miles south of Corpus Christi, while the Aransas National Wildlife Refuge — winter home to the endangered whooping crane — lies 35 miles north of Rockport. Both parks give visitors a good look at what coastal Texas looked like before Spanish and American settlers began pouring into the area. The variety of birds and plant life in the parks can't be found in most areas of the United States.

The Coastal Bend also is home to several state, county and municipal parks. The following is a list of many of the better parks in the area.

North Bay Area

Aransas National Wildlife Refuge
F.M. Rd. 2040, Austwell • (512) 286-3559

The endangered whooping crane is the star of this 70,504-acre wildlife refuge 35 miles north of Rockport. These shy birds, which make the refuge's saltwater marshes their winter feeding grounds, have made a comeback since their numbers dwindled to as few as 15 in 1941. Much of that success is due to the creation of the refuge in 1937 to protect the vanishing wildlife of coastal Texas. For more information about the whooping cranes, see our Birding chapter.

But there's more to the refuge than whooping cranes. This remote refuge on Blackjack Peninsula (named for its blackjack oaks) also is home to alligators, deer, javelina, coyote, bobcat, raccoon and feral hogs (see The Natural World chapter for more about these creatures). Grasslands made up of bluestem and other prairie grasses, live oaks and redbay thickets cover deep sandy soils ringed by tidal marshes and broken by long, narrow ponds.

Thousands of migratory birds are attracted to the refuge's brackish tidal marshes on their journey between North America and Central America. Birders have spotted as many as 392 species at the refuge, including pelicans, herons, egrets, spoonbills, shorebirds, ducks and geese. Warblers are abundant from mid-April to early May (see our Birding chapter). Freshwater ponds farther inland are home to alligators, turtles, frogs, snakes and birds.

The refuge is open between sunrise and sunset; public camping is not allowed. All visitors must register daily. Public facilities include a 16-mile paved tour road, Wildlife Interpretive Center, 40-foot observation tower, several miles of walking trails and a picnic area.

Food and fuel are not available on the refuge. Bring mosquito repellent, watch for poisonous snakes, and keep an eye out for wildlife on the roads. Pets must be on a leash at all times.

The Wildlife Interpretive Center is open daily from 8:30 AM to 4:30 PM. The entrance fee is $5 per carload or $3 if you're visiting the refuge alone. The refuge is 7 miles south of Austwell.

Goose Island State Park
Texas Hwy. 361, off Texas Hwy. 35, Lamar • (512) 729-2858

This 314-acre state park is at the conjunction of the Aransas, Copano and St. Charles bays about 10 miles north of Rockport. It's a pleasing mix of shoreline and woodlands with camping facilities (127 sites) available in both areas (see our Campgrounds and RV Parks chapter). The park stretches inland from the bayfront to thick brush and live oak and mesquite trees.

The park is known for "Big Tree," the largest coastal live oak tree in the state (see our Attractions chapter). Anglers will love the fishing opportunities. Cast for speckled trout, redfish, drum, flounder and sheepshead from your boat or from the park's 1,620-foot fishing pier. The park also is a good site for crabbing and oystering.

Water birds, waterfowl, shore birds and passerines (birds that perch) are common at the park.

Campsites have picnic tables, barbecue grills and water. Park amenities include group facilities, a recreation hall, youth group area, a short, paved hike-and-bike path, two playgrounds and a two-lane boat ramp with loading dock.

Bring insect repellent and firewood. Canvas shoes are recommended for bayfront activities. Reservations are recommended and can be made as many as 90 days in advance. Expect to pay an entry fee of $2 per person per day for anyone between the ages of 13 and 65.

The park office is open from 8 AM to 5 PM. The gate leading into the park is open from 7 AM to 10 PM.

Rockport Beach Park
210 Seabreeze Dr., Rockport • (512) 729-9392

The 61-acre Rockport Beach Park near the city's downtown came into being in the 1950s when the Aransas County Navigation District No. 1 dredged the adjacent Little Bay (now a bird sanctuary) and placed the material on a sandbar jutting out into Aransas Bay.

In 1988 the city developed the park for day use and began charging an entrance fee. Facilities include two pavilions with upstairs verandas, restrooms and party rooms, playground equipment for both older and younger children, a band shell, an 800-foot fishing pier, a lighted fishing jetty (open 24 hours a day) and a walking trail. The park has a four-lane boat ramp, a separate launch for sailboats and catamarans and watersport rentals (see our Beaches and Watersports chapter). Other amenities include a saltwater pool with concrete bulkhead, 75 picnic tables (many with covered cabanas), volleyball courts and handicapped-accessible picnic cabanas and water fountain.

The park's mile-long beach is a great place for children to swim. There are no undertows, high tides or rough waves, and the water is shallow for about a quarter-mile from shore.

The park is open from 5 AM to 11 PM Monday through Friday and 5 AM to midnight on weekends. Admission is $3 per vehicle per day or $5 for a three-day pass. A six-month pass costs $10, and a one-year pass is $15. Those wanting to bring more than one car to the beach can get as many as three annual permits for $25.

Aransas Pass Community Park
Two blocks east of Texas Hwy. 361, Aransas Pass • (512) 758-3111

This park, established in 1993, serves as the site for Aransas Pass's annual Shrimporee Festival to celebrate the city's ties to the shrimping industry (see our Annual Events and Festivals chapter). It's also home to the Aransas Pass Little League and hosts softball tournaments and soccer matches.

Located near two saltwater ponds, the park features a pavilion, covered picnic tables, barbecue grills, restrooms, playground equipment for both little tykes and older children and playports with stairs, slides and tunnels. Concession stands are open when Little League teams are playing or when a softball tournament is under way.

Admission is free. The park is open from 8 AM to 9 PM every day.

Live Oak Park
East of F.M. Rd. 1069, Ingleside • (512) 776-2517

This park's major claims to fame are the live oak trees for which the park is named and the nine-hole disc golf course, one of only two in the Coastal Bend. (The other course is in West Guth Park in Corpus Christi.) Disc golfers use flying discs instead of golf balls and aim at baskets instead of holes. Plans have been drawn up to expand the course to a full 18 holes. Meanwhile, locals enjoy the park's picnic tables, barbecue pits, playground equipment, three tennis courts, basketball court, baseball field and small lake with a hike-and-bike trail around it.

Live Oak Park, which became an official city park in 1995, is included on The Great Texas Coastal Birding Trail (see our Birding chapter). Admission is free. The park is open 24 hours a day. Farm-to-Market Road 1069 is 2 miles south of Texas Highway 361.

Portland Municipal Park
Lane Rd. and Memorial Pky., Portland
• (512) 777-3301

Locals refer to this park as "13-acre park" even though it now covers more than 21 acres on Portland's northside. You'll find wide-open spaces at this community park, with a mostly flat landscape and mesquite trees throughout.

Facilities include an amphitheater, three sets of restrooms, two lighted tennis courts, a basketball court, two baseball fields, playground equipment and a group pavilion with electricity and a barbecue pit that's available for rent.

The park is open from 6 AM to 11 PM Sunday through Thursday and from 6 AM to midnight on Friday and Saturday. Admission is free.

Corpus Christi

Cole Park
1500 block of Ocean Dr., Corpus Christi
• (512) 880-3461

You can't beat the view from this 43-acre park on the Corpus Christi bayfront. Developed in 1969, this park sits at the bottom of a steep hill sloping down from the city's scenic thoroughfare known as Ocean Drive. Look east and you're confronted with the beauty and grandeur of Corpus Christi Bay; turn west and admire the beautiful homes. Look north and you'll see the city skyline, the Harbor Bridge and the Nueces Bay Causeway in the distance.

Cole Park is a popular attraction for people from all over the city. No other city park comes close to matching this one for beauty and fun activities for children. The main attraction for the little ones is KidsPlace, an 18,000-square-foot wooden play area (see our Kidstuff chapter). Cole Park also is a great place to fly a kite or hold a barbecue.

The Cole Park Amphitheater is the site of the city's annual Thursday Night Concert Series. The music offered is an eclectic mix rang-ing from jazz, reggae and rock to blues and Texas folk and country.

The southern portion of the park, known by many locals as Oleander Point, is the site of the annual U.S. Open Sailboarding Regatta (see our Annual Events and Festivals chapter and the Spectator Sports chapter).

Admission is free. The park is open from sunrise to sunset.

West Guth Park
On Up River Rd. north of Rand Morgan Rd., Corpus Christi • (512) 880-3461

This 80-acre park on the city's northwest side has two things you won't find in most other parks: hills and a disc golf course. The Texas Coastal Bend is mostly flat, so when you find a hilly spot it's a nice change of pace.

West Guth also is home to the area's only 18-hole disc golf course (there's a nine-hole course in Ingleside's Live Oak Park). Disc golfers use flying discs instead of golf balls and aim at baskets instead of holes.

West Guth also has a swimming pool, senior center, duck pond, jogging trail, group pavilion, playground equipment and restrooms. Turkey Creek runs through the property. Admission is free. The park is open from sunrise to sunset.

To get here take Interstate Highway 37 north to the Rand Morgan Exit. Turn left, go under the interstate and turn right on Up River Road. The park will be on your left.

Hazel Bazemore County Park
F.M. Rd. 624, Corpus Christi
• (512) 949-8122

This 77-acre park just outside the Corpus Christi city limit is a haven for bird watchers, especially hawk watchers (see our Birding chapter). Every year thousands of hawks roost in the park's abundant trees to rest on their long migration. This 25-year-old park, named after a longtime bird watcher, has two nature trails, including one that leads to a blind overlooking a marsh.

Facilities include picnic tables, a shelter with barbecue pit, playground equipment, restrooms, observation tower and public boat ramp. You can fish or swim in the Nueces River. The park is open from 7 AM to 7 PM during standard time and 7 AM to 10 PM during daylight-saving time. The park lies a mile west of U.S. Highway 77.

Port Aransas to Padre Island

Roberts Point Park

East of south ferry landing, Port Aransas • (512) 749-4158

You can't get any closer to the water than Roberts Point Park in Port Aransas. This 50-acre park dedicated in 1991 sits on a peninsula overlooking the Corpus Christi Ship Channel, where cargo ships, pleasure boats and dolphins are common sights. The park was named after longtime residents Elda May and George E. "Florida" Roberts, who built a driftwood house there in 1931.

The park is due east of the ferry landing adjacent to the city marina. Facilities include a fishing pier, fish-cleaning station, observation tower, picnic pavilion, amphitheater, boat slips, soccer field and playground equipment for toddlers and older children. The park has restrooms, sand volleyball, horseshoe pits, basketball court, shuffleboard and a fishing ramp for the handicapped.

Admission is free. The park is open 24 hours a day.

Port Aransas Park

End of Cotter Ave., Port Aransas • (512) 749-6117

The great thing about this park is that you can enjoy the beach and still be less than a mile from your favorite restaurants. It's on the beach at the end of Cotter Avenue, southeast of the ferry landing past the University of Texas Marine Science Institute.

The park has camping and RV sites (see our Campgrounds and RV Parks chapter), flushing toilets, showers, bathhouse, picnic shelters and the lighted 1,245-foot Horace

Caldwell Pier. The snack bar/convenience store on the pier sells fast food, ice and basic groceries. You can also rent fishing tackle there. You'll pay a $1 entrance fee to get on the pier. Entry to the park is free, and it's open 24 hours a day.

Mustang Island State Park

Texas Hwy. 361, 14 miles south of Port Aransas • (512) 749-5246, (800) 792-1112

This 3,703-acre park on the southern end of Mustang Island has been owned and operated by the state of Texas since the land was purchased from private owners in 1972. Its primary draw is the relatively unpopulated beaches that stretch 5.5 miles along the Gulf of Mexico. Most of this park 14 miles south of Port Aransas is undeveloped. The bulk of activity occurs along a short section of beach near the park headquarters and a 48-site RV park and campground (see our Campgrounds and RV Parks chapter).

Recreational activities include swimming, sunbathing, camping, picnicking and fishing. Facilities include parking, restrooms, dressing rooms, showers, shade shelters, picnic tables, pay phones and a Texas State Parks Store, where you can buy ice and souvenirs.

The park is open from 7 AM to 10 PM. Office hours are 8 AM to 5 PM. The park charges an entrance fee of $3 per person older than 12.

Nueces County Padre Balli Park

15820 Park Rd. 22 • (512) 949-8121

This 374.5-acre park is just outside the Corpus Christi city limit and a few miles north of the Padre Island National Seashore. Padre Balli (pronounced bay-YEE) is operated by Nueces County and is popular among anglers, surfers and sunbathers.

Anglers are drawn to the lighted, 1,240-foot Bob Hall Pier, dedicated by the county in the fall of 1983 after Hurricane Allen destroyed

---

INSIDERS' TIP

You can purchase a Gold Texas Conservation Passport for $50. The passport enables cars to enter state parks and wildlife management areas without paying a per-person admission price. Call (800) 792-1112.

Photo: Greater Corpus Christi Business Alliance

Visitors can tour numerous historic homes in Heritage Park.

its predecessor three years earlier. Surfers also find the pier to their liking. Waves breaking near the structure are considered especially nice among the waxed-board set.

Facilities include RV and tent sites (see our Campgrounds and RV Parks chapter), restrooms, hot showers, concession stand, picnic shelters, laundry facilities and first-aid station. Park rangers are on duty 24 hours a day.

Padre Balli is open 24 hours a day year round. Park admission is free, but the charge is $1 per person to enter the pier plus a $1 fee per fishing pole.

Padre Island National Seashore
9405 S. Padre Island Dr., Corpus Christi • (512) 949-8068

Padre Island National Seashore was founded in 1968, six years after President John F. Kennedy signed a bill authorizing the purchase of 80.5 miles of Padre Island

for a national seashore. Padre Island is one of a chain of islands that stretches along the Atlantic and Gulf coasts of the United States from Maine to Texas.

The national seashore is undeveloped other than facilities to accommodate visitors on its northern edge. It's one of the longest stretches of primitive, undeveloped ocean beach in the United States. You'll see white sand-and-shell beaches, picturesque dunes, grassland and tidal flats (see our Beaches and Watersports chapter).

You can swim or fish in the Gulf of Mexico or the Laguna Madre, the area between the island and the mainland. Gulls, herons, ducks, sandpipers, terns and egrets are among the 350 species of birds that inhabit the island. Inland you'll find killdeer, meadowlarks and sandhill cranes. Animals that make the island their home include coyotes, blacktailed jackrabbits, lizards and Western diamondback rattlesnakes.

Facilities include RV and camping sites (see our Campgrounds and RV Parks chapter), toilets, cold showers, shaded picnic tables, nature trails, summer interpretive programs, a boat launch and a visitors center.

The first 5 miles of beach are accessible by two-wheel-drive vehicles; the next 60 miles are accessible via four-wheel-drive only.

The park charges a $10 entrance fee good for seven days; an annual pass is available for $20. An additional $5 fee is charged for anyone wishing to visit the popular windsurfing site known as Bird Island Basin; an annual pass sells for $10. Discount passes for senior citizens and the handicapped are available.

The park is open 24 hours a day. The visitors center is open every day from 9 AM to 4 PM except Christmas and New Year's Day.

Kingsville Area

Dick Kleberg Park
U.S. Hwy. 77 at Escondido Rd., Kingsville • (512) 595-8591

This park named after a member of the King Ranch family is on the south side of Kingsville between U.S. Highway 77 bypass

and Business U.S. 77. The park has plenty of wide-open spaces and is home to the J.K. Northway Exposition Center, where the annual George Strait Team Roping Classic and Concert is held (see our Annual Events and Festivals chapter).

Inside the park you'll find six soccer and eight softball fields, five baseball fields, a sand volleyball court, a swimming pool, a basketball court and two tennis courts. Other facilities include picnic tables, a 1-mile hike-and-bike trail along Escondido Creek, a large playground and two smaller playgrounds, a recreation hall, a pier and barbecue equipment. Escondido Creek is listed on The Great Texas Coastal Birding Trail (see our Birding chapter).

The park is open from 7:30 AM to 11 PM. Admission is free. Between November 15 and January 15, the park has a lighted Christmas display in a portion of the park for which admission is $8 per car.

Kaufer-Hubert Memorial Park
F.M. Rd. 628, Loyola Beach • (512) 297-5738

This waterside park east of Loyola Beach in Kleberg County is a long drive from just

Free concerts are held several nights each week during the summer at the Cole Park amphitheater, located on Corpus Christi's Ocean Drive.

Photo:Daniel Fielder

about anywhere in the Coastal Bend — but don't let that stop you. Anglers and nature lovers will love this facility, which is part of a 137-site RV park known as SeaWind Resort (see our Campgrounds and RV Parks chapter). The drive from Corpus Christi will take about an hour.

Kaufer-Hubert overlooks the Cayo del Grullo, which feeds into the popular fishing sites of Baffin Bay and the Laguna Madre. Facilities include campgrounds, group picnic shelters, single picnic tables with grills, two freshwater lakes, restrooms and a two-story observation tower overlooking the bay. Other facilities include a 500-foot lighted fishing pier, four-lane boatramp/parking, sand beach with shower, birding overlook, 1-mile walking/jogging trail with 12-station senior fitness course, playground, horseshoe pits and soccer/softball fields.

The park is close to the renowned Kings Inn Restaurant (see our Restaurants chapter) and is open from 7:30 AM to 11 PM. Admission is free.

The Texas Coastal Bend, with its nearly year-round subtropical climate and tremendous variety of birds, is rapidly becoming known as a birder's paradise.

Birding

Birds have been wintering in South Texas for many years, so it should be no surprise that birders — that binocular-toting population of folks who follow, track, chart and simply enjoy birds — have followed suit.

And the Texas Coastal Bend, with its nearly year-round subtropical climate and tremendous variety of birds, is rapidly becoming known as a birder's paradise.

Of the nearly 800 species of birds that live in North America, almost 500 are present at some time during the year in the Coastal Bend. Some of the birds that people travel great distances to see here are the least grebe, white-tipped dove, couch's kingbird, green jay, pyrrhuloxia, great kiskadee, tropical parula and ferruginous pygmy owl. And that's not even mentioning the hummingbirds and the whooping cranes, both of which are the focus of entire celebrations and seminars because of their annual visits here. (See our Close-up on whooping cranes in the Annual Events and Festivals chapter.)

What makes the Texas Coastal Bend so popular with birds? Well, several elements combine to attract such large numbers and varieties of birds, according to the avian experts. Geography plays a large role in enticing a wide variety of birds to either settle or winter here: Because we're on the coast, we have seabirds, shorebirds and marsh waders, as well as songbirds, game birds and raptors.

In addition, South Texas draws thousands of migrant birds along what is known as the Central Flyway — kind of a flight plan for avian travelers. Other birds traveling the Mississippi Flyway choose to circle around the coast rather than risk the Gulf crossing, and still others are diverted eastward from the Rocky Mountain Flyway. Tropical species from Mexico also frequently cross the Rio Grande into our region.

Climate and weather contribute to the situation. In the summertime, birds from Central and South America that come to nest here join resident species. In the winter, birds from northern breeding grounds — some as far away as the Arctic — come to spend the mild winter months with us. And the spring and fall migrations are spectacular, making the region a premier destination for birders around the country.

It's easy enough to spot these birds. There are city parks and hot spots, state and county parks, a national seashore, a national wildlife refuge, bird sanctuaries and more. The most grueling part of your visit may be deciding where to go and how long to stay!

Although birds have long been visiting South Texas, the business of courting birders and other nature-loving travelers has only begun to take flight in the past decade. Cities and counties now recognize the value of promoting and protecting their natural resources, including birds and other wildlife, as an economic safeguard. The community of Kingsville has even adopted its own "city bird" — the emerald-colored green jay.

All of which is good news to birders. It means that birds and their homes will be better cared for. And that means there will be more birds to see.

If you're new to the birding game, have no fear. You'll find maps and guidebooks aplenty to acquaint you with the resident and visiting species.

You can also take a birding tour with a local nature group, such as the Audubon Outdoor Club of Corpus Christi, which celebrates the spring migration with bird walks in Blucher Park every Saturday and Sunday morning (except Easter) in April and May.

The privately operated Rob and Bessie Welder Wildlife Foundation Refuge offers free tours on Thursday afternoons. A 12-mile loop on the Santa Gertrudis Division of the King Ranch is open to the public daily, with free maps available at the ranch entrance on Texas Highway 141 at Kingsville.

There are also paid tours, on land and on the water, to help you locate specific species. Among the more popular are boating trips to see the whooping cranes and other birds, available in winter from Rockport and Port Aransas. Other tours by local birding experts are additional options, and these usually offer half-day or full-day trips into the wilderness to find some of the more elusive species. We've included a listing of guided tours, with prices when available, at the end of this chapter.

A recommended birding guide for this area is *A Birder's Guide to the Texas Coast* by Harold Holt, published by the American Birding Association. To order a copy, call (800) 634-7736.

In this chapter we also try to acquaint you with some of the most popular birding sites in the Coastal Bend, including information about which birds can be seen there. Admission is free at city parks; however, state and county parks generally charge a small fee.

This is not an all-encompassing list of birding sites in the Coastal Bend. We've tried to hit some of the highlights, but the many places where you can bird in the Coastal Bend are simply too numerous to mention. More detailed guides are available from local chambers of commerce, as well as in many of the books about birding on the Texas coast. In addition, the state has published one of the more comprehensive and easy-to-use maps of the Coastal Bend's birding hot spots in literature about the Great Texas Coastal Birding Trail (Central Texas Coast). Texas officials created this 500-mile birding trail, the first of its kind in the United States, to guide birders through the Texas coast and its diverse bird population. This map represents Texas' officials recognition of the importance and growing interest in Texas birding — said to be among the nation's best. For information about statewide birds and maps, contact the Texas Parks and Wildlife Department at (800) 792-1112 or the Texas Department of Transportation at (800) 452-9292. Local chambers of commerce also have copies of the map.

Dozens of Coastal Bend sites are included on the state map. Each site is marked with a trail number and a logo, and some sites are enhanced with observation platforms, boardwalks and kiosks. In addition, local chambers of commerce also publish birding lists and maps to help visitors find the birds that visit their city or town.

The statewide Rare Bird Alert hotline, (218) 992-2757, sponsored by the Houston Audubon Society, is a good source for the most recent information about unusual birds seen along the coast. For more information about birding in the Coastal Bend, call the Coastal Bend Bird Hotline, (512) 265-0377; Coastal Bend Audubon Society, (512) 882-7232; Kingsville Bird and Wildlife Club, (512) 592-7558; and the Convention and Visitors Department of the Greater Corpus Christi Business Alliance, (512) 881-1888 or (800) 766-BEACH.

www.insiders.com

See this and many other **Insiders' Guide®** destinations online — in their entirety.

Visit us today!

Birding Sites and Resources

North Bay Area

Aransas National Wildlife Refuge
F.M. Rd. 2040, Austwell
• (512) 286-3559, (512) 286-3533

This is the winter home of the whooping crane, which attract thousands of birders annually. But it's also known among birders for its exceptional variety of resident and transient birds, including roseate spoonbill, reddish egret, white and white-faced ibis, and a variety of ducks, grebes and shorebirds. Look for hummingbirds from late spring through the fall.

A variety of other wildlife, including wading birds, alligators, crested caracara, javelina and armadillos, is active in early morning and late evening. You can pick up a map and bird checklist from the wildlife interpretive center, near the refuge's entrance; the center is open 8:30 AM to 4:30 PM. The refuge itself is open daily from sunrise to sunset. It is 7 miles south of Austwell. See our Parks chapter for more information.

Connie Hagar Cottage Sanctuary
E. First and Church Sts., Rockport
• **(512) 729-6445, (800) 242-0071**

A 6½-acre sanctuary managed by the Friends of Connie Hagar, this site pays homage to a longtime birder who essentially put the Coastal Bend on the birding map. (See our Close-up on Connie in this chapter.)

Hagar, born in 1886, moved with her husband to Rockport in 1934 and soon began birding. Her reports of birds sighted in the Coastal Bend were the first that alerted the national birding world to the tremendous variety and wealth of birds in the Coastal Bend, particularly during the migratory season. This site is where Hagar and her husband Jack owned and operated a small hotel, Rockport Cottages, for birders in the 1930s. Although the sanctuary is small, it contains a wide variety of birds. Vireos, warblers, grosbeaks and flycatchers can fill the woods, and the grassy fields have dickcissels, sparrows and buntings. A daily bird list in the kiosk identifies what others have seen there.

4 The Birds
92 S. Austin St., Rockport
• **(512) 790-9700**

A birding headquarters for visitors and locals, 4 The Birds offers custom-blended and bulk birdseed, birdhouses and feeders; CD-ROM programs to help you identify birds; books and identifying guides; updated information about tours and trips; and a selection of candles, T-shirts, kites, windsocks, art and photography.

Goose Island State Park
Off Texas Hwy. 35, Lamar
• **(512) 729-2858**

This live oak-draped state park serves as a migratory stop for many land birds, while a variety of waterfowl (loons, grebes, common goldeneye, red-breasted merganser and redhead) make appearances along the shores. Don't forget to visit Big Tree, the nation's largest live oak with an estimated 1,000 years under its bark. Rails, gallinules, common yellowthroat and marsh wrens frequent this area along the marshes.

Campsites are available, and the park has a nature trail. The park is 2.6 miles east of Park Road, 13 miles from Texas Highway 35. See our Parks chapter for more information.

Live Oak Park
East of F.M. Rd. 1069, Ingleside

Within the city of Ingleside is this community park that offers outdoor recreation and a nature trail. The park is a remnant of the extensive oak forest that once bordered Redfish Bay. Among birds you may encounter here are thrushes, thrashers and ground-dwelling warblers such as worm-eating, hooded and Swainson's. Farm-to-Market Road 1069 is 2 miles south of Texas Highway 361. See our Parks chapter for more information.

Rockport Demo Bird Garden and Wetlands Pond
Intersection of Texas Hwy. 35 and F.M. Rd. 3036, Rockport

This hummingbird garden is jointly maintained by the Texas Department of Transportation and the community of Rockport. It serves as a stopping point for thousands of mostly ruby-throated hummingbirds in early September and October. The garden also features educational information about the hummingbird and a boardwalk that extends into a huge patch of trumpet creeper plants, a favorite of hummingbirds.

Rob and Bessie Welder Park
U.S. Hwy. 181 N., 2.5 mi. north of Sinton
• **(512) 364-2381**

The City of Sinton recently dedicated these 45 acres — within this 300-acre multi-use park named for the Welders — as a natural preserve. The area contains open grasslands, scattered trees and an observation platform that overlooks a pond. Birds you may see here include common yellowthroat, marsh wren and migrant land birds.

INSIDERS' TIP

Hummingbirds are attracted to the color red, so birders in the know put a drop of red food coloring in the sugar water used to fill their feeders.

Connie Hagar: Spotlight on Birds

She was "a wren of a woman" — 97 pounds — and given to wearing dresses even in the field. Her first reports of the birding abundance on the Texas coast met with overwhelming skepticism, but when the experts arrived to question her numbers, she calmly led them to see the birds she had described — and quelled all doubts.

Connie Hagar devoted her life to birds in the tiny community of Rockport, where  today a sanctuary is named after her. And after 35 years of daily record-keeping on hundreds of birds, she is now recognized as one of the state's first and premier birders. The first book about her, *The Life History of a Texas Birdwatcher*, was written by Karen Harden McCracken and published in 1986. It is remarkable in its detail and in the sheer force of its subject's personality.

As McCracken herself writes in the preface, "Hers was the most phenomenal memory I have ever encountered. I was constantly amazed by her vivid recollections of events, people, details, even dialogue — she could remember what was said and who said it."

McCracken, who knew Hagar, based her book on hours of interviews and Hagar's own daily note taking, letters and photographs. Another book about Hagar is in the works as well, according to the Friends of Connie Hagar, a Rockport-based group dedicated to preserving Hagar's history and contributions — and to furthering public awareness and appreciation of the birds in Texas.

Noted ornithologists have also given widespread recognition to Hagar's research. The late Roger Tory Peterson, the highly respected author of birding field guides, called her "the wonder-woman of Rockport." Ornithologist Harold Holt wrote that Hagar "opened the eyes of the growing numbers of birdwatchers to the fact that Rockport is one of the most productive areas on the entire Texas coast. The diminutive Connie Hagar put Rockport on the birding map, and by the time she died, in 1973, the place had become a magnet for birders as well as for birds."

Born in the north Texas town of Corsicana in 1886, Martha Conger Hagar moved to Rockport in 1934 after spending a month there with her sister. Her husband Jack bought the Rockport Cottages, a motel complex, which soon became a coveted vacation spot for the nation's birders.

Hagar's love of nature came from her father, who introduced her early to the beauty of the birds and plant life. As an adult, she and her sister formed a nature study group that was intended as a memorial to their beloved father. In 1928, she began to make daily observations of her birding expeditions in what she called the "Nature Calendar," a practice she continued for 35 years. Those notes, written on pages in blank ledgers, became a source of scientific record for future ornithologists. She wrote about wildflowers, her daily life and always of the birds — the painted buntings, humming-birds, cactus wrens and bluebirds, that she so loved.

Hagar was a sweet and intelligent woman who dedicated herself to the study of nature, particularly birds. She mentored many young birders, and she readily deferred to the scholars — even when they were skeptical about her ability. Her solution was always to show them what she had seen, and she turned all her doubters into fans and defenders by her simple, straightforward manner and her dedication.

As a Rockport resident, she and her husband soon became intimately involved in the community's life. The locals grew accustomed to seeing Connie Hagar and her

— continued on next page

This is a copy of a photo taken by Alfred Eisenstadt that appeared in Life magazine on September 10, 1956. The photographer wanted Connie Hagar to wear pants — but she insisted on wearing a dress, her normal birding attire.

dog, Fuzzy, looking for birds. They were probably quite a pair — Hagar in her dresses and with the snake stick she used to fend off rattlers and other reptiles, and the dog, who alerted his beloved mistress to the presence of snakes and other dangers.

As for Hagar's attire, she apparently once tried wearing jeans in the field but felt too uncomfortable, due to her genteel upbringing — and a photo taken by her brother meant to poke fun at the pants only confirmed her dislike of the outfit. She wore dresses from then on, much to the dismay of famed *Life* photographer Alfred Eisenstadt, who came to Rockport to photograph her for a spread in the magazine in 1956.

Hagar was also notable for her willingness not only to learn about birds, but also to share what she knew. For decades, she volunteered to speak at social gatherings, schools and other public forums as part of her fervent desire to acquaint people with the natural world and its avian inhabitants on the Texas coast. She also worked to band birds for years, and often wrote articles and columns about her research for newspapers and magazines.

Despite her active schedule, Hagar was not always in good health. She courageously battled blindness during much of her adult life.

When she died, at age 86, in 1973, family, friends and birders throughout the nation mourned her. The extraordinary national and even international recognition she received during her lifetime led the Texas State Historical Commission to dedicate a

— continued on next page

state marker in her honor — waiving the customary requirement that the designee be deceased no less that 20 years.

A citation from the National Audubon Society summed up her life's contributions with eloquence: "You opened our eyes to that great miracle of the natural world, the migration of birds. You enriched our knowledge by patient, open-minded and courageous observation and reporting of the facts — so many of them unbelievable. In your selfless devotion to the truths of nature, you have literally discovered the link between heaven and earth."

Visitors to Rockport can see the Connie Hagar Cottage Sanctuary, the site of the Rockport Cottages she and her husband managed. It now consists of a 6 ½-acre nature preserve, maintained by the Friends of Connie Hagar. There is also the Connie Hagar Wildlife Sanctuary, designated in December 1943 and managed by the Texas Parks and Wildlife Department.

In addition, you can view a state marker, the graves of Connie and Jack Hagar and a demonstration hummingbird and butterfly garden in Rockport, which is maintained by the Friends of Connie Hagar. For more information about any of these sites, call the Rockport Chamber of Commerce, (512) 729-6445 or (800) 242-0071.

Rob and Bessie Welder Wildlife Foundation Refuge
U.S. Hwy. 77, 7.5 mi. north of Sinton
• (512) 364-2381

This privately owned wildlife refuge occupies 7,800 acres, a small portion of a large ranch that has been in the Welder family for more than 150 years. The refuge, which opened in April 1961, is dedicated to wildlife research and education. It operates as a working cattle ranch and oil field.

Sixteen plant communities exist on the refuge, including about 1,400 species of native plants. More than 380 species of birds, 55 species of mammals and 55 species of reptiles and amphibians have been recorded on the refuge. About 1,000 deer live on the refuge along with javelinas, Río Grande wild turkeys, Northern bobwhites and several species of ducks and geese.

Visitors can take a free public tour at 3 PM Thursdays that includes a walk through the compound of buildings, then a driving tour of the refuge. No reservations are required. The refuge also hosts an annual Bird and Field Day, usually at the end of February or early March, that attracts many birders and nature lovers.

Welder Park
700 N. Rachal Ave., Sinton

Tucked away in a remote corner of Sinton, this park (not to be confused with the Rob and Bessie Welder Park listed above) is closed to

vehicular traffic. Park at the entrance and walk in to find migrating land birds, water thrushes (prothonotary warbler and common yellowthroat), warblers and a number of species along the fence, such as the blue-gray gnatcatcher and Bewick's wren.

Corpus Christi

Blucher Park
100 block of Carrizo St., Corpus Christi

This little park adjacent to Corpus Christi Central Library is filled with dense woods and a small creek that attracts plenty of migrating land birds, including flycatchers, thrushes, vireos and warblers. Some of the city's original families lived along this street, and several of its homes have been restored, including one that's been turned into an environmental education center.

The Audubon Outdoor Club conducts birding tours through this park at 7:30 AM every Saturday and Sunday in April. One caveat on this park: It seems to also attract a number of vagrants, so we recommend that predawn birders bring a buddy for security.

Corpus Christi Botanical Gardens
9545 S. Staples St., Corpus Christi
• (512) 852-2100

An assortment of native habitats, including a wildflower field, nature trail through

Photo: Greater Kingsville Economic Development Council

Roseate Spoonbills are year-round residents along the Coastal Bend.

mesquite woods, an alligator lake and a bird and butterfly trail, attracts birds and birders. You'll be able to see species such as groove-billed ani, long-billed thrasher, curve-billed thrasher, pyrrhuloxia and olive sparrow, as well as water birds such as least grebe and Couch's kingbird. See our Attractions chapter for more information.

Fred Jones Nature Sanctuary
Moore Ave. (F.M. Rd. 893) and County Rd. 69, Portland

This nature sanctuary is an oasis of vegetation in the middle of an agricultural region. Privately maintained by the Audubon Outdoor Club of Corpus Christi, it's worth a visit during migration, particularly for vireos and warblers. Donations are requested. This is also a great place to view spring wildflowers.

Hans A. Suter Wildlife Area
Ennis Joslin Rd. at Oso Bay

A boardwalk provides access to the lagoon, where you can spot dozens of shorebirds as well as land birds in migration. Shorebirds can be seen here all year, including white pelicans, spoonbills, egrets, herons, gulls and terns. Migratory birds also arrive in winter. Check the newspaper for the tide tables, as these birds are best seen as the tide is falling.

Hazel Bazemore County Park
F.M. Rd. 624 at Nueces River, half-mile west of U.S. Hwy. 77

Hawk migration in September and October brings tens of thousands of hawks through this brushy park — and attracts birders worldwide. The hawks tend to migrate on the season's first cold fronts, often in September or October. Also look for bluebirds in the winter, as well as owls, paraques, warblers, hummingbirds and shorebirds. The park has a nature trail and restrooms. Ask for a map and bird checklist. It's is open 7 AM to 10 PM daily. See our Parks chapter for more information.

Nature's Bird Center
5830 McArdle Rd. at Airline Rd., Corpus Christi • (512) 992-2473

This store specializes in items intended for birds and birders, including guidebooks, binoculars, feeders, baths, seed, houses and T-shirts with — what else? — birds on them. Owner Vicki Simon also offers an array of gift items, such as wind chimes, and provides information about birding sites, bird sightings and tours.

Pollywog Pond
Upriver Rd. at Sharpsburg Rd., Corpus Christi

A collection of lakes and pools creates a

habitat for numerous water birds, songbirds and migrants. These old Water Department settling ponds can attract black-bellied whistling ducks, least grebe, least bitterns, white-winged doves, great kiskadee and groove-billed anis. Walking can be rough in some places.

Port Aransas to Padre Island

Aransas Pass Wetlands
Conn Brown Harbor, Texas Hwy. 361 between Aransas Pass and Port Aransas

Best in the winter, Conn Brown Harbor attracts shorebirds such as loons, grebes, diving ducks and pelicans. The stretch of state highway between the two towns is bordered by Redfish Bay and lots of tidal flats and sandy spots, where you can find waterfowl, shorebirds and species such as loons, grebes, American oystercatcher, snowy plover and sooty tern.

Port Aransas Birding Center
Ross Ave., Port Aransas
• (512) 749-5919, (800) 45-COAST

This facility includes a boardwalk that extends into a freshwater marsh that attracts waterfowl such as black-bellied whistling ducks, cinnamon teal, grebes, heron and egrets, cormorants and shorebirds such as black-necked stilt and roseate spoonbill.

Mustang Island State Park
Texas Hwy. 361, 14 mi. south of Port Aransas • (512) 749-5246

Look for gulls, terns and shorebirds along this beach where the birds you're likely to see include lesser black-backed gull, glaucous gull, piping and snowy plovers, red knots and Wilson's plover. Camping facilities are available at this state park (see our Parks chapter).

Padre Island National Seashore
Park Rd. 22, Corpus Christi
• (512) 949-8068

The nation's longest barrier island, this 133,000-acre national park extends from Corpus Christi to Port Isabel, 80 miles to the south. Most of the beach is accessible only in a four-wheel-drive vehicle, but you can see plenty of birds along the entrance road and the visitors center. Expect to see peregrine falcons, migrant land birds, gulls, terns and shorebirds and a variety of raptors, including white-tailed kite, white-tailed hawk and ferruginous hawk. Primitive and developed camping facilities are available. For more information about this park, see our Parks chapter.

Kingsville Area

Dick Kleberg Park
U.S. Hwy. 77 and Escondido St., Kingsville

A trail along the lake provides a perfect vantage point to see vermilion flycatcher, a variety of waterfowl and nesting sparrows. Resident species include golden-fronted and ladder-backed woodpeckers, green jay, great kiskadee and curve-billed and long-billed thrashers. You can also see both pipits, although the Sprague's is rare. For more information, see our Parks chapter.

Drum Point (Baffin Bay)
F.M. Rd. 772 and County Rd. 1132

Follow this unpaved road to look for herons, egrets, pelicans, waterfowl and shorebirds. Especially of interest is the white form of the reddish egret, a type of heron which favors saltwater. In April and September migrations, you can see millions of swallows and

---

INSIDERS' TIP

Two rare birds seen on the King Ranch include the jabiru (a South American stork photographed on the ranch) and the only North American record of the double-striped thick-knee, a chicken-sized tropical bird that resembles some sandpipers and plovers.

martins along the bluff here. This is a good fishing spot, too.

Hawk Alley
Texas Hwy. 285 between Kingsville and Falfurrias

This stretch of road is so named by local birders for the multitudes of raptors spotted here. Resident species include white-tailed hawk, Harris' Hawk, crested caracara, red-tailed hawk and ferruginous hawk, while migratory species include Mississippi kite, broad winged hawk and Swainson's hawk.

Kaufer-Hubert Memorial County Park
F.M. Rd. 628, Loyola Beach

Look for herons, egrets and shorebirds in the wetlands and mudflats at the mouth of Vattman Creek in this county park. Also, you can find waterfowl such as greater scaup, black scoter and surf scoter at the ponds, and ground-dove, green jays and olive sparrows in the brush. Camping facilities are available. Also, you can fish from the lighted pier.

King Ranch
King Ranch Visitors Center, Texas Hwy. 141 W., Kingsville • (512) 592-8055

This is one of the largest working ranches in the world, specializing in longhorn cattle and quarter horses. Its 825,000 acres also attract thousands of birds, including some of the more rare species. A number of South Texas specialties, which you're unlikely to see elsewhere in the United States, are commonly seen here. You can take one of the hourly bus tours along the loop road in the ranch and find anhinga, kingfisher, black-bellied whistling ducks, cactus wrens, curve-billed thrashers, green jays (the city's official bird) and great kiskadees. Private birding tours into the exterior of the ranch will bring you more variety (see our listing of guided tours below).

Louise Trant Bird Sanctuary
U.S. Hwy. 77 near Riviera

This is a marsh maintained by the Audubon Outdoor Club of Corpus Christi. You can find soras wintering here, and yellow-headed blackbirds make their appearance in the cattails in spring. Rare species sighted here are the red-billed pigeon and masked duck.

Santa Gertrudis Creek Bird Sanctuary
U.S. Hwy. 77 at F.M. Rd. 1717, Kingsville

This is an extensive marsh inhabited by species including least grebe, black-bellied whistling duck, purple gallinule, marsh and sedge wrens and a variety of herons and egrets. Also look for great kiskadee and green jay in the surrounding mesquite woodlands, as well as cave swallows nesting in the culverts during summer.

Birding Tours

Even the most experienced birders often choose to have a tour guide during their birding adventures so they can more quickly locate a particular species. Tours are also helpful when the area you want to bird is closed to the public. And last, but not least, there are the boat tours that allow birders access to remote areas and rare species.

We've described some of the more popular tours in the Coastal Bend and provided telephone numbers for more information or reservations. Please call ahead for reservations to make sure that there is a place for you on these trips.

Bird Song Natural History Adventures
(512) 882-7232

Guided tours are with Gene W. Blacklock, co-author of *Birds of Texas: A Field Guide'* (Texas A&M Press, 1995) and *Birds of the*

INSIDERS' TIP

The late birder and researcher Roger Tory Peterson published 34 birding guidebooks, but the only state with such birding diversity that it merited its own book was Texas. Peterson's *Field Guide to the Birds of Texas* was published in 1963 and contains a wealth of information.

Texas Coastal Bend" (Texas A&M Press, 1985). Blacklock was curator of the natural history museum and coordinator of environmental education at the Welder Wildlife Foundation for 20 years. He has been leading bird tours in North America for more than 30 years.

A half-day tour is $95 for two people plus $30 for each additional person; a full-day tour is $175 for two and $50 for each additional person.

Capt. John Howell's *Pisces*
1015 N. Allen St., #B, Rockport Harbor, Rockport • (800) 245-9324

The *Pisces* offers two daily tours, from 8 AM to noon and 1 to 5 PM, to Aransas National Wildlife Refuge. The tours are conducted November through April. The 58-foot boat holds 49 passengers. There is a limited supply of binoculars for rent on board, so it's probably wise to bring your own pair. You'll be able to see brown pelicans, roseate spoonbills, great blue herons and, of course, whooping cranes. Hot and cold beverages and snacks available for sale on the boat. The cost is $25 per adult and teen ($2 discount on the adult fare for seniors) and $17 for children younger than 12.

Capt. Ted's Whooping Crane Tours
Sandollar Pavilion, Fulton Beach Rd., Fulton • (512) 729-9589, (800) 338-4551

For more than 20 years, Capt. Ted Appell has been guiding tourists through the Coastal Bend wetlands to see endangered whooping cranes and nesting areas of other birds. His boat, the *M.V. Skimmer*, operates the whooping crane tours from November 1 through April 1 and tours of the rookery islands in April and May. During the three-hour trip through wetlands and bays, Capt. Ted provides an entertaining narrative about the Coastal Bend birds and their habits. Conti-

nental breakfast is also provided. Price is $33 per person.

Coastal Bend Birders
5030 N. Texas Hwy. 35, Fulton
• (512) 790-8884

Full and half-day guided tours of the Coastal Bend are led by longtime guide Michael Marsden. Michael and his wife, Donna, also run Cayman House, a bed-and-breakfast inn for birders in Rockport (see the Bed and Breakfast Inns chapter). These tours are suitable for everyone from beginners to advanced birders. Transportation is in a seven-seat minivan equipped with telescopes, binoculars and identification guides. A half-day tour for one person is $40; the cost is $80 for a full-day tour. The rates go down with the size of your group — for example, it costs $20 per person for a group of six to take a half-day tour. A lunch is provided with the full-day tour.

Fennessey Ranch Nature Tours
F.M. Rd. 2678, 10 mi. north of Bayside
• (512) 529-6600

This private ranch is open for tours by reservation only. The ranch, east of Refugio, offers birders an array of wildlife including black-bellied whistling duck, mottled duck, masked duck, least bittern, purple gallinule, common moorhen and marsh wren in the marshes; sparrows in the grasslands; hummingbirds in migration; and sandhill cranes, geese and other waterfowl. For more information see our Attractions chapter.

King Ranch Nature Tours
King Ranch Visitor Center, Texas Hwy. 141 W., Kingsville • (512) 592-8055

This 825,000-acre private ranch has only recently ventured into the ecotourism business, offering nature and birding tours that range from half-day to four-day retreats. The half-

The tiny, speedy hummingbird is honored each September in Rockport at the annual Hummer/Bird Celebration.

day wildlife tour is 3½ hours long and takes visitors through a variety of habitats on the ranch. Offered October through March, it costs $17.50 per person plus tax.

The full-day birding tour (nine to 10 hours) takes you from one end of the ranch to the other, where you'll see ferruginous pygmy owls, tropical parula, Audubon's oriole and northern beardless tyrannulet. Lunch is provided. It costs $99 per person plus tax.

For those who want total immersion in South Texas life and nature, try the four-day retreat package. Participants stay at cottages on the ranch, and meals and transportation are included. The cost is $589 per person plus tax.

There are also customized or private tours that can cost up to $100 per person. These offer glimpses of a specific bird, such as the ferruginous pygmy owl, white-tailed hawk or LeConte's sparrow.

Reservations are required for all the tours, and the number of people allowed per trip is limited. Some tours are seasonal so please call in advance. See our Attractions chapter for more information.

Lucky Day Charters, Rockport
Rockport Harbor, Rockport
• (512) 729-GULL, (800) 782-BIRD

The 75-foot catamaran *M.V. Wharf Cat* departs daily from both Rockport and Port Aransas on whooping crane tours November through March. The four-hour trip takes birders through Aransas Bay to the Aransas National Wildlife Refuge, while the captain provides a narrative. Binoculars and spotting scopes are on board, as well as a snack bar with refreshments. The *Wharf Cat* is a twin-hulled boat with covered lower deck and an outdoor observation deck. The cost is $25 for adults and teens and $17 for children 12 and younger.

For fishing and hunting enthusiasts, the Texas Coastal Bend offers a veritable bounty on sea and land.

Fishing and Hunting

For fishing and hunting enthusiasts, the Texas Coastal Bend offers a veritable bounty on sea and land. Anglers have long known about the abundant marine life found in the waters off the Texas coast, traveling here for deep-sea excursions as well as excellent bay fishing. Among the most prominent of visitors were President Franklin D. Roosevelt, who fished for tarpon here during his vacations from the White House, and President George Bush, who shot quail here during presidential getaways.

The good news for anglers is that the area's populations of redfish, speckled trout and black drum are at record highs — the best since the 1970s — thanks to strict regulations and catch limits that have helped increase the species' numbers. In addition, the state has been restocking the bays and the results have been spectacular.

The area offers several types of fishing. You can go offshore fishing in the Gulf of Mexico or bay fishing in the nearby, shallower waters. In addition, anglers can try their hand at surf fishing, fly fishing and fishing from piers or jetties. Serious anglers will want to head over to Port Aransas, one of the state's premier headquarters for offshore fishing. With more than a dozen fishing tournaments and countless fishing guides and charter services, you can easily fish all year in Port Aransas.

If you're lucky enough to have your own boat, then all you need is to find a public launch site and some bait, and you're set to go. Other visitors may want to avail themselves of a guide service, a charter boat or a party boat. A party boat generally takes 25 to 80 people out for a half-day or daylong trip; the per-person rate can range from $22 to $75, depending on if you go into the bay or the Gulf of Mexico. The boat operator furnishes all your tackle and other equipment. A charter boat outing is more expensive. You arrange with a boat captain for a private, guided group trip of four to six people. It can cost $350 to $700 a day.

An abundance of wildlife, particularly waterfowl, makes the Coastal Bend popular as well with duck, dove and quail hunters. Many locals have private leases on some of the sprawling ranches that extend across South Texas; others will opt to sign on with a guided tour or take their chances on public lands that are overseen by the Texas Parks and Wildlife Department. There are also several hunting lodges in the Coastal Bend that offer packaged hunts for those interested in duck, dove, quail, feral hogs or deer. At a cost of several hundred dollars per day, a hunter will receive a guided hunt, meals and lodging at a quality resort in the great outdoors.

Obviously, you will need a fishing or hunting license from the Texas Parks and Wildlife Department to participate in any of these activities. Licenses are available from marinas, sports stores and other sites throughout the Coastal Bend. In addition, you can obtain current information about season, size, bag and possession limits on saltwater fish, freshwater fish, waterfowl and other animals. A resident combination hunting and fishing license for Texans is $32, and you'll pay additional fees for saltwater stamps, tarpon tags and red drum tags. Nonresidents can get a license for $30, or a temporary (five-day) license for $20. For more information about fishing and hunting licenses or to purchase licenses by credit card, contact the state at (800) TX LIC 4 U or (800) 895-4248.

A good place to keep abreast of the latest in hunting and fishing news is to check out newspaper columnist Buddy Gough, who writes about the South Texas outdoors for the *Corpus Christi Caller-Times*. His column is published on Thursday and Sunday.

Fishing

For each of our four geographic areas in the Texas Coastal Bend, we include a summary of the fishing scene and offer recommendations for businesses you can contact if you are planning to ply area waters for that trophy catch — or some salty sea yarns about the one that got away.

www.insiders.com

See this and many other **Insiders' Guide®** destinations online — in their entirety.

Visit us today!

North Bay Area

Aransas Pass

Aransas Pass offers countless bait and tackle shops that supply all your angling needs, including rental equipment. From shore, wharves, piers and jetties, anglers can expect to catch redfish, speckled and sand trout, sheepshead, flounder, croaker, skipjack and drum.

Group boats provide bay and deep-sea fishing for half or full days, while charter cruisers are available for offshore sport. Species caught from group or charter boats may include tarpon, sailfish, marlin, kingfish, mackerel, ling, pompano, bonito, red snapper, warsaw, and many others.

As for fishing from piers, check out the Conn Brown Harbor piers in Aransas Pass at the Harbor Park.

Guides and Equipment

Hampton's Landing
430 Ransom Ave., Aransas Pass
• **(512) 758-1562**
Hampton's Landing is the main fishing dock in the area. Here you'll find launch sites, ice, bait and some of the city's best fishing guides. The boats from here go into Aransas Bay and Redfish Bay.

The Crabman Marina and Seafood Market
Texas Hwy. 361 E., Port Aransas Causeway, Aransas Pass
• **(512) 758-0294**
This marina offers the equipment to get your own fresh catch – and it even sells fresh shrimp and oysters if you come back empty-handed. Among the services it offers are a free boat ramp, charter boats, live bait and tackle, guide services, boat rentals and personal watercraft rentals (during the summer).

Fin & Feathers Marina and RV Park
Texas Hwy. 361, Aransas Pass
• **(512) 758-7414**
You can pitch your tent at the water's edge, hook up your recreational vehicle, take a hot shower, have a picnic or launch your boat from this marina. Other amenities include a 600-foot lighted fishing pier and boat slips. You can also buy fresh shrimp for eating, live and dead bait, tackle, beer, ice, soft drinks and snacks.

South Bay Bait and Charters Redfish Bay Marina
1950 Texas Hwy. 361 E., Port Aransas Causeway, Aransas Pass
• **(512) 758-2632**
You can get rental boats, charter deep-sea and bay fishing trips, use the free boat ramp and buy bait, sodas, beer, ice. About a dozen charter companies work from here. There's also an RV park here.

Rockport

You would be hard-pressed to find more fishing guides than there are in Rockport, considered one of the best bay fishing sites along the Texas coast. From here, you can fish in Aransas Bay, Redfish Bay, Copano Bay, Mesquite Bay and San Antonio Bay. Guide boats

Fishermen flood the waters of the Coastal Bend year-round
to reel in varieties like flounder, redfish and trout.

operate from Goose Island State Park, Rockport Beach Park and Cole Harbor.

The jetty sheltering Rockport Yacht Basin is a popular spot for bay fishing; dawn hours generally are the most productive. Many hotels and motels on the bayfront maintain private fishing piers for guests. Depending upon the season and proverbial luck, catches may include redfish, sand and speckled trout, catfish, croaker, sheepshead, flounder and drum.

Group-boat bay fishing is also available at the yacht basin. Offshore species may include tarpon, sailfish, marlin, ling, wahoo, king mackerel, bonito, pompano, red snapper, warsaw and others.

Public fishing piers are the Fulton Harbor Pier on Fulton Beach Road and the piers at the north and south ends of Rockport Beach Park. Another popular fishing pier is Copano Bay State Fishing Pier, (512) 729-8519 or (512) 729-7762, a lighted facility with a public boat

ramp, concessions and restrooms. Admission is $1.75 per fishing pole. For more information, see our Attractions chapter.

Guides

The best place to start looking for a guide is the Rockport-Fulton Area Chamber of Commerce, (512) 729-6445 or (800) 242-0071, which offers a regularly updated list of the city's fishing guide services. In addition to bay fishing, Rockport guides also offer fly fishing — a relatively new phenomenon on the Gulf Coast, but one that is increasingly popular among anglers who like the challenge of laying a lure atop an unsuspecting fish.

Redfish Lodge on Copano Bay
940 Rattlesnake Point Rd., Rockport
• (512) 729-8100

For a packaged fishing experience, check out the Redfish Lodge on Copano Bay. This is where anglers can get the full and deluxe treatment: all meals, transportation to and from the airport, lodging and guided fishing trips for redfish and trout in nearby Copano Bay. The 14-person lodge caters mostly to corporate groups, and the cost is $410 per day per person. The lodge also offers duck hunting packages.

Port Aransas to Padre Island

Port Aransas bills itself as a fishing capital, and there's plenty of evidence to support that claim. The height of the offshore fishing season extends from Memorial Day to Labor Day, when drift fishing and troll fishing for king mackerel is popular, as is blue-water fishing for dolphin, marlin and sailfish.

However, offshore fishing is also popular during the fall and winter months. In the fall and spring, you can catch tuna, amberjack or red snapper, and in the winter, red snapper is the primary attraction. If you're fishing in the bay, you can expect to catch trout and redfish most of the year, although spring and summer are the best times.

Surf fishing is also a popular activity, particularly in the summertime. Some of the best places to try surf fishing are Horace Caldwell Pier in Port Aransas Park on Mustang Island, and Mustang Island State Park, south of Port Aransas. Anglers will find trout and redfish during the right conditions, when the surf is clear and calm.

Other popular fishing sites include Redfish Bay Pier on Texas Highway 361, east of Port Aransas, and the rock jetties, which extend a mile into the Gulf of Mexico and form the entrance to the Corpus Christi Ship Channel.

Over on Padre Island at Nueces County Padre Balli Park, fishing is particularly popular at Bob Hall Pier, especially at night during the summer months. The area is also good for surf fishing.

Head over to Malaquite Beach at Padre Island National Seashore for surf fishing. There is a 60-mile stretch of beach that's accessible only by four-wheel drive vehicle and is excellent for surf fishing of sharks, Spanish mackerel, redfish, trout and tarpon.

The area's one and only professional surf fishing guide on the national seashore is Billy Sandifer, (512) 937-8446. Sandifer offers anglers guided tours as well as nature tours of the pristine and rugged beach area along the national seashore. The daylong nature tours, which can include birding, beach combing or whatever the customer wants, cost $150 for two people, and $25 additional for every other person with a maximum of five. The fishing tours, which include everything except food and drinks, often last more than 12 hours, Sandifer says. He charges $350 for two people, $75 for a third and $50 each for a fourth and fifth person. Sandifer knows the surf: He says 64 species of fish have been caught there, and one of his customers once caught an 820-pound shark.

Party Boats and Charters

If you're interested in either a party boat or charter boat from Port Aransas, we offer you several choices for locating guides or other services. We also include choices that specialize in inshore and bay fishing.

Dolphin Docks
300 W. Cotter Ave., Port Aransas
• (512) 749-6624, (800) 456-9156
A good spot for party boats and charters, Dolphin Docks attracts the more salty fishermen with a wide variety of bait and other equipment.

Deep Sea Headquarters
416 W. Cotter Ave., Port Aransas
• (512) 749-5597, (800) 705-3474
Party boats are the main attraction here, but Deep Sea Headquarters also has some charters. Plenty of boats are available, from the largest to the smaller ones.

Fisherman's Wharf
900 N. Tarpon St., Port Aransas
• (512) 749-5448, (800) 605-5448
Fisherman's Wharf offers both party boats and charter boats. Some of the largest boats, big catamarans, operate out of this marina, and it attracts a lot of tourists.

Island Queen
Woody's Sports Center, 136 W. Cotter Ave., Port Aransas • (512) 749-5252
Among the boats that operate from here is the *Island Queen*, a bay-fishing party boat that

Bird hunting draws enthusiasts from all over the world to South Texas.

is an old, converted ferry. You can climb aboard for a four-hour fishing trip at the rate of about $23 per adult, while children younger than 12 go for half-price. The price includes rod, reel, bait and tackle.

Woody's Sports Center
136 W. Cotter Ave., Port Aransas
• (512) 749-5252

For those interested in inshore or bay fishing, Woody's Sports Center is the place to go for equipment, boat charters and guided tours. For 30 years Woody's has been a sports lover's headquarters. This store also offers amenities including rental slips, a seafood market, fuel, T-shirts, hats and other fishing accessories.

Corpus Christi

The headquarters for fishing in the Laguna Madre is the John F. Kennedy Causeway, which is lined with piers, opportunities for bank fishing and marinas. There are about a dozen good guides who work along the Laguna Madre. In the following listings, we describe several of the major marinas for launching a boat, buying bait and finding a guide.

Conventional bait fishing as well as fly fishing is available here. Longtime guide Don Hand of the Coastal Bend Guides Association, (512) 993-2024, can recommend some reputable fishing guides.

Fly fishing has been growing in popularity here, with many anglers trying their luck at catching a redfish in the shallow surf waters along the Laguna Madre and Redfish Bay. Several recently established businesses cater to this growing trend.

If you don't have a boat, you can still go fishing at some of the rock jetties and piers in the area. During the spring and summer, it's common to see young kids walking down the street in the bayfront area, toting their fishing rods and sometimes the catch of the day.

Fishing Piers and Jetties

Corpus Christi Municipal Marina
Lawrence Street T-Head, Corpus Christi
• **(512) 882-7333**

Folks can fish for free at many spots along this marina area: in the little park at the waterfront-end of Peoples Street, along the seawall, on the rock jetty that extends from the Memorial Coliseum area and at the wooden fishing pier on Powers Street at Shoreline Drive.

The Coliseum area jetty, 520 S. Shoreline Boulevard, (512) 881-9122, also is the site of a Wienerschnitzel, a fast-food chain that features mostly hot dogs. This jetty also has public restrooms and showers.

Cole Park Pier
1500 block of Ocean Dr., Corpus Christi
• **(512) 880-3461 city, (512) 884-7275 amphitheater**

This wooden pier is a favorite free fishing spot for many local residents. And if the kids get bored with fishing, they can always play on the playground — called KidsPlace — at the park. The pier area has restrooms and a concession stand, but the concession stand's hours are unpredictable (city officials say they open it if weather permits).

Indian Point Park and Pier
U.S. Hwy. 181 between Corpus Christi and Portland • (512) 643-8555

On Corpus Christi Bay, this pier is a favorite fishing site for local anglers as well as visitors. You can catch drum, redfish and gafftop here, depending on the season. The park and pier are owned by the city of Portland and include a 720-foot fishing pier with a 280-foot T-head, restrooms and a concession stand that sells bait, tackle, snacks and drinks. Birdwatching jetties are near the pier for when you tire of fishing.

The pier fee is $1 per person and $1 per fishing pole, but you can get an annual pass for $100, or $50 for senior citizens. Children younger than 5 get in free when accompanied by an adult. The park and pier are open 24 hours a day.

Charter and Party Boats

Captain Clark
Peoples Street T-Head, Corpus Christi
• **(512) 855-7089**

This 65-foot boat carries large groups, usually about 65 people, into Corpus Christi Bay to catch sand trout, whiting, gafftop, drum and small sharks. The *Captain Clark* goes out on three four-hour trips per day, but the schedule can vary by season. It's best to call ahead to get the week's schedule. The cost is $15 per adult and $10 for children ages 4 to 11, with an additional $4 fee to rent tackle, or you can bring your own. Bait is provided. The *Captain Clark* is also available for private charters.

Star Trek
Peoples Street T-Head, Corpus Christi
• **(512) 883-5031, (800) 293-3506**

Great for short fishing excursions into the bay, this 71-foot boat makes three daily trips into Corpus Christi Bay. Anglers are taken to any of 50 sites from 2 to 12 miles into the bay. The cost is $15 per person. A rod and reel rents for $3, or you can bring your own. Bait is furnished. Snacks and drinks are available, but you can also bring your own ice chest. The *Star Trek* is also available for private charter or groups.

Marinas

Copeland's Marina
4041 S. Padre Island Dr., Corpus Christi
• **(512) 854-1135**

You can sign up for a chartered deep-sea fishing or scuba diving trip at this shop. The fishing trips, which include all your equipment, bait, tackle and lunch, range in price from $40 per person for a five-hour trip and $60 per person for a nine-hour trip to $75 for a 12-hour trip. The shop also sells scuba diving and snow skiing equipment.

INSIDERS' TIP

Saltwater fly fishing was first popularized in Florida and has moved over to the Texas coast, where an increasing number of anglers are trying their hand at it.

Marker 37 Marina
13317 S. Padre Island Dr., Corpus Christi
• **(512) 949-8037**

This full-service marina, on the upper Laguna Madre, has been in business since 1988, offering fuel, bait, tackle, a guide service and fish cleaning. You can sign up for a half-day charter fishing trip at a cost of $250 for two people, or a full day for $350 (the price includes everything except your lunch). Anglers catch trout, redfish, flounder, drum and sheepshead.

Land and Sea Marina
10857 S. Padre Island Dr., Corpus Christi
• **(512) 939-9296**

Ten fishing guides operate out of this full-service marina on the Laguna Madre. Established in 1982, the marina offers fish cleaning, RV hookups, boat slips and a boat ramp, and it sells bait, tackle, sandwiches and drinks. The fishing guides will take you into the Laguna Madre and Baffin Bay at a rate of $350 for two people all day, or $250 for a half-day. All equipment is furnished, but customers do have to bring their own food and drinks.

Outfitters

Bradford Outfitters
5425 S. Padre Island Dr., Corpus Christi
• **(512) 985-2278**

This fly-fishing store, established in July 1997, carries some of the more well-known names in fly-fishing equipment including Thomas and Thomas fly rods, Winston fly rods, Tibor reels and Billy Pate reels. You can also purchase outdoor clothing or kayak gear and obtain information about local as well as international fly-fishing excursions.

Gruene Outfitters
1233 Airline Rd., Corpus Christi
• **(512) 994-8361**

You can buy fishing gear, outdoor clothing, Wilderness Systems kayaks and more at this fly-fishing specialty shop. The store concentrates on saltwater fly fishing, but also has gear for freshwater fly fishing. While you're here, you can test out a new rod in the outdoor casting pond, pick up some tips on fly fishing and grab a list of guides for this area. The staff also offer casting seminars, fly-tying

classes and kayak demonstrations, as well as information about where to go for wade fishing (for those who don't have a boat).

Kingsville Area

For fishing in the Kingsville area, your best bet is Baffin Bay, which is renowned for its large trout. The Riviera area, south of Kingsville on U.S. Highway 77, is where you'll find guides, lodges and a good fishing pier.

Baffin Bay, in contrast to Port Aransas and Rockport, offers a quieter fishing environment and tends to draw serious anglers who want to devote their entire time to fishing. On the one hand, there aren't as many distractions and the fishing areas are less likely to be crowded. On the other hand, if you're with family members who aren't into fishing, they won't find quite as many activities such as shopping, museums or recreation as in the area's more bustling communities.

Try the Kaufer-Hubert Memorial Park for a launch ramp to fish on Baffin Bay.

The area is home to one really fine restaurant, King's Inn, which draws customers from wide and far for its delectable fried seafood and avocado salads. For more information see our Restaurants chapter.

Fishing Pier

Kaufer-Hubert Memorial Park
East on F.M. Rd. 628, Loyola Beach
• **(512) 297-5738**

This waterfront park overlooks the Cayo del Grullo, which feeds into Baffin Bay and the Laguna Madre, and offers some of the best fishing in this area. The facility is part of a 137-site RV park known as SeaWind Resort (see our Campgrounds and RV Parks chapter). You'll find a 500-foot lighted fishing pier as well as campgrounds, restrooms, picnic tables and a boat ramp.

Fishing Lodges and Guides

Baffin Bay Lodge
Riviera • (800) 609-4868

This lodge is situated on 3 acres on Baffin Bay, which is home of Texas' speckled-trout record. Accommodations are for groups of two to 16 people. Amenities include a private lighted 300-foot fishing pier, kitchen and laundry facilities, and access to fishing guides. Baffin Bay Lodge charges $100 per night for up to two people and $25 for each additional person.

Charter fishing trips in Baffin Bay are $350 per day for up to two people, and $50 for each additional person.

B Bar B Ranch Inn
County Rd. 2217 off U.S. Hwy. 77, 8 mi. south of Kingsville • (512) 296-3331

Guide Luther Young offers hunting and fishing tours as well as a stay at a restored old ranch house. The B Bar B Ranch Inn was originally part of the nearby historic King Ranch, and it still retains a rustic and isolated feel. An all-day guided fishing trip in Baffin Bay is $300 per person, with a minimum of two people, and the price includes room and board (see our Bed and Breakfast Inns chapter).

Wild Horse Lodge
Riviera • (512) 584-3098

The Wild Horse Lodge consists of three houses on the water at Baffin Bay that provide accommodations for hunting and fishing parties. You can rent a house and fish on your own for $100 per night for one or two people ($25 for each additional person) plus tax. You can also arrange a chartered day of fishing, including a guide, tackle, artificial bait and cleaning of your catch for $325 to $425 per day, depending on how many people are in the boat.

Hunting

Dove and quail are the most popular birds for hunters in South Texas, although duck and other waterfowl are also abundant. Turkey, deer, feral hog and nilgai (an exotic antelope) are also sought after by hunters, but they can be more expensive to shoot when you take into account the cost of deer leases and guided tours running in the thousands of dollars.

As for deer hunting, the brush country of South Texas produces most of the states' trophy bucks and also offers some of the most expensive hunting in the state. Locating a place

to hunt can be the most arduous part of the experience, particularly for hunters coming from states with large tracts of public land that are open to all comers. Since some 97 percent of Texas' land is privately owned, you generally have to find private land on which to hunt. Leasing hunting rights is a firmly established practice in which many folks share in a seasonal hunting lease on a specified pasture or area. Others do day leasing or pay a fee to the owner for each day of hunting; still others opt for a package lease, paying for a guided hunt or a weekend at a ranch that offers a packaged hunt.

Under a program launched recently by the state, public lands are now set aside for hunting. A list and map of these lands is available to anyone who purchases a $40 public hunting permit from the Texas Parks and Wildlife Department, (800) TX LIC 4 U or (800) 895-4248. South Texas has 20 public dove hunting sites within an 80-mile radius of Corpus Christi. If you choose to use these public lands, you'll fare best if you visit the prospective site before your hunt to check out the availability of your quarry.

Under Texas regulations, youngsters (16 and younger) can hunt for free with a licensed adult.

For a guided tour, check out the following guide services, lodges and ranches.

North Bay Area

Waterfowl hunting is particularly popular in Aransas Pass and Rockport. In Rockport, you can hunt in the bay or in the marshes.

Guides

Guides in addition to the company described below include Tommy Ramzinsky, (512) 729-4493, and Brad Smythe with Web Foot Guide Services, (512) 790-8354. You can also acquire a list of local guides from the Rockport-Fulton Area Chamber of Commerce, (800) 826-6441.

South Bay Hunting Club
Aransas Pass • (512) 758-1432

Hunters who want basic ferry service to an already prepared blind or guide services can call Gordon Spears of the South Bay Hunting Club. Spears heads up a family-owned business that consists of guides who use air boats to ferry hunters to duck blinds already set up in the South Bay, which is between Aransas Pass and Port Aransas.

Longtime guide Spears has been operating this service since 1963, and much of his business is from repeat customers who've been coming to them for decades. The company has five air boats and 35 duck blinds that are fully decoyed. The cost is $65 per person per hunt, either in the morning or evening, and hunters can expect to get teal, widgin, pintails and redheads. Additional guide services are available for those who can't identify the birds in flight. Spears is a fishing guide from March through October and a hunting guide from October through January.

Corpus Christi Area

Fennessey Ranch
F.M. Rd. 2678 10 mi. north of Bayside • (512) 529-6600

The Fennessey Ranch offers a wide array of recreational opportunities, including hunting, fishing, birding and nature viewing. The ranch is part of a legendary 750,000-acre land empire that has been in the same family for 165 years. Today it consists of 4,000 acres of wetlands, meadows, natural lakes and Mission River frontage. It's in Refugio County, about 45 minutes north of Corpus Christi.

You can hunt for 15 species of ducks, including gadwalls, canvasbacks, teals, wood ducks, pintails, northern shovelers and fulvous tree ducks. You can also arrange a quail hunt with a trained dog, hunt a Russian boar from an African-style duck blind or bag a trophy whitetail deer. The cost of a one-day wild-hog hunt is $350; a one-day hog/duck combination hunt is $400. A half-day duck hunting trip costs $135. In addition, the ranch offers Copano and Mission Bay fishing trips for up to six anglers at a cost of $350.

The ranch has also teamed with the Red-

fish Lodge on Copano Bay to offer fishing packages for redfish and speckled trout. You can find more information about the lodge's services in the previous Fishing section of this chapter.

Knolle Ranch
F.M. Rd. 70, Sandia • (512) 547-2546

The Knolle Ranch offers private dove, duck and goose hunting during the season. This ranch, which also operates a bed and breakfast inn (see our Bed and Breakfast Inns chapter), is 35 miles west of Corpus Christi in the Nueces River Valley. Long a dairy farm, the owners transformed it into an English country-style inn that caters to horse owners, hunters and other visitors.

The rates per gun, per day, are $25 for dove, $70 for duck, $100 for geese and $125 for a duck and goose combination. Hunters bring their own shotguns and gear, while field work is done by the guides. Staff clean the gear and guns after the hunt and process the birds for you.

Knolle Ranch also offers cross-country riding, lodging for horses, riding instruction, birding, canoeing, skeet shooting and gourmet meals.

Kingsville Area

The B Bar B Ranch Inn
County Rd. 2215 off U.S. Hwy. 77, 8 mi. south of Kingsville • (512) 296-3331

The inn is a restored ranch house that doubles as a bed and breakfast (see our Bed and Breakfast Inns chapter). Owner and guide Luther Young offers a two-day, two-night dove hunt for $350 per person and quail hunts for $750 per person per day that includes the use of his professionally trained bird dogs. Also available are a two-day, two-night spring turkey hunt for $800 per person and a two-day, two-night nilgai bull hunt for $1,300 per person. The nilgai is an exotic antelope found in South Texas.

The Coastal Bend is the best place along the Texas coast to stroll along the beach, sail across calm waters or zip around on a personal watercraft.

Beaches and Watersports

The Texas Coastal Bend is a mecca for beach and watersports enthusiasts drawn to the area's water, sand and warm weather. There's no better place along the Texas coast to stroll along the beach, sail across calm waters or zip around on a personal watercraft.

The beaches are concentrated along the barrier islands that extend from north of Corpus Christi to the Padre Island National Seashore to the south. The North Bay area has one real beach, a 1-mile-long, man-made beach built with dredge material. The Kingsville area has no beaches; much of the Padre Island National Seashore is in the same county as Kingsville, but to approach them by road you have to go through Corpus Christi. Corpus Christi has three small beaches that pale in comparison to those found on Mustang and Padre islands.

When you talk about beaches in the Coastal Bend you're really talking about one beach stretching the length of Mustang and Padre islands. The beaches look pretty much the same: white sand stretching 50 yards or so from the water's edge to sand dunes. What's different is the development that has sprung up around them. The northern end of Mustang Island is packed with high-rise condos and other tourist-oriented businesses in the city of Port Aransas. On the opposite side of the spectrum is the undeveloped Padre Island National Seashore, where development is limited to the visitors center on the northern tip.

Many visitors are surprised to learn that cars are allowed on most area beaches. The speed limit is 15 mph, and Texas motor vehicle laws are enforced. A beach parking sticker is required for all Nueces County and Port Aransas beaches. The fees fund beach improvements. The Nueces County Parks and Recreation Department issues 30-day permits for $5 and annual permits for $10. You can buy permits from convenience stores, county offices, beach vendors, parks and recreation employees on the beach and at the Beach Service Office, (512) 949-8122, 15820 Park Road 22.

Beach parking permits are also required at most beaches within the Port Aransas city limits. The cost is $6 per calendar year. Beaches at the southern end of town do not require permits.

Lifeguards staff most area beaches between Memorial Day and Labor Day. You'll also find lifeguards on Nueces County beaches during spring break. We've noted exceptions to these guidelines in the listings.

Watersports run the gamut from fishing and sailing to riding personal watercraft and paddleboats. The vast majority of watersports take place in Rockport, Aransas Pass, Port Aransas and Corpus Christi. Watersports equipment can be rented at many beaches from vendors. You also can find equipment at the businesses and municipalities listed in this chapter. We've divided beaches and watersports equipment rentals into two sections. The prices listed should be considered approximations, as prices could change by the time this book is published. Call ahead to get the latest figures. Businesses that rent watersports equipment either close down in the winter or work reduced hours. In the winter they can be hard to reach. We've noted their months of operation and change in hours wherever possible.

The Corpus Christi Municipal Marina, a service of the City of Corpus Christi Park & Recreation Department, offers water-related activities for residents and nonresidents. Activities include fishing, sailboat races and sailing classes. For information or to obtain registration forms, visit the Corpus Christi Municipal Marina office on the Lawrence Street T-Head or call (512) 882-7333.

Beaches

North Bay Area

Rockport Beach
210 Seabreeze Dr., Rockport
• (512) 729-9392

This man-made beach built on a spoil island is part of the 61-acre Rockport Beach Park near the city's downtown. Although in existence since the 1950s, it wasn't until 1988 that the city developed it for day use and began charging an entrance fee (see our Parks chapter). The 1-mile-long beach overlooking Aransas Bay is a great place to take the kids. The water is shallow for a quarter-mile into the bay, there are no undertows, and high tides and rough waves are scarce.

Facilities include two pavilions with upstairs verandas, restrooms and party rooms; playground equipment for older and younger children; a band shell; and an 800-foot lighted fishing pier. Other amenities include a lighted fishing jetty (open 24 hours a day); a walking trail; a four-lane boat ramp and separate launch for sailboats and catamarans. You'll also find watersports rentals; a saltwater pool with a concrete bulkhead; 75 picnic tables, many covered with cabanas; volleyball courts; and wheelchair-accessible picnic cabanas and a water fountain.

The park is open from 5 AM to 11 PM Monday through Friday and 5 AM to midnight on weekends. Admission is $3 per vehicle per day or $5 for a three-day pass. There are no lifeguards.

Corpus Christi

Corpus Christi Beach
North of the Harbor Bridge, Corpus Christi

This former residential neighborhood fell into decline over the years only to be revived when it was chosen as the site for the Texas State Aquarium. The Lexington Museum on the Bay (a decommissioned aircraft carrier) soon followed, and it wasn't long before other tourism-related businesses moved in. Corpus Christi Beach (often referred to as North Beach by city old-timers) is on the north side of the Port of Corpus Christi across the towering Harbor Bridge. The beach isn't as large and the sand isn't as fine as those on Mustang and Padre islands, but you don't have to drive far to get there. The sand is not native to this area. It was brought in after hurricane Celia destroyed the beach in 1970.

Attractions include the International Kite Museum, miniature golf, restaurants, gift shops, hotels, motels and condominiums (see our Attractions chapter).

Emerald Beach
East side of Holiday Inn Emerald Beach, Corpus Christi • (512) 883-5731

Don't let the location fool you — this is a

public beach. It's right outside the back door of the Holiday Inn, which leads many to believe it's private property. It isn't. This may be the smallest beach you've ever seen; it runs the length of the Holiday Inn. The water is shallow and protected on the sides by seawalls extending 50 yards or so into the bay, which helps keep it calm. Facilities include rinse showers, sun deck, bar, lounge chairs, beach umbrellas and, in the summer months, an enormous trampoline in the bay. Jumping privileges cost $5 per person per day. Beach umbrellas rent for $8 a day, and lounge chairs go for $3 a day.

Port Aransas to Padre Island

Nueces County Park
End of Cotter Ave., Port Aransas
• (512) 749-6117

The beaches along Mustang Island are pretty much the same in terms of surf and sand. What makes this area different is the proximity to area condos and the restaurants and shops in Port Aransas. It's accessible from Port Aransas via Cotter and Beach streets or Avenue G off Alister Street. The park has camping and RV sites (see our Parks and Campgrounds and RV Parks chapters), toilets, showers, bathhouse, picnic shelters and the lighted 1,245-foot Horace Caldwell Pier. The snack bar/convenience store on the pier sells fast food, ice and basic groceries. You can also rent fishing tackle here. It costs $1 to get on the pier. Entry to the park is free; it's open 24 hours a day.

Mustang Island State Park
Texas Hwy. 361, 14 miles south of Port Aransas • (512) 749-5246, (800) 792-1112

The state of Texas owns and operates this 3,703-acre park on the southern end of Mustang Island. That means two things: They charge an entrance fee, which limits crowds, and they keep the beach in good shape, removing trash and sea waste and smoothing the sand with heavy machinery. The beach, which runs for 5.5 miles along the Gulf of Mexico, is popular with families because no cars are allowed.

Sites for tent and RV camping are nearby

(see our Campgrounds and RV Parks chapter). Other facilities include restrooms, dressing rooms, showers, shade shelters, picnic tables, pay phones and a Texas State Parks Store, where you can buy ice and souvenirs. The park is open from 7 AM to 10 PM. Office hours are 8 AM to 5 PM. The park charges an entrance fee of $3 per person for those 13 and older. There are no lifeguards on duty.

J.P. Luby Park
Southern tip of Mustang Island, Corpus Christi

This beach on the southern end of Mustang Island is a favorite among surfers, young people and skimpy bathing suit fans. To get there from Corpus Christi, head north on Park Road 53 (also known as Texas Highway 361) and turn right at the first road. The beach is dead ahead. Facilities include portable toilets, covered picnic tables, showers, lights and a covered pavilion.

Nueces County Padre Balli Park
15820 Park Rd. 22, Corpus Christi
• (512) 949-8121

This 374.5-acre park is just outside the Corpus Christi city limits and a few miles north of the Padre Island National Seashore. Padre Balli is especially popular among anglers and surfers. Anglers are drawn to the lighted, 1,240-foot Bob Hall Pier. Surfers are attracted to the waves that break near the pier, a situation that in the past has resulted in conflicts as surfers became entangled in fishing lines.

Facilities include RV and tent sites (see our Campgrounds and RV Parks chapter), restrooms, hot showers, concession stand, picnic shelters, laundry facilities and first-aid station. Park rangers are on duty 24 hours a day.

Padre Balli is open 24 hours a day year round. Admission is free. There is a $1 charge per person to enter the pier and a $1 fee per fishing pole.

Padre Island National Seashore
9405 S. Padre Island Dr., Corpus Christi
• (512) 949-8068

"Secluded" best describes the Padre Island National Seashore. The barrier island south of Corpus Christi retains much of the unspoiled grandeur that prompted President

John F. Kennedy to authorize its purchase in 1962. It's one of the longest stretches of primitive, undeveloped ocean beach in the United States. You'll see white sand-and-shell beaches, picturesque dunes, grassland and tidal flats.

Malaquite Beach is near the visitors center as you enter the park. Here you'll find lifeguards, umbrella rentals, toilets, cold showers and shaded picnic tables. The first 5 miles of beach are accessible by two-wheel-drive vehicles; the next 60 miles are accessible via four-wheel-drive only.

The park charges a $10 entrance fee good for seven days; an annual pass is available for $20. Discount passes for senior citizens and handicapped individuals are available. The park is open 24 hours a day. The visitors center is open every day from 9 AM to 4 PM except Christmas and New Year's Day.

Equipment Rental and Sales

Boat Rentals

Little Bay Marine
1838 Broadway, Rockport
• **(512) 729-7409, (512) 729-7461**
Little Bay Marine has 12 boats available for rent, ranging from a 15-foot Boston Whaler to a 22-foot Mowdy shallow boat. Prices for a five-hour, half-day range from $100 to $150 and from $145 to $220 for a full, 10-hour day. Boats come with a full tank of gasoline, instructions, compass, fishing chart and life jackets. You'll be charged for fuel used.

South Bay Bait and Charters
Texas Hwy. 361 between Aransas Pass and Port Aransas • (512) 758-2632
South Bay has nine 16-foot Sea Ark aluminum boats with 15-horsepower Yamaha motors for rent. A five-hour half-day costs $45 for two people and $10 extra for more than two adults. A full day costs $70 for two people and $10 extra for more than two. The company furnishes gasoline, life jackets, paddles and an anchor.

Personal Watercraft

Paradise Jet Ski Rentals Inc.
136 Cotter Ave., Port Aransas
• **(512) 749-6904**
Paradise Jet Ski Rentals is on the docks of Woody's Sports Center just east of the ferry landing. You can rent a Jet Ski for one to three people by the hour or by the day. They go for about $40 a half-hour and $65 an hour. Call for daily rates. Gas and life jackets are furnished. You must leave an open credit card or personal check of $500 per machine as a safety deposit. Paradise is open from 9 AM to sunset every day between March 1 and October 31.

Island Watersports Center
1102 S. Shoreline Blvd., Corpus Christi
• **(512) 880-8901**
3938 Surfside Blvd., Corpus Christi
• **(512) 880-8901**
Generally open from Memorial Day weekend to Labor Day weekend, Island Watersports rents Yamaha Waverunners from two bayfront locations. The first, 1102 S. Shoreline Boulevard, is on Emerald Beach outside the Holiday Inn bearing the same address. The second is on the beach outside the Villa del Sol Condominiums. Island Watersports is open from 9 AM to dusk during the summer.

Depending on the weather, Island Watersports is sometimes open during spring break or other times during the spring. Call ahead. Waverunners at the Holiday Inn-Emerald Beach rent for $20 for 15 minutes, $30 for 30 minutes and $60 for an hour. Prices at the Villa del Sol are $5 cheaper for each category. A life jacket and gasoline are included in the price. A deposit is not required.

Paddleboats

Rent a paddle boat, motor boat or bumper boat at the Peoples Street T-Head along the Corpus Christi Bayfront. On most summer days the water is relatively calm in Corpus Christi Bay, and the T-Head and rock breakers ringing the Corpus Christi Marina make the water near the rentals even calmer. Drop by the T-Heads in warmer months to check

Tourists from all over the world travel to the Coastal Bend
each year to enjoy its pristine beaches.

on availability and prices. In Rockport visit
the Rockport Beach Park in downtown
Rockport or call (512) 729-9392. Paddleboats
rent for about $10 per half hour.

Sailing

Wednesday Night Sailing Regatta
Lawrence Street T-Head, Corpus Christi

The Wednesday Night Sailing Regatta is
held every Wednesday beginning at 6 PM from
the Lawrence Street T-Head. Races are held
on varying courses on Corpus Christi Bay.
While they await the signal to start, boats criss-
cross inside the rock breakers that form a semicircle around the Corpus Christi Marina. The
regatta is open to all boaters. Registration takes
place at the marina office 30 minutes before
the race begins. There is no entry fee.

Rockport Sailing School
and Charter
Rockport Harbor, Rockport
• (512) 729-0226

Richard Lamb, a U.S. Coast Guard-li-
censed captain with more than 30 years of
sailing experience, runs this school and charter service out of Rockport Harbor. Lamb

sails an 18-foot fiberglass Cape Cod Cat-
boat built in the 1960s. Its single sail makes
it an easy boat on which to learn. Lamb
teaches an eight-hour beginning sailing
course for $99. A chartered trip costs $25
an hour with a two-hour minimum.

Lamb can suggest a trip or help you design one to suit your interests. Rockport Sailing School and Charter is open year round by
appointment.

Rockport Yacht Club
Rockport Harbor, Rockport
• (512) 729-3115, (512) 729-5622

The Rockport Yacht Club is a fancy name
for a bunch of folks who like boats. You don't
have to have a fancy yacht to join — all you
need is a boat, a love for the water and a $150
initiation fee. Annual dues are $150 for indi-
viduals and $180 for families. Nonresident dues
are $100 for singles and $120 for families. Both
sailors and power boaters are welcome here.

The club meets at 6:30 PM on the third
Thursday of each month at its clubhouse at
Rockport Harbor. The club sponsors bay sailboat races every spring, summer and fall, a
race/cruise from Port Aransas to Port Mansfield
on Labor Day Weekend, a race from Corpus
Christi to Rockport during the October Seafair

(our Annual Events and Festivals chapter), a Christmas Light Parade and a Sunfish sailing instructional program.

Corpus Christi Municipal Marina
Lawrence St. T-Head • (512) 882-7333

The Corpus Christi Municipal Marina offers sailing lessons each summer. Learn to sail on a Sunfish or Dolphin sailboat. Basic and intermediate lessons are available to anyone 10 and older. Basic classes include instruction in Marlinespike Seamanship, righting a capsized boat, boarding a capsized boat and rigging/derigging a sailboat. All participants must pass a swimming test. Fees are $60 per person per session plus $10 for a textbook. Class size is limited to 12 students.

Corpus Christi Sailing Center
200 S. Shoreline Blvd., Corpus Christi
• (512) 881-8503

Sail on vessels from 30 to 46 feet with captained charters or under your own guidance for four hours to a week. The sailing center also offers sunset supper cruises, Sunfish sailboat rentals, new boat sales, basic keelboat sailing instructions and a Sunfish sailing school for children and adults. Sunset supper cruises include a four-course dinner at a seafood restaurant on a boat in Corpus Christi Bay, followed by a two-hour sailing trip on the bay. Tickets (dinner included) are $55 for adults and teens, $25 for children ages 6 to 12 and $10 for children younger than 6.

Sunfish sailboats rent for $50 for four hours; Sunfish lessons are $30 for three hours. A basic keelboat sailing course is held from 9 AM to 5 PM on Saturday and Sunday. The cost is $150, including textbook. A three-day basic coastal sailing course takes you along the Texas coast as you learn to sail and live aboard the boat. The cost is $500, including food and textbook. During this five-day live-aboard course, you'll develop skills necessary to sail 30- to 48-foot sailboats. The cost is $825, including food and textbook.

Scuba Diving

Copeland's Marine
4041 S. Padre Island Dr., Corpus Christi
• (512) 854-1135
134 W. Cotter Ave., Port Aransas
• (512) 749-7464

Copeland's Marine offers scuba diving lessons, daytrips and sleeper trips throughout most of the year. A new scuba diving class starts up about once a month throughout the year, while dive trips leave from Port Aransas each week except in December and January. *The Adventurer* takes divers to offshore oil rigs and the 7 ½-Fathom Reef Flower Garden Marine Sanctuary, where fish gather in large numbers. The air-conditioned and heated 85-foot custom dive boat comes with a full galley and room to sleep 33. A daytrip aboard *The Adventurer* costs between $45 and $119 per person. Sleeper trips range from $99 to $299.

See Sea Divers
4020 Weber Rd., Corpus Christi
• (512) 853-3483

This Corpus Christi dive shop, which rents and sells scuba equipment, organizes weekend trips to the Gulf of Mexico throughout the summer. Boats leave from Fisherman's Wharf in Port Aransas and take divers to offshore oil platforms where fish congregate. Dive trips cost as little as $89. See Sea also offers diving trips to the Caribbean throughout the year. Private and group lessons are available.

A basic certification course costs $169. Lessons are given at indoor, heated swimming pools throughout the city. The shop is open from 10 AM to 7 PM Monday through Friday and 10 AM to 5 PM on Saturday.

Surfing

The best places to surf in the Coastal Bend are Bob Hall Pier at Nueces County's Padre Balli Park, Mustang Island State Park and Horace Caldwell Pier in Port Aransas.

Port Aransas

Bo Jon's
100 E. Cotter Ave., Port Aransas
• **(512) 749-5365**
220 E. Ave. G, Port Aransas
• **(512) 749-6478**

Bo Jon's is really two stores in one, situated side-by-side and offering much of the same merchandise. One store serves as a "half-off" store while the other sells at normal retail prices. Both sell sportswear, T-shirts, bathing suits and suntan products. They also sell and rent surf boards and Boogie Boards. Surf boards are available for rent; Boogie Boards go for $4 a day with a $15 deposit. Hours are 9 AM to 9 PM in the summer.

Pat Magee's
101 Ave. G, Port Aransas
• **(512) 749-4177**

Pat Magee's has been in business here since 1969. His island shop offers swimwear, sportswear, T-shirts and watersports equipment, including surf boards, Boogie Boards and skim boards. Rental prices are as follows: surf boards, $10 a day; Boogie Boards, $5 a day; skim boards $7 a day. You must have a valid driver's license to rent equipment.

Corpus Christi

Wind and Wave Water Sports
10721 S. Padre Island Dr., Corpus Christi
• **(512) 937-9283**

Wind and Wave rents all sorts of water toys, including surfboards, Boogie Boards, sailboards and kayaks. They also give windsurfing lessons. Surfboards rent from $15 to $25 a day; Boogie Boards go for $10 a day. Sailboards will run you $45 a day, and kayaks rent for $25 to $45 a day. The shop is open from 9 AM to 7 PM on weekends throughout the year and 9 AM to 7 PM Monday through Friday in the spring and summer. In the fall and winter it's open 10 AM to 6:30 PM on weekdays.

Windsurfing

People come from all over the world to windsurf in the Coastal Bend. Corpus Christi is one of the windiest cities in the nation. The annual U.S. Open Windsurfing Regatta is held at South Cole Park, known by longtime locals as Oleander Point, and attracts professional windsurfers from all over the world.

In addition to South Cole Park, popular windsurfing spots include the Laguna Madre and Bird Island Basin at the Padre Island National Seashore. South Cole Park, it should be noted, is not a place for beginners. They're better off learning in the Laguna Madre or Bird Island Basin, where the water is relatively shallow and calm.

Bird Island Basin is perhaps the most favored windsurfing location in the area. The water is flat and chest deep. Beginners feel safe knowing they can stand up if they fall in, while more experienced windsurfers like it because the calm water allows them to go faster.

Wind and Wave Water Sports
10721 S. Padre Island Dr., Corpus Christi
• **(512) 937-9283**

Wind and Wave rents an assortment of water equipment (see the previous entry), including windsurfing equipment. The shop also offers lessons. Windsurfing equipment rents for $45 a day, and lessons cost $45 for a three-hour class. Lessons and equipment are dispensed on South Padre Island Drive along the Laguna Madre west of the John F. Kennedy Causeway Bridge.

Wind and Wave is open from 9 AM to 7 PM on weekends year round and from 9 AM to 7 PM weekdays in the spring and summer. Fall and winter weekday hours are 10 AM to 6:30 PM.

Worldwinds Windsurfing
Bird Island Basin • (512) 949-7472, (800) 793-7471

Worldwinds rents windsurfing equipment and gives lessons from March through November at Bird Island Basin, a popular windsurfing spot at the Padre Island National Seashore. A three-hour class (including equipment) costs $45. Equipment for beginners rents for $20 for two hours and regular equipment rents for $30. Regular equipment rents for $55 a day or $275 for a week. The shop is open from 10 AM until around 5 PM.

The Coastal Bend offers everything from archery to volleyball, plus team sports for all ages through local recreation departments.

Recreation

Maybe it's the year-round warm weather or maybe perhaps it's being so close to nature, but whatever the reason, Coastal Bend residents participate in a wide of variety of recreational activities throughout the year.

Hunting and fishing are such popular activities here that we've devoted an entire chapter to them. See our Fishing and Hunting chapter for details on fishing spots, guides and stores as well as favored hunting spots in the area. And as you might imagine, watersports also are popular here, so we've set aside a chapter for those activities as well. For more information see our Beaches and Watersports chapter.

What's left? Plenty. The Coastal Bend offers everything from archery to volleyball, along with youth leagues, little leagues and a vast selection of classes and leagues offered by local parks and recreation departments. If you don't see your favorite activity listed in this chapter, call the park and recreation department of the city nearest you and ask about it.

Corpus Christi has the most to offer with leagues and classes throughout the city. The athletic/recreation office of the Corpus Christi Park & Recreation Department operates the Corpus Christi Gym and the Ben Garza Gym. Each offers a variety of athletic programs open to youth. Volleyball, basketball, weightlifting and martial arts are offered throughout the year. The Corpus Christi Park & Recreation Department also offers adaptive programs for people with disabilities. For more information on these or other activities call the athletics office at (512) 880-3460.

Other park and recreation departments in the region also cater to the public's fun and fitness needs: Rockport, (512) 729-2213; Aransas Pass, (512) 758-5301; Ingleside, (512) 776-2517; Portland, (512) 777-3301; Port Aransas, (512) 749-4111; and Kingsville (Kleberg County), (512) 595-8591.

Recreational activities are listed in alphabetical order to make it easier to find an activity in which you are interested. Entries in each category are then divided into geographic regions under appropriate headers.

Archery

Clyde's Archery Lanes
5564 Ayers St., Corpus Christi
• (512) 855-3116

Clyde's Archery Lanes has been in business since 1981 and is the third-oldest archery shop in Texas. It has 20 indoor ranges and a full-service repair shop and carries major brand-name bows. You'll also find videos and camouflage clothing here, and you can sign up to go bow hunting. The shop is open from 11 AM to 9 PM Monday through Friday and from 10 AM to 4 PM on Saturdays.

Texas Archery Club
5564 Ayers St., Corpus Christi
• (512) 855-3116

The Texas Archery Club is the oldest archery club in Texas. Its charter dates back to the 1930s. Men, women and children comprise its 50 members. Dues are $50 a year. Members participate in leagues and tournaments.

Baseball

South Texas Adult Baseball League
Corpus Christi • (512) 241-5949

This men's league began its sixth year in March 1998 with 16 teams playing a 12-game season. Keep in mind that this is baseball — known by enthusiasts as "hardball" — and not the softer, slower softball. The league has two seasons: The spring season runs from March to May, while the fall season runs from August to October. Both seasons include playoffs and an all-star game. Players can participate in the 18-and-older category or in the 30-and-older category.

All games are played at Oxy Park on McKenzie and Haven roads in northwest Corpus Christi. You can be matched with a team or organize your own. Teams hold tryouts to determine whether you're qualified to play. Fees are $75 per person to pay for umpires, use of the field, baseballs and maintenance. Team managers participate for free, and player/managers are allowed.

Billiards

Clicks
4535 S. Padre Island Dr., Corpus Christi
• (512) 851-2680

Throw your pool cue in the back seat and head for Clicks, where chances are you won't have to wait for a table. Clicks, which you'll find along Corpus Christi's main shopping and dining district, has 18 Brunswick pool tables, including one 9-foot-long Gold Crown, the Cadillac of pool tables. At Clicks you rent a table by the hour. The cost is $6 an hour at most times, although you can find cheaper rates.

Clicks also has a full-service bar, video games, three electronic dart boards, two foosball tables, a CD jukebox, electronic interactive trivia, nine midsize televisions and one big-screen TV. Clicks sponsors pool leagues and pool and dart tournaments. It's open from 11 AM to 2 PM every day of the year.

Bowling

You won't regret packing that 18-pound bowling ball when you visit the area. Bowling is a popular sport here, and bowlers have five bowling centers to choose from, including four in Corpus Christi. At least two bowling associations have formed for people who share a common interest in the game. You can reach the Corpus Christi Women's Bowling Association at (512) 852-2871 and the Senior All Star Bowling Association at (512) 265-0774.

The Corpus Christi Park & Recreation De-

partment offers bowling for adults with mobility difficulties. The program is designed for adults having problems with balance and mobility, including those using a wheelchair walker or cane and anyone suffering stiffness from arthritis or recent surgery. Spouses, care providers and assistants also may participate. The group meets at 10:30 AM Monday at Saratoga Lanes, 6116 Ayers Street.

Sully's Bowling Lanes
2285 W. Wheeler Ave., Aransas Pass
• (512) 758-3225

Sully's, the only bowling center in the North Bay area, has 16 lanes, a video/game room and a snack bar. Rates are $2.40 a game and $1.85 to rent shoes. On weekends ask for the special and get three games and shoe rental for $7.

Sully's has league play Monday through Friday beginning at 7 PM. Call the bowling center to join up. A few lanes usually are available for open play even on league nights.

Sully's is open every day from noon until 11 PM. Senior and military discounts are available Monday through Thursday until 6 PM.

AMF Saratoga Lanes
6116 Ayers St., Corpus Christi
• (512) 857-2695

AMF owns three bowling centers in Corpus Christi, including the AMF Saratoga Lanes on the city's south side. Its 40 lanes are the most in the Texas Coastal Bend. The center also has a snack bar, lounge, video/game room, billiards, darts and automatic computerized scoring. Fees for adults are $2.40 a game until 5 PM and $2.95 a game thereafter. Shoes rent for $1.85. Kids bowl for $2.10 a game. League play is held several nights a week, and open lanes are available most nights.

The center opens at 9 AM on Monday, Tuesday, Wednesday and Saturday and at noon on Thursday, Friday and Sunday. Closing time is around 11 PM depending on how busy they are.

AMF also operates two other centers: AMF Riviera Lanes, (512) 883-5481, 3211 Ayers Street, Corpus Christi; and AMF Is-

Photo: Greater Corpus Christi Business Alliance

Sailing can be enjoyed year-round in windy, warm South Texas.

land Bowl, (512) 937-1445, 1601 Flour Bluff Drive, Corpus Christi. Prices, hours and facilities are similar here.

Hilltop Lanes
12150 IH-37, Corpus Christi
• (512) 241-2700

Hilltop Lanes bills itself as "the coolest bowling center in South Texas" thanks to the $100,000 air-conditioning unit that was installed in 1997. Hilltop offers another form of "cool" with its Lunar Bowling from midnight to 3 AM every Saturday when you can bowl for three hours for $10.

This 40-lane bowling center in northwest Corpus Christi has youth bowling on Saturday mornings, 99¢ bowling after 9 PM on Wednesday and league bowling every day except Sunday.

Games are $2 each before 6 PM and $2.85 from 6 PM on. Hours are 11 AM to midnight Monday and Wednesday, 9 AM to 11 PM on Tuesday, 9 AM to 1 AM on Thursday, 9 AM to 2 AM on Friday, 9 AM to 3 AM on Saturday and noon to 11 PM on Sunday.

Facilities include a game room, lounge, snack bar and automatic scoring. Military discounts are available.

Cycling

The Texas Coastal Bend could either be considered a great place for cycling or one of the worst, depending on whether you're headed into the wind or have it at your back. The relatively flat landscape makes cycling long distances a breeze (no pun intended), unless you find yourself battling against the ever present wind.

The Coastal Bend has few biking lanes and established cycling paths. In Corpus Christi, you can cycle along the seawall or along the special bike path on Ocean Drive. But be careful. The speed limit here is 40 miles per hour, and many motorists exceed that. Port Aransas is a great place to ride. The city itself is so small that a bicycle is a legitimate transportation option. And if you're into long-distance cycling, ride the 26-mile length of Mustang Island from Port Aransas to Padre Island. Again, be careful. Drivers along this stretch of Texas Highway 361 often reach speeds in excess of 70 miles per hour.

Port Aransas

Island Bikes
520 Cut-off Rd., Port Aransas
• **(512) 749-6566**

Island Bikes rents old-fashioned single-speed beach cruisers year round from its Port Aransas shop. The shop has 25 to 30 bikes available to rent for one hour to one month. It also sells bikes and accessories, rents bike trailers and repairs bikes. Bikes rent for $4 an hour, $10 a half day, $15 a day, $25 a week or $35 a month. Island Bikes provides free pickup and delivery within the Port Aransas city limit for anyone who spends $25 or more. The shop is open noon to 6 PM on Sundays and 9 AM to 6 PM on Monday and Wednesday through Saturday. It's closed on Tuesdays.

Corpus Christi

Corpus Christi Bicycle Club
(512) 883-4517, (512) 980-9909

Hop on your bike and join the Corpus Christi Bicycle Club for its weekend rides around town. They meet every Saturday at Jason's Deli, 5325 Saratoga Boulevard, to commune with fellow pedal pushers and pursue their passion for cycling. The club also participates in special events. The most notable is the annual Island Breeze, a 68-mile ride around Corpus Christi Bay held the last weekend in October. The club also promotes cycling safety and cycling education in local schools. Membership dues are $15 a year for individuals and $25 a year for families. Children are welcome, and helmets are required for club rides.

Corpus Christi BMX
6429 Ayers St., Corpus Christi
• **(512) 814-4269, (512) 852-6374**

We decided to include this in the main listing even though most participants are kids. The reason? BMX bicycle races are open to people of all ages. Organizers say they've seen riders as young as 3 and as old as 45 at their weekly dirt-track races. For those unfamiliar with the sport, BMX bicycle racing mimics dirt-bike motorcycle racing with riders providing the horsepower instead of an engine. Racers ride on a dirt track made more difficult by hills, valleys and hairpin turns. Contestants are placed in divisions based on sex, age and experience. Races are held on Thursdays beginning at 8 PM. To race you must sign up between 6:30 and 7:30 PM. A helmet, long pants and a long-sleeved shirt are required. Handlebars must be padded. To participate in races you have to be a member of the American Bicycle Association. Dues to the association are $15 for a one-month trial membership or $35 for one year. The entry fee to race is $10 each week.

Disc Golf

Bay Area Disc Golf Association
(512) 758-6466

The 100 or so members of the Bay Area Disc Golf Association sponsor weekly tournaments open to players of all skill levels. Want to learn? Just show up at their weekly tournaments and someone will loan you a disc or two. Disc golf is played like regular golf using flying discs instead of a ball and club. It's cheap and easy to learn. You can make do with one $10 disc, although four is considered the minimum number required to play a good round.

The Coastal Bend has two disc golf courses. A nine-hole course is in Live Oak Park in Ingleside east of Farm-to-Market Road 1069 and 2 miles south of Texas Hwy. 361. An 18-hole course is in Corpus Christi's West Guth Park on Up River Road north of Rand Morgan Road. (For more information see our Parks chapter.)

One-round tournaments are held beginning at 3 PM on the first, third, fourth and fifth Saturdays of each month at West Guth Park. A two-round, all-day tournament is held on the second Saturday of the month at Live Oak Park. Rounds begin at 10 AM and 1 PM.

Golf

Year-round warm weather makes the Coastal Bend a great place for golfers. Even in the middle of winter it's usually warm enough to play a round of golf at one of the area's several courses. You can even play in shorts on many winter days.

Want to hit a few practice shots before heading out to the course? Head to the driving range. Many courses have their own driving ranges. Stand-alone driving ranges include: Tee Time, (512) 790-5115, 3451 Texas Highway 35 S., Rockport; Cimarron Golf Driving Range, (512) 993-8180, 3752 Cimarron Road, Corpus Christi; Paradise Golf Center, (512) 939-7333, 9449 S. Padre Island Drive, Corpus Christi; The Kingsville Ballpark, (512) 592-2444, 2520 E. Santa Gertrudis Avenue, Kingsville.

Following is a list of courses open to the public.

Corpus Christi

Gabe Lozano Sr. Golf Center
4401 Old Brownsville Rd., Corpus Christi
• (512) 883-3696

Gabe Lozano Sr. Golf Center has both a regulation 18-hole course and a nine-hole executive course. It also has a pro shop, snack bar and lighted driving range. The 6900-yard, par 72 course is open seven days a week. The course is long and flat with lots of water and a little sand. The greens are usually in excellent shape, and wind conditions are generally breezy. Greens fees for the 18-hole course are $11.25 weekdays and $13.50 on weekends. Senior citizens 60 and older pay $8.25 on weekdays. Fees for the executive nine are $6.25 weekdays and $7.50 on weekends. Cart rentals are $7.50 per person for two people and $10 for singles. Walking the course is allowed.

Oso Beach Municipal Golf Course
5601 S. Alameda St., Corpus Christi
• (512) 991-5351

This municipal golf course on the city's southside has an 18-hole course, pro shop and snack bar. It's open every day. This 6223-yard, par 70 course is flat with small greens, lots of water and breezy conditions. Greens fees on weekdays are $11.25 ($9.25 after 3 PM). Weekend fees are $13.50. Carts rent for $15.

Pharaohs Country Club
7111 Pharaoh Dr., Corpus Christi
• (512) 991-1490

This country club on the city's southside offers an 18-hole course, country club facilities, driving range, pro shop and restaurant. This 6000-yard, par 70 course has water on 15 of 18 holes. It's mostly flat with lots of palm trees, narrow fairways and midsize greens. Public play is welcome. Fees are $13.20 on weekdays. Weekend fees are $19.95. Carts rent for $10 per rider.

Kingsville Area

L.E. Ramey Municipal Course
U.S. Hwy. 77 S. at F.M. Rd. 3320,
Kingsville • (512) 592-1101

This 18-hole municipal course is about a half-mile southeast of Kingsville near the naval air station. It includes a pro shop, driving range and snack bar. It's open every day. Greens fees are $8.54 weekdays and $10.68 weekends for unlimited golf. Cart fees are $10 for nine holes and $15 for 18. Monthly memberships are available for $64 for singles and $95 for families. This 7100-yard, par 72 course is flat and open with lots of mesquite trees.

Horseback Riding

Mustang Island

Mustang Ranch Riding Stable
Mustang Island • (512) 991-7433

The Coastal Bend adds its own particular spin on this popular activity by offering horseback riding on the beach. For more than 10 years the Mustang Ranch Riding Stable has been offering horseback riding on the beach on Mustang Island. The ranch has horses to suit everyone from children on their first ride to experienced horsemen. It also offers hay rides, beach parties, catering, live music and dancing. Mustang Ranch is open year round beginning at 9 AM and closing at around 5 or 6 PM. The cost is $20 an hour for adults, $15 an hour for children 12 and older and $5 for a child riding with an adult.

To get there from Corpus Christi, take S. Padre Island Drive south across the John F. Kennedy Causeway to Padre Island. Turn left on Texas Highway 361 and drive 6.5 miles. The riding stables will be on your right.

Corpus Christi

Painted Dreams Riding Facility
6201 Bradley Dr., Corpus Christi
• **(512) 991-3474, (512) 812-0936**

Corpus Christi resident Glen Bertrand started this riding facility for the enjoyment of the local Texas Special Olympics chapter. It soon grew into a full-fledged riding business. Painted Dreams teaches riding lessons to children, hosts birthday parties and offers private trail rides for an hour or several hours. Riding fees are $20 an hour per person or $15 an hour for rides of four hours or more. Regular customers also are charged the $15-an-hour fee. Frequent customers receive discounts. Call for an appointment.

Martial Arts

North Bay Area

Master Lenny's Tae Kwon Do
2818 Texas Hwy. 35 N., Rockport
• **(512) 790-9710**

Master Lenny strives to instill discipline, self-confidence and self-control in his students through the Korean martial art of tae kwon do. This defensive art emphasizes kicking techniques designed to give the user an advantage over larger opponents. Students, who range in age from 5 to 75, participate in local tournaments for trophies and medals. Beginning and advanced classes are available for children and adults. Most classes are held in the evening. Master Lenny also teaches classes in Portland and Sinton. Call for locations and times.

Corpus Christi

Texas BlackBelt Academy
4701 Ayers St., Ste. 301, Corpus Christi
• **(512) 852-4299**

The Texas BlackBelt Academy emphasizes the enhancement of life skills over kicking and punching. The school has a theme each month with a lesson plan and drills designed to emphasize that theme. It strives to teach children and adults to set and achieve goals for themselves. Adults can also improve their aerobic conditioning and learn self-defense. Classes are offered in the mornings and evenings in private or group settings.

Kim Soo Karate
4705 S. Alameda St., Corpus Christi
• **(512) 993-7127**

Kim Soo Karate combines Japanese, Chinese and Korean arts into one system known as chy yon ruy. Chy yon ruy is designed to build internal and external power and to control anger. It is taught as a discipline rather than as a sport, stressing becoming a mentally and physically balanced and responsible person rather than winning trophies and medals. Classes are offered for men, women and children in the afternoon and evening. Day classes are offered during the summer.

Paintball

Corpus Christi

C.C. Paintball Park
7901 McGloin Rd., Corpus Christi
• **(512) 758-2181**

Paintball is a harmless form of warfare in which participants "shoot" one another with

Photo: Greater Corpus Christi Business Alliance

Padre Island offers off-season visitors a peaceful place for relaxation under the sun.

paintballs instead of bullets. Paintball enthusiasts break up into teams and chase each other around a field trying to capture their opponent's flag. You can get a gun, mask and 100 paintballs for $21.45 ($26.81 for 200 balls). A 100-ball refill costs $5 plus tax. Those with their own equipment are charged $10 for use of the field.

Parachuting

North Bay Area

Sky's the Limit
1508 F.M. Rd. 351, Beeville
• (512) 358-9330

Drop in for an adrenaline rush at Sky's the Limit in Beeville. Your first jump will be as a rider secured to a jump master. Fifteen minutes of instruction is all that's needed to experience the sport without having to worry about doing anything your first time out. The cost is $140.

For those who want to become certified to skydive alone, Sky's the Limit offers an eight-hour program with seven levels of instruction and one jump for $1,000. Post-certification jumps are $13 each. Jumps take place on weekends and holidays in a big field near Beeville. They're open from sunrise to sunset.

To get to Beeville from Corpus Christi, take U.S. Highway 181 north across the Harbor Bridge. The highway will take you northwest through Portland, Gregory, Taft, Sinton and Skidmore before coming to Beeville, 60 miles away.

Racquetball

Corpus Christi

YMCA
417 S. Upper Broadway, Corpus Christi
• (512) 882-1741

You don't have to be a member to play

racquetball or handball on one of the Y's four courts. All you need is $10 or a Y card from anywhere in the world to gain access to courts, whirlpool, steam room, Nautilus machines, free weights, cardiovascular room, indoor pool and fitness classes. The complex is open from 5:45 AM to 10 PM Monday through Friday, 8 AM to 6 PM Saturday and noon to 6 PM Sunday.

Running/Walking

Popular running/walking areas in Corpus Christi are along the 2-mile-long seawall and Ocean Drive, which runs along the bayfront. The beach is popular, too, as is the 2-mile-long West Guth Park running trail. West Guth Park is on Up River Road north of Rand Morgan Road.

Corpus Christi

Corpus Christi Roadrunners
(512) 881-6166

This nonprofit club of 300 organizes several local races each year and donates the proceeds to charity. Races include 5K runs, half-marathons and the increasingly popular Beach-to-Bay Marathon, a relay race from Padre Island to Corpus Christi's Cole Park. Fees are $10 for singles and $15 for families. You can get a membership application at Fleet Feet Sports, (512) 225-3338, 514 Everhart Road, or by leaving a message on the group's answering machine.

Shooting

Corpus Christi

Corpus Christi Pistol & Rifle Club
F.M. Rd. 763 on Oso Creek, Corpus Christi • (512) 852-1212

This club on the city's far south side offers sporting clays, skeet and trap on their outdoor range. Nonmembers shoot for $7.50 a 25-target round for skeet and trap; sporting clays are $9 a round. To shoot a rifle or pistol

you must be a member of the club. Dues are $96 a year, and you must go through a 10- to 15-minute safety orientation.

The site is open five days a week: Wednesday and Friday from 3 PM until sunset, Thursday from 3 PM to midnight and Saturday and Sunday 9 AM to sunset.

The Sharp Shooter
2033 Airline Rd., Bldg. K, Corpus Christi • (512) 980-1190

The Sharp Shooter offers indoor pistol, rifle and reactive ranges. It has a total of 15 shooting bays. Fees for both rifles and pistols are $12 an hour per person, not per gun. Two people can shoot in one lane for $18 an hour. The price is the same for all three ranges.

The Sharp Shooter carries a full supply of ammunition, holsters, reloading supplies, gun-cleaning supplies and guns. A top-of-the-line air ventilation system keeps the air clean. You can rent guns, targets and ear protection. The complex includes a lounge and viewing windows. A retired Texas Ranger — the law enforcement agency, not the baseball team — teaches a one-day concealed-handgun class for $100. Shooting lessons cost $25 per lesson.

The Sharp Shooter is open from noon to 8 PM Tuesday through Friday, 10 AM to 8 PM Saturday and noon to 6 PM on Sundays.

Shuffleboard

Port Aransas
to Padre Island

Roberts Point Park
Waterfront, Port Aransas • (512) 749-4148

Shuffleboarders can borrow equipment without charge from the harbormaster's office next to Roberts Point Park in Port Aransas. Playing at these outdoor shuffleboard courts will give you a great view of the Corpus Christi Ship Channel and the Port Aransas Harbor.

Roller-Skating

Corpus Christi

Cityskates
8051 S. Padre Island Dr., Corpus Christi
• (512) 993-7456
This old-fashioned skating rink has a 14,000-square-foot hardwood maple skating area, snack bar and video games. It offers free beginning skating lessons, ladies night, private company and school parties, birthday parties, tiny tots skating, teen night and aggressive skating using ramps, rails and quarter-pipes.

Soccer

Corpus Christi

Coastal Bend Women's
Soccer Association
(512) 992-3141
The Coastal Bend Women's Soccer Association has begun rebuilding in recent years and is now up to seven teams. Ages of participants range from 18 to 55 (you have to be at least 16). The spring season begins in February and runs until the beginning of June, while the fall season begins in September and runs until December. Games are played on Sundays at Oso Soccer Field on S. Padre Island Drive near Oso Bay. There are no playoffs. The cost is $16.75 per person. The association holds monthly meetings.

Softball

North Bay Area

Aransas County
Softball Association
1300 N. Live Oak St., Rockport
• (512) 729-4011
This nonprofit league supports and promotes adult softball (16 years and older) in Aransas County. The association offers co-ed and men's leagues and sponsors a senior citizen's tournament each summer. Games are played between March and November in spring, summer and fall seasons. Each team plays about 10 games per season. The men's league has a playoff system. Registration fees are $290 a team for men's teams and $225 for co-ed teams. Games are played at Tiger Field in Rockport.

Corpus Christi

Corpus Christi Softball Association
5230 Kostoryz Rd., No. 17, Corpus
Christi • (512) 852-8776
This nonprofit organization promotes a family environment (no alcohol) at its softball games held throughout most of the year. Divisions include 55-and-older men's, 60-and-older men's, church, co-ed, men's open, men's industrial (players must work 30 hours or more for the company that sponsors them) and church boys and girls. The cost is $295 per team for a six-game season plus playoffs. The association sponsors four seasons: one each in the spring and fall and two in the summer. The cost for teams in the men's 55-and-older league is $265 and $225 for the men's 60-and-older. Teams must win 50 percent of their games to qualify for the playoffs.

Square Dancing

North Bay Area

It all began in the early 1960s when Richard "Blackie" Handy, a new young caller from Corpus Christi, was asked to teach a class for beginners in Aransas Pass. Two couples enrolled in the class loved it so much they decided to organize classes in Rockport. Square dancing flourished in Rockport and continues to do so to this day. The original group adopted the name Paws & Taws, square dancing terms denoting the man, Paw, and the woman, Taw.

In 1965 the group finished the Paws and Taws Convention Center on Fulton Beach Road. Approximately 14 square-dancing weekends are held there each year by groups from throughout the state. The building is home to the Ocean Waves Square Dance Club, (512) 729-2828 or (512) 729-9158. You can try your hand (or foot) on the center's wooden floor from 8 to 10 PM every Wednesday night. Admission is $2 a person.

Swimming

People might go crazy if they didn't have a place to cool off in the middle of the long, hot summer. Fortunately the Coastal Bend has several swimming pools (not to mention the bays and Gulf of Mexico) in which to escape the heat.

The cities of Portland and Ingleside have public swimming pools. Admission to the Portland pool, (512) 777-3301, one block west of U.S. Highway 181 on Moore Avenue, is $1 for children and adults. Admission to the Ingleside pool, (512) 776-7972, 400 Mustang Drive, is $1.50 for children and adults.

The Corpus Christi Park & Recreation Department offers several ongoing swimming programs. They include lap and general swimming, swim league practice, Masters and U.S. Swimming programs, Red Cross and Gus and Goldie swimming lessons, Red Cross lifeguarding and water safety instructors courses, and water aerobics. Pools are also available for private swimming parties.

The department offers swimming for the disabled of all ages, a program that incorporates lessons, water games and practice. An adult or older sibling must accompany the swimmer in the pool. The program begins in June at Collier Pool, 3801 Harris Street. Call (512) 852-0243.

Corpus Christi has nine swimming pools in all. For information call (512) 880-3481. We've featured two swimming pools in the following entries.

Collier Pool
3801 Harris Dr. , Corpus Christi
• (512) 852-0243

This outdoor heated pool in a small city park in the center of the city is open year round. General swim, lap swim and swim leagues are available. Pools are open all day during the summer season; hours are limited during

the off-season. Admission is $2 for adults, $1 for seniors and 50¢ for youths. Season and annual passes also are available.

Corpus Christi Natatorium
3202 Cabaniss Pkwy., Corpus Christi
• (512) 878-2337

The city's only natatorium is a climate-controlled, indoor state-of-the-art facility with two swimming pools. One is an Olympic-size pool and the other a 25-yard instructional aerobic exercise pool. General swim, lap swim, swimming leagues and step and splash aerobics are available. Admission is $2 for adults, $1 for seniors and 50 cents for youth. Season and annual passes also are available.

Tennis

North Bay Area

Rockport Fulton Tennis Center
5102 Texas Hwy. 35 N., Rockport
• (512) 729-2742

This public tennis facility is a combination tennis center and school. The school is a non-profit entity that aims to promote tennis among area youth. It raises money, holds youth tournaments and offers scholarships for those who can't afford to play. The tennis center has six courts (four lighted) and a pro shop and sponsors tournaments and leagues. The center is open from 8 AM to 8 PM every day. Fees are $4 a day, $15 a week or $40 a month. It has women's, mixed doubles, men's and senior leagues.

Corpus Christi

H.E.B. Tennis Center
1520 Shely St., Corpus Christi
• (512) 888-5681, (512) 882-6013

This city-owned facility has 24 outdoor lighted courts and a full-service pro shop. It rents rackets and balls and strings rackets. In-house and citywide leagues are available. Fees are $2.35 per person for 90 minutes. Six-month permits offering unlimited play are available for $31 for juniors and $67 for adults. Annual permits are $55 for juniors and $130 for adults.

Naval Air Station - Corpus Christi is a great place to see a Navy jet up-close.

The center also offers private, semiprivate and group lessons. Civic and corporate tournament rates are $2.50 per court per hour. The whole facility can be rented for $140 for a half-day and $280 for a full day. The center holds about 30 tournaments throughout the year. Hours are 9 AM to 9:30 PM weekdays, 9 AM to 6 PM Saturday and 1 to 6 PM on Sunday.

Al Kruse Municipal Tennis Center
502 King St., Corpus Christi
• **(512) 883-6942**

This city-owned tennis center in South Bluff Park has 10 courts, a full-service pro shop, equipment rental, professional instruction and stringing service. In-house and citywide leagues are available. The cost is $2.35 per person for 90 minutes. A six-month permit is $31 for juniors (18 and younger) and $67 for adults. An annual permit is $52 for juniors and $130 for adults. The center is open every day of the year except Christmas, New Year's Day, Easter and Thanksgiving. It's open from 8:30 AM to 9 PM on weekdays and 8:30 AM to 6:30 PM on weekends.

Volleyball

Port Aransas
to Padre Island

Roberts Point Park
Port Aransas • (512) 749-4148

Volleyball equipment is available for use without charge from the Harbormaster's office next to Roberts Point Park in Port Aransas. This sand volleyball court offers a great view of the Corpus Christi Ship Channel and the Port Aransas Harbor. Expect windy conditions. The park is adjacent to the south ferry landing. When you exit the ferry, look to your left. You can't miss it.

Youth Activities

Recreational activities for youths are not hard to find in the Coastal Bend. Schools, parks and recreation departments, little leagues, churches and youth groups provide a wealth of opportunities for young people. We've accumulated a vast list of groups offering recreational activities for youngsters, but it is by no means all-inclusive.

Many parks and recreation departments offer activities for youths. The Corpus Christi Park & Recreation Department, (512) 880-3480, is particularly active. Activities offered by the city include a baseball league for high school boys (registration is by team only). Also available is a summer youth basketball league for boys and girls entering the 7th grade through grade 12. A fast-pitch softball league for girls between the ages of 8 and 18 requires team registration; the season runs from May through July. A slow-pitch softball league for boys and girls between the ages of 9 and 14 holds games on Saturdays for six to eight weeks beginning in March; call (512) 880-3479 for this league.

Youth Groups

The Coastal Bend has numerous youth groups offering a variety of recreational activities, and we've included many of them in this section.

In the North Bay area, contact Aransas County Youth Support Center, (512) 729-2200, Texas Highway 35 N., Rockport; YMCA of Rockport-Fulton, (512) 790-9622, 644 E. Market Street, Rockport; Aransas Pass Scout Center, (512) 758-7398, 259 S. McCampbell Street, Aransas Pass; and (Portland) Youth Football, (512) 643-1390.

In Corpus Christi, contact Boy Scouts of America, (512) 882-6126, 144 Baldwin Boulevard; Boys & Girls Club of Corpus Christi, (512) 853-2505, 3902 Greenwood Drive; Camp Fire Council of Corpus Christi Area, (512) 887-1601, 1601 N. Chaparral Street; Girl Scouts, (512) 883-3611, 1620 S. Brownlee

INSIDERS' TIP

Pedal-powered surreys can be rented along the Corpus Christi Bayfront. Four people can fit in these four-wheeled, covered vehicles. They're a great way to take in the bayfront.

Boulevard; Nueces County 4-H & Youth Development Program, (512) 767-5220, 710 E. Main Street, Robstown; YMCA, (512) 882-1741, 417 S. Upper Broadway; YMCA Flour Bluff Teen Center, (512) 855-9592, 9801 S. Padre Island Drive; and YWCA, (512) 857-5661, 4601 Corona Drive

In Kingsville, the Boys & Girls Club of Kingsville, (512) 592-2100, 1238 E. Kenedy Avenue, provides activities for youths.

Soccer

The following organizations, all in Corpus Christi, are available for youth soccer: Coastal Bend Youth Soccer Association, (512) 992-8299; Oso Soccer League, (512) 939-7795; Padre Soccer League, (512) 994-7810; and Santa Fe Soccer League, 4401 Little John Drive, (512) 857-8217.

Baseball and Softball

Baseball and softball leagues for children can be found throughout the Texas Coastal Bend. The following is a list of most of the leagues found here.

In the North Bay area, contact the Rockport-Fulton Little League Association, (512) 729-6424; Aransas Pass Little League, (512) 758-5644; Port Aransas Little League, (512) 749-6310, 257 N. Station, Port Aransas; San Patricio Girls Softball Association, (512) 643-5027; and Portland Little League, (512) 643-1390.

In Corpus Christi, contact the Gulf Coast Southside Girls Fast-Pitch League, (512) 857-0740; International Pony League, (512) 855-3100; International Westside Pony League, (512) 855-4050; National Little League, (512) 993-8862; Oil Belt Little League, (512) 241-8854; Oso Pony Baseball Inc., (512) 980-1108; Southside Pony League, (512) 857-5714; Southside Youth Sports Complex, (512) 851-0207; and Universal Little League, (512) 855-4272.

In Kingsville, contact the American Little League, (512) 592-7134; National Little League, (512) 595-1700; and Brush Country Girls Softball, (512) 592-8445, (512) 592-8450.

Sports fans in the Coastal Bend will find plenty to cheer about — everything from windsurfing and hockey to college tennis and high school football.

Spectator Sports

Sports fans are plentiful in the Coastal Bend, but unfortunately the area has few professional sports teams. Still sports fans will find plenty to hold their interest — you can watch and cheer for everything from windsurfers to high school football teams.

Water-based sports, obviously, are going to be as near as the bayfront. You can see windsurfing, sailing and surfing all year round. High school sporting events are also as near as the closest stadium, and with 10 high schools in Corpus Christi alone, you're likely to have plenty of teenage teams to choose from.

College sports are a little more limited. Texas A&M University-Corpus Christi, which became a four-year institution in the fall of 1994, plans to add 14 intercollegiate sports programs beginning in the fall of 1998 and continuing through 2001. First on line will be women's golf and men's and women's tennis. In the fall of 1999, the university will add baseball, softball and men's and women's basketball, and in the fall of 2000, it will add men's and women's cross-country teams and women's volleyball. Men's and women's indoor and outdoor track and field will round out the new programs in the fall of 2001. The teams will participate in the NCAA Division I.

Texas A&M University-Kingsville, about 45 miles from Corpus Christi, does have intercollegiate athletics, and the university's 10 athletic teams draw plenty of spectators from around the Coastal Bend, particularly for the top-ranked Javelinas football games. The Javelinas — also known as the Hoggies — have been ranked one of the nation's best football teams since the program began in 1925. The Javelinas compete in the NCAA Division II Lone Star Conference and have won seven national titles. More than 100 Javelinas have gone on to the professional ranks, including NFL Hall of Famer Gene Upshaw, Darrell Green, James Jefferson, Johnny Bailey, Heath Sherman, John Randle and Earl Dotson. Games are played in the 15,000-seat Javelina Stadium, on the northeast corner of the campus.

At Texas A&M University-Kingsville, you'll also find men's teams competing in baseball, basketball, cross-country and track; women's teams here compete in volleyball, basketball, softball, cross-country and track. The university's Nolan Ryan Baseball Field was completed in 1994 with fund-raising help from its great namesake pitcher, and a new softball facility was finished in 1997.

The good news for sports lovers is the recent advent of a new professional team, the Corpus Christi IceRays hockey team. Season ticket sales for the IceRays' first season in late 1998 were going well, and the Western Professional Hockey League appeared strong.

However, other professional sports ventures have proved unsuccessful, namely the now defunct Barracudas baseball team and the disbanded Sharks basketball team, which didn't last a single season.

Many Coastal Bend sports fans take to the highways to cheer for their favorite out-of-town professional teams in Houston and San Antonio, about 3½ and 2½ hours away, respectively. In Texas, where football is more than a passion for many folks, it's no big deal to travel hours to see a game played by alma mater Texas A&M University in College Station or The University of Texas at Austin. You can also check out the Houston Astros baseball team, the San Antonio Spurs basketball games or even the Dallas Cowboys and Texas Rangers in the Dallas area — as long as you don't mind the drive.

For information about these out-of-town matchups, check the local newspapers' sports sections. Closer to home, here is the lowdown on some of the more popular local and regional teams and how to go about seeing a game or event.

Auto Racing

Crash Carlock Speedway
241 Flato Rd., Corpus Christi
• **(512) 289-8847**

Bring your earplugs and watch stock-car racing every Saturday night between April and August at Crash Carlock Speedway, formerly Corpus Christi Speedway, the self-proclaimed fastest quarter-mile asphalt track in Texas. Gates open at 6 PM, with races starting at 8 PM. General admission tickets are $8 and pit passes are $15. Children 12 and younger get in free with a paying adult.

South Texas Speedway
6701 Old Brownsville Rd., Corpus Christi
• **(512) 814-4100**

South Texas Speedway offers several classes of racing including stock, super stock, modified, dwarf and late model on its quarter-mile banked dirt oval. Racing begins in mid-March and continues through November. Races are held on Saturdays only. Track owners recently acquired sponsorships from major corporations to build one of the largest points funds ever for a dirt short track its size. The $18,500 points fund is to be divided among the points leaders of its five car classes following the 1998 season.

Gates open at 5:30 PM and racing begins at 7:30 PM. Admission is $10 for adults, $3 for children ages 7 to 12 and free for children 6 and younger. Military and seniors receive a $2 discount.

Greyhound Racing

Corpus Christi Greyhound Park
5302 Leopard St., Corpus Christi
• **(512) 289-9333**

This $18 million complex offers year-round parimutuel greyhound racing with 450 race programs — 300 evening and 150 matinee programs, with 13 races per program. Post time is 7:30 PM Tuesday through Saturday. Matinees are 1:30 PM Wednesday, Saturday and Sunday. Odds are available daily at the track. There is also a restaurant here.

Hockey

IceRays
Sunrise Mall (team offices), 5858 S. Padre Island Dr., Corpus Christi
• **(512) 814-PUCK**

Corpus Christi's newest sports team is the IceRays, part of the Western Professional Hockey League, which had its inaugural season in 1996. The league has 14 professional teams in four Southwestern states.

The IceRays inked a five-year contract with a five-year option to play in the city's Memorial Coliseum on Shoreline Boulevard. Head coach is Taylor Hall, a native of Regina, Saskatchewan, who served as head of the New Mexico Scorpions during the 1996-97 hockey season. Hall's playing experience spanned 12 years and included a five-year stint in the National Hockey League with the Vancouver Canucks and the Boston Bruins. He completed his playing career with the Tulsa Oilers of the Central Hockey League as the team's all-time leading scorer, with 269 points, and was first in all-time goals with 124.

The local team will play its first game in October 1998, and the season should last through March. Season tickets are $389 to $589. For more information and sports paraphernalia, check out the team's offices at Sunrise Mall, or call (512) 814-PUCK.

Seasonal bird hunting is a popular pastime along the Coastal Bend.

Rodeo

Both of the following events are held at the J.K. Northway Exposition Center at Dick Kleberg Park, which is on the south edge of Kingsville between the U.S. Highway 77 Business and U.S. Highway 77 Bypass.

George Strait Roping Classic and Concert
J.K. Northway Exposition Center, Kingsville • (512) 592-8516, (800) 333-5032

This annual three-day roping event draws thousands of country-and-western fans to Kingsville to see superstar George Strait roping by day and singing by night. Usually scheduled for June or July, the event features Strait and his relatives in competition with roping teams from across the country. For more information, see our Annual Events and Festivals chapter.

Tuff Hedeman Professional Bull Riders Challenge
J.K. Northway Exposition Center, Kingsville • (512) 592-8516, (800) 333-5032

This professional bull-riding competition began in 1997. The three-day event, held the first weekend in January, attracts professionals from all over the country and is a national final qualifying event. Admission is $10 and $15. For more information, see our Annual Events and Festivals chapter.

Running

Beach-to-Bay Marathon
Corpus Christi • (512) 225-3338

Jogging is seldom considered a spectator sport, but Corpus Christi's annual Beach-to-Bay Marathon may be worth watching. Held on the third Saturday in May (Armed Forces Day), this relay marathon draws thousands of runners from all over the state and nation. Each team of six runners must complete a marathon-length course (26.2 miles), with the six runners each logging approximately 4.4 miles each. For more information see our Annual Events chapter.

Sailing

Every Wednesday evening, sailors converge on Corpus Christi's downtown marina and yacht basin for their weekly escape — the evening sailboat races. You can watch from the yacht basin or the seawall. Corpus Christi Bay is a great place for sailing because it has protected waters and good breezes.

If you want to sail yourself, small sailboats and catamarans are available for rent in season. You can also rent captained boats and bare-boat charters. For a list of rental and charter companies throughout the area, contact the Corpus Christi Business Alliance's convention and visitors department at (512) 881-1888.

You can also learn to sail at the Corpus Christi Sailing Center, on the L-Head, (512) 881-8503. A Saturday and Sunday basic course costs $150, a three-day live-aboard course costs $500, and a five-day, live-aboard course costs $825 (see our Beaches and Watersports chapter).

Tennis

HEB College Team Championships
H.E. Butt Tennis Center, Corpus Christi • (512) 882-6013

Considered the first of its kind in the United States, this college tennis championship tournament has been held here since 1968. There's a waiting list to enter each year, with the nation's top-ranked university teams lined up to attend more than a year in advance.

Of the 11 conferences represented in the

INSIDERS' TIP

One of the state's most fervent rivalries is that between college football teams at The University of Texas at Austin (the Longhorns) and Texas A&M University in College Station (the Aggies).

1998 tournament, most teams were conference champions or runners-up. Participating teams included 1996 champion Southern Alabama, 1997 defending champion Middle Tennessee, Clemson, Tulsa, Virginia Tech, Ball State, Texas Tech, Tulane, University of Washington, Baylor, Minnesota, Colorado, Oklahoma, Southern Methodist and University of Nevada Las Vegas.

The tournament, held annually in March, is free to spectators. All matches are held at the HEB Tennis Center, beginning on Friday and ending with the finals Sunday afternoon.

Windsurfing

Drive along Ocean Drive in Corpus Christi any day of the week and you're likely to see windsurfers toting their boards to the water and braving the bayfront waves. Windsurfing — the sport of riding an enlarged surfboard that's equipped with a sail — is an extremely popular sport here. Oleander Point, at Cole Park in the 2000 block of Ocean Drive, is the most common gathering place.

With its mild climate and consistent winds of 15 to 25 mph blowing across the bayfront, the city has positioned itself to become a windsurfing capital.

U.S. Open Windsurfing Regatta
Oleander Point, Cole Park, Corpus Christi • (512) 985-1555

You may want to check out this colorful regatta held on Memorial Day weekend each year. The four-day event, begun in 1987, attracts some of the nation's best windsurfers as well as plenty of enthusiastic amateurs. Winners can receive up to $70,000 worth of prizes during the weeklong competition. For more information see our Annuals Events and Festivals chapter.

If you have the time and want to see other parts of the Lone Star State, hop in the car and hit the road for one of the destinations listed in this chapter.

Daytrips and Weekend Getaways

The Texas Coastal Bend is two to four hours away from several attractive tourist destinations. So if you have the time and want to see other parts of the Lone Star State, hop in the car and hit the road for one of the destinations listed in this chapter.

We've included popular tourist destinations within a reasonable driving distance. Note that this chapter is entitled "Daytrips and Weekend Getaways," which means that some trips can be completed in a single day while others require a more lengthy commitment of time. Our six destinations are San Antonio, South Padre Island, Goliad, Matagorda Island, Austin, Houston and Laredo. Each write-up contains a brief introduction followed by sections on History, Attractions, Restaurants and Accommodations. The Austin and Laredo write-ups include sections on Nightlife.

San Antonio, home to the beautiful Riverwalk, is the No. 1 tourist destination in Texas. It's also a great place to witness the influence of Mexican and Spanish culture on South Texas. South Padre Island, renowned for its beautiful beaches, is another popular tourist destination, so much so that it's the city's only industry. Goliad is the site of the most fought-over fort in Texas history, while Matagorda Island offers visitors a look at a relatively unspoiled coastal ecology. Austin, the Texas state capital, is one of the fastest-growing cities in the country, while Houston, one of America's largest cities, boasts a varied and sophisticated culture. And, finally, Laredo, on the border across from Nuevo Laredo, Mexico, offers visitors a quick and safe trip to another country.

Enjoy your travels!

San Antonio

A little more than two hours from Corpus Christi, San Antonio offers a glimpse into the state's history as well as its future. This city of more than a million is one of the nation's 10 most populated and is a major tourist destination. The historic Alamo, the graceful Riverwalk, an array of historic Spanish missions, plenty of theme parks and a fleet of museums attract thousands of visitors.

You can drive to San Antonio from the Coastal Bend, taking U.S. Highway 37 N. Or you can travel by air via most major airline carriers.

History

The first settlers here were the Native Americans, who lived along the San Antonio River and called it *Yanaguana*, which means "clear waters." In 1691, a group of Spanish missionaries came upon the river, and since their arrival coincided with the feast day of Saint Anthony, they named the river "San Antonio." The city was actually founded in 1718 with the establishment of Mission San Antonio de Valero — known later as the **Alamo** — where 189 Texas defenders held the old mission against 4,000 Mexican soldiers for 13 days. "Remember the Alamo" became a rallying point for the Texas revolution against Mexico, and the Alamo today is a shrine and museum dedicated to Texas history.

Historical attractions abound here, starting with the downtown area. Check out **La Villita**, one of the original settlements of Spanish soldiers, and the **Spanish Governor's Pal-**

ace, which served as the seat of government when San Antonio was capital of the Spanish Province of Texas. You can also visit the **San Fernando Cathedral**, constructed in 1731, and the **José Antonio Navarro State Historical Park**.

Just northeast of downtown is **Fort Sam Houston**, where military greats like Pershing and Eisenhower served. San Antonio was also a training site for the Buffalo Soldiers, famed African-American cavalry fighters who helped bring peace to the western frontier a century ago. Today Fort Sam Houston is headquarters for the Fifth U.S. Army and the Health Services Command and home to the **Fort Sam Houston Museum** and the **U.S. Army Medical Department Museum**.

www.insiders.com

See this and many other **Insiders' Guide®** destinations online — in their entirety.

Visit us today!

Attractions

The Paseo del Rio, or **Riverwalk**, is a cobblestone and flagstone-covered path that borders both sides of the San Antonio River downtown. It's 20 feet below street level. There are plenty of European-style cafes, specialty boutiques and high-rise hotels along the walk, as well as quiet park areas. The scenic walkway is 2.5 miles long, bordered at the north end by the Municipal Auditorium and Conference center and at the south by the King William Historic District.

For sightseeing from the water, take the **Yanaguana Cruise** barge, (210) 417-4139, down the river. You can also dine aboard open-air, candlelit barges as they wind their way along the scenic waterway. The cruises are available Monday through Sunday, 9 AM until 11 PM. Admission is $4 for adults, $1 for children 5 and younger and $3 for active military and seniors.

The **King William Historic District**, on the south bank of the San Antonio River, is a 25-block area that was zoned as the state's first historic district. This neighborhood, originally settled by prominent German merchants in the 1800s, is still graced by stately mansions. A self-guided walking tour brochure is available from the San Antonio Conversation Society, 107 King William Street, (210) 224-6163.

Guided tours are available from 10 AM until 4:15 PM daily, and tickets are $2 for adults and free for children younger than 12.

Visitors should be sure to journey to the **San Antonio Missions National Historical Park**, (210) 932-1001, an 819-acre park that retraces the historic Mission Trail. Included in the park are four Spanish Colonial missions — Mission Concepcion, Mission San José, Mission San Juan and Mission Espada — as well as the Rancho de las Cabras in Floresville, the historic ranch site that supplied livestock for the missions. The chain of missions established along the San Antonio River in the 18th century are reminders of one of Spain's most successful attempts to extend its New World dominion northward from Mexico. They were the greatest concentration of Catholic missions in North America. The missions are open daily from 9 AM until 5 PM, except for Thanksgiving, Christmas and New Year's Day. Admission is free, but donations are accepted.

Don't forget the most famous of all the missions, Mission San Antonio de Valero, or the **Alamo**. After losing San Antonio to the Texans during the siege of Bexar, Mexico's General Santa Anna decided to retake this key location and at the same time impress upon the Texans the futility of further resistance to Mexican rule. When Santa Anna's army arrived in San Antonio in February 1836, some 145 Texans took refuge in the mission under joint command of William B. Travis and Jim Bowie. Over a two-week period, Mexican forces increased to 2,000, while a few Texans managed to enter the Alamo grounds and brought the number of defenders to 189.

Finally, the Mexican army stormed the fortress on the morning of March 6, 1836, and killed all the Texan defenders, sparing only a few noncombatants including Susanna Dickenson, wife of one of the Texans, her baby and a servant of Travis. To reinforce his goal of terrorizing Texan colonists, Santa Anna released this group to spread the word about what had happened. Losses in the battle were placed at 189 Texans to 1,600 Mexicans. In spring and summer, the Alamo is open Monday through Saturday 9 AM to 6:30 PM Sunday from 10 AM until 6:30 PM. It closes at 5:30 PM during the fall and winter months. Admission is free, but donations are accepted.

Also on Alamo Plaza are three popular stops for visitors. The popular **Cowboy Museum**, (210) 229-1257, charges $3 admission for adults and $2 for children. The **Plaza Theatre of Wax** and **Ripley's Believe It or Not!**, (210) 224-9299, can provide hours of entertainment. Admission to the Plaza Theatre of Wax is $7.95 for adults and $4.95 for children, while admission to Ripley's is $8.95 for adults and $4.95 for children. You can also get a combination ticket to visit both that costs $11.95 for adults and $7.95 for children.

For family activities, head to the **San Antonio Zoo**, (210) 734-7183, in Brackenridge Park, a 433-acre refuge in the city's center. The zoo is ranked as one of the nation's best, with more than 3,000 animals in its collection. Admission is $6 for adults and $4 for children ages 3 to 11. Nearby is the **Witte Museum**, (210) 357-1900, which contains exhibits that explore Texas history and science. Admission is $5.95 for adults and $3.95 for children ages 4 to 11.

Be sure to take the kids for a ride on the **Brackenridge Eagle Miniature Train**, (210) 736-9534, and check out the carousel, skyride and Kiddie Park. The train ride is $2.25 for adults and $1.75 for children.

San Antonio is also home to two major theme parks, **Sea World of Texas**, (210) 523-3611, and **Six Flags Fiesta, Texas**, (210) 697-5050. Sea World is the world's largest marine life park. Days and hours of operation vary by season. Admission is $29.95 for adults, $19.95 for children ages 3 to 11 and $26.95 for senior citizens. Six Flags is made up of four themed areas, including the Mexican town of Los Festivales, the German village of Spassburg, the 1920 cowboy boom town of Crackaxle Canyon and the small Texas town of Rockville during the golden age of rock 'n' roll. It's open in the spring and summer, but the days and hours vary by season. Admission is $31 for adults, $21.50 for children and senior citizens.

On a cultural note, be sure to plan a visit to the **McNay Art Museum**, (210) 824-5368, which is set in a Mediterranean-style mansion and has wide-ranging collections (admission is free). Also see the **San Antonio Museum of Art**, (210) 978-8100, housed in the castle-like former headquarters of the Lone Star Brewery. This museum is noted for its antiquities collections, Mexican folk art, modern art, pre-Colombian art and Spanish colonial art. Admission is $4 for adults, $1.75 for children and $2 for senior citizens. Admission is free on Tuesdays.

You may also want to check out the action with the **San Antonio Spurs** basketball team, (210) 554-7787, the **San Antonio Dragons** hockey team, (210) 737-7825, and the **San Antonio Missions** minor league baseball team, (210) 675-7275.

Shopping

San Antonio is also a good place to do some serious shopping. There are a number of major malls, including the beautiful **Rivercenter Mall** in the middle of downtown. The largest department stores here are Dillard's and Foley's, while other stores include The Limited, Gap, Victoria's Secret, Banana Republic, Express, Gymboree, Bath and Body Works, the Disney Store, Project Earth, Godiva Chocolatier, Latin Gold Cigar Company, Sports Fantasy and Brentano's bookstore.

If you want a more colorful shopping experience, be sure to hit **El Mercado**, (210) 207-8600, 514 W. Commerce St., a Mexican-style market area downtown. Billed as the largest Mexican marketplace outside of Mexico, the area is bustling with shops selling such items as leather goods, blankets, clothing, jewelry, pottery and other curiosities. Nearby is the **Farmers Market Plaza**, which features food, cafes and a stage for weekend entertainment.

Restaurants

You won't go hungry in this city, which has a number of notable restaurants and offers Mexican, German, French, Chinese and American cuisine. The following are just a few of our favorites. All prices listed below are the average cost of a dinner for two, excluding drinks, appetizers, desserts, tax and tip.

The Barn Door, (210) 824-0116, 8400 N. New Braunfels Avenue, offers real Texas-style steaks in a rustic atmosphere. You can also get quail, pork chops, catfish or flounder. Dinner for two is about $40.

Biga Restaurant, (210) 225-0722, 206 E. Locust Street, is an elegant restaurant that serves Southwestern and Mediterranean cuisine in a renovated century-old mansion. Seasonal specialties include items such as antelope, pheasant, seared sea bass and grilled oysters, as well as exotic breads and pastries. It's open for dinner Monday through Saturday. A dinner for two costs $40 to $60.

Casa Rio, (210) 225-6718, 430 Commerce Street, serves Tex-Mex dishes on the Riverwalk. It also offers dining on floating barges along the river. It's open daily. A dinner for two is less than $20.

Earl Abel's, (210) 822-3358, 4200 Broadway Street at Hildebrand Avenue, is an old-fashioned eatery that serves great chicken-fried steak, fried chicken, burgers and steaks — as well as fabulous homemade desserts such as lemon chess pie, maple pecan pie and chocolate layer cake. It's open daily. A dinner for two costs about $20.

Drive out to the **Grey Moss Inn**, (210) 695-8301, 19010 Scenic Loop Road, for a romantic evening. About 45 minutes from downtown, this restaurant has an outdoor patio and more than 500 wines. The specialties are mesquite-grilled seafood, steaks, lamb chops and chicken. Reservations are taken for seating from 5 to 10 PM. Dinner for two is about $50.

La Fogata, (210) 340-1337, 2427 Vance Jackson Road, may be the city's most popular Mexican restaurant. You can dine in the courtyard or inside on delectable Mexican entrees, including a tasty chicken in mole sauce. It's open daily and can be crowded on the weekends, when reservations are recommended. Dinner for two costs about $35.

For a fun after-hours dining experience, try **Mi Tierra Café and Bakery**, (210) 225-1262, 218 Produce Row. This is practically a late-night institution, with its colorful atmosphere and wide-ranging menu. Open 24 hours daily, this restaurant has been serving up Mexican specialties and mariachi music since 1941. Two can dine here for less than $20, and don't forget to pick up some pan dulce or sugary pralines on your way out.

Paesano's Classic Italian restaurant, (210) 227-2782, 111 W. Crockett Street, has traditional Italian specialties served in an old-World ambiance. Especially good are the veal dishes, snapper and an excellent shrimp Paesano. There are two locations: one on the Riverwalk and another on the city's north side, at 555 E. Basse Road. Dinner for two is about $35.

Also downtown is **Schilo's German Delicatessen**, (210) 223-6692, 424 E. Commerce Street. Authentic, old-style German decor and fare are hallmarks of this longtime delicatessen. We recommend the hearty split-pea soup, homemade root beer, Reuben sandwiches and cheesecake. It's open Monday through Saturday. Two can easily dine here for $20.

Accommodations

San Antonio has a wide array of hotels, bed and breakfast inns and motels, offering accommodations that can fit into any traveler's budget. A complete listing of the city's hotels is available from the **San Antonio Convention and Visitors Bureau**, (800) 447-3372. Here are a few of the city's most famous and prestigious hotels, as well as several less pricey establishments.

The **Menger Hotel**, (210) 223-4361, 204 Alamo Plaza, offers history and luxury to visitors. Opened in 1859 by W.A. Menger, it offered 19th-century visitors a taste of history and elegance and enjoyed visits from some of the era's most prominent people. O. Henry favored the hotel and included it in several of his works. General Robert E. Lee rode his horse, Traveller, into the lobby. General Ulysses S. Grant tipped a few at the Menger Bar. President Dwight D. Eisenhower enjoyed strolling the gardens. It was the San Antonio home of Sarah Bernhardt, Judge Roy Bean's Lilly Langtry and movie vamp Mae West.

Today the Menger Hotel is a National Historic Landmark, and it even offers Victorian-style lodging rooms that are available by special request. More modern amenities include in-house movies, room service, valet parking, a spa and the downtown's largest heated swimming pool. A double room costs $132 per night.

Another hotel that offers a taste of history is the **Crockett Hotel**, (210) 225-6500, 320

Mission Concepcion and other missions are popular stops for tourists in San Antonio.

Bonham Road, near Alamo Plaza. This elegant hotel, which has 206 guest rooms, has a historic flavor, from its frosted-glass lobby paneling to the adobe-colored atrium. A double room costs $149 per night.

Or try **La Mansion del Rio**, which overlooks the historic Riverwalk. Built in 1852 as a private boys school, La Mansion has 337 luxury guest rooms, many with balconies and views of the San Antonio River. A double room costs $220 to $290 per night.

The **Radisson/Market Square**, (210) 224-7155, 502 W. Durango Street, has 250 guest rooms, a swimming pool and a health center. A double room is $125.

The **Days Inn Alamo Riverwalk**, (210) 227-6233, 902 E. Houston Street, has 50 guest rooms and is near many of the city's downtown attractions. A double room costs $74 to $94 per night.

Near the downtown convention center is one of the city's 10 La Quinta hotels, **La Quinta**

Convention Center, (210) 222-9181, 1001 E. Commerce Street. It has 190 hotel rooms, and a swimming pool. A double room costs $109 per night.

South Padre Island

A 34-mile stretch of beach just a half-hour's drive from Mexico, this community is home to about 2,000 residents and nearly 2.5 million annual visitors. To get there, take Texas Highway 77 south, then take Texas Highway 100 through Port Isabel and over the Queen Isabella Causeway bridge to South Padre Island. It takes about 3½ hours to drive here from Corpus Christi — and you'd better stick to the speed limits, because the small towns along the route strictly enforce them. You can also fly into **Harlingen's Valley International Airport**, 45 minutes away, or **Brownsville/ South Padre Island International Airport**, 25 minutes away.

History

According to legend, Caribbean pirates first discovered Padre Island nearly 500 years ago. As they searched for ports to pillage, they were thwarted at the tip of Texas: The coastline that confronted them was actually a 100-mile-long barrier sand dune created by nature to protect the Texas coastline from erosion, wind, storm and sea. Officially claimed by the Spaniards in 1519, it was named Isla Blanca, or White Island. In the 1800s, the first settlement on the island was named after its founder, Padre José Nicolas Balli.

South Padre Island is a much younger entity, created in 1964 when the Port Mansfield Channel divided Padre Island into two parts, creating a more convenient passage for ships and barges into the Intracoastal Waterway. The move also created a tropical island retreat that had a few hundred permanent residents by 1973 and self-government. Because it was separated from the rest of the big island, this community established its own identity as a coastal resort town focused on fun in the sun. Many residents are transplanted Northerners who came south searching for warmth and stayed to establish businesses, captivated by the Tex-Mex lifestyle and ambiance.

The town itself is totally focused on tourism — that's literally the only industry here. And with 5,000 hotel and condo units, more than 300 varieties of birds and an abundance of fish in the Gulf of Mexico and the Laguna Madre bay, South Padre Island has plenty to offer tourists. City officials play their welcoming role to the hilt. They recently declared neckties illegal on the island. The penalty for wearing a tie is a written notice and a free South Padre Island T-shirt.

The climate is subtropical, with an average high of 82 in the summer and a low of 65 in the winter, plus an average of 27.6 inches of rainfall each year.

More importantly when planning your trip, remember that South Padre Island is a hugely popular destination for college students on spring break. An estimated 130,000 students were expected in March 1998, bringing with them headliner bands, games, beachside events, basketball and volleyball tournaments, surfing, sumo wrestling, partying and more. This small community swells at the seams during this rowdy time of year, and if you're looking for a quiet vacation, you might want to select a different time to visit.

Attractions

Fishing is a major draw here, with 800-pound marlins in the Gulf of Mexico. The Laguna Madre bay is filled with speckled trout, redfish and flounder. Check out fishing guides and charter boats to get the best fishing information and guidance. For information call the **South Padre Island Convention and Visitors Bureau**, (956) 761-6433 or (800) SO-PADRE.

Surfing on South Padre Island is considered the best on the Texas coast. Fall through spring is the best time of year for the biggest waves, while summer offers smaller waves that are good for newcomers. Surfboard sales, rentals and lessons are available at Isla Blanca Park and at a variety of shops along Padre Boulevard.

Windsurfing is increasingly popular here, with plenty of rentals and lessons available at local shops. You can also rent sailboats, personal watercraft, paddleboats and bumper boats. Bicycling, pedal-powered buggy rides, miniature golf, shuffleboard, horseback riding and sandcastle building are among other recreational opportunities.

Golfers have plenty of courses from which to choose. Several are in Brownsville, about 25 minutes from South Padre Island, while others are in Harlingen, about 45 minutes away. Among courses open to the public is the newly opened **South Padre Island Golf Club**, (956) 943-5678, in Laguna Vista about 20 minutes from South Padre Island. It has an 18-hole, par 72 championship course. In Brownsville, golf courses open to the public are the **Brownsville Golf and Recreation Center**, (956) 541-2582; **Fort Brown Municipal Golf Course**, (956) 541-0394; and the **Riverbend Golf Course**, (956) 548-0191.

Peek into the **Coastal Studies Laboratory**, (956) 761-2644, at the southern end of the island in Isla Blanca Park. This laboratory, operated by the University of Texas-Pan American, features aquariums of fish and native marine life, as well as a vast shell collection. It's open Sunday through Friday afternoons and admission is free.

Camping, picnic pavilions, jetty fishing and RV hookups are available at **Isla Blanca Park**, (956) 761-5493. The day-use fee is $3 per vehicle.

Laguna Atascosa National Wildlife Refuge, (956) 748-3608, 25 miles northwest of South Padre Island, is a 45,000-acre refuge filled with birds, nature trails and wildlife. Tour roads, including a 15-mile bayside drive, are accessible from sunrise to sunset. Admission is $2 per vehicle.

The **Port Isabel Lighthouse**, on the mainland near the foot of the Queen Isabella Causeway, offers a panoramic view of the Laguna Madre. The 1853-era lighthouse is open 10 to 11:30 AM and 1 to 5 PM daily.

You should also visit the **Port Isabel Historical Museum**, (956) 943-7602, in one of the area's oldest structures which is famous for its fish murals. The two-story museum contains interactive exhibits that teach about the area's colorful past, including archaeological findings of coins that date back to before 1810 and both the Mexican and Civil wars. Admission is $3 for adults, $1 for students and $2 for senior citizens. It's open Wednesday through Sunday.

Sea Turtle Inc., (956) 761-1720, 5805 Gulf Boulevard, a sea turtle conservation group, offers educational shows featuring endangered sea turtles cared for by organization members. Shows are at 10 AM Tuesday and Saturday, and with a requested donation of $2 for adults and $1 for children.

See a live shark up close and personal at the **South Padre Island Aquarium**, (956) 761-7067, 105 W. Marlin Street. The aquarium lets you look at the marine life through 42-inch portholes, and you can even go underwater with a shark in a shark cage, if you want.

Internationally known environmental artist Wyland painted his 53rd Whaling Wall — the only one in Texas — on the exterior of the South Padre Island Convention Centre, 7355 Padre Boulevard. The wall features whales frolicking in an undersea environment. Wyland intends to paint 100 such walls to educate people about marine conservation.

Restaurants

In addition to a vast array of fast-food eateries, the island offers several options for fine dining. Many restaurants specialize in fresh seafood, while others offer Mexican fare. Here is a listing of some of the most popular restaurants in town. All prices listed below reflect the average cost of a lunch or dinner for two, excluding drinks, appetizers, desserts, tax and tip.

Amberjack's Bayside Bar & Grill, (956) 761-6500, 209 W. Amberjack Street, serves seafood, steaks, pasta, hamburgers and sandwiches in a casual setting. The Rasta-style shrimp is a house specialty, featuring shrimp in a tasty cream-of-coconut and curry sauce. It's open daily for lunch and dinner during the season, and closed on Mondays during the winter months. A dinner for two costs about $25.

Blackbeard's, (956) 761-2962, 103 E. Saturn Street, serves seafood, burgers and steaks in a pirate-themed, casual setting. It's open daily. Two can dine here for about $25.

Browse among the Harley-Davidson accessories and funky clothing while you're waiting for your food at **Blue Rays Diner**, (956) 761-7297, 410 Padre Boulevard. The restaurant is open for lunch and dinner and specializes in burgers and other diner-style fare. Dinner for two costs about $20.

For a bayside buffet, check out **Louie's Backyard**, (956) 761-6406, 2305 Laguna Boulevard. This is a popular summertime stop for many visitors and residents, who swear by Louie's seafood and prime rib. It's closed in the winter. The average cost of a buffet dinner for two is $35.

You can get premium hand-crafted beer at the **Padre Island Brewing Company**, (956) 761-9585, 3400 Padre Boulevard. The kitchen serves pizza, sandwiches, seafood and burgers. It's open for lunch Tuesday through Sunday and dinner every day. A dinner for two costs about $25.

Try the **Palmetto Inn**, (956) 761-4325, 1817 Padre Boulevard, for Mexican specials and seafood. The Carrasco family has been serving up steaks and nightly specials, such as fresh red snapper and fajitas, since 1956. This is the oldest restaurant on the island, and it's open daily. Two can dine here for less than $20.

Kids love to watch the electric train travel around the front room at **Rovan's Restaurant and Bakery**, (956) 761-6972, 5300 Padre Boulevard. This longtime restaurant is known for homestyle breakfasts, baked goods and mesquite-pit barbecue. A breakfast for two costs about $10; dinner for two is about $15.

For elegant bayside dining, try **Scampi's Restaurant and Bar**, (956) 761-1755, 206 W. Aires Street. You can get seafood, pasta and prime steaks at this upscale restaurant, which offers an extensive wine list. It's open for dinner only, and a meal for two costs about $32.

Accommodations

There are more than 5,000 hotel, motel and condo units in South Padre Island, and it would be impossible to list them all here. However, a comprehensive list is available from the local chamber of commerce, (956) 761-6433 or (800) SO-PADRE. Bear in mind that room prices vary with the season: Hotels will be cheapest here between the off-season fall and winter months. In addition, many hotels require damage deposits and key deposits, particularly during spring break, when thousands of college students converge on this town.

Bahía Mar Resort, (800) 99-PADRE, 6300 Padre Boulevard, is a 15-acre resort with a 12-story hotel, condominiums and meeting rooms. It's also the official hotel for contestants in the Miss Texas USA Pageant. You can walk down to the beach, play tennis, lounge by either of two large pools and eat in the Bahía Breeze Restaurant. The nightly rate for a standard room with two queen beds is $75 to $135, depending on what time of year you visit.

Many national hotel chains offer accommodations here: The **Holiday Inn Sunspree Resort**, (956) 761-5401 or (800) 531-7405, 100 Padre Boulevard; **Radisson Resort**, (956) 761-6511 or (800) 333-3333, 500 Padre Boulevard; **Sheraton Fiesta Beach Resort**, (956) 761-4913 or (956) 761-6551 or (800) 222-4010, 310 Padre Boulevard; **Best Western Fiesta Isles**, (800) 528-1234, 5701 Padre Boulevard; **Days Inn South Padre Island**, (956) 761-7831 or (800) 329-7466, 3913 Padre Boulevard; and **Ramada Limited**, (956) 761-4097 or (800) 2-RAMADA, 4109 Padre Boulevard.

Goliad

Head over to the town of Goliad and the **Goliad State Historical Park**, (512) 645-3405, for a look at one of the most fascinating and bloody chapters in Texas history. The **Presidio La Bahía**, designated a National Historic Landmark, is considered the world's finest example of a Spanish frontier fort. It is also the most fought-over fort in Texas history, having been a participant in six national revolutions and wars for independence.

To get to Goliad from Corpus Christi, take U.S. Highway 77 north, then take Texas Highway 183 N. to Goliad. Driving time is about 1 ½ hours. The park has wheeled camper sites with electricity, water and sewage facilities; primitive camping sites; and screened shelters. There are also toilets, showers, a playground, picnic sites along the San Antonio River and a restored museum/interpretive center, the **Mission Espíritu Santo**.

Goliad, with a population of 2,026, has several fast-food restaurants and about a dozen cafes and restaurants. Many campers like to bring their own food and cook outdoors.

History

Strategically situated on an elevation overlooking the surrounding area, this site was established by the Spanish, who arrived in 1749. They found evidence of an Indian village they named Santa Dorotea. The Spanish settlers founded the town around the protection of the fort, renaming it La Bahía, (The Bay).

This town was the original Goliad. Its name was changed in 1829 as an anagram for Hidalgo, in honor of the patriot priest of the Mexican Revolution, Father Miguel Hidalgo, who sounded the famous "Grito de Delores"

Photo: Austin Chamber of Commerce

The majestic pink granite capitol building is Austin's centerpiece.

in 1810 for Mexican Independence from Spain. Goliad became the second-largest populated settlement in Spanish Texas.

In 1721, the Royal Presidio La Bahía was established in response to encroachment by the French. Built on the banks of the Garcitas Creek, the fort was later moved inland near Mission Valley, and in 1749, relocated to its present position.

The Royal Presidio La Bahía became the only fort responsible for the defense of the coastal area and eastern province of Texas. Soldiers from Presidio La Bahía assisted the Spanish army fighting the British along the Gulf Coast during the American Revolution. This action gives Goliad the distinction of being one of the only communities west of the Mississippi River to have participated in the American Revolution.

It's also considered the birthplace of the Texas Revolution. On October 9, 1835, a group of Texas citizens attacked the Mexican garri-son stationed at the presidio and seized the fort. This action followed the incident at Gonzales, Texas, one week earlier. It was at the presidio that the first Declaration of Texas Independence was drawn up on December 20, 1835, signed by 92 citizens and distributed throughout Texas. Along with it flew the first flag of Texas independence. Nothing short of full independence from Mexico would satisfy those who had suffered under the injustices of a dictatorial government led by the self-styled "Napoleon of the West," General Antonio Lopez de Santa Anna.

The darkest day in Texas history, the Goliad Massacre, took place here on Palm Sunday, March 27, 1836, when Col. James Walker Fannin and 341 men under his command were executed a week after their capture at the Battle of Coleto, under Santa Anna's orders. There was twice as much loss of life here at Goliad than at the Alamo.

Nothing had touched the raw nerve of the

American character as the news of the large numbers of men who were slaughtered in one execution. As grim details reached the United States, volunteers streamed forth for Texas. This one single event, the Goliad Massacre, more than any event in the Texas Revolution, proved to the people of the United States what manner of warfare confronted the Texans.

Attractions

The Presidio La Bahía (Fort of the Bay) is the oldest fort in the western United States and the only Texas Revolution site that has retained its original 1836 appearance. Nine flags have flown over the presidio, and it was the site of the saddest chapter in Texas history, the massacre of Fannin's troops — the single largest loss of life during the war for Texas' independence.

The presidio was restored in the 1960s to stand as a memorial for Texans, along with its sister shrines, the Alamo and San Jacinto. Local artisans supplied the labor for the project, and the noted restoration architect, Raiford L. Stripling, directed the project to its completion. It is today considered one of the most authentic restoration projects in the United States. The presidio compound is a self-sustaining private institution operated under the administration of the Diocese of Victoria Catholic Church. Tax deductible contributions are accepted and can be given through the fund-raising campaign, "Friends of the Fort." The fort is open daily, and admission is $3 for adults and $1 for children. To arrange guided tours for large groups or schools, call (512) 645-3752.

Visit the **Our Lady of Loreto Chapel**, the oldest building in the old fort compound, which has been in continuous use since the 1700s. Although the presidio is a fort, not a mission, a chapel was erected inside the quadrangle for the sole use of the soldiers and Spanish settlers living in the town of La Bahía surrounding the fort. The religious needs of the Indian tribes were served by the missions of Rosario, Espirtu Santo and Refugio.

One of the oldest churches in America, it is also one of the only buildings in existence to retain its groin-vaulted ceiling. The striking fresco at the back of the altar was created in 1946 by the "Michelangelo of South Texas,"

Corpus Christi artist Antonio Garcia. In the niche above the chapel entrance is the statue of Our Lady of Loreto made by Lincoln Borglum, of Mount Rushmore fame.

This centuries-old chapel was where Fannin's men were held for part of their captivity before they were massacred. The First Declaration of Texas Independence was signed inside the chapel on December 20, 1835.

Another attraction is the **Mission Espíritu Santo**, which was founded in 1722 near Matagorda Bay to serve the Karankawa Indians and their allies. The Indians abandoned the mission in 1724, however, and two years later the missionaries moved to Mission Valley near modern Victoria, in the territory of the Aranama and Tamique Indians.

In 1749 the mission was relocated to its present site on the San Antonio River near modern Goliad. Mission Espíritu Santo was granted jurisdiction over all land between the Guadalupe and San Antonio as far north as Capote Hills near modern Gonzales. On this land grazed the mission's cattle herds, which soon grew to approximately 40,000 head. The first large cattle ranch in Texas, Mission Espíritu Santo supplied its own needs and those of Spanish colonial settlements as far away as Louisiana. Destruction and theft by civilians and hostile Indians eventually depleted the herds.

Espíritu Santo served as a mission for 110 years, longer than any other Spanish colonial mission in Texas.

Yet another mission nearby is **Mission Nuestra Señora del Rosario**. This one was founded in 1754 by Franciscan missionaries from Mexico in an attempt to settle the Karankawa Indians. The Rosario ruins are about 4 miles west of Goliad State Historical Park headquarters and 6 miles west of the city of Goliad off U.S. Highway 59. In 1776 the superior of Franciscan missions in Texas, Father José De Solis, reported of Mission Rosario: "As far as the temporal goods are concerned, it is in a flourishing condition. It possesses two droves of asses, forty tame horses, thirty tame mules, twelve teams of oxen, five thousand head of cattle, two hundred milk cows, and seven hundred sheep."

This temporal success, which was only momentary, did not guarantee spiritual success.

When secularization of Texas missions was ordered in 1794, missions Espíritu Santo and Rosario were permitted to continue because their Indians had not yet adapted to civilized life. The missionaries feared that they would return to nomadic life, fears that were well-grounded. Later, the Indians deserted the mission, and its lands were distributed to colonists.

General Ignacio Zaragoza's birthplace, across from the presidio, is another stopping point during your visit to this state historical park. Zaragoza was born at this site in 1829 and lived in the area as a child. Educated in Mexico, he joined the Mexican army and worked his way to the rank of general. At the Battle of Pueblo, Mexico, on May 5, 1862, Gen. Zaragoza's outnumbered forces defeated a French army of intervention. To commemorate the event, May 5 — or *Cinco de Mayo* — became a Mexican national holiday and is celebrated each year in Goliad.

Also at the park, you can take a nature trail that heads from the mission buildings and picnic grounds and traverses typical South Texas brushland, or chaparral. The brushland contrasts sharply with the woodlands of the San Antonio River floodplain. Bird life along the trail is especially varied due to proximity of diverse habitats and to the mild regional climate.

You'll find the ruins of an old quarry, thought to date to the early mission period, in the park. Stone from the quarry was used in construction of the mission church, granary, priests' quarters, workshop, the exterior compound wall and other structures. Other buildings of wood and adobe also once existed inside the compound wall. A brick kiln, which can be seen from the nature trail, was built in the late 1930s during reconstruction of the mission. Near it is an older kiln, probably used for making lime for mortar of for firing bricks and tiles.

The workshop is a reconstruction of a previous structure. Here, under supervision of the missionaries, the Indians learned cattle-raising, farming, spinning and weaving, carpentry and blacksmithing.

In the granary, a display of Indian and Spanish colonial artifacts and interpretive exhibits is of special interest. In addition, slide and film presentations on the history of the area after the Spanish period, together with artifact exhibits, can be seen in the park headquarters.

Once you've finished with the park, be sure to head into the town itself for another dose of historical attractions. The **county courthouse** in Goliad is listed on the National Register of Historic Places. The Second Empire Style-style courthouse, designed by noted Texas architect Alfred Giles, was completed in 1894. Limestone used in the construction was hauled from Austin by oxcart. Restored and enlarged in 1964, the courthouse is also a Recorded Texas Historic Landmark.

Other 19th- and 20th-century buildings, many of which are in the National Registry, can be seen downtown as well. The **Market House Museum**, which was designated a State Archaeological Landmark in May 1981, was built by the city in the early 1870s. It contained stalls, which were rented to farmers for the sale of meat and produce. Firehouse hook and ladders were added in the 1880s. Today it is a museum and houses the Goliad County Chamber of Commerce.

On the north courthouse lawn is the **Hanging Tree**, an oak tree that served as the site of court sessions between 1846 and 1870 and is now a Recorded Texas Historic Landmark. Death sentences pronounced by the court were carried out immediately with a rope and a strong limb. During the 1857 Cart War, in which Texan freighters perpetrated a series of vicious attacks against Mexican cart drivers along the Indianola-Goliad-San Antonio Road, this site witnessed a number of unauthorized lynchings before the conflict was ended by Texas Rangers. Approximately 70 men lost their lives during the conflict, some of them on this tree.

Accommodations

Goliad State Park, (512) 645-3405, is open all year with facilities for picnicking, hiking, tent and trailer camping, and both history and nature study. The campsites range from primitive to those with water, sewer and electrical connections. Restrooms are in picnic and camping areas; showers are included in the camping area restroom.

Screened shelters with electricity, water, tables and cooking grills are available. Fishing and boating are permitted in the San Antonio River. A playground and 2 miles of hiking trail provide further activities. You can get entrance and camping permits from park headquarters. The park entrance fee is $2 per person 12 and older; children younger than 12 get in free.

For overnight stays, the cost is $12 a night for RV hookups. Screened shelters are $18 per night. Other nightly fees include those for trailer sites, including water and electricity, $10; water-only sites, $8; and primitive sites, $4. A group dining area with a complete kitchen, a grill, microwave, refrigerator, picnic tables and a large fireplace rents for $65 a day.

If you want lodging in an 18th-century Spanish colonial fort, try staying at **The Quarters**, within Presidio La Bahía, (512) 645-3752. The price is $150, and the fort accommodates up to four people. It has a fully equipped kitchen, bathroom with shower, master bedroom with queen bed, a second bedroom with twin beds and a living-dining area with a table, chairs and a couch.

You can also stay at the **Goliad Inn Motel**, (512) 645-3251, 105 S. Jefferson. A room for two people costs $38 per night.

Matagorda Island

One of the wildest sites maintained by the state of Texas is the **Matagorda Island State Park and Wildlife Management Area**, (512) 983-2215, 16th Street and Intercoastal Canal in Port O'Connor. Separated from the mainland by San Antonio and Espíritu Santo bays, Matagorda Island is one of the barrier islands that borders the Gulf of Mexico. It also protects the mainland from the great tides and strong wave action of the open Gulf.

With Gulf beaches, uplands and tidal marshes, the island serves as home to more than a dozen species of endangered and threatened wildlife. There is no daily user fee, and the facilities are open year round.

To get to Port O'Connor from Corpus Christi, take U.S. Highway 181 north to Texas Highway 35 and continue north to Texas Highway 185, then head east through Seadrift to Port O'Connor.

The island is accessible only by boat and has no telephone, electricity, food concession or drinking water. The state ferry from Port O'Connor runs Thursday through Sunday and costs $10 for adults, $5 for children under 12. Camping is $4 per night for four people. Visitors must bring an ample personal water supply.

Although the southern tip of this Gulf of Mexico barrier island is privately owned, the remainder — about 51,000 acres — is state and federal land administered by the Texas Parks and Wildlife Department. The island's primary management goal is preservation and conservation, with emphasis on endangered and threatened species. Within the wildlife management area, a 36,568-acre area offers limited recreational use such as nature study, birding and fishing. Supervised hunts are held here, and fishing is permitted under state regulation. All of the activities can be restricted or prohibited if state authorities decide they are endangering the species.

In the park area, there are 2 miles of beach open to year-round picnicking, fishing, hiking, beach combing, nature study, swimming and primitive camping. All access to the island is by chartered or private boat. Pit toilets and an outdoor shower are also available. However, visitors are warned that shade is limited and you should bring sun or shade protection, as well as insect repellent.

For several years, beginning in 1942, a portion of Matagorda Island was used for practice bombing by the U.S. Air Force. Now, as a state park, the 7,325-acre area has largely returned to its natural state as a haven for migratory waterfowl and deer. The park is seven miles south of Port O'Connor, separated from the mainland by Espirito Santo and San Antonio bays.

Attractions

Wildlife is abundant here, and visitors can glimpse 19 species that are on state or federal endangered lists, including the whooping crane, brown pelican, piping plover, peregrine falcon, eskimo curlew and the Kemp's ridley sea turtle.

More than 300 species of migratory and resident waterfowl, shorebirds, songbirds, raptors and other birds which inhabit the island at various times throughout the year. Every spring and fall, the area serves as a critical stopover site for numerous migrating birds. Matagorda Island is also an important wintering home for many avian species, including the whooping crane.

Alligators also reside here, as do 19 species of snakes, including the western diamondback rattlesnake. The island's marshes provide habitat and nourishment for shrimp, oysters, crabs and a wide variety of sportfish. Bottle-nosed dolphins frolic in the Gulf.

There's plenty to do on Matagorda Island in addition to observing nature. Historical sites range from an 1852 lighthouse to an abandoned air base. Human habitation here goes back to the time of the Karankawa Indians, whose height, giant bows and mosquito repellent — a coating of alligator grease and dirt — impressed European settlers.

Eighty miles of beach, roadway and mowed paths are available for hiking and biking. Surfing, swimming and beach combing are all popular. Bicycles and surfboards can be brought over on the state ferry.

Anglers come for a wide variety of sportfish, including redfish, trout, flounder and whiting.

The island has two campgrounds. A 2-mile stretch of Gulf beach open for primitive camping is served by a shuttle vehicle making the 3.5-mile connection to the boat dock. The cost of being ferried in this truck by the park rangers is included in the state ferry fee you already paid to get to the island. At the boat dock is the **Army Hole Campground**, equipped with pit toilets, a cold-water shower and other amenities. There are also a 14-bed group barracks and a smaller overflow barracks. The campground is open Fridays and Saturdays only, and an overnight stay costs $12 per person. To make reservations call (512) 983-2215.

Austin

Austin is a 3½-hour drive from Corpus Christi via interstate highways. You'll begin on Interstate 37 to San Antonio where you'll connect with Interstate 35, which will take you to Austin. Traffic from Corpus Christi to San Antonio is generally light. You'll find highways in San Antonio more congested but manageable.

However, once you reach the northern outskirts of San Antonio you'll find the going a bit slower. Traffic between San Antonio and Austin has doubled in the past decade, making it the most congested and accident-prone section of Interstate Highway 35 between Mexico and Canada.

An alternative route you might want to consider is more scenic and takes you through several small towns. Driving time is about the same, but you won't get as bored or frustrated. To get there take U.S. Highway 181 across the Harbor Bridge. Stay on U.S. 181 as you head northwest, passing through Sinton, Beeville, Kenedy and, finally, Karnes City. At Karnes City take Texas Highway 123 north through Stockdale and Sequin until you connect with IH-35 in San Marcos. From there, follow IH-35 until you reach Austin.

Austin, the capital of Texas, is home to the University of Texas at Austin, a thriving technology industry and one of the best live music scenes in the country. The city recently surpassed Seattle as the 22nd-largest city in the nation, with a population of 540,000, and, by the end of 1998, census figures project Austin's population will outstrip those of Boston and Washington, D.C.

As the state capital, Austin has always had more than its share of government employees and buildings. The most prominent structure is the Texas Capitol Building, which opened in 1888 and is designed after the U.S. Capitol. It's in the center of Austin just north of downtown. A few blocks north of the capitol is the University of Texas at Austin, one of the largest universities in the nation with an enrollment of more than 48,000. Its 357-acre campus is home to the Lyndon Baines Johnson Library and Museum, the Harry Ransom Humanities Research Center and the Archer M. Huntington Art Gallery. See Attractions, below, for tour details of these sites.

Austin calls itself the "Live Music Capital of the World," and although that may be a stretch, it's fair to say that few cities can match it for

---

INSIDERS' TIP

Taxis in Nuevo Laredo should be approached with caution: They are not metered, and fares can get expensive. Make sure you and the driver agree on a price before you get in a cab.

the quality and quantity of music. Janis Joplin earned her stripes in Austin clubs before hitting it big. So did Willie Nelson and the late blues-rock guitarist Stevie Ray Vaughan.

Austin is home to Dell Computer Corporation, maker of personal computers, and founder and chairman Michael Dell, who at $4 billion and growing is the wealthiest person in Texas, surpassing Ross Perot. More than 900 software companies occupy Austin and its suburbs — the largest concentration of microchip plants outside California's Silicon Valley.

Despite the city's booming growth, it's still a great place to enjoy the outdoors. The Colorado River (known as Town Lake inside the city) weaves its way through Austin on its way to the Gulf of Mexico, and the Texas Hill Country provides a lush backdrop on the city's west side. From atop Mount Bonnell (a large hill overlooking the Colorado River) you can see the UT campus, the Texas Capitol, downtown, Lake Austin and the Texas Hill Country. Take a scenic drive on Loop 360 and enjoy the view or head out on Farm-to-Market Road 2244 (also known as Bee Cave Road) or Farm-to-Market Road 2222 and enjoy the Lake Austin scenery. Better yet, take a short drive (or walk if you're staying nearby) to Town Lake, where you can walk or ride a bike along the 11.5-mile hike-and-bike trail.

Attractions

Austin has its share of fun things to do and see. Start with a tour of the **Texas Capitol Building**, (512) 478-0098 or (800) 926-2282, at the northern end of Congress Avenue and downtown Austin. It was built in the 1880s out of pink granite from a quarry in nearby Marble Falls. An $81 million restoration project completed in 1995 returned the building to much of its original state. Free daily tours of the 26-acre complex and its grounds are available. And as long as you're in the area why not tour the nearby **Governor's Mansion**, (512) 463-5518, 1010 Colorado Street, home of the state's highest officeholder since 1856.

Barton Springs Pool, (512) 476-9044, 2200 Barton Springs Road, is a great place to cool off in the summer. This 1,000-foot-long, spring-fed pool is a constant 68 degrees year round. It's an ideal spot to catch some rays,

bodywatch and marvel at nature's handiwork (we're talking about the pool here) without straying far from the big city. Admission on weekdays is $2.50 for adults, 75¢ for youths ages 12 to 17 and 50¢ for children younger than 12. Weekend admission is $2.75 for adults, youths and children. You'll be charged a $2 parking fee on weekends if you park near the north gate. Parking adjacent to the south gate is free.

The **Town Lake Greenbelt** serves as a meeting place for runners, walkers and cyclists. This 11.5-mile hike-and-bike trail circles a portion of Town Lake. You can rent a mountain bike at the **Bicycle Sport Shop**, (512) 477-3472, 1426 Toomey Road (Lamar Boulevard at Riverside Drive). A hiking and biking guide is available from Austin Parks and Recreation, (512) 499-6700, 200 S. Lamar Boulevard.

The **Lyndon Baines Johnson Library and Museum**, (512) 916-5136, 2313 Red River Street on the UT campus, houses more than 36 million personal and official documents and historical and cultural exhibits pertaining to the former president. The library and museum chronicle Johnson's rise from obscurity to the American presidency.

Shopping

For an interesting culinary shopping experience try **Central Market**, (512) 206-1000, 4001 N. Lamar Boulevard, a warehouse-sized grocery store specializing in health and exotic foods. While you're there, walk a few paces over to the **Clarkesville Pottery** store, in the same shopping center, and take a look at the selection of plates, glasses, jewelry and pottery. Prices tend to be high here, but you can still find earrings for less than $20.

And, finally, nothing sums up the Austin experience more than a visit to the corner of N. Lamar Boulevard and Sixth Street. Here you'll find a **Whole Foods Market**, (512) 476-1206, a popular natural food grocery store chain, and the **Book People Bookstore**, (512) 476-1206. Book People, a locally owned store, has managed to capture the small-bookstore feel and place it inside one of the largest bookstores in Texas. Inside you'll find thousands of books and magazines, comfortable antique chairs for sitting and reading, gift items like

Photo: San Antonio Convention and Visitors Bureau

San Antonio's riverwalk is the hub for shopping, dining and nightlife in the Alamo City.

candles and jewelry, CDs and a coffee shop. Give yourself plenty of time.

You could easily spend an entire day here.

Restaurants

Austin has a good mix of restaurants for a town of its size.

For good Italian food try **Mezzaluna**, (512) 472-6770, 310 Colorado Street, in the downtown area, where dinner for two averages around $50.

Those wanting to sample the local Tex-Mex cuisine will want to visit **Matt's El Rancho**, (512) 462-9333, 2613 S. Lamar Boulevard. Matt's has been in business since 1952, serving what it claims is the "best Mexican food and Margaritas in the world." Dinner for two ranges from $15 to $25.

If Thai jungle salsa and spicy peanut sauce are more to your liking, try **Satay**, (512) 467-6731, 3202 W. Anderson Lane, where you'll find more than 100 dishes from Singapore, Indonesia, Cambodia, Laos, Vietnam and the Philippines. Dinner for two averages around $20 to $30.

If you're looking for hot chili and rustic atmosphere, duck into the **Texas Chili Parlor**, (512) 472-2828, 1409 Lavaca Street, not far from the Texas Capitol. Here you'll find great burgers, cold beer and some of the best chili around, with a choice from mild to very hot. Dinner for two is $20 or less.

Nightlife

Austin isn't short on nightlife, either. Downtown's E. Sixth Street is the city's center for live music venues, dance clubs, restaurants, bars and lounges that tend to appeal to a younger (read: college) crowd. You'll find plenty to do there every night, and if you like crowds you'll love Sixth Street on the weekend. While you're there, check out **Esther's Follies**, (512) 320-0553, 525 E. Sixth Street, for a lighthearted spoof of local, Texas and national events.

Antone's, (512) 320-8424, 215 W. Fifth Street, is a legendary Austin blues club, booking well-known blues musicians from around the country. **La Zona Rosa**, (512) 472-9075, 612 W. Fourth Street, is known for booking big-name acts into its fairly small venue, attracting a variety of artists from Sarah Hickman to David Byrne. The music varies quite a bit here, including rock, blues, country, modern folk and conjunto.

The **Warehouse District** west of Congress Avenue and south of Sixth Street has in recent years become a hot spot for nighttime fun, featuring clubs, bars and upscale restaurants that appeal to an older, professional crowd. **Speakeasy**, (512) 476-8017, 412 Congress Avenue, is a sophisticated jazz lounge featuring the best in local jazz musicians. At Speakeasy you'll find people dressed to the nines, smoking cigars and drinking martinis.

Accommodations

Austin has a wealth of accommodations to meet just about any budget. And because Austin is still fairly small, no matter where you stay you're not far from the city's main attractions. Austin has the usual chains as well as a few locally owned lodgings and several bed and breakfasts. Prices listed are for two adults.

For first-class accommodations try the **Driskill Hotel**, (512) 474-5911, 604 Brazos Street, in downtown. Cattle baron and businessman Jesse Driskill built the hotel in 1886 for the then-lofty sum of $400,000. Politicos and other VIPs have made the Driskill their home away from home ever since. Room prices range from $155 to $185 a night.

For more economical accommodations try **The Habitat Suites**, (512) 467-6000 or (800) 535-4663, 500 Highland Mall Boulevard, where you'll find a family atmosphere for families on a budget. The Habitat Suites has 96 suites with kitchens, a breakfast buffet and happy hour every afternoon. Room prices range from $85 to $107.

Homegate Studios & Suites on Town Lake, (512) 326-0100, 1001 IH-35, offers efficiencies and suites at even lower prices. Close to downtown and Town Lake, Homegate offers 143 efficiencies, six suites and eight disabled-equipped rooms. Room prices range from $69 to $79.

The **Miller-Crockett House**, (512) 441-1600, 112 Academy Drive, is a bed-and-breakfast two blocks from downtown Austin. It offers three large rooms with private baths and balconies, two corporate bungalows and spectacular views of the Austin skyline. Room prices range from $99 to $129 per night.

Want to stay in a funky old hotel where touring musicians like to hang out? Then try the **Austin Motel**, (512) 441-1157, 1220 S. Congress Avenue, south of the Congress Avenue Bridge. You'll discover interesting shops and restaurants all along this section of Congress Avenue. Inside the hotel restaurant you'll often find runners recuperating from their trek around the Town Lake hike-and-bike trail. Room prices range from $46 to $99 per night.

Houston

Driving to Houston from Corpus Christi takes about three hours depending on how fast you drive (the speed limit is 70 now in many areas) and whether you run into heavy traffic as you near the nation's fourth-largest city. To get there take U.S. Highway 181 across the Harbor Bridge and veer to the west through Taft and Sinton. In Sinton take a right on U.S. Highway 77, which will take you through Refugio to the outskirts of Victoria. There you'll connect with Loop 175, which will take you to U.S. Highway 59. Follow U.S. 59 until you reach Houston.

Houston has several major highways running through and around it. U.S. 59 (known as the Southwest Freeway in Houston) will take you into the heart of the city, inside Loop 610. Downtown Houston and many of the city's major attractions are inside the loop.

Houston is twice the size of Rhode Island and home to more than 4.1 million people of more than 100 nationalities. This international flavor has led more than 60 nations to set up consular offices in this city whose residents speak more than 90 languages.

Houston also is home to headquarters for America's manned spaceflight effort (Space Center Houston), the world's largest medical center (The Texas Medical Center), the world's richest rodeo (the Houston Livestock Show and Rodeo) and the international energy industry. Museums, art galleries, the symphony and the Theatre District add a touch of class to this rough-and-tumble oiltown. Houston is one of only a few cities to have permanent theater, opera, symphony and ballet compa-

nies. You'll also find hundreds of city parks, more than 8,000 restaurants, the Houston Zoological Gardens, the Astrodome and Six Flags Astroworld and WaterWorld among the attractions. Houston's downtown area is booming with about $1 billion in renovation and new construction projects designed to make the area an attractive entertainment and residential district.

Attractions

To help you narrow your list of things to see and do in the city, here are some of our favorites.

The **Museum of Fine Arts, Houston**, (713) 639-7300 or (713) 639-7379 (Spanish), 1001 Bissonnet, houses the largest art collection in the Southwest. Permanent exhibits include Renaissance, impressionist and post-World War II American art. Admission is $3 for adults, $1.50 for seniors 65 and older and children ages 6 to 18 and free for children younger than 6. Admission is free on Thursday.

Learn about manned space flight at **Space Center Houston**, (281) 244-2105 or (800) 972-0369, 1601 NASA Road 1. Activities include tours of NASA's Johnson Space Center, interactive exhibits, IMAX films and live demonstrations exploring the past, present and future of manned space flight. While you're there you can land the space shuttle, cruise the surface of the moon or touch a moon rock. Admission is $12.95 for adults, $8.95 for children ages 4 to 11 and free for children younger than 4.

Experience Chinese culture, history and landmarks at **Forbidden Gardens**, (281) 347-8000, 23500 Franz Road in Katy. Forbidden Gardens is an outdoor museum with 40 acres of lakeside walks and miniaturized exhibits of the Great Wall of China and the Forbidden City. Admission is $10 for adults, $5 for children ages 6 to 18 and free for children younger than 6.

The **Houston Museum of Natural Science**, (713) 639-4600 or (713) 639-4603 (Spanish), One Hermann Circle Drive, houses a museum, planetarium, IMAX Theater and three-level butterfly tropical rain forest. The nation's fourth most visited museum is near Hermann Park. Admission to the museum is $3.50 for adults, $2 for children ages 3 to 11 and free for children younger than 3. Admission to the planetarium is $3 for adults, $2 for seniors and free to children ages 3 to 11. Admission to the IMAX Theater is $6 for adults, $3.50 for seniors and children ages 3 to 11 and free to children younger than 3. Admission to the butterfly rain forest is $3.50 for adults, $2.50 for seniors and children ages 3 to 11 and free to children younger than 3.

Moody Gardens, (409) 744-4673 or (800) 582-4673, One Hope Boulevard in Galveston, offers visitors a variety of experiences ranging from a tropical rain forest to a ride on a paddlewheel boat. Build sandcastles on a white-sand beach, experience a jolting adventure in the IMAX Ridefilm Theater or watch butterflies hatch in the Butterfly Hatching Hut. Admission is $6 per person per attraction.

Now more than 30 years old, the **Astrodome**, the world's first domed stadium, is still worth a visit. Its history is outlined in a high-tech video as part of a tour of the dome. The Astrodome, (713) 799-9595, 8400 Kirby Drive and Loop 610 S., was once dubbed the "eighth wonder of the world." Tours are given at 11 AM and 1 PM Tuesday through Saturday. Admission is $4 for adults, $3 for seniors 65 and older and children ages 4 to 11 and free to children younger than 4. You must be part of a tour to go inside. Parking is $5.

Six Flags Houston AstroWorld and WaterWorld, (713) 799-8404, is next to the Astrodome. The more than 100 rides and attractions and 15 acres of water rides are among the reasons it's the most visited amusement park in the Southwest. It features the most roller coasters and rides of any theme park in Texas. It also has shows and water rides, including the Edge, an 83-foot slide, a wave-pool, beach and rushing stream. A recent addition is the Dungeon Drop, a 23-story free-fall at 60 miles per hour. Admission to Six Flags Houston AstroWorld is $34.59 for people 48 inches and taller and $22.68 for anyone less than 48 inches tall. Admission to WaterWorld is $18.35 for

people 48 inches and taller and $15.10 for anyone less than 48 inches tall. A two-day pass to both attractions is $40 for people 48 inches and taller and $34 for people less than 48 inches tall.

Shopping

You would be hard-pressed to find a city anywhere with more shopping opportunities than Houston. Shoppers have more than 30 malls to choose from. The place to start is the Post Oak-Galleria area, at Westheimer Road and Post Oak Boulevard.

The Galleria, 5075 Westheimer Road, has more than 300 stores and restaurants offering mostly upscale merchandise. Stores include Lord & Taylor, Macy's, Neiman Marcus and Saks Fifth Avenue. Other amenities include an ice skating rink and two hotels.

Across the street from the Galleria is the **Centre at Post Oak**, featuring such stores as FAO Schwarz, Barnes & Noble Booksellers and Old Navy.

The Montrose area west of downtown offers shoppers more offbeat choices, while the immense **Antique Center**, (713) 688-4211, off Loop 610, is a don't-miss destination for antique lovers.

Bargain hunters need not fear: Houston has something for you, too. Reduced prices on clothing and other merchandise are available at several area outlets: the **Conroe Outlet Center**, 45 miles north on IH-45; **The Strand Outlet Shops**, (409) 765-7199, on Galveston Island; and the **Sealy Outlet Center**, (409) 885-3200, west on IH-10.

And because Texas is known for its cowboys, no trip to the Lone Star State would be complete without a trip to a western-wear store. **Cavender's Boot City**, (713) 952-7102, 9525-B Westheimer Road, and **Stelzig's of Texas Western Store**, (713) 629-7779, 3123 Post Oak Boulevard, will have the duds needed to turn you into a real live cowpoke.

INSIDERS' TIP

To get tickets for the Houston Ballet, Houston Grand Opera, Houston Symphony and Society for the Performing Arts, call (713) 227-ARTS or (800) 828-ARTS.

Restaurants

Houston has more than 8,000 restaurants offering every sort of food imaginable. We've chosen several established restaurants with good reputations to meet a variety of budgets.

Brennan's, (713) 522-9711, 3300 Smith Street, combines Louisiana Cajun with Texas-style cooking to produce spicy and creative dishes. Try the mesquite-grilled veal chop, complimentary pralines and Ramos gin fizz and milk punch. Jacket is required. Dinner for two excluding drinks is $60 to $80.

Houston's rich and powerful can often be found at **Tony's**, (713) 622-6778, 1801 Post Oak Boulevard. Don't miss out on Tony's wonderful desserts. Jacket and tie are required. Dinner for two excluding drinks is $80 and up.

Butera's, (713) 523-0722, 4621 Montrose Boulevard, is an open-air cafe offering patrons traditional deli food along with a few unusual items. Dinner for two is $40 or less.

D'Amico's Italian Market Cave, (713) 526-3400, 510 Morningside Street, is a combination deli and specialty store offering great food at low prices. Don't miss the fish of the day and the crab claws. Dinner for two is $40 or less.

Ninfa's, (713) 228-1175, 2704 Navigation Boulevard, is the original restaurant in what has become a successful chain of Mexican-food restaurants. Ninfa Laurenzo, the restaurant's founder, now owns several restaurants, but the original is still considered the best. Dinner for two is $40 or less.

Take an hour-long drive from downtown Houston to **Gaido's of Galveston**, (409) 762-9625, 3800 Seawall Boulevard in Galveston. Galveston is on an island with the same name 50 miles southeast of Houston. To get there take IH-45. Gaido's has been in business since 1911 and continues to pack customers into its cavernous dining room. Take in the ocean view as you dine on Gulf seafood. Dinner for two will run you $40 to $60.

At **Brenner's**, (713) 465-2901, 10911 Katy Freeway, you can enjoy a great view of the garden and pond while dining on steaks and other offerings. Try the homemade salad dressings. Order wine and you'll get a trip to the wine cellar to select your choice. Dinner for two costs $60 to $80.

Nightlife

For the greatest number of entertainment options in the smallest area, you'll want to try the Richmond Avenue entertainment district, which runs from the 5600 block to the 6500 block of Richmond Avenue, west of Loop 610. This dining and entertainment district offers food, dancing and live entertainment at some of Houston's most popular nightspots. Restaurants in this area range from casual to elegant, the food from steaks to Lebanese cuisine.

Club-hopping along Richmond Avenue will expose you to the range of musical genres, everything from rock 'n' roll to blues to country. Shopping and accommodations are here, too. And while you're in the area, pop into **Dave and Buster's**, (713) 952-2233, 6010 Richmond Avenue. Here you'll find 50,000 square feet of billiards, shuffleboard, bowling, play-for-fun blackjack, golf, Skeeball and a midway filled with more electronic games than you've ever seen in one place. For more information on the Richmond Avenue area, call the Richmond Avenue Merchants Association at (713) 974-4686.

Accommodations

Houston has more than 38,000 hotel/motel rooms to offer. Choosing from among the many fine hotels isn't easy. The major hotel and motel chains are represented here — Comfort Inn, Hilton, Days Inn, Holiday Inn, Omni, Hyatt and others — as well as a number of locally owned lodgings. Following are a few we think you'll like. Remember to add a 15 percent hotel/motel tax to all prices.

Shoppers will enjoy our first listing, which is really two hotels in one. The **Westin Galleria & Westin Oaks Hotels**, (713) 960-8100 or (800) 228-3000, 5060 West Alabama, are in the renowned Galleria shopping center. The Westin Galleria has 485 rooms; the Westin Oaks, 406. All rooms have private balconies; penthouse suites are available. Room prices are around $205 a night.

Sheraton Astrodome Hotel, (713) 748-3221 or (800) 552-0942, 8686 Kirby Drive, is across the street from the Astrodome. It's also close to the Texas Medical Center, Hermann

Park (where the zoo and other attractions are located) and the Museum District. This nine-story building and three additional buildings hold 631 rooms, including 44 suites. Room prices range from $90 to $165 a night.

The **Houstonian Hotel, Club & Spa**, (713) 680-2626 or (800) 231-2759, 111 N. Post Oak Lane, is Houston's only member of Preferred Hotels & Resorts Worldwide. Nestled amid 18 wooded acres in the Galleria area, the Houstonian provides seclusion from big-city stress yet is near shopping and restaurants. Room prices range from $199 to $239 a night.

The 12-story white-marble **Wyndham Warwick Hotel**, (713) 526-1991 or (800) 996-3426, 5701 Main Street, was built in 1926, and, although fully updated, still retains its earlier charm. This 308-room hotel is next to the Museum of Fine Arts and Natural Science Museum. Rooms range from $165 to $185 a night.

Homestead Village, (713) 797-0000, 7979 Fannin Street, offers an apartment-like setting for people planning to stay a night, a week or longer. Rooms come with a fully equipped kitchen and free local calls. Laundry facilities are on the premises. Homestead Village is across the street from the Astrodome. Room prices are $50 to $75 a night or around $219 weekly.

Laredo

Laredo is really two cities: Laredo on the U.S. side of the Río Grande and Nuevo Laredo on the Mexico side. Los dos Laredos (the two Laredos), as they call themselves, work closely to promote international trade and tourism. Three international bridges link the two cities, providing access to tourists and business people alike. Laredo feels larger than its population warrants because of international trade and the large Mexican population across the border. Laredo's population in 1996 stood at 166,000, while the population of Nuevo Laredo was 575,000.

Laredo is a 2½-hour drive from Corpus Christi via two-lane highway through South Texas brush country. To get there take N. Padre Island Drive (Texas Highway 358) to Texas Highway 44 W. Stay on Texas 44 through Robstown, Agua Dulce, Alice and Freer. When you get to Freer, Texas 44 joins with U.S. High-

way 59, which takes you through 65 miles of desolate cactus and brush country to the border town of Laredo. It's sister city — Nuevo Laredo, Mexico — lies across the Río Grande.

You'll quickly understand why the town of Freer adopted the rattlesnake as its school mascot: The brush and cacti that cover the area are the perfect habitat for the venomous rattler. When you reach Laredo stay on U.S. 59, which becomes Saunders Street inside the city limits, until you reach IH-35.

You'll know you're near the border when you hear all the horn honking. Laredo and Nuevo Laredo residents seem to find lots of reasons to lean on their horns, a practice most Texans frown on. Maybe it's the narrow streets in both downtowns that lead so many drivers to vent. Whatever the reason, don't take it personally. You may find that the traffic in Laredo moves at a snail's pace in certain areas and at certain times of the day. You should also remember that the best times to visit weatherwise are in the winter and spring when temperatures are bearable.

Laredo is one of the oldest cities in the United States and the oldest independent city in Texas. Today it is one of the fastest growing cities in the nation. The North American Free Trade Agreement and cross-border production sharing (known as *maquiladoras*) have spurred Laredo's growth. A maquiladora uses inexpensive Mexican labor to assemble items that are then returned to the country of origin, where they are sold or exported. More than 100 are in the Nuevo Laredo area. They've contributed to making Laredo the nation's largest commercial inland port, handling 35 percent of all U.S. exports into Mexico. At the southern end of IH-35, it marks the entrance to the Panamerican Highway, which extends through Central and South America. It's also the distribution point for 190 maquiladoras in neighboring Mexican states.

Laredo is part Texan, part Mexican, with a large, bilingual Hispanic population that speaks English as a second language. Tourists flock to the two Laredos from both sides of the border. U.S. citizens are drawn to Nuevo Laredo to find bargains on furniture, artwork, liquor, jewelry, prescription drugs, silver and Mexican curios. Mexicans cross into Laredo to buy electronics, perfume and clothes at rates

Photo: South Padre Island Convention and Visitors Center

The 2.6-mile Queen Isabella Causeway links South Padre Island to the mainland.

20 percent to 30 percent below normal, and to shop at the upscale **Mall del Norte**, where they can buy items unavailable in Mexico.

The downtowns of the two cities are connected by a pedestrian bridge (International Bridge No. 1) at the south end of Convent Street. U.S. citizens can visit within a 26-mile area inside Mexico for as long as 72 hours with no paperwork. You must carry proof of U.S. citizenship such as a birth certificate or a drivers' license.

International Bridge No. 2 is a few blocks to the east at the end of Interstate 35. A third bridge is on the far west side of Laredo and is used mostly by trucks carrying cargo across the border. Both downtown bridges are open to vehicular traffic, and both collect a toll each way. Tolls are $1.35 on the U.S. side and $1.60 on the Mexico side, or $2.95 for a round trip. If you're planning to drive across the border, it's a good idea to buy Mexico insurance from a company in Laredo.

To walk across from Laredo, park in the free public lot below International Bridge No. 1 on Salinas Avenue and Water Street. Pedestrians pay 35¢ to enter Nuevo Laredo and another 35¢ to return to Laredo. The bridge connects Convent Street with Avenida Vicente Guerrero on the Nuevo Laredo side. This is the city's main tourist attraction with shops along either side.

These days it's not necessary to change your money into pesos. Most Nuevo Laredo retailers accept U.S. currency, and many post prices in dollars. Credit cards and travelers checks are widely accepted. Most merchants speak English, and many will haggle with you over prices. Each visitor to Mexico can bring back as much as $400 worth of duty-free (tax-free) retail items for personal use every 30 days. The next $1,000 is taxed at a flat rate of 10 percent. You can bring into the United States one carton of cigarettes and one quart or liter of alcohol per adult every 30 days. IRS tax and a federal duty will be collected on quantities over the one duty-free quart. Some prescription drugs may be purchased in Mexico (often at much lower prices) and brought into the United States, provided you have a valid U.S. doctor's prescription for a reasonable amount.

Calling into and out of Mexico requires the use of certain access numbers. When calling from Mexico to Laredo, dial 95-956 and then the Laredo number. Local calls within Nuevo Laredo from public phones require Mexican pesos or a phone card that can be purchased at pharmacies. To call Nuevo Laredo from the United States you must dial international code 011, country code 52, city code 87 and then the Nuevo Laredo number. Each city has a different code. The Laredo area code is 956.

Attractions

Of course there's more to do in Laredo than shop, eat and drink (although some people do nothing else). It should come as no surprise that the Spanish influence extends to other areas as well.

Been to a bullfight lately? Then cross the border to Nuevo Laredo for an old-fashioned *corrida* (bullfight). Traditional bullfights in which the bull is killed are held at the **Plaza de Toros Lauro Luis Longoria**, (52) (87) 12-71-92, (52) (87) 12-71-93 or (888) 240-8460. Toreadores (bullfighters) from throughout Mexico and Spain appear here. Ticket prices range from $3 to $17 depending on the view and whether you sit in the sun or the shade.

If you're in Laredo between mid-March and late July or early August take in a baseball game featuring the only binational sports franchise in the world. The **Tecolotes de los dos Laredos** (the Owls of the two Laredos), (956) 795-2350, is a Mexican League AAA baseball team that plays half its home games in Laredo and the other half in Nuevo Laredo.

Laredo prides itself on having lived under seven flags during its history: Spain, Mexico, Texas, the Republic of the Río Grande, the Confederacy, the United States and France. Laredo served as the capital of The Republic of the Río Grande when Federalist leaders proclaimed independence from Santa Anna's Centralist Mexican government. The republic lasted a mere 283 days, but Laredoans have commemorated the moment with the **Republic of the Río Grande Museum**, (956) 727-3480, 1005 Zaragoza Street. Admission is $1 for all ages.

To learn more about Laredo's history take the **Heritage Trolley Tour**, (956) 727-0977, from 9 AM to 11 AM on Tuesday, Thursday or Saturday. Tickets are $8 for adults and $4 for children younger than 12, students with valid ID and guests in wheelchairs. A turn-of-the-century trolley will pick you up at the Río Grande Museum and take you on a two-hour tour of the 242-year-old city's historic district.

Shopping

Laredo is home to two shopping malls: **Mall del Norte**, the ninth-largest in Texas, is an upscale mall that caters to Americans and well-to-do Mexicans, and **Riverdrive Mall**, near the border. You'll find many of the usual chains — Dillard's, The Gap, Victoria's Secret — represented at Mall del Norte, on Interstate 35 north of U.S. Highway 59. Shoppers looking for bargains should head to Riverdrive Mall near the border where you'll find chains like JCPenney, Bealls and lower-end stores.

Ueta Inc., (956) 722-4684, 1208 Zaragoza Street, is one of several duty-free stores in Laredo that sell everything from DKNY sunglasses and brand-name perfumes to Swiss Army Watches and Cross pens. Liquor and cigarettes are also available at reduced prices. One caveat: Items sold in duty-free stores are intended for export and are not to be returned to the country of purchase.

In Nuevo Laredo, shopping opportunities are plentiful. Vendors ply their wares along busy streets, and children offer everything from necklaces to gum.

Among those shopping experiences you won't want to miss are **El Mercado**, a two-story outdoor market on Avenida Vicente Guerrero, four blocks from International Bridge No. 1. You'll find all sorts of Mexican art and curios in these small, jam-packed shops, which open up on a courtyard. Here you'll find everything from gaudy sombreros and fake designer watches to authentic Mexican artwork and Tiffany-style lamps.

Be sure to visit **Marti's**, 12-33-37, Calle Victoria 2923. Marti's is known locally as the Neiman Marcus of the border, and its selection and prices bear that out. This three-floor shop carries everything from designer clothing and jewelry to furniture and home decorations.

Another shop to check out is **Rafael**, Avenida Vicente Guerrero at Sonora Street. You can tell this is a great place by the fact that it's so hard to find. Owner Rafael Costilla hasn't bothered to put up a sign advertising his store nor installed a business phone. That's because his reputation is so great people find him anyway. Inside you'll find lanterns, hand-blown glass, carved masks and metal furniture stacked to the rafters. You'll also find a plentiful supply of doors made from weathered mesquite, punched-tin lamp shades and hand-forged metal drawer pulls.

Restaurants

When it comes to dining out, Mexican food is the specialty on both sides of the border, but you'll also find many popular chain restaurants such as Tony Roma's, Pelican's Wharf and Tokyo Gardens. Restaurants serve everything from Tex-Mex (a form of Mexican food eaten by Mexican immigrants living in Texas) to offerings from Mexico's interior.

Victoria's 3020, 13-30-20, at the corner of Victoria and Matamoros streets in Nuevo Laredo, offers a good representation of food from throughout Mexico. The glass-walled restaurant overlooking a lush, Spanish-style courtyard is a hotspot for food, drinks and socializing 2½ blocks from the border. Dinner for two, including appetizers, dessert and coffee, ranges from $25 to $50.

Laredo Bar and Grill, (956) 717-0090, 102 Del Court, serves steaks, chicken, seafood, burgers, salads and other American food in a quiet dining atmosphere. The food is prepared and presented well. Dinner for two, including appetizers, dessert and coffee, costs around $35.

Toño's Bar & Grill, (956) 717-4999, 120 W. Del Mar Boulevard, combines dishes native to Mexico with original recipes concocted by Toño himself. The menu includes typical Mexican foods — enchiladas, tacos — as well as more exotic meats such as pheasant and dove.

For nightlife try **Señor Frog's**, 13-30-31, 351 Ocampo Street, Nuevo Laredo. Señor Frog's can best be described as Mexico's version of The Hard Rock Cafe, with trendy videos playing on screens throughout the restaurant/bar. The restaurant portion is open throughout the week. The bar is open Thursday through Saturday, attracting a younger crowd.

El Dorado, 12-00-15, Beldon and Ocampo streets, Nuevo Laredo, has been in business since 1922, operating until recently as the Cadillac Bar. The restaurant portion of this restaurant/bar offers interesting specialties like frog legs, quail, cabrito (goat) and traditional Mexican food. El Dorado's bar claims to make the best Margaritas in the world and touts its "famous Ramos Gin Fizz."

On the U.S. side try **Guapos Sports Cafe**,

(956) 791-5918, 107 Calle Del Norte. Guapos serves food and drinks at its popular restaurant and bar. It has music, a live deejay and several TV monitors tuned to sports programs.

Accommodations

Laredo has a variety of accommodations available, most within a few minutes drive of the border. Remember that a 14 percent hotel/motel tax will be added to the rates quoted.

La Posada Hotel/Suites, (956) 722-1701 or (800) 444-2099, 1000 Zaragoza Street, is the most renowned hotel in the area. The 208-room Spanish-style building overlooks the Río Grande River and downtown Nuevo Laredo, one block from International Bridge No. 1. The former 19th-century Spanish-Colonial convent offers a tropical courtyard, swimming pool, fitness center and free airport transportation. Nightly rates range from $99 for a standard room to $169 a night for a deluxe suite.

The **Red Roof Inn**, (956) 712-0733 or (800) 843-7663, 1006 West Calton Road, is one of the most recent additions to the city's accommodations offerings. Rooms are comfortable if unspectacular and offered at a reasonable price. Amenities include a swimming pool, lighted work area and sitting area. This 150-room hotel is a short drive from the border and Mall del Norte. Prices range from $39 to $50.

The **Best Western Fiesta Inn**, (956) 723-3603 or (800) 460-1176, 5240 San Bernardo Street, is 2.5 miles from the border and across Interstate 35 from the Mall del Norte. Amenities at this 151-room motel include a free continental breakfast, swimming pool, courtesy van, lounge and meeting rooms. Weekend rates range from $49 to $55.

As the name suggests, **Family Gardens Inn**, (956) 723-5300 or (800) 292-4053, 5830 San Bernardo Street, caters to families with decent, moderately priced rooms, a general store in the lobby and free hot dogs, nachos, popcorn, lemonade and beer in the evenings. Some rooms come with a living room and small kitchen. This 193-room hotel offers a swimming pool, playground, courtesy van and meeting rooms. It's a two-minute drive from Mall del Norte and a five-minute drive from the border. Room prices are around $55 a night.

The military's arrival changed the complexion of the community, transforming it almost overnight from a rural outpost to a major city.

The Military

Evidence of the Coastal Bend's close ties with the military is as near as the skies and seas, where you'll find a multitude of aircraft and ships used by our armed forces.

Residents and visitors become accustomed to seeing the distinctive orange-and-white training aircraft overhead. The sounds, too, are different from that of commercial aircraft — you'll likely hear the drone of propeller-driven planes used by beginning student aviators at Naval Air Station Corpus Christi and the deeper roar of training jets flown by advanced students at Naval Air Station Kingsville.

Boaters and fishers may encounter some of the more than two-dozen mine warfare ships stationed here. The mine warfare ships are ported at Naval Station Ingleside, across the bay from Corpus Christi, as part of the Navy's recently established mine-warfare headquarters here.

And with the Corpus Christi Army Depot (the Army's largest helicopter repair and maintenance facility) here, you're also likely to see several different types of helicopters. The Depot, as it is called, is one of South Texas' largest industrial employers, with 2,772 civilian employees. Its steady workforce and good wages have been credited with establishing a Hispanic middle class in this region.

As the chamber of commerce puts it, "South Texas is Navy country." That sentiment was never more heartfelt as when city leaders and state politicians battled successfully to retain their military presence in the light of recent Defense Department downsizing. After three rounds of base closures, the Coastal Bend lost one air-training base but gained a mine-warfare center and strengthened its missions at several existing bases.

Some credit the Coastal Bend's long-standing loyalty to the armed forces, particularly the Navy, with helping to preserve its military presence through the decades. The rela-

tionship has certainly benefited both the community and the military — the military's arrival helped foster development and growth of the Coastal Bend, particularly Corpus Christi. The Coastal Bend itself, with its unique geographic and meteorological assets, has aided the Navy's task of training student pilots.

The roots of this relationship can be traced back more than half a century. In 1938, as America became increasingly involved in the ongoing war in Europe, a Navy survey team came to South Texas to scout possible locations for a pilot-training base.

The sleepy fishing town of Corpus Christi (then-population 60,000) caught the attention of Navy planners because of three key assets: a moderate year-round climate, miles of available land for future expansion and plenty of open, uncluttered air space.

In June 1940, President Franklin D. Roosevelt, an avid supporter of aviation and former secretary of the Navy, signed a bill approving funds for construction of the $100-million Naval Air Station Corpus Christi.

It was to be the single biggest economic boost that the city had ever known, transforming a sandy expanse of snake-infested flatlands and fishing shacks into a busy complex of runways, barracks, seaplane hangars and paved roads.

Construction began immediately, and planes began flying at the newly built base an astonishing nine months after the first spadeful of dirt had been turned. Originally planned for completion in three years, the base was finished in two years — due at least in part to the U.S. government's haste to get pilots in the air after the December 1941 bombing of Pearl Harbor.

During World War II 600 pilots per month completed their training and received their wings at what was known as "The University of the Air." More than 35,000 naval aviators graduated from this base during the war. At that time Corpus Christi was the only primary, basic and advanced training base in the nation — and the largest pilot training facility in the world.

The local newspaper used to devote entire pages to publishing the photographs and names of every new graduate, in recognition and support of the war-bound young men whose smiling faces were pictured wearing leather aviators' caps and goggles. Among the more well-known people who trained as pilots at Corpus Christi are former president George W. Bush, game show host Bob Barker and astronaut John Glenn.

www.insiders.com

See this and many other **Insiders' Guide®** destinations online — in their entirety.

Visit us today!

The military's arrival changed the complexion of the community, transforming it almost overnight from a rural outpost to a major city. Hotels, restaurants, stores and entertainment halls were created to meet the demands of the energetic new arrivals.

Celebrity visits became a matter of course. Among the most prominent during the war years were President Franklin D. Roosevelt, Rear Adm. Chester W. Nimitz, and heads of state including King Ibn Saud of Saudi Arabia.

There were even celebrities-turned-naval aviators among those stationed at the base. For example, Ted Williams, the Boston Red Sox star hitter, was a physical fitness instructor at Corpus Christi after he received his wings. Hollywood film star Tyrone Power was at the base for months while learning to fly. Entertainers such as Bob Hope, Frank Sinatra, Louis Armstrong, Ginger Rogers, Rita Hayworth and Katherine Hepburn came to the new base to entertain the young recruits.

The growth extended to neighboring communities, as auxiliary naval air stations were built in the nearby towns of Kingsville and Beeville to assist in pilot training.

After the war, the Navy's need for pilots decreased dramatically, and the Corpus Christi base was downgraded to a smaller facility.

The bases in Kingsville and Beeville were shut down until 1948, when the Navy decided to use the South Texas complex, which includes Corpus Christi, Beeville and Kingsville, as headquarters for its air training command and for teaching jet pilots to fly.

Today, there are an estimated 11,000 military and civilian employees at South Texas' four military facilities in Corpus Christi, Ingleside and Kingsville.

The Corpus Christi base continues to teach beginning naval aviators how to fly, and has gained increasing importance as a headquarters for joint training of students from the Navy, Marine Corps, Air Force, Coast Guard and foreign countries.

The auxiliary training base in Beeville was shut down by the Base Closure and Realignment Commission in 1991, but the Kingsville base continues to train the Navy's advanced students to fly high-tech combat jets.

Also in 1991 the Coastal Bend gained another military mission when the Navy decided to base its mine-warfare operations at Ingleside. The base at Ingleside now serves as home to more than two-dozen mine-warfare ships and is used as a centralized location to train and deploy the Navy's mine-warfare fleet and personnel.

The Ingleside base, with its fast-growing population and modern facilities, is one of the Navy's most progressive installations. In 1997 the base won the Commander-in-Chief's Installation Excellence award for its innovative programs, conservation of natural resources and partnering programs with the local community.

Today the Coastal Bend continues to nurture its relationship with its military neighbors, considered key economic assets for the region. A local task force remains vigilant in its efforts to protect local bases from closing.

For its part, the military cherishes its rela-

INSIDERS' TIP

The weather is one of the reasons that the Coastal Bend was chosen as a home for three Navy bases — clear skies are the norm, for an average of 328 to 345 days per year.

Photo: Naval Air Station Corpus Christi

Naval Air Station Corpus Christi is the home of Naval Air Training Command and Corpus Christi Army Depot.

tionship with the community as well. Aviators and sailors are active in the community and often serve as volunteers at local schools and charitable events. Navy officers say the Coastal Bend is one of the most welcoming destinations for personnel, and there are plans to establish the Corpus Christi-Ingleside area as a fleet concentration area, similar to San Diego, California, and Norfolk, Virginia.

The Navy has also expanded its operations here, sending a squadron of mine-hunting helicopters to the Corpus Christi base and building the first two projects in an ongoing series of joint-partnership housing ventures — which pair Navy funds with private money — in the Coastal Bend.

A detailed description of each of the military bases, their missions and availability of access to the public follows.

Naval Air Station Corpus Christi
19 Ocean Dr., Corpus Christi
• **(512) 939-3420 public affairs office**
The primary mission of this 4,400-acre naval base is pilot training, overseen by the Chief of Naval Air Training, Rear Adm. Michael Bucchi. Beginning flight students come to Corpus Christi to start their training and, depending on their performance, to determine which aircraft they will eventually fly on active duty in the Navy.

Three training squadrons, overseen by Training Air Wing Four, teach students the various stages of flight — VT-27 and VT-28, used for training primary students in a single-engine turboprop; and VT-31, where students do advanced flying in a larger, twin-engine turboprop. Students train for approximately 18 months before they receive their wings, and approximately 400 students graduate from the program each year.

The base is also home to one of the Navy's two mine-warfare helicopter squadrons, Helicopter Mine Countermeasures Squadron 15, which uses massive Sea Dragon helicopters to sweep the seas for underwater mines.

Other tenants at the base are the Commander of the Navy's Mine Warfare Command; the U.S. Coast Guard; the Corpus Christi Army Depot; U.S. Customs; and the U.S. Naval Hospital.

There are 1,619 active-duty personnel on base, 2,500 reservists and 5,404 civilians. The estimated annual economic impact of the base is $333 million. Commanding officer of the base is Capt. Richard W. Strickler.

The base has two entrances, one at the southernmost end of Ocean Drive and the

Plane Spotting

Look overhead — it's a bird! It's a plane! It's a . . . T-45 Goshawk training jet!

Astonish your friends and neighbors by being the first on your block to identify most of the military aircraft used in the Coastal Bend — thanks to your handy *Insiders' Guide®* instructions.

It's easy to distinguish military aircraft from their civilian counterparts. With the clear skies here, you can see the color of the planes easily as they fly overheard, especially if you're near the bayfront. (That's because several of our local military installations are on the water's edge.)

Close-up All the aircraft used to train student pilots are orange and white, to make them more visible — sort of like the signs on the student driver cars. Coast Guard search-and-rescue helicopters are also orange and white, for greater visibility. Other military aircraft are pale gray or dark olive-green.

There are also distinctive noises to the different types of aircraft used here — the low drone of propeller planes used by beginning students, the roar of high-tech fighter jets used by advanced students, and the rhythmic chop of helicopter blades.

Here's a photo and brief description of several of the more common aircraft you're likely to see.

T-34C Turbo Mentor

The T-34C Turbo Mentor is a small orange and white, single-engine, turbopropeller aircraft used to train beginning students at Naval Air Station Corpus Christi. It is the very first military airplane that the students learn to fly. Manufactured by Beech Aircraft, it has two seats, so the student and the instructor can sit in tandem beneath a glass cockpit canopy. The Navy has used this trainer since 1973, and by mid-1987, it had logged the lowest accident rate of aircraft in the Navy's inventory. It has a distinctive high-pitched drone.

T-44A Pegasus

The T-44A Pegasus is an orange and white, twin-engine, turboprop plane used for more advanced training at Naval Air Station Corpus Christi. Manufactured by Beech Aircraft, it is a militarized version of the King Air 90. An instructor and student sit side-by-side on the flight deck, with dual controls and instruments. The plane can carry up to 13 passengers.

T-45A Goshawk

These sleek orange and white jets are the newest and most high-tech trainers in the naval training command's inventory. A two-seat intermediate and advanced training jet, it costs $20 million and is manufactured by McDonnell Douglas. Since February 1994, students at Kingsville have flown the jets to learn instrument navigation, air-to-air combat, bombing and how to take off and land from the aircraft carrier at sea. The maximum level speed is 543 knots, or 625 mph.

MH-53E Sea Dragon

A dark green, three-engine, heavy lift helicopter used to search the seas for underwater mines, the MH-53E Sea Dragons are among the largest helicopters in the world. When they pass overhead, you can pick them out easily by the roof-rattling

— continued on next page

Photo: Courtesy Naval Air Station Kingsville

A T-45 Goshawk on final approach.

sound of the powerful chopper blades. A dozen of these aircraft belong to Helicopter Mine Countermeasures Squadron, based at Naval Air Station Corpus Christi. Manufactured by Sikorsky, the helicopters tow a water hydrofoil sledge that carries mechanical, acoustic and magnetic sensors. Each of the 73,500-pound helicopters costs approximately $24 million.

P-3 Orion

The P-3 Orion is an airborne early warning aircraft, recognizable by the circular radar that sits atop the light-gray plane's body. There are eight P-3 Orion aircraft at the U.S. Customs branch, Naval Air Station Corpus Christi. Four of the aircraft have a dome used to scan up to 200,000 square miles with one radar sweep. The other four Orion aircraft have an infrared detection system, intercept radar and an intelligence gathering system used to videotape and transmit images to other aircraft or ground stations.

other from South Padre Island Drive. There are security guards posted at each entrance, and although the base is open to the public, unchaperoned sightseeing is not permitted. The base, however, is available for pre-arranged tours and for special events, such as concerts and the occasional air show that features the Navy's flight demonstration team, the Blue Angels. Call the public affairs office for more information.

Naval Air Station Kingsville
554 McCain St., Ste. 309, Kingsville
• (512) 516-6146 public affairs office

The best and brightest flight students are assigned to this air training base, on nearly 4,000 acres about 45 miles south of Corpus Christi.

During their yearlong training stint, Navy and Marine Corps students learn to fly jets, to engage in air-to-air combat, to drop bombs and — most crucially — to land on the Navy's principal warships, aircraft carriers.

There are two training squadrons, VT-21 and VT-22. Both use the same syllabus and same aircraft, the T-45A Goshawk, to train student pilots. When the students graduate and receive the wings of gold that mark them as naval aviators, they go to the fleet for further training in fighter jets such as the F-14 Tomcat and the FA/18 Hornet.

Established in July 1942, the base first provided a home for four squadrons that trained pilots in fighter and bomber tactics and a gunnery school for combat aircrew men. After World War II, training was reduced and the land leased to Texas A&I College in Kingsville for use as an agricultural station.

In 1951 the base was reopened as an auxiliary station, and in 1969, it was redesignated as a naval air station.

The base boasts four 8,000-foot runways, an auxiliary landing field in nearby Orange Grove and a target range in McMullen County. Its assets are valued at more than $300 million.

Tenant commands are the Naval Oceanographic Command Detachment, the Naval Air Maintenance Training Group Detachment, the Mobile Mine Assembly Group Detachment, the Relocatable-Over-the-Horizon Radar, and U.S. Border Patrol sector offices and headquarters.

There are 786 officers and enlisted personnel on base, and 1,042 civilians, with Capt. Patrick Twomey as Commanding officer of the base.

Again, this base is not open for general sightseeing. There are special events during which the public is invited aboard the base, including a Fourth of July celebration with aircraft flybys and static displays of vintage aircraft. You can also arrange a tour for your school or tour group by calling the public affairs office in advance.

Naval Station Ingleside
1455 Ticonderoga Rd., Ingleside
• (512) 776-4206

Located on the northern shore of Corpus Christi Bay, this base sits astride the Corpus Christi ship channel, a deep-water artery linking the city to the Gulf of Mexico. Originally planned as a Navy homeport, the base had its groundbreaking in February 1988. The area was first chosen to serve as home for the battleship USS *Wisconsin* and the aircraft carrier USS *Lexington*. However, in April 1991, the Navy changed its plans for the base and instead designated it as the headquarters for the Navy's mine-warfare fleet.

The change in its mission came as Navy leaders increased attention on mine warfare in the wake of the Persian Gulf War, when the United States' weak minesweeping capabilities forced cancellation of planned amphibious landings.

The base was officially dedicated on July 6, 1992, and the first mine-countermeasures ship, USS *Scout*, arrived in June 1992. The ship has the distinction of being the first U.S. Navy ship homeported in Texas since World War II.

Since then, Navy officials have consolidated their mine-warfare assets — ships, aircraft, divers and training headquarters — at Ingleside so personnel can train and work nearby to improve their capabilities. Recent international mine-hunting exercises have allowed the U.S. Navy to demonstrate its new prowess in the field of mine warfare.

There are 3,650 personnel assigned to Ingleside, including 3,300 military personnel and 350 civilians. The base boasts a state-of-the-art 4,600-foot waterfront with a 1,100-foot double-deck pier.

Tenant commands include the Regional Support Group, which provides maintenance and training for the ships at Ingleside; Mine Countermeasures Squadrons One and Two, deployable squadrons sent to mine-warfare ships overseas; Shore Intermediate Maintenance Activity, which makes special and advanced ship repairs; and a branch medical and dental clinic.

There are now 22 mine countermeasures ships at the base, including the Navy's first command and control ship, USS *Inchon*; 12 Avenger-class mine countermeasures vessels; and nine Osprey-class coastal mine hunters. A total of 25 ships is scheduled to be stationed here by 1999. Base commander is Capt. Nancy Honey.

This is an open base — you can drive onto it at any time. Also, the public affairs office offers a free "windshield" tour of the base at 1:30 PM every Tuesday. Reservations are not required.

Once a month, usually on a Saturday, a ship is designated for free public visitation.

The ships are also available for pre-arranged tours for groups and organizations.

Corpus Christi Army Depot
308 Crecy St., Corpus Christi
• **(512) 939-2749**

In the 1940s the Navy operated an aircraft overhaul and repair facility to maintain the seaplanes and carrier-based aircraft used to teach World War II-era pilots. The operation was shut down on June 30, 1959, putting 3,000 people out of work.

The facility sat idle for two years, until the Army took over the large hangars and other buildings and opened its U.S. Army Aeronautical Depot Maintenance Center in 1961. The facility began by repairing fixed- and rotary-wing aircraft. In 1967, the fixed-wing aircraft repairs were phased out because of increased demand for helicopter service.

By 1968 the depot was repairing more than 400 helicopters per year; in 1974, its name was changed to Corpus Christi Army Depot.

Today the depot has more than 100 production shops and 2,772 civilian employees. Although the facility began with employees working mostly on Army helicopters, today's employees work on rotary wing aircraft from all branches of the armed services, including Air Force, Marine Corps and Navy.

The 154-acre depot operates on $600 million worth of facilities at Naval Air Station Corpus Christi.

The Corpus Christi depot is the Army's largest helicopter repair depot and, as such, is considered a key player in the country's military readiness. Depot commander is Col. Dennis A. Williamson.

The depot is not open to the public; however, organizations and clubs can schedule pre-arranged tours of the facility. Call the public affairs office for more information.

As in other Sunbelt regions, one of the main attractions for retirees is the warm weather in the Texas Coastal Bend, attracting thousands of "winter Texans" from the Midwest and other cold areas.

Retirement

The Texas Coastal Bend, as you will discover in the pages that follow, has plenty to offer retirees. As in other Sunbelt regions, one of the main attractions here is the warm weather. Each year thousands of "winter Texans" close up their homes in the Midwest or other cold regions, climb into recreational vehicles and begin their long journey to the Coastal Bend in search of sunshine and streets free of ice and snow. Some stay in the many campgrounds and RV parks in the Coastal Bend (see our Campgrounds and RV Parks chapter), while others prefer to stay in one of the many condominiums available here (see our Weekly and Long-Term Rentals chapter).

And while many spend only their winters here, others decide to make the Coastal Bend their full-time homes, including many retired military who were stationed at one of the local military bases at some point during their careers (see our Military chapter).

Retirees who decide to live in Coastal Bend communities full time will find many fine neighborhoods from which to choose. Rockport is an especially popular home for retirees, who enjoy its small-town lifestyle, art galleries, fishing, watersports and attractive views of Aransas Bay. Corpus Christi is another popular retirement area. Corpus Christi has many of the amenities people enjoy in larger towns — restaurants, museums, the arts — without sacrificing its small-town appeal. Retirees (and anyone else tired of the rat-race) will enjoy the ease with which one can move around in Corpus Christi. Both the Aransas Pass and Corpus Christi housing authorities can help low-income retirees find subsidized housing (see the listings that follow).

Kingsville also draws its share of military retirees. Many retired jet pilots settle here; two have served as mayor in recent years, while seven former chamber of commerce presidents have been retired aviators.

Other retirees will want to look into the several independent and assisted-living facilities in the area, several of which we describe in the "Housing" section of this chapter. Assisted-living facilities and home-healthcare providers have increased tremendously in the Coastal Bend during the past few years. Their growth is a response to the growing number of seniors here and their desire to stay out of nursing homes as long as possible.

Organizations, agencies and senior centers further bolster the quality of life for older adults in the Coastal Bend. Seniors will find several chapters of the American Association of Retired Persons (AARP) meeting in the Coastal Bend. The Area Agency on Aging of the Coastal Bend, (512) 883-5743 or (800) 817-5743, provides a wide range of services to seniors in a 12-county area. You can also call the Port Aransas Senior Services, (512) 749-4111, for information on activities and services in that area. The Coastal Bend has numerous senior centers, including eight in Corpus Christi, each offering activities for older adults along with daily lunches.

Following is a description agencies that help retirees and seniors meet their needs, including a breakdown of the American Association of Retired Persons (AARP) chapters in the area. They're listed in alphabetical order instead of by geographic region because many are regional or statewide resources. Sections on area senior centers and housing options follow.

Organizations and Services

American Association of Retired Persons

The AARP serves the needs and interests of people 50 and older through legislative advocacy, research, informative programs and community services provided by local chapters and volunteers throughout the country. To join an AARP chapter you must first join the national organization. National dues are $8 a year or $20 for three years. You do not have to belong to a chapter to join the national organization.

Members can receive free tax assistance by calling (512) 985-8230. During tax season volunteers staff 13 sites throughout the Coastal Bend, helping seniors and others prepare income tax forms. The AARP also administers the Prescription Drug Program, (800) 456-2277, which provides prescription and nonprescription products at discount prices.

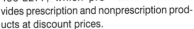

In this section we fill you in on the AARP chapters in the Coastal Bend.

Rockport-Fulton AARP Chapter No. 1536
Paws & Taws Convention Center, 400 Fulton Beach Rd., Rockport
• (512) 729-3443

This active group meets at 10:30 AM on the second and fourth Thursday of each month. The first monthly meeting is reserved for business, and the second is set aside for a covered-dish lunch. Entertainment is included at both meetings. The group's board of directors meets on the first Thursday of the month.

Chapter members play bridge at 1 PM every Thursday and hold a country-and-western dance every Thursday night. Although the chapter doesn't meet in June, July and August, bridge players still get together on Thursdays at Norwest Bank, One Broadway Plaza. Members collect trash along a 2-mile stretch of Texas Highway 35 as part of the state's litter control program. Proceeds from the dances and bridge games go toward college scholarships and local charities.

South Corpus Christi AARP Chapter No. 1778
Briarwood Senior Center, 1701 Thames Dr., Corpus Christi • (512) 854-1715

Meetings are held at 1:30 PM on the sec-

ond and fourth Thursday of the month. The first meeting is held to conduct chapter business, and the second is a covered-dish lunch. Members play bingo, dominoes and cards. They also contribute to Alzheimer's research and the Salvation Army.

AARP Senior Citizens Group Chapter No. 1855
Senior Citizens Center, 720 E. Lee Ave., Kingsville • (512) 592-8049

The 35 to 40 seniors who belong to this group meet at 6:30 PM on the third Thursday of each month. They bring sandwiches, cake and coffee or have a covered-dish supper. Speakers are often invited to address the group on current issues.

Corpus Christi Northwest AARP Chapter No. 1907
Hilltop Community Center, 11425 Leopard St., Corpus Christi
• (512) 241-2364

Members of this Corpus Christi chapter meet at 10 AM on the first Monday of each month. Meetings combine business, entertainment, group participation and a covered-dish meal. The group also participates in fund-raising activities and holds an annual Christmas party.

Portland AARP Chapter No. 2901
Senior Citizens Center, Wildcat and Fifth Ave., Portland • (512) 643-2317

The Portland AARP chapter is active in fund-raisers to support such worthy causes as the public library, emergency medical services, the Portland Police Department and drug prevention programs. They also collect food and clothes for the needy, especially around Thanksgiving and Christmas. The group meets at 6 PM on the fourth Friday of the month. The group's program usually includes AARP business, entertainment, speeches and bingo.

Southeast AARP Chapter No. 2939
The Garden Center, 5325 Greely Dr., Corpus Christi • (512) 855-5827

Southeast AARP members meet at 1 PM

on the first and third Wednesday of each month at the Garden Center, a facility owned by the local garden club and administered by the city of Corpus Christi. A covered-dish lunch is held at the first monthly meeting; cookies and bingo are on the agenda for the second monthly meeting. Business is discussed at both meetings. Guest speakers and entertainment are common. Each year the group holds a spaghetti dinner to benefit the Corpus Christi Council on Literacy, and the group regularly contributes a part of its budget to charity.

Greenwood AARP Chapter No. 4386
Greenwood Senior Center, 4040 Greenwood Dr. • (512) 853-2167

This group strives to live up to the AARP motto: "To serve and not to be served." They do this by being self-sufficient and helping the needy whenever possible. They meet at 10 AM on the first and third Thursday of each month. Members discuss chapter business, community activities and volunteer opportunities. They socialize, eat sweets and drink coffee. They also raise funds through raffles and sales.

Agencies and Programs

Adopt A Nursing Home Volunteer Program
(512) 878-3546

This program uses volunteer groups of at least three people to visit nursing homes four times a year. They take residents on outings, help them with arts and crafts, play table games and visit them in their rooms.

Adult Protective Services
(800) 252-5400

This state-licensed agency investigates reports of abuse, neglect or exploitation of elderly or disabled people.

Alzheimer's Association of the Coastal Bend
3216 Reid Dr., Ste. H, Corpus Christi • (512) 854-3887, (800) 460-3887

This support group provides information, education and financial assistance for respite care to Alzheimer's victims, families and caregivers.

American Red Cross — Coastal Bend Texas Chapter
1721 S. Brownlee St., Corpus Christi • (512) 887-9991, (800) 656-9991

The local chapter of this nationwide group offers a 25 percent senior discount on first aid, CPR and other classes.

American Red Cross "I'm OK" Program
1721 S. Brownlee St., Corpus Christi • (512) 887-9991, (800) 656-9991

Volunteers in this program call seniors once or twice a week and sometimes visit them in their homes if no relative lives in the area. The service is free; bilingual volunteers available.

Area Agency on Aging of the Coastal Bend
2910 Leopard St., Corpus Christi • (512) 883-5743, (800) 817-5743

One of the most dynamic forces for senior services in the region, this agency plans, coordinates and funds nutrition and other support services for residents 60 and older in 12 Coastal Bend counties. Services include meals, transportation, senior center activities, legal services and Alzheimer's support services.

Area Agency on Aging Case Management
2910 Leopard St., Corpus Christi • (512) 883-5743, (800) 817-5743

This program buys in-home services for the elderly including personal care, home-

INSIDERS' TIP

Fifteen years ago, Corpus Christi had eight home-healthcare agencies. Now there are more than 200 in the Corpus Christi area.

maker, personal response units and bathroom safety bars from home health agencies when all other avenues of help are exhausted.

Arthritis Foundation
(800) 364-8000

Warm water therapy and arthritis self-help courses are two of the services the Arthritis Foundation provides to arthritis sufferers.

Coastal Bend Legal Services Metro Corpus Christi
(512) 883-3623, (800) 840-3379

Low-income seniors receive assistance from Legal Services with problems that cannot be handled without legal expertise, such as appealing denied Medicare or Medicaid benefits, reviewing insurance or pension benefits and preparing wills. This agency also conducts community education programs on legal rights and responsibilities.

Corpus Christi Central Library Career Center
805 Comanche St., Corpus Christi • (512) 880-7004

Employment is a vital aspect in the lives of many older adults, and this center, at the Corpus Christi Central Library, provides local job listings for those seeking jobs, along with resources to explore careers, prepare resumes, write cover letters and hone interviewing skills. The center, which serves the general population as well as older adults, offers free workshops to help job hunters and people changing careers.

Del Mar College Senior Education Program
Baldwin and Ayers Sts. • (512) 886-1298

This community college program encourages lifetime learning for older adults by allowing people 65 and older to audit classes without paying tuition. The program also offers free, volunteer-taught classes of interest to persons 55 and older and enrichment seminars for seniors.

Eldercare Locator
(800) 677-1116

This national information and referral service helps find community resources for elderly individuals throughout the United States. Call between 8 AM and 8 PM (CST) Monday through Friday.

Elderhostel Programs
National office (617) 426-7788

This worldwide program provides non-credit courses, lodgings and meals for people 60 and older. This educational program offers participants the chance to combine study and the exploration of new places in an academic environment. In addition to calling the national office, above, you can call Del Mar College, (512) 886-1514; Texas A&M-Corpus Christi, (512) 994-5967; and Texas A&M-Kingsville, (512) 593-2861.

Foster Grandparent Program
(512) 844-7625

This federally funded program sponsored by the Corpus Christi State School provides volunteer opportunities for seniors 60 and older who meet federal income guidelines. Volunteers are matched with individuals ages 1 month to 21 years to provide one-on-one companionship. Volunteers receive an hourly stipend for 20 hours a week, transportation to the work site, training and insurance.

Hearing Aid Helpline
(800) 521-5247

Callers to this helpline receive information on signs of hearing loss and can request a free consumer kit that answers questions about hearing aids, including how to shop for them and what to look for. The helpline also puts callers in touch with a reputable, qualified hearing-aid specialist in their area.

Home Provider Program/ Community Care for Elderly and Disabled
(512) 855-9924

This service is designed to provide in-home assistance with personal care and household tasks to seniors who are unable to perform those tasks themselves. Personal care may include help with bathing, dressing and meal preparation. Housekeeping may include tasks like washing dishes, doing laundry, cleaning and shopping. Other services include home-delivered meals, respite services and adult day care.

Photo: Daniel Fielder

Area retirement communities offer retirees in the Coastal Bend a safe, structured living enviroment.

Housing and Community Development Program
1201 Leopard St., Corpus Christi
• (512) 880-3010

A city of Corpus Christi initiative, the Housing and Community Development Program provides loans and grants to rehabilitate owner-occupied housing for low-income, elderly and disabled people. It also runs a grant program for emergency repairs for the elderly and disabled.

Jewish Community Council of Corpus Christi
750 Everhart Rd., Corpus Christi
• (512) 855-6239

This Corpus Christi-based group provides basic computer instruction, low-impact aerobics and counseling for seniors. They have facilities available for social activities, and provide speakers who can discuss issues important to seniors. The council's services are available to people of all faiths.

Medicare
Claims (800) 442-2620
Eligibility (800) 772-1213
Fraud/Abuse (800) 368-5779

The federal Medicare program provides insurance for both hospital and medical coverage to people who are disabled or 65 and older and who have paid into the Social Security System. The government has put several resources at the disposal of older adults, including numbers to call for the status of pending claims and general information on eligibility. In cases of suspected fraud and abuse related to health and human services for Medicare recipients, a special arm of the program will evaluate and process complaints.

National Association of Retired Federal Employees Sparkling City by the Sea Chapter 91
Lindale Senior Center, 3135 Swantner Ave. • (512) 852-6658

This organization strives to preserve federal retirement benefits for civilian employees and retirees. Officers help members and nonmembers with insurance, pay or the filing of documents when a spouse dies. The local chapter meets from 1:30 to 3:30 PM on the first Tuesday of each month. Every Wednesday from 10 AM to 2 PM it operates a service center to help federal retirees or their survivors. The service center is held at the Corpus Christi Army Depot, Building 1727, Room 102A, 308 Crecy Street, Naval Air Station-Corpus Christi. Call 939-3112.

National Health Information Center
(800) 336-4797

Information on general health, Lyme disease, cancer, health insurance, Medicaid, Medicare and more is available by calling this toll-free number. Callers can also receive a list of health publications.

New Horizons of Corpus Christi
4455 S. Padre Island Dr., Corpus Christi
• (512) 853-9355

This counseling service helps the seniors who are experiencing emotional problems. Its clinical staff contributes to mental wellness through a comprehensive treatment program.

North American Senior Citizens
Lindale Senior Center, 3135 Swanter Rd., Corpus Christi • (512) 888-0503

This group's goals include better housing, healthcare, services, economic conditions and education for all senior citizens.

Nueces County Senior Citizens Association
Greenwood Senior Center, 4040 Greenwood Dr., Corpus Christi
• (512) 991-8514

This senior advocacy group promotes low-income housing, elderly rights and healthcare. It meets at 2:30 PM on the first Tuesday of the month.

Ombudsman Long-Term Care Program
(512) 883-5743, (800) 817-5743

This program sponsored by the Area Agency on Aging investigates and acts on complaints by nursing home residents or their families. Volunteers who staff this program go through special training and certification. The Blue Angel Volunteer Program works in conjunction with the ombudsman program. Blue Angel volunteers visit nursing home residents on a weekly basis.

Operation Heat Help
(512) 885-6900

This program run by the city of Corpus Christi Gas Department helps low-income seniors pay their winter gas bills.

Port Aransas Senior Services
710 W. Ave. A, Port Aransas
• (512) 749-4111

This program run by the city of Port Aransas provides meals delivered to seniors' homes, transportation and other assistance.

Project Ayuda Employment Program
(512) 887-7071

Project Ayuda provides employment and training for economically disadvantaged senior citizens 55 and older. Services include temporary part-time, minimum-wage work, job-search counseling and educational opportunities.

Retired and Senior Volunteer Program
(512) 880-3149

RSVP provides volunteer opportunities for people 55 and older, retired or still working. RSVP volunteers serve with nonprofit, private and public community organizations in Corpus Christi and rural Nueces County.

Retired Teachers' Association
(512) 852-6763, (512) 992-8330

This former teachers group holds monthly meetings to give seniors the chance to socialize and remain informed on topics related to teaching and the teacher retirement system. Members also perform community service projects. National, state and local dues are $20 per year.

Salvation Army Home League
1507 Mestina St., Corpus Christi
• (512) 884-9497

These meetings for older women consist of fellowship, service, education and worship.

INSIDERS' TIP

Central Power & Light, the local electric company, in conjunction with Nueces County Community Action Agency, provides emergency assistance with utility bills for low-income elderly. Call the Neighbor to Neighbor program at 882-4193.

Senior Community Services
1201 Leopard St., Corpus Christi
• (512) 814-1681

This city-sponsored program is designed to foster independence for individuals 60 and older who are homebound and isolated. Staff members provide hot lunches to seniors Monday through Friday.

Senior Community Services Meals in Senior Centers
(512) 880-3150

This city-sponsored program is designed to reduce isolation among seniors by providing a nutritious lunch to people 60 and older at eight senior centers in Corpus Christi.

Senior Companion Program
(512) 880-3154

This program is designed to help adults maintain their independence by providing volunteers to give them a hand with their daily needs. Assistance includes housekeeping, meal preparation, respite care, social recreation and home management. Volunteers receive an hourly stipend for a 20-hour work week, meal and mileage money, insurance and training.

Senior Employment Project
(512) 880-3304

This federally funded program sponsored by the city of Corpus Christi provides employment training for economically disadvantaged senior citizens 55 and older. Services include temporary part-time, minimum-wage work, job-search counseling and educational opportunities.

Senior Friends
Sunrise Mall, 5858 S. Padre Island Dr., Corpus Christi • (512) 993-4288, (800) 445-5280

This seniors association is designed to meet the special needs of older adults, such as insurance claims counseling, physician referral and regular health screenings. The organization also provides monthly membership meetings, guest speakers, social events, field trips, volunteer opportunities and a bimonthly newsletter.

Senior Friends also is available in northwest Corpus Christi, 3151 McKinzie Road, (512) 241-4407, and in Aransas Pass, 1560 W. Wheeler Avenue, (512) 758-8585, extension 222.

Senior Link/Elder Link/ Gray Gazette
710 Buffalo St., Corpus Christi
• (512) 884-1755

The Senior Link is a group of nonprofit services for seniors, their families and professionals in the aging field. Services include the *Gray Gazette*, a newspaper published each month; HalloFest, an annual fund-raising festival; and Elder Link, a program designed to help older adults stay in their homes.

Seniors Assisting Seniors
3312 Wayside Dr., Corpus Christi
• (512) 886-2782

This program operated with the assistance of the Corpus Christi Police Department gives seniors 55 and older the chance to help seniors whose homes have been burglarized. Members conduct a free home safety check to deter future burglaries.

Seniors Awareness & Safety Facts Education
(512) 887-2260

This educational program sponsored by the Nueces County Sheriff's Department makes presentations before groups of 10 and more on crimes against the elderly, travel safety, frauds and scams, 911 education and personal safety in the home.

Service Corps of Retired Executives Association
(512) 888-4322, (512) 888-3331

Retired corporate and business managers serve as volunteers providing free counseling to people planning to start a new business and to business owners who need help to make their business grow.

Silver Haired Legislators
(512) 883-5743, (800) 817-5743

This senior advocacy group convenes in Austin to discuss issues important to senior citizens. Members 60 and older elect four representatives from the Texas Coastal Bend. The group debates issues and established priorities for consideration by the Texas Legislature.

Spohn Healthwise 55
(512) 881-3733, (800) 451-3631

Healthwise 55 is a club for seniors sponsored by Spohn Health System. Healthwise 55 benefits include trips, 24-hour membership infoline, exercise and strengthening classes, lectures, dances and socials, club calendars, health screening and seminars and membership luncheons. Members receive discounts on items such as eyewear, hearing aids, medical equipment, prescriptions and gifts. Seniors also benefit from discounts at local restaurants and florists.

State Long-Term Care Ombudsman
(800) 252-2412

Provides assistance with those needing an ombudsman (someone who assists in investigating and solving complaints) to deal with long-term care needs. It also provides local numbers seniors may call for help.

Texas Attorney General — Elder Law Section
(800) 621-0508

This section of the state attorney general's office is a part of the Consumer Protection Division. It investigates and prosecutes people who defraud or abuse elderly Texans.

Texas Department on Aging
(512) 424-6840, (800) 252-9240

This is the state-level focal point for all activities related to the needs and services of older persons throughout Texas. It provides funds for local aging services through Title III of the Older Americans Act. Call for information on elderly services at the Area Agency on Aging nearest you.

Texas Department of Human Services Bureau of Long-Term Care
(800) 458-9858

This regulatory agency surveys and investigates compliance of long-term care facilities with Medicare and Medicaid standards. Call for information on facilities or to voice a complaint. They cover all nursing homes, private and nonprivate.

The Porch Handcrafts Consignment Store
5488 S. Padre Island Dr.
• (512) 991-3217

Volunteers staff this nonprofit retail outlet in Padre Staples Mall, which provides a place for seniors to display and sell their homemade crafts.

United Way INFO•LINE
(512) 882-4636, (800) 421-4636

The United Way of the Coastal Bend operates this information and referral service for people needing help from health and human service agencies in the Texas Coastal Bend. With assistance from local volunteers, the service has helped seniors get their lawns mowed and obtain wheelchair ramps.

Vineyard Employment Ministry
(512) 888-5161

Corpus Christi Metro Ministries runs this employment program to help anyone seeking employment, including seniors. It provides networking with other agencies to develop job opportunities and other support services.

Volunteer Center
505 S. Water St., Corpus Christi
• (512) 887-8282

The Volunteer Center places people of all ages as volunteers for 250 agencies throughout the Coastal Bend. Volunteers are assigned according to their interests, abilities and skills they would like to develop.

Workforce Development Corporation
(512) 889-5315

This federally funded program helps economically qualified Nueces County residents 55 and older find a job. They provide

By the year 2000 the senior population in Nueces County is projected to have grown by 13.7 percent during the preceding five years.

job leads, employer incentives, job-search workshops, resume services, computer training, GED classes and testing. They also offer physicals, eye exams, glasses and uniforms. All services are free of charge.

YMCA
417 S. Upper Broadway, Corpus Christi
• (512) 882-1741

The YMCA offers wellness programs for all ages. Senior activities include water exercise classes, fitness evaluations, aerobic fitness classes and personalized exercise programs.

YWCA
4601 Corona Dr., Corpus Christi
• (512) 857-5661

The YWCA has a variety of low-impact aerobic and water fitness classes. Classes are designed to increase flexibility, fitness, toning and endurance. The Y also offers classes designed for arthritis sufferers and people concerned about osteoporosis.

Senior Centers

Texas Coastal Bend region senior centers are scattered throughout the Texas Coastal Bend. They offer activities designed to benefit the health and well-being of adults 60 and older. Activities vary from center to center, but all focus on providing nutritionally balanced meals on weekdays. Activities include health screenings, benefits counseling, recreation, health promotion programs, physical fitness, legal assistance and transportation.

Senior centers in the Texas Coastal Bend, excluding those in Corpus Christi (see subsequent information), include: Council on Aging Senior Center, 912 S. Church Street, Rockport, (512) 729-5352; Fulton Community Church, Third and Chaparral streets, Fulton, (512) 729-2180; Kleberg County Human Services, 720 E. Lee Avenue, Kingsville, (512) 595-8572; Ricardo Senior Center, U.S. Highway 77 S., Ricardo, (512) 595-8572; Ingleside Senior Center, Avenue E and Seventh Street, Ingleside, (512) 776-3136; McSwain Senior Center, 254 13th Street, Aransas Pass, (512) 758-3669; Senior Citizens Community Center, 250 S. 13th Street, Aransas Pass, (512) 758-2939; and Portland

Senior Center, 1100 Moore Avenue, Portland, (512) 643-6501, extension 257.

In Corpus Christi, Senior Community Services, (512) 880-3150, a division of the Corpus Christi Park and Recreation Department, provides recreational programs for seniors at eight senior centers. Activities include fitness classes, dances, senior group meetings, community organization meetings and arts and crafts classes. Staff members are available to help with benefits counseling, housing, letter writing and reading, volunteer opportunities, home visits, telephone reassurance, nutrition education and health screening. The centers also host visits from local speakers.

Adults 60 and older may eat lunch at the centers Monday through Friday. The department publishes a monthly activity calendar detailing activities, including classes, at the city's senior centers. To receive a calendar call Senior Community Services at the number above. To register for classes, call or drop by the center offering the class.

These programs are available at all Corpus Christi senior centers: Briarwood Senior Center, 1701 Thames Drive, (512) 991-8081; Broadmoor Senior Center, 1651 Tarlton Street, (512) 888-7012; Ethel Eyerly Senior Center, 654 Graham Road, (512) 937-3218; Greenwood Senior Center, 4040 Greenwood Drive, (512) 854-4628; Northwest Senior Center, 11425 Leopard Street, (512) 241-3956; Lindale Senior Center, 3135 Swanter Road, (512) 854-4508; Oveal Williams Senior Center, 1414 Martin Luther King Drive, (512) 887-7633; and Zavala Center, 510 Osage Street, (512) 882-1561.

Housing

North Bay Area

Rockport Retirement Village
900 Enterprise St., Rockport
• (512) 729-5254

This 34-unit retirement village sits between the local post office and Rockport High School in a residential neighborhood. It offers senior citizens assisted and unassisted living in one- and two-room apartments. Staff provides personal care — bathing, dressing, grooming and medication supervision — for those who need it. Rockport Retirement Village offers residents three meals a day, daily housekeeping, telephone, cable television, transportation, group activities, a beauty salon, 24-hour staff, laundry facilities and laundry service. In-house activities include line dancing, sing-alongs, fitness classes and music. The complex also provides transportation to area senior centers or Senior Friends meetings where they can participate in more structured programs.

Monthly prices range from $1,495 to $2,895 depending on room size and required services.

Housing Authority of Aransas Pass
254 N. 13th St., Aransas Pass
• **(512) 758-3032**

Eighty family units and 38 units for elderly or disabled individuals are available through this city agency. It also has 126 units available through a federally funded program to supplement rental payments of low-income families.

Corpus Christi

Housing Authority of Corpus Christi
3701 Ayers St., Corpus Christi
• **(512) 884-3801**

This housing authority serving Corpus Christi was established in 1938 to provided help to low-income families seeking a place to live. The authority operates low-rent public housing developments and facilitates a federally funded program to supplement rental payments of low-income families.

Homewood Residence at Corpus Christi
6410 Meadowvista Blvd., Corpus Christi
• **(512) 985-0555**

This retirement community offers independent living for seniors in an apartment setting. Homewood Residence offers unfurnished apartments with all utilities included. It also offers a dining service, courtyards, private patios and housekeeping and linen services. Homewood offers an emergency alert system, kitchen and laundry appliances, transportation, a hair salon and advocacy and social activities. Other amenities include covered

parking and maintenance and staff on site 24 hours a day.

Monthly rates for one-bedroom apartments begins at $1,290 a month.

Esplanade Gardens
5813 Esplanade Dr., Corpus Christi
• **(512) 991-9600**

This exclusive retirement community on the city's southside offers assisted living in an attractive, homey apartment-like setting near Spohn Hospital South. Esplanade Gardens has 56 suites that can be set up with one large bedroom or a bedroom and living area, and all suites have private bathrooms. Amenities include three meals a day in its formal dining room, an atrium with 30-foot ceiling, a courtyard, library, beauty salon, barber shop, cable television, utilities, transportation and 24-hour emergency response. Weekly housekeeping and linen service are other conveniences. Activities include bingo and other games, Bible study, church group meetings, parties, dances and field trips to local attractions. Ice cream socials welcome new residents.

Monthly fees range from $1,250 to $1,425 depending on the size of the room. These prices do not include the cost of any in-house care residents might request.

Trinity Towers
101 N. Upper Broadway, Corpus Christi
• **(512) 887-2000**

You won't find a better view than the one offered by Trinity Towers. This 19-story high-rise in downtown Corpus Christi offers views of Corpus Christi Bay from each of its 200 units. Three blocks from the bay, Trinity Towers allows residents to choose from 10 floor plans ranging from a studio efficiency to 1,500-square-foot, two-bedroom apartments. It also offers three levels of care: independent living, assisted living and residence in its skilled nursing unit.

A five-story addition is under construction across the street from Trinity Towers. When completed in 1998, the addition, which is connected to the main facility via a skywalk, will house assisted-living and skilled-nursing units.

For those who choose the independent-living arrangement, one meal a day in Trinity Towers' dining room is included in the cost, and residents can pay for additional meals as needed. Others receive three meals a day. Amenities in-

The Rockport-Fulton RV Association has more than 1,500 RV sites to accommodate visitors.

clude transportation, a beauty salon, library, billiard room, health club and 24-hour security. Activities include musical programs, book reviews, art demonstrations, fashion shows and games.

Monthly fees range from $1,275 to $3,000.

Heartland of Corpus Christi
202 Fortune Dr., Corpus Christi
• (512) 289-0889

Heartland provides more hands-on care to residents than many senior facilities in the Coastal Bend. This assisted-living and skilled-nursing facility is near West Oso High School in northwest Corpus Christi. Heartland has a high number of residents in need of personal care, along with several who need the round-the-clock care required for skilled-nursing residents.

Residents eat three meals a day in a restaurant-style dining room, and all medications are administered by staff. Heartland's director of assisted living is a registered nurse who can make working with doctors easier and less time consuming. All assisted-living residents pay the same fee regardless of their level of care.

Activities include exercise classes, church services, Bible study, bingo and other games and field trips to movies, lunch, shopping or more distant destinations such as Sea World in San Antonio. Heartland has 50 one-bedroom, private apartments with 321 square feet

of space, a full bath and large closet. Most apartments are private, but the complex recently began offering companion living. Amenities include a coin laundry, beauty salon, barber shop and cable television.

The cost is $2,100 a month for an assisted-living private room.

Mount Carmel Home
4130 S. Alameda St., Corpus Christi
• (512) 855-6243

This assisted-living home is run by the Carmelite Sisters in an attractive mission-style building in central Corpus Christi. It is not affiliated with the Diocese of Corpus Christi and welcomes residents of all faiths. Mount Carmel has 70 private one-bedroom, one-bath apartments. Some have living areas, too. Residents must be recommended by a doctor and be able to perform personal care services or arrange for a home-health agency to provide them. The staff does not perform nursing procedures.

Residents eat three times a day in the Mount Carmel dining room, and residents are free to come and go as they please. The staff provides housekeeping, clean linens and towels. Activities include exercise classes, sing-a-longs, Bible classes, church services and crafts classes.

Monthly fees range from $700 to $1,200.

The number of homes
sold in the Coastal Bend
has been on a steady,
annual increase for the
past few years — and
so has the average price
of those homes.

Neighborhoods and Real Estate

The sun and saltwater work their magic on many visitors, who decide that they want to make their stay in the Texas Coastal Bend permanent. If you're one of those who choose to adopt South Texas as a home, you're in for good news. The real estate market here is booming, and it is rich with variety. Realtors say there truly is something for every taste, and the price ranges vary tremendously — meaning there will likely be something to suit your budget as well.

Annual statistics from the Corpus Christi Board of Realtors indicate that the number of homes sold has been on a steady increase — and so has the average price of those homes. The real estate market did $283 million worth of business in 1997, and 1998 promised to be even better.

The caveat here is that the rental market is not quite as upbeat. Although there is an increase in apartment construction, prices remain relatively high and in some areas apartment vacancies are scarce to nonexistent. Many people find they are better off renting a home than an apartment — the price may be about the same, and you'll end up with more space and more options.

Before you set out in search of that "For Sale" sign that may be sitting in front of your dream house, take a minute to get acclimated to the vagaries of the region. First, let's explain why the real estate market is doing so well. Realtors say that recent years, including 1996, 1997 and so far in 1998, have recorded an increasingly large number of home sales here. Why? Well, the economy is very good, not only nationally but locally. There are lots of jobs, and the U.S. Navy's increasingly large presence has helped to not only bring more people to the area, but also to supply additional work for local industry, retailers and service professionals.

Secondly, interest rates are extremely good, hovering in the 7-to-8 percent range. Realtors says that's what the interest rates were 25 years ago.

Thirdly, the city has provided some incentive programs to first-time buyers, such as low down payments, low interest rates and other financial bonuses.

And finally, the tight apartment market means that many would-be renters have chosen instead to purchase. Newcomers figure that if they're going to pay $800 a month in rent, they might as well put that money into a mortgage payment.

For many newcomers, the Coastal Bend real estate market also offers an important advantage: low prices, particularly for waterfront property. The down side is that homeowner's insurance rates can be higher than in other areas because the area is subject to hurricanes and storms.

If you do decide to become a permanent resident of the Coastal Bend, there are a few peculiarities of the local real estate scene that you should be aware of. Obviously, any house you select should undergo several inspections: for termites, which are a common menace in this moist, warm climate; for plumbing problems, which can be particularly important if you're looking at an older house; and for structural concerns, which are also an issue here because of soil and climate conditions.

The plumbing test is important, too, because the cast-iron pipes in older houses tend to rot, at least partly because of the salt in the soil. A plumbing static test should be part of any inspection before you purchase a house because it tells you whether the pipes leak and if any need to be replaced. Replacement means taking out the cast-iron pipes and replacing them with the more lasting PVC pipes — another costly job.

All these concerns are certainly workable and can be overcome by thorough inspections and investigations on your part or the part of your broker. Doing the necessary homework before you buy a house here will pay off in the long run.

We've provided you with a description of towns and neighborhoods, plus listings of real estate professionals in each area. Remember, these listings are not all-inclusive but should give you a good place to begin your home hunting here. So, come on. Join the many other transplanted Texans who have decided to settle in the Coastal Bend, where the climate, the economy, the quality of life and the housing prices combine to entice thousands each year.

North Bay Area

Rockport

The Rockport-Fulton area sits on the coastline and has long been known as a haven for vacationers and nature lovers. Increasingly popular with birders, the area also attracts retirees who want to make their stay here a permanent one.

One of the most popular and well-known areas is **Key Allegro**, an island of canal-front lots with vacation/resort homes. Established about 30 years ago, this development now has about 700 homesites. The homes are usually stucco with tile roofs, most of them two-story with upstairs living areas, waterfront views and boats docked in the back for quick access to fishing and birding. Prices can range from $100,000 to $1 million.

Another popular part of town is the **Rockport Country Club Estates** subdivision,

where oak trees abound and the golf course is the neighborhood's centerpiece. There are many new homes here, with more under construction. Prices range from $130,000 to $1 million.

Old Rockport neighborhoods display classic Victorian beach-style architecture, including high ceilings, crown molding and large open windows originally designed to permit the cooling sea breezes through the houses. Many of these homes line Fulton Beach Road, which overlooks Aransas Bay, and range in price from $50,000 to $400,000, depending on age and condition.

Among real-estate publications available for buyers are Rockport's *Property Previews*, which is published eight times a year. Another is *Corpus Christi Homes*, published weekly. Both publications are free and available from real estate offices as well as at many local business and restaurants. You can also scan the real estate sections of the town's weekly newspapers, the *Rockport Pilot* and *The Herald*.

Real Estate Companies

Century 21-Emery Real Estate
501 S. Austin St., Rockport
• **(512) 790-9500**
Owner Barbara Emery has been running this company since 1991. It employs six full-time agents and specializes in waterfront properties.

Coldwell Banker Myers-Gallagher
3002 N. Texas Hwy. 35, Ste. D, Rockport
• **(512) 729-6060**
This is a branch office with six agents, managed by broker Pam MacLure-Stanley, who also oversees a branch office in Aransas Pass.

Key Allegro Real Estate Co.
1798 Bayshore Dr., Rockport
• **(512) 729-3691**
With 14 full-time agents, this is the city's largest real estate company. Owned by Carla Krueger Rinche, it has been in business for about 35 years and was the original devel-

oper of the Key Allegro Island subdivision. This firm handles residential property in Aransas County and Live Oak Peninsula and is known for handling some of the larger, pricier homes in the area.

Ledbetter's Key Allegro Sales
1809 Bayshore Dr., Rockport
• **(512) 729-2772**

Established in 1978 on Key Allegro, this firm is headed by principal broker Jerre Ledbetter. It employs seven agents and specializes in property on Key Allegro Island, although it is not limited to this subdivision.

Sipe Real Estate
546 Texas Hwy. 35 S., Rockport
• **(512) 729-2603**

Established in 1945 by Winnie Sipe, this is the oldest real estate company in Aransas County. It has been owned since 1966 by Juanita Wagley, Mrs. Sipe's daughter. With five full-time agents, this company specializes in channel and waterfront homesites, but it sells property all over the county.

Aransas Pass, Ingleside, Gregory and Portland

Continuing in a southerly direction toward Corpus Christi on Texas Highway 35, you come to the communities of Aransas Pass, Ingleside, Gregory and Portland. Many of the real estate firms in this area serve all these towns, so it seems logical to include them together. Still, each town has its own flavor.

Aransas Pass, a town built on the shrimping industry, is a waterfront community of mostly modest homes. Obviously, the residences on the waterfront are more costly and more exclusive. One of the newer and more popular neighborhoods here is **Pelican Cove**, a waterfront community of new homes that are approximately 2,000 square feet. These residences are on the upscale side, ranging from $120,000 to $300,000.

Nearby Ingleside has seen a steady growth in its population since the expansion of the naval mine warfare base here. That has meant an increased demand for housing — and a corresponding increase in the num-

ber of new homes and developments that have been built in the past five years. Among the newer subdivisions are **Lakeview** and **Parkside Terrace**, both of which offer new homes that are approximately 1,200 square feet. These homes tend to sell for $60,000 to $80,000. Nearby is the separate community of **Ingleside on the Bay**, which has older waterfront homes. The prices here go from $60,000 to $200,000. A two-bedroom, canal front home was listed for $75,000, while a four-bedroom was listed for $155,500.

The Gregory-Portland area shares a public school district and many of the same real estate characteristics. Newcomers, particularly those from the military and outlying areas, tend to move here because of the reputation of the school district. One of the most popular subdivisions is **Northshore**, which is a country-club neighborhood of large, new homes, usually in excess of 2,000 square feet. A brand-new three-bedroom, two-bath brick home here was listed for $148,900, while a house with four bedrooms, five bathrooms, a fireplace, cathedral ceilings and a swimming pool was listed for $389,000.

Newcomers can find a listing of properties available in *The Real Estate Book*, which is published quarterly, and *Corpus Christi Homes*, a newspaper published every two weeks. Both publications are free and available from real estate agents as well as at local businesses and restaurants.

Real Estate Companies

Associated Brokers Group
614 Eighth Ave., Portland
• **(512) 643-3031**

Established in 1985, this firm is owned by John Thomas and employs eight full-time agents. They handle mostly residential properties in Portland, Ingleside and Aransas Pass as well as some commercial properties.

Century 21 Bay Area Realtors
1559 S. Commercial St., Aransas Pass
• **(512) 758-7506**

With six agents, this office sells properties in Rockport, Portland, Port Aransas, Aransas Pass and occasionally Ingleside. Co-owners Ivah Mircovich and Virginia Bufkin have been in the real estate business for more than 25 years, and this office has been affiliated with Century 21 since 1992.

Century 21 Myers-Lee Real Estate
921 Houston St., Portland
• **(512) 643-2591**

Co-owned by Joe Myers and Phyllis Lee, this office employs 23 agents. They sell properties in Aransas, Kleberg, Nueces and San Patricio counties. The agency was established more than 25 years ago and is one of the largest real estate firms in the North Bay area.

Coldwell Banker Myers Gallagher
264 S. Commercial St., Aransas Pass
• **(512) 758-7534**

Formerly Aransas Real Estate, this is a branch office affiliated with the Corpus Christi main office. It has six agents and covers the North Bay area.

McAllister and Associates
106 Amarillo St., Ingleside
• **(512) 776-3550**

A husband-and-wife team, Billie and Shirley McAllister, operates this real estate office. They employ seven agents and have been in business since 1993.

North Bay Properties
720 Dallas St., Portland • (512) 643-8525

Owned by Eileen Morris, this office employs six agents. They handle residential properties, rentals and commercial properties. This company was established in 1997, but Morris has been handling real estate in Portland since 1978.

Port Aransas to Padre Island

Port Aransas

This area is a resort vacation community with many neighborhoods inhabited by both full-time and part-time residents. The lifestyle is extremely casual here, and it shows in the architecture: The homes are simple, many offering views of the waterfront and the wetlands.

The **Port Aransas Private Marina** is a neighborhood near the beach and adjacent to the Corpus Christi Ship Channel, and residents enjoy waterfront views of the channel and nearby St. James Island. These wood-frame homes were built in the late 1950s and 1960s and are on the canal with a boat slip at each address. An on-site manager controls access to the marina. A five-bedroom, three-bath home here is listed for $550,000.

Island Moorings is another popular neighborhood, 2 miles south of town on the canal. Many homes have a Southwest flavor, with stucco and tile roofing. And the residents are strict about adhering to this style — an architectural committee has to review all new home construction. Prices in this neighborhood range from $230,000 for a three-bedroom, two-bath home to $549,000 for a four-bedroom, five-bathroom house.

Channel Vista neighborhood is south of the ferry landing and near the ship channel, providing convenient access to town and schools. Mostly permanent residents live here, and a new city park and swimming pool are under construction nearby. A three-bedroom, three-bath home was listed for $129,900.

A new development is **Beachwalk**, which offers homes that are less than a year old but are modeled after Victorian cottages. The homes feature wide porches and picket fences, and residents have amenities that include a boardwalk to the beach, swimming pool and clay tennis court. A three-bedroom, two-bath home is listed for $150,000.

Port Aransas' brokers have their own listing service, called Port Aransas Listing Service, and the real estate offices produce brochures on available listings. Usually the brochures are divided by price and type of property, such as residences, condominiums and lots. The real estate market is strong, but it is mostly a seller's market: little inventory and high demand. New construction is ongoing, so there should be more properties available soon.

Real Estate Companies

Coldwell Banker Island Realtors
821 Alister St., Port Aransas
• **(512) 749-6000, (800) 580-6600**

This is the only franchise company in the

Multimillion-dollar homes line Corpus Christi's famous Ocean Drive.

city, offering eight full- and part-time agents. The owner is Jack Ponton, who has been in the real estate business for more than 25 years.

Mark R. Grosse Real Estate
211 W. Cotter Ave., Port Aransas
• (512) 749-6603

One of the oldest real estate companies on the island, this firm was established in 1978. It's owned by Mark and Carolyn Grosse and employs two additional full-time agents.

Islander Real Estate
108 S. Alister St., Port Aransas
• (512) 749-6996, (800) 749-6996

An older, established company with new owners, Jack and Helen Jameson, this firm was established in 1968. It has five full-time agents. This company handles residential and commercial properties, and also leasing of properties.

Port Aransas Realty
111 E. Cotter Ave., Port Aransas
• (512) 749-4000, (800) 242-3480

This is the city's largest real estate company, with two locations and nine full-time agents. One office is in the city harbor, while the other is at Island Moorings. It is known for its service and professionalism.

Padre Island

If you continue through Port Aransas and head to Corpus Christi along the coastline, you'll arrive at Padre Island. This area offers fairly expensive waterfront homes, with $109,000 being the lowest price you'll likely find. The homes here are more costly at least in part because the residences require sturdier construction because they're on the coastline and therefore will bear the brunt of a tropical storm or hurricane. The area tends to attract a lot of retirees, particularly those who enjoy fishing or boating.

That said, Realtors also point out that these waterfront homes are among the most reasonably priced in the United States. You can buy a lot on the waterfront, with a bulkhead already built in, for $30,000 or so. We were told by one real estate broker that the prices are good because the company that originally developed the island went bankrupt. An increasing number of foreign investors, particularly Canadians, have come to buy property here — and, again, many retirees look at the prices and decide this is where they'll locate their retirement home.

The **Padre Isles Property Owners Association**, (512) 949-7025, is a very strong and active organization here, and they do have architectural restrictions for new construction.

A popular island neighborhood is **Point Tesoro**, where we found a listing for a two-story, three-bedroom waterfront home for $125,000. A four-bedroom stucco home on the main channel was listed for $219,000.

Real Estate Companies

Coldwell Banker Island Realtors
14613 S. Padre Island Dr., Corpus Christi • (512) 949-7077

With 15 full-time agents, this company has been in operation since 1985. Owner Terry Cox specializes in sales on the island.

Prudential Real Estate Center
14200 S. Padre Island Dr., Corpus Christi • (512) 949-7033

The oldest real estate company on the island, this firm employs 15 full-time agents. It is owned by Jacqueline Svoboda.

Corpus Christi

The region's largest city, Corpus Christi has the most diverse real estate offerings in the area. You can buy an older frame home and remodel it, or you can opt for a brand-new house in what passes for the suburbs — new developments on the south side of town. You can choose to live in an older, quiet, oak tree-shaded neighborhood or in a modern subdivision built around a golf course and tennis courts.

Among the city's most opulent residences are the mansions that line **Ocean Drive**, the city's showcase street that fronts Corpus Christi Bay. It was once described by *Texas Monthly* magazine as the most beautiful street in Texas. These are the area's multimillion-dollar homes, and although there are other areas that attract the city's wealthy, this is the most well-known neighborhood for the very affluent.

The rest of the city offers a wide variety of price ranges, depending on the size, location and condition of the home you select. It's probably best to make some decisions before you begin your search. For example, do you want to live near the waterfront? Would you prefer an older home or a new one? This can help you and your Realtor narrow the search and focus on the type of residence you want.

The local board of Realtors divides the city into six areas, each with a distinct personality and attractions: the southside, near southside, central city, northwest, Flour Bluff and Padre Island. We discussed homes on Padre Island in the section that includes Port Aransas and Padre Island, so we won't repeat that information here.

Of all the city's neighborhoods, the southside has the largest number of new homes. A variety of new developments attract many of the mid- to upper-income home buyers. The area's largest neighborhood is **Country Club**, a golf course-centered neighborhood with large homes that were built in the 1970s. Most of them are ranch-style residences, many in excess of 2,000 square feet. A three-bedroom, two-bath brick home was listed for $109,900. A four-bedroom, 3½-bath, two-story brick home was listed for $139,900.

Another well-known southside neighborhood is **King's Crossing**, another golf-course neighborhood with a lot of new construction, large homes and contemporary designs. We found a three-bedroom, two-bath home with a swimming pool, fireplace, built in 1995, listed for $215,000. A four-bedroom, 2½-bath, two-story brick home was listed for $139,900.

Yet another popular southside neighborhood is **The Lakes**, with man-made lakes, lots of new construction and large residences aimed at an upper-middle income population. A four-bedroom, 2½-bath home, built in 1990, with a fireplace was listed for $143,900. A three-bedroom, four-bath waterfront home with a swimming pool was listed for $329,500.

Not all the southside neighborhoods are so pricey. In **Bear Creek** subdivision, established about a decade ago, you'll find new homes that are smaller and more affordable. A three-bedroom, two-bath brick home was listed for $78,400, while another with three bedrooms and two baths was selling for $97,900.

The area known as the near southside extends from the outskirts of downtown to the city's main throughway, S. Padre Island Drive. This area includes the mansion-lined Ocean Drive homes as well as some of the city's older, historic neighborhoods. Many of the homes, while not on the waterfront, are within a few blocks of Corpus Christi Bay. And, obviously, the price of real estate does tend to go up with proximity to the bayfront.

One of the most popular neighborhoods in this area is the **Del Mar** subdivision, which contains some of the city's oldest homes, built in the 1930s and 1940s. These homes, mostly wood-frame structures, are flanked by large live oak trees and characterized by hardwood floors, high ceilings and expansive windows. There is very little new construction here, although several Realtors noted a trend of young professionals who purchase old homes and renovate or tear them down and rebuild. An English Tudor-style home with three bedrooms, two baths, fireplace and hardwood floors was listed for $104,900, while a two-story, three-bedroom with 1½-baths was listed for $139,900. At the higher end, we found a lovely Austin stone two-story with four bedrooms, two baths on three lots that was listed for $310,000.

Adjacent to Del Mar is the **Morningside** neighborhood, another one that features mostly older homes. We found a two-story, three-bedroom, two-bath house on a corner lot for $109,900.

Other popular and longtime neighborhoods in this area are **Bessar Park** and **Aransas Cliffs**, close to the bayfront and featuring older homes, lots of trees and mostly spacious lots. Many of these homes have been renovated and are quite beautiful; just a few blocks away, you'll find homes that are badly in need of renovation. We found a two-bedroom that listed for $66,500; we also found a Colonial-style three-bedroom, two-bath advertised here for $149,000.

One of the more exclusive addresses in this area is **Hewitt Drive**, where the city's millionaires dwell in houses that take up several lots and sit well back from the roadway. A four-bedroom, five-bath home on Hewitt was recently listed for $525,000, while a five-bedroom, four-bath residence was listed at $835,000. This area also includes the elaborate waterfront homes along the city's showpiece street, Ocean Drive, which also tend to be pricey. We found a three-bedroom for $695,000 and a four-bedroom for $649,000.

Lamar Park is another well-known and pricey area of town, although not nearly as exclusive as Ocean Drive. The homes here were built in the 1950s and are generally one-story brick or stone residences with spacious yards. Prices range from $129,900 for a modest three-bedroom, two-bath home with fireplace to $375,000 for a four-bedroom, four-bath home with a swimming pool.

South Shores is another high-priced neighborhood that borders the bayfront, with homes that tend to be newer, more elaborate and larger than other homes in this part of town. A four-bedroom, three-bath home was listed for $205,000; a five-bedroom, four-bath house was listed for $498,500.

The downtown area of the city has very few residences for sale. It includes central city housing for low- to moderate-income residents as well as a lot of older homes that once were beautiful but now need a lot of work. Realtors say this is a fairly inactive market, meaning that few homes come up for sale here.

The city's northwest area is often known by the names of the two school districts out here, **Calallen** and **Tuloso-Midway**. The area has a fair amount of new construction and is considered the city's more rural section, with many of the homes on large lots or acreage. People often move out here for the school districts, which are small but affluent, with a tax base that includes the city's petrochemical plants. Prices range from $62,000 for a two-bedroom country home on a half-acre with a horse barn to $349,000 for a four-bedroom, two-story brick home with 5,728 square feet and an acre lot.

The northwest area's crown jewel neighborhood is **Wood River**, with a golf course, hills and lots of native mesquite trees. A three-bedroom, two-bath brick home on a cul de sac here was listed for $104,900. We also found a 5,000-square-foot, two-story Colonial-style mansion on the golf course that has four bedrooms, 3½ baths, a swimming pool and an exercise room. It was listed for $395,000.

Another subdivision out here is **Solar Estates**, which is not quite as expensive. We found a brick three-bedroom, two-bath home for $92,900 and a four-bedroom, two-bath for $105,900.

The area of the city to the south, past the shopping malls, is known as **Flour Bluff**. This area has its own school district, like the northwest neighborhoods, but it is more eclectic. There are some very low-income residences here as well as some very expensive homes.

Bordered on one side by the Laguna Madre and on the other by Oso Creek, this area offers a sort of waterfront or rural lifestyle for some folks who don't want to live in the city. Some people buy homes with acreage out here so they can keep horses; others buy canal lots with boat slips in the back.

One neighborhood in the Flour Bluff area is **Tropic Isles**, which offers houses on the water that range from $73,000 to $398,000. A three-bedroom, two-bath home facing the waterfront was listed for $89,900. We also found a four-bedroom, three-bath home with a fireplace listed for $115,500.

Another established area is **Roscher Estates**, where we found listings that included a custom-built, three-bedroom, three-bath brick home on an acre lot offered for $265,000 and a huge five-bedroom, 3½-bath brick home listed for $398,900.

Real Estate Companies

Berney Seal Co. Realtors
601 Everhart Rd., Corpus Christi
• (512) 992-9000

This company is owned by Berney Seal, a Realtor who gained local fame with a now-defunct morning talk show that was popular with local listeners. Seal has been selling real estate since 1965, and his company has 20 full-time professional Realtors. The company specializes in residential property in all price ranges.

Century 21 — Best of the Best
7110 S. Staples St., Corpus Christi
• (512) 994-0204

This is the largest of several Century 21 offices here, with about 30 agents. Owner Lowell Gaut has been in the real estate business since 1990, and the office became affiliated with Century 21 in 1997. The agency specializes in relocation and residential property, although it also handles commercial, farm and ranch listings. Gaut says his company deals a

lot with military newcomers and offers in-house mortgage financing.

Garron Dean and Associates
4817 Saratoga Blvd., Corpus Christi
• (512) 992-4182

Established in 1972, this firm is owned by Garron Dean. It employs 20 agents and serves all of Corpus Christi as well as the neighboring communities of Portland and Rockport.

Alfred Edge Realtors
4466 S. Staples St., Corpus Christi
• (512) 993-3343

Owner Alfred Edge marked his 51st year as a broker in 1998, so he definitely has plenty of experience in the real estate business. At one time, Edge had 10 offices throughout this area; now he runs just one office with 32 agents. They handle residential, farm and ranch, and some industrial properties, focusing primarily on the southside of the city.

ERA Windward Properties
5801 S. Staples St., Corpus Christi
• (512) 994-1089

This company advertises a sale guarantee — if it doesn't sell your house, then the company will purchase it (at a discounted price). Owner David Wallace says it's an example of the company's service-oriented attitude. Wallace has 30 agents at this company, which was established about three years ago. It handles residential properties throughout the city and is one of the 200 top-selling ERA companies in the United States.

Group One Real Estate
5302 Everhart Rd., Corpus Christi
• (512) 991-9111

Owner Sarah Graham runs one of the city's largest real estate firms, with approximately 20 agents. Graham has been in the business for 32 years, and her company handles residential, farm and ranch, and commercial properties throughout the city.

INSIDERS' TIP

Corpus Christi's southside recorded more home sales in 1997 than any other part of town: 898 homes sold for an average price of $111,287, according to the Corpus Christi Board of Realtors.

Home building is currently experiencing a boom on the canals of Padre Island.

Holtzclaw Herrmann
4040 Five Points Rd., Corpus Christi
• (512) 241-5363

This firm, which specializes in property on the city's northwest side, is owned by Judy Herrmann, Darlene Holtzclaw and Doug Holtzclaw. Established in October 1992, it employs 10 agents and sells mostly residential properties as well as some farm, ranch and commercial land.

Main Realty
1601 S. Alameda Ave., Corpus Christi
• (512) 883-9209

Established in 1975 by Mary and Sam Main, this father-daughter company handles both residential and commercial property. Mary conducts the residential portion of the business, and her father deals with the commercial properties.

Martin Company
13525 F.M. Rd. 624, Corpus Christi
• (512) 241-6001

Specializing in the northwest area of town, this company handles residential, commercial and farm and ranch properties. Owner Gary Martin has 10 agents working with him at this office, which was established in 1985.

Pacesetter
6116 S. Staples St., Corpus Christi
• (512) 992-9231

Co-owned by Anne Davis and Beth Wollitz, this is the city's largest real estate company and consistently records the highest volume of sales in the area. Established in 1978, it employs 35 full-time agents and has been voted "Best of the Best" by the local newspaper, the *Corpus Christi Caller-Times*, two years in a row. Pacesetter agents specialize in residential properties, but it also has a property management division, a relocation division and a commercial division.

RE/MAX Metro Properties
5890 Everhart Rd., Corpus Christi
• (512) 994-9393

This is one of the city's largest companies, with 44 agents. Owner Tim Teas says the company handles mostly residential property as well as some commercial, farm and ranch listings. Property listings range from all over town to Padre Island and Ingleside.

Arlene Steel Realtors
5525 S. Staples St., Corpus Christi
• (512) 993-3117

This is a family operation, owned by Arlene and Bob Steel and their daughter, Lynda Steel

Photo: Daniel Fielder

Kings Crossing Country Club is an exclusive south Corpus Christi neighborhood, complete with 18-hole golf course, tennis courts, pool and dining facilities.

Martin. Arlene Steel has been in the real estate business since 1967, forming her own company in 1984. Today, the agency has two offices: one in the northwest part of town with eight agents, and this office, which has about 32 agents. The Steels handle mostly residential properties, although they do offer some commercial properties.

Kingsville

Local Realtors describes this community as one in transition. Its economy was originally centered on ranching and railroads but is now driven by the U.S. Navy's largest jet training facility and one of the world's largest petrochemical plants. The city is in the midst of some of the finest recreational areas in the United States, yet its land value and cost of living remain comparatively moderate.

Kingsville is home to Texas A&M University-Kingsville, the aforementioned Naval Air Station and an increasing number of manufacturing facilities. The city is poised for growth,

and a housing task force has set a goal to build an average of 20 new homes a year through the year 2000. The military's growing presence, the expanding number of manufacturing facilities and the increase in U.S. trade with Mexico mean that there is a need for housing here. That said, there are still homes to be purchased and rented. The apartment market remains tight, and many newcomers, particularly those from the military, find it preferable to rent a house or to buy, even if they are here for only a short time.

Many people come here for the recreational opportunities of fishing and hunting. Other newcomers are winter Texans who buy property here or retired military folks who decide to settle down in South Texas.

Housing options vary widely here. You can find a historic Victorian-style home in town or a newly built ranch house with acreage right outside the city limits. Prices are just as varied. We found a one-story, three-bedroom brick house in town for $72,000 and a four-bedroom new home with a fireplace for $83,500.

In the more rural areas around Kingsville, including **Riviera** and **Ricardo**, we found a three-bedroom, two-bath home on 30 acres for $148,000. Another rural home was a three-bedroom, 2½-bath house with a screened porch, hot tub and Italian tile floors for $169,000.

Real Estate Companies

Betty Haas Realtors
1921 King Ave., Kingsville
• **(512) 592-3321**

Formerly Alfred Edge Realtors, this firm is now owned by Betty Jo Haas. It employs five agents and handles residential and commercial properties as well as property management.

Century 21 Myers Real Estate
2701 U.S. Hwy. 77 S., Kingsville
• **(512) 595-7653, (800) 333-9318**

Owned by Joe Myers and Bubba Evans, this office employs 18 agents. They offer full-service real estate marketing for buyers, sellers, builders, investors and renters. The company handles properties throughout the Coastal Bend, from Rockport to Kingsville.

Coldwell Banker Homestead Properties Inc.
515 E. King Ave., Kingsville
• **(512) 592-4343**

This firm is the one of the largest real estate companies in Kingsville, with 12 full-time agents whose combined experience totals more than 185 years. Established in 1960, the firm became affiliated with Coldwell Banker in 1985. Their motto is to "Make Real Estate Real Easy" for their clients and they specialize in offering state-of-the-art technology, such as computerized listings. Co-owners are manager Patti Wolfe and broker Ricki Cunningham.

Kingsville Realtors Group
1314 E. King Ave., Kingsville
• **(512) 592-8282**

Formerly Kingsville Real Estate, this office is run by a trio of broker-owners who have more than 30 years in the business. Odis Michalk, Bev Nielsen and Julia Wade specialize in residential properties, although they also handle farm and ranch land, and investment properties. Two of the owners are natives of Kingsville, while the third has lived here 20 years, so they know the area well.

The area has two four-year universities, Texas A&M University-Corpus Christi and Texas A&M University-Kingsville, as well as one junior college, Del Mar College.

Child Care
and Education

The Coastal Bend offers many options for child care and education, from day-care facilities to universities. Not only does the region have more than a dozen public school districts, it also has a host of private schools. We've separated the school districts by geographic region, as we've done with other categories in this book, to make it easier for you to find a school in a particular area or city. We end the chapter with the three universities in the region, which offer more than 200 degree programs.

Child Care

The Coastal Bend has four child-care centers that are accredited by the National Academy of Early Childhood Programs. The accreditation program, run by the National Association for the Education of Young Children (NAEYC), ensures that participating centers have met national standards that include curriculum, interaction between children and adults, safety, child-to-teacher ratio, nutrition and communication with parents. Centers that have received the accreditation in Corpus Christi are First Presbyterian Church Day School, First United Methodist Church Vincent Morris Children's Center, and Naval Air Station Corpus Christi's Child Development Program. In Kingsville, Naval Air Station Kingsville's Child Development Center has also

been accredited by the NAEYC. For more information about these centers, including addresses and phone numbers, see the listings in the "Education" section of this chapter.

The area has many excellent, nonaccredited day-care homes that provide warm, safe environments for just a few kids. There are also many topnotch facilities and preschools that haven't gone through the fees, paperwork and visits required for official accreditation. As always, your best sources are friends, neighbors and others whose judgment you trust. Talk to the people you know, ask them about the places you want to visit, and then go in person to check it out.

You can obtain a free list of licensed day-care facilities by calling the Texas Department of Protective and Regulatory Services in Corpus Christi, (512) 854-2011. Licensed facilities are listed by county.

For low-income families, Corpus Christi has several well-established day-care facilities that are licensed by the state. The Mary McLeod Bethune Day Nursery, 900 Kinney Street, (512) 882-7326, takes infants through school-age children for full- and part-time care. Open since 1942, it also offers summer camp programs, before- and after-school care and transportation. It is open 7:15 AM to 5:30 PM Monday through Friday.

Two other well-respected, low-income facilities include Dos Mundos Day School, 849

Erwin, (512) 884-7062; and Brooks Chapel Early Childhood Development Center, 1517 Winnebago Street, (512) 884-8861.

When you're looking for a school or day-care center, be sure to make several visits. Meet with the teachers and inquire about the student-to-teacher ratio. Ask about accreditation, programs, staffers' backgrounds and activities. Trust your instincts and don't be afraid to ask questions. You, better than anyone else, know what your child needs.

We have included child-care listings in the Early Childhood section of this chapter because so many of the programs are also for school-age youngsters.

Education

In the arena of higher education, the outlook here is far brighter than it has been in past decades. For many years, community leaders had complained that the state gave short shrift to higher education in South Texas, which translated to a lack of funding and political support. A legislative study in 1988 showed that the state spent $43 per college student in South Texas, compared with $103 per college student in the rest of the state. As a result of these studies, attorneys for the Mexican American Legal Defense and Educational Fund (MALDEF) filed suit against the state on behalf of the League of United Latin American Citizens. A judge ruled that the state had discriminated against South Texas residents in its distribution of higher educational funding and initiatives. In 1993, lawmakers passed several bills that began the process of sending more dollars to South Texas colleges and universities. Officials with MALDEF have estimated it will take 10 years and $2 billion to bring the area's higher education institutions up to par with the rest of the state; however, many see the progress made so far as a good starting point.

The area has two four-year universities, Texas A&M University-Corpus Christi and Texas A&M University-Kingsville, as well as one junior college, Del Mar College.

Texas A&M University-Corpus Christi and Texas A&M University-Kingsville both have some history in this region; both have grown since becoming affiliated with the prestigious Texas A&M University System in 1989. Both universities also changed their names in 1993 to reflect their affiliation with the Texas A&M University System. It's also worth noting that TAMU-Corpus Christi became a four-year university in 1994, which means it's undergoing expansion in many areas, including academics and sports.

Del Mar College, a junior college in Corpus Christi, often serves as a starting point for youngsters who want to begin their college education in an affordable setting, then continue their degree program at a larger university. Del Mar also offers a number of vocational programs that are quite popular.

Our listings are by no means all-inclusive, particularly when it comes to private day-care facilities, but they give you a good starting point for recommendable centers and schools.

Early Childhood

Corpus Christi

Central Christian Children's Academy
6301 Weber Rd., Corpus Christi
• (512) 851-8747

This Christian day-care program, open since 1980, averages about 110 children daily, ages 6 months to kindergarten. The program includes chapel time, one Montessori class, a latchkey program and a Mother's Day Out program. It's open 7:30 AM to 6 PM for the day-care program and 9:30 AM to 2:30 PM for the Mother's Day Out program.

Early Childhood Development Center
Texas A&M University-Corpus Christi, 6300 Ocean Dr., Corpus Christi
• (512) 980-3366

Opened in August 1996 as a venture between the city's largest public school district and Texas A&M University-Corpus Christi, this

Photo: Greater Kingsville Economic Development Council

Texas A&M University - Kingsville has a reputation for academic excellence and athletic success.

center enrolls 132 children ages 3 through the 3rd grade. It emphasizes dual-language learning, multi-age grouping and team teaching. It is open to all students in the Corpus Christi Independent School District; applicants are chosen through a lottery system.

First Baptist School
3115 Ocean Dr., Corpus Christi
• (512) 884-8931

With approximately 225 students, this private day-care/school offers Christian-based education for children ages 2½ through the 8th grade. The curriculum is A-Beka, a Christian-based educational program, and classes include music, computer, Bible and chapel. The school has been in operation for almost 25 years.

First Christian Day School and Child Care Center
3401 Santa Fe St., Corpus Christi
• (512) 854-1241

This school has been operating for nearly 30 years and enrolls approximately 160 students, ages 2 through kindergarten. Officials pride themselves on their low teacher-to-student ratio: 1-to-8 for the 2-year-olds; 1-to-12 for the 3-year-olds; 1-to-14 for the 4-year-olds; and 1-to-16 for the kindergartners. The school also offers special programs for music, science and cognitive skills development.

First Presbyterian School
430 S. Carancahua St., Corpus Christi
• (512) 887-7116

This popular day-care program enrolls approximately 72 students, ages 2 through 5. The program is half-day and is accredited by the NAEYC. Registration for the fall is held in March, and some classes fill up fast.

First United Methodist Church Vinson Morris Children's Center
900 S. Shoreline Blvd., Corpus Christi
• (512) 884-9211

This is a full-time church-run facility that enrolls 82 children, ages 18 months to 5 years. The day-care center offers both half-day and full-day programs, and it is open from 6:30 AM to 5:45 PM. It has been in operation since 1965 and is NAEYC-accredited. Like the facility listed above, there can be a waiting list for some classes, particularly the 18-month-old group. Student-to-teacher ratios are way below the state requirement, and the teachers tend to have a lot of longevity here.

Jewish Community Council of Corpus Christi
750 Everhart Rd., Corpus Christi
• (512) 855-6239

As many as 150 students are enrolled at this 25-year-old school, which offers a manipulative-based program for youngsters ages 2 through 5. Each class has a teacher and an assistant, and the student-to-teacher ratios tend to be lower than the state requirements. The school is open in the morning and offers a structured enrichment program and free play in the afternoons. Only a third of the students are Jewish; the remainder are from other religions and varying nationalities.

Montessori School of Corpus Christi
2205 16th St., Corpus Christi
• (512) 883-9306

This year-round school, opened in 1981, enrolls about 70 students in a Montessori-based curriculum where the emphasis is on individualized learning within a prepared environment. Children can progress through the curriculum at their own pace, in multi-age classrooms. The school also offers creative arts courses, such as art, music, drama and song, and field trips.

In addition, there is an extended care program, summer camp and day care during the school's break.

Naval Air Station Corpus Christi Child Development Center
Ninth and E Sts., Blg. 1782
• (512) 939-7843

Open to military personnel only, this NAEYC-accredited facility has the capacity to care for 117 youngsters. It enrolls children ages 2 through school age. It's open daily from 6:45 AM to 5:15 PM.

Naval Air Station Kingsville Child Development Center
742 Rosendahl St., Ste. 101, Kingsville
• (512) 516-6176

This facility is open to military personnel and civilian employees at this Navy base, south of Kingsville. It has the capacity to care for 63 youngsters, ages 6 weeks to 6 years. It also offers family child care, where youngsters are taken care of in private homes; an after-school program for children ages 6 to 12; and a summer camp program. The center is accredited by the NAEYC.

Public Schools

North Bay Area

Aransas County Independent School District
1601 Pirate Blvd., Rockport
• (512) 790-2212

The Aransas County Independent School District is a 4-A school system serving a 280-square-mile area including the communities of Holiday Beach, Lamar, Fulton, Rockport and a small portion of northern Aransas Pass. The district serves approximately 3,500 students on six campuses: one early childhood, two elementaries, one intermediate, one junior high and one high school, encompassing more than 73 acres. Among special programs are gifted/talented, special education, GED, vocational, high school honors, advanced placement and community education.

Aransas Pass Independent School District
244 W. Harrison Blvd., Aransas Pass
• (512) 758-3466

This school district serves 2,231 children residing in the eastern end of San Patricio County, a 53.1-square-mile area. The system is composed of five campuses that encompass kindergarten through grade 12, including three elementary schools, one intermediate school and one high school.

The public school system curriculum includes not only special programs for students who plan to attend college, but also courses and training for those planning to enter the work force immediately after graduation from high school. These include correlated vocational academics and vocational office education. Other special programs offered include: all University Interscholastic League (UIL) academic and extra curricular activities, a gifted and talented program, art, speech and hearing therapy, all levels of special education, band, choir and all sports.

Gregory-Portland Independent School District

308 N. Gregory, Gregory
• **(512) 643-6566**

Students from the neighboring communities of Gregory and Portland attend schools in this district north of Corpus Christi.

The district enrolls about 4,300 students and includes four elementary schools (grades pre-K through 4); one intermediate school (grades 5 and 6); one junior high school (grades 7 and 8); and one high school (grades 9 through 12).

Ingleside Independent School District

2807 Mustang Dr., Ingleside
• **(512) 776-7631**

Approximately 2,000 students attend the district's two elementary schools, one junior high and one high school. The district is bordered on the south and west by Corpus Christi Bay and includes several petrochemical plants as well as the Naval Station Ingleside, the Navy's Mine Warfare Center. The district has a gifted and talented program, a special education program, and a Tech-Prep program designed to give high school graduates job-entry, college or trade-school skills.

Port Aransas to Padre Island

Port Aransas Independent School District

100 S. Station St., Port Aransas
• **(512) 749-5500**

Situated on the island, this school district has one elementary school, one junior high and one high school, serving about 530 students. It has a staff of 80 employees. The district has received awards for academic excellence and for meeting the needs of parents. In addition to academics, the Port Aransas Marlins are competitive in a number of extracurricular areas, including girls and boys basketball, tennis and drama. It is one of the few school districts in the area that does not boast a football team — a testimony to the part that watersports, particularly surfing, play in the lives of the community's students.

Corpus Christi

Corpus Christi Independent School District

801 Leopard St., Corpus Christi
• **(512) 886-9200**

This is the largest of five public school districts within the city limits of Corpus Christi as well as the largest in the Coastal Bend. It has 63 campuses with approximately 41,000 students in prekindergarten through grade 12. An instructional staff of more than 2,800 teachers is complemented by a support staff of 2,500.

The district has five senior high schools, 12 middle schools, 40 elementary schools and six special campuses. The high schools all have regular and honors programs. Roy Miller High School was revamped as the Miller High School Center for Communications and Technology in 1996 and now offers course work that focuses on engineering and computer science, technology and business, and communications.

The middle schools contain grades 6 through 8. Baker Middle School is part of the Athena Program for gifted and talented students, with enrollment determined by scores on tests administered each spring, summer and fall, and by teacher recommendation. Wynn Seale Middle School Academy of Fine Arts is for students interested in the arts as well as academics, with a curriculum that integrates band, orchestra, art, dance, choir, piano and theater arts with the general curriculum of math, science, English and social studies.

One of the elementary schools, Windsor Park, also has a program for the gifted and

INSIDERS' TIP

The John E. Conner Museum at Texas A&M University-Kingsville features a display of a 1910-era kitchen that includes period utensils such as a butter churn and hand-cranked washing machine.

talented. Admittance, again, is by test scores and teacher recommendation. Another elementary school, Chula Vista Academy of Fine Arts, emphasizes art, music and drama in addition to reading, mathematics and composition. Students must demonstrate interest in the arts and apply for admission.

There are also seven special-emphasis schools, based on the belief that some students do best in a highly structured curriculum, with emphasis on basic skills, good citizenship and discipline.

Other special campuses include the Adult Learning Center, Human Development Center, Teenage Mothers School and the Student Learning and Guidance Center.

Flour Bluff Independent School District
2505 Waldron Rd., Corpus Christi
• **(512) 937-2681**

The approximately 5,200 students enrolled in this district attend classes on five campuses, including an early childhood center for prekindergarten and kindergarten, a primary school for grades 1 and 2, an elementary school for grades 3 and 4, an intermediate school for grades 5 and 6, a junior high for grades 7 and 8 and a high school for grades 9 through 12. The district also has two alternative centers, one to educate students who are behind in credits and need extra assistance to graduate with their class and another for students with disciplinary problems. The district includes the southern portion of Corpus Christi, near Naval Air Station Corpus Christi.

Calallen Independent School District
4205 Wildcat Dr., Corpus Christi
• **(512) 241-9321**

This district in the northwestern part of the city has six campuses, including four elementary schools, one middle school and

one high school. It enrolls approximately 4,706 students. The district's 75-member jump rope team, the Calallen Hop-A-Longs, has won state, national and international awards, traveled to 10 foreign countries and served as a state demonstration team for the American Heart Association.

Tuloso-Midway Independent School District
9760 LaBranch St., Corpus Christi
• **(512) 241-3286**

This district has four campuses: one elementary, one intermediate, one middle and one high school. It is in the city's northwestern end and enrolls approximately 3,000 students. This district has received state recognition for its academic achievements.

West Oso Independent School District
5050 Rockford Dr., Corpus Christi
• **(512) 855-3321**

This district has five campuses, including three elementary schools, one junior high and one high school. It is on the city's west side and enrolls 1,900 students.

Kingsville Area

Kingsville Independent School District
207 N. Third St., Kingsville
• **(512) 592-3387**

This is the largest of four public school districts in the area and serves approximately 5,000 students. Facilities include six elementary schools, one intermediate school, one middle school, one traditional high school and an alternative high school. There is also a Life and Academic Skills Education Reinforcement (LASER) School that provides services to students who would normally be expelled.

In addition to standard academic

courses, the high school offers a strong vocational program with seven career pathways that include agricultural science and technology, business and marketing, health science technology, industrial and engineering technology, automotive/aircraft technology, law enforcement and home economics. The high school was also the first in the nation to offer a jet maintenance class, using a Navy jet housed at the school.

The system also offers a Challenge program, open to gifted and talented students.

Ricardo Independent School District
W. County Rd. 2160, Ricardo
• (512) 592-0471

This district south of Kingsville educates children through the 8th grade. Students then can transfer to high schools in Kingsville or nearby Riviera. Riviera Independent School District, in the southern part of Kleberg County, goes through the 12th grade and has a 2-A high school.

Santa Gertrudis Independent School District
King Ranch, Texas Hwy. 141, Kingsville
• (512) 592-7582

This small school district takes the ranch's students through the 8th grade. The Learning Academy, established in the 1994-95 school year, is a joint venture between Santa Gertrudis Independent School District and nearby Driscoll Independent School District. The Academy, on the campus of Texas A&M University-Kingsville, began with 9th grade and will expand to a four-year high school as the students progress. The system serves 135 students beginning in prekindergarten.

Private and Parochial Schools

The largest group of private schools in the Coastal Bend are the parochial campuses run by the Catholic Diocese of Corpus Christi, 3036 Saratoga Boulevard, (512) 814-0444. The diocese operates 26 private Catholic schools in an area that extends from the Coastal Bend all the way south to Laredo. Approximately 6,000

The Dr. Hector P. Garcia Plaza is a focal point on the campus of Texas A&M University - Corpus Christi.

students attend these schools, many of which use a year-round schedule.

Corpus Christi has nine Catholic elementary schools: Central Catholic, Christ the King, Holy Family, Incarnate Word Academy Elementary, St. Patrick's, St. Pius, Most Precious Blood, Our Lady of Perpetual Help and Saints Cyril & Methodius. There are also two middle schools, Bishop Garriga Middle School and Incarnate Word Academy Middle School, and one high school, Incarnate Word Academy High School.

In Kingsville, there are two Catholic elementary schools. They are St. Gertrude and St. Martin.

Other Catholic elementary schools in the area include St. Anthony's in Robstown and Sacred Heart in Rockport, as well as seven schools in Laredo, on the Texas-Mexico border.

All these institutions are known for their emphasis on Catholic education, as well as for their smaller class size and a high level of parent involvement. Several schools have won national recognition for their programs, including St. Patrick's Elementary in Corpus Christi, which is one of only 15 schools in the nation to have twice received the prestigious Blue

Ribbon Award from the U.S. Department of Education, in 1986 and 1997.

The three campuses at Incarnate Word Academy, (512) 883-0857, 2910 S. Alameda Street, Corpus Christi, attract students from throughout the area. Although they are considered part of the diocesan school system, they are actually owned by the Sisters of the Incarnate Word and Blessed Sacrament, a religious order that started in 1625 in Lyon, France. The school, founded in 1871, began as an all-girl high school; it later expanded to include elementary students, both boys and girls. The high school became coeducational in 1975. Today, the academy is composed of three campuses: one elementary school that has a Montessori program, a middle school for students in grades 6 through 8 and a high school.

The following listings describe some of the other private schools in the city and area.

St. James Episcopal School
602 S. Carancahua St., Corpus Christi
• (512) 883-0835

Near downtown, this private school has a reputation for academic excellence. It enrolls about 348 students, ages 2½ through 8th grade. Class sizes run around 18 in middle and lower school and 12 in the preschool. Founded in 1946, the school was separated and incorporated in 1995 but remains affiliated with the Episcopal Church of the Good Shepherd. Students start each day with spiritual reflection. In 1992, the school won the nation's Blue Ribbon of Excellence Award.

Kingsville Area

Epiphany Episcopal School
206 N. Third St., Kingsville
• (512) 592-2871

This is a nondenominational Christian private school that has been in operation since 1950. It enrolls children ages 3 through the 5th grade for a total enrollment of 150 students. After-school care is also available, from 3:15 to 5:30 PM.

Presbyterian Pan American School
U.S. Hwy. 77 and F.M. Rd. 772, Kingsville
• (512) 592-4307

A fully accredited college prep school, this facility has boarders as well as day students in grades 9 through 12. A self-described "community of worship, study and work," it has gained a reputation for recruiting international students who are interested in an American education. Originally founded in 1918 as a missionary school for Mexican boys, it became coeducational in 1957. It now enrolls local and area students as well as a number of international students. The enrollment is approximately 100 students.

Colleges and Universities

Del Mar Community College
Baldwin and Ayers Sts., Corpus Christi
• (512) 886-1254 admissions/registrar

This is a technical and junior college with two campuses and outreach programs that provides academic, occupational and continuing education classes to more than 28,000 students each year. Founded in 1935, the college was originally under the control of the Corpus Christi Independent School District and designed to provide two years of post-secondary education. It started with 154 students in borrowed classrooms. The college became an independent political subdivision in 1951.

As one of the state's most affordable colleges, Del Mar allows students to take a full-time course load for about $300 in tuition and fees each semester. The college also distributes more than $8 million in financial aid each year.

Del Mar offers programs to earn associate degrees in art, science and applied science; certificates of achievement; and enhanced skills certificates in more than 100 fields of study. More than 75 percent of students who plan to transfer and complete their bachelor's degree do so within one year. The average passing rate for Del Mar graduates in licensed occupational programs is 92 percent.

Texas A&M University-Corpus Christi
6300 Ocean Dr., Corpus Christi
• (512) 994-2624, (800) 4TAMUCC

Situated on a 240-acre island campus that fronts Corpus Christi Bay, this four-year university specializes in business, education, science and the arts. It is a member of the Texas

A&M University System, enrolls approximately 6,000 students and employs 250 full-time teachers. Nicknamed the Island University, it was ranked one of the nation's best public regional universities by *U.S. News and World Report*, in the magazine's 1998 guide, America's Best Colleges. It is also a fast-growing university: It was expanded from a two-year to four-year university in 1994, and student enrollment has nearly doubled. The university is also now looking to add intercollegiate athletics to its roster of recreational activities. Still, classes tend to be small, with an average 15-to-1 student-teacher ratio.

The university is on Ward Island, which was used as a top-secret radar installation during World War II. The Defense Department was persuaded to relinquish the island so it could be used as the site of a university, sponsored by the Baptist General Convocation of Texas. The first university on Ward Island, called University of Corpus Christi, was a private, liberal arts college that opened in 1947. Through the years, its name was changed to Texas A&I University-Corpus Christi and Corpus Christi State University. It joined the Texas A&M University System in 1989, and changed its name to Texas A&M University-Corpus Christi in 1993. Today, it offers more than 50 degree programs.

Among its more well-known efforts are those in environmental research, particularly appropriate because of the school's location along the coast. In 1997, the university's $10 million Center for Environmental Studies opened with 18 state agencies and research organizations. The building provided a new home for the university's Center for Coastal Studies, which has specialized in research on the coastal environment and with state and federal regulatory agencies. Among research projects that have been conducted at the center are a study of the environmental effects of oil spills and the resulting cleanup, and a study on the invasion of brown mussels along the Texas coast and marshes.

Texas A&M University-Kingsville
Office of School Relations, MSC 116, 700 University Blvd., Kingsville
• **(512) 593-3907, (800) 687-6000**

This longtime four-year university is de-

voted to educating students from South Texas, and offers 56 undergraduate degree programs in subjects including engineering, business, science, agriculture and education. Its mission is to foster the growth of a middle class in South Texas; currently 65 percent of its students are Hispanic, and many are first-generation college students, which means that the university experience is new to them as well as to their families.

The campus consists of 1,625 acres on five sites in South Texas, including a main campus, a university farm, a Citrus Research Center in Weslaco and buildings in Baffin Bay and Kleberg County. It also offers 57 graduate degrees in 40 areas, including three doctorates. Among its more renowned activities are agricultural research — its citrus center developed the well-loved Rio Red and Star Ruby varieties of grapefruit — and athletic achievement, having produced a football program that has won seven national titles and sent more than 100 players to the pros, including Darrell Green, Earl Dotson, John Randle and Jermane Mayberry.

Established in 1925 as South Texas State Teachers College, it joined the Texas A&M University system in 1989. Texas A&M University-Kingsville enrolls more than 6,000 students annually and specializes in developing programs for minority students in agriculture, science and engineering. The university is also one of the community's major employers, with 815 employees, including 260 faculty members, 450 staff members and more than 100 part-time employees, most of whom are instructors.

The university is also known for research into wildlife science, conducted at the Caesar Kleberg Wildlife Research Institute. Ongoing research focuses on such topics as big cats, including ocelots and mountain lions in South Texas, and on helping ranchers manage habitats so they can utilize the wildlife as an economic resource.

A final claim to fame: The university says it is the only one in the United States with the javelina as its mascot. The javelina, also called the collared peccary, is a sort of wild pig that is known for its aggressiveness.

Corpus Christi has experienced an explosion of hospital mergers, expansions and new construction during the past few years.

Healthcare

Corpus Christi serves as the healthcare center for the Texas Coastal Bend. Fourteen of the 16 hospitals listed in our four geographical areas are in Corpus Christi. The Spohn Health System and Columbia/HCA Healthcare System dominate the local industry, operating all but five of the 16 hospitals.

Corpus Christi has experienced an explosion of hospital mergers, expansions and new construction during the past few years. And now a nationwide trend to open new hospitals devoted to specific healthcare needs has led both Spohn and Columbia to open cardiology centers.

In the Coastal Bend, Spohn Health System has four major hospitals — Spohn Shoreline, Spohn South, Spohn Memorial and Spohn Kleberg Memorial — 18 primary-care centers and several medical, educational and wellness services. Established in 1905, Spohn is a member of Incarnate Word Health System, a nonprofit healthcare system based in San Antonio and sponsored by the Sisters of Charity of the Incarnate Word.

Columbia is one of the largest hospital networks in the United States. It operates seven full-service and specialty hospitals in our four geographical areas, along with one psychiatric center. In the past few years it has expanded facilities at three hospitals and built two new ones.

Both Spohn and Columbia say they're expanding to provide needed healthcare services to the Coastal Bend, a region that traditionally has been underserved by the healthcare industry. Their recent emphasis on cardiovascular care is in response to the needs of an aging population that is experiencing more heart problems.

In this chapter, along with writeups on full-service and specialty hospitals, you'll find information on physician referral services, telephone numbers to call in a medical emergency or when you need medical information, walk-in clinics, mental health facilities, hospices and alternative healthcare.

Our listings are divided into the four geographical areas and are then listed alphabetically within those areas.

Hospitals

North Bay Area

Columbia North Bay Hospital
1711 W. Wheeler Ave., Aransas Pass
• (512) 758-8585, (800) 400-3742

Columbia North Bay Hospital is the only fully accredited acute-care hospital in the North Bay area. It provides outpatient and inpatient care for people needing surgery, obstetric care, orthopedics, urology services and complete diagnostic radiology services.

The hospital recently expanded its emergency room space. It's emergency room and emergency-medicine-trained doctors are available 24 hours a day.

Corpus Christi

Columbia Bay Area Medical Center
7101 S. Padre Island Dr., Corpus Christi
• (512) 985-1200, (800) 265-8621

This 141-bed facility at the corner of S. Padre Island Drive and Rodd Field Road is a full-service, acute-care hospital employing more than 700 healthcare workers. Facilities include the hospital, medical offices, The Cancer Center, The Breast Center and Coastal Bend Women's Center. It recently added a new neonatal intensive-care unit that complements its labor-delivery, recovery-postpartum rooms that allow mothers to spend their entire hospital stay in the same room.

Columbia Bay Area has a 24-hour emergency room and a residency program. It's on Corpus Christi's southside and is particularly accessible to residents in Flour Bluff and Padre Island.

Columbia Doctors Regional Medical Center
3315 S. Alameda St. • (512) 857-1400, (800) 442-2512

Set in the middle of several residential neighborhoods, Columbia Doctors Regional Medical Center is a full-service, acute-care hospital. This 282-bed hospital offers a complete range of inpatient and outpatient services. The first area hospital to open a neonatal intensive-care unit, it also organized a Women's Pavilion, 3240 Fort Worth Street, bringing together obstetricians, gynecologists, women's health education resources and a diabetes management program.

This hospital also has a 24-hour emergency room, MRI diagnostic center and an adjacent office building for physicians.

Columbia Northwest Regional Hospital
13725 F.M. Rd. 624, Corpus Christi • (512) 241-4243

Formerly known as Riverside Hospital, Columbia Northwest was purchased by Columbia in September 1995 and is the only acute-care medical facility in northwest Corpus Christi. Recent construction that doubled the hospital's size updated its 24-hour emergency services and added surgical suites and high-tech diagnostic and treatment services.

The hospital campus also houses physician offices and the Calallen Orthopedic and Sports Medicine Center, a treatment and rehabilitation center serving orthopedic cases, sports injuries and outpatient cardiovascular patients. Its wellness/fitness center is open to both corporations and individuals.

Columbia Rehabilitation Hospital
6226 Saratoga Blvd., Corpus Christi • (512) 991-9690

Columbia Rehabilitation Hospital provides inpatient and outpatient treatment for traumatic brain injury, stroke, spinal cord injury, neurological disorders, orthopedic and amputation needs, as well as chronic pain management.

The Arthritis Foundation, South Texas chapter, sponsors programs for arthritis patients here called People With Arthritis Can Exercise (PACE). The facility also features a modern rehab gym, mobility track duplicating everyday obstacles and a heated indoor therapy and exercise pool.

Multidisciplinary teams work together to create individual treatment plans for each patient. They include a rehabilitation physician, certified rehab registered nurses, occupational and physical therapists, speech-language pathologists, neuropsychologists and psychological diagnosticians.

Corpus Christi Naval Hospital
10651 E St., Naval Air Station, Corpus Christi • (512) 961-2688

Situated on Naval Air Station Corpus Christi, this ambulatory care facility serves active-duty military and their family members as well as military retirees and their dependents. Built in 1974, this five-story hospital employs approximately 400 military personnel and civilians. The hospital houses outpatient clinics on two floors and administrative offices.

A snack bar, galley, store and optometry shop are in the basement.

Spohn Hospital Shoreline
600 Elizabeth St., Corpus Christi • (512) 881-3000, (800) 247-6574

Licensed for 458 beds, Spohn Hospital Shoreline is the largest hospital in Corpus Christi. A new $28.8 million addition, Spohn Shoreline Pavilion, houses the Spohn Heart Institute and the Spohn Shoreline Surgery Center. It also is home to the Spohn Cancer Network, including the Radiation Therapy Center and Spohn Hospice.

The Spohn Diabetes Center, Spohn Neuroscience Center, a Sleep Disorders Lab, Spohn Orthopedics, Spohn Rehabilitation Center, and the Spohn Women's Center provide other health services. The hospital also pro-

---

vides a complete array of outpatient services, including outpatient surgery and 24-hour emergency physicians. Spohn Hospital Shoreline employs 1,700 people.

Spohn Hospital South
5950 Saratoga Blvd., Corpus Christi
• **(512) 985-5000, (800) 247-6574**

Spohn Hospital South opened in 1994 to meet the medical needs of Corpus Christi's fast-growing Southside area. It has 102 private rooms, an array of inpatient and outpatient services and the largest medical professional building in the city, Spohn South Health Plaza.

Hospital facilities include day surgery, 24-hour physician-staffed emergency room, cardiopulmonary services, 27 birthing suites and gynecological, medical/surgical and inten-sive-care services. The hospital also offers an MRI facility.

Spohn Health Plaza is home to the LifeCenter, which includes Spohn Wellness Services, counseling, a resource library, mammography, massage therapy and sports physical therapy.

Spohn Hospital South employs 250 people.

Spohn Memorial Hospital
2606 Hospital Blvd., Corpus Christi
• **(512) 902-4000, (800) 247-6574**

Spohn Memorial Hospital is a 397-bed acute-care hospital providing a full range of medical services. The city's second-largest hospital provides emergency, critical care, medical/surgical and diagnostic services. It also serves as the region's burn and trauma center. Additional services include 24-hour physician-staffed emergency services, a 24-bed coronary care unit, a 24-bed intensive-care unit, labor-and-delivery services, diabetes treatment, rehabilitation services and complete diagnostic services, including MRI and accredited mammography.

Spohn Memorial, a teaching hospital affiliated with The University of Texas Health Science Center at San Antonio, employs 1,600 people.

Kingsville Area

Spohn Kleberg Memorial Hospital
1311 E. General Cavazos Blvd.
• **(512) 595-1661, (800) 247-6574**

Spohn Kleberg Memorial Hospital is an acute-care facility serving residents in Kleberg, Kenedy, Brooks, Jim Wells and southern Nueces counties. This 100-bed medical center has a 24-hour emergency room, inpatient and outpatient surgical services, an ambulatory care unit, pediatric services and a skilled nursing unit.

Other services include a full range of treatment and diagnostic capabilities, obstetrics, mammography, intensive care, a health and wellness center and home health services. It also operates six Spohn Family Health Clinics and employs 500 people in its hospital, home-health services and family medical clinics.

Specialty Hospitals

Corpus Christi

Columbia Surgicare Specialty Hospital
718 Elizabeth St., Corpus Christi
• **(512) 882-3204**

Just down the street from Spohn Hospital, Columbia Surgicare Specialty Hospital, which opened in 1993, is an ambulatory surgery center equipped with four operating rooms and an emergency treatment room.

This six-bed hospital offers a wide variety of surgical services in a quiet environment. It employs specialists in dentistry, general surgery, gynecology, ophthalmology, orthopedics, pain therapy, podiatry, plastic surgery and urology.

Corpus Christi Warm Springs Rehabilitation Hospital
2606 Hospital Blvd., Corpus Christi
• **(512) 888-4458, (800) 500-0107**

Although on the first and eighth floors of

Spohn Memorial Hospital, Warm Springs is a separate medical facility specializing in treating catastrophic neurological injuries. It provides inpatient and outpatient services to people with brain injuries, burns and strokes, and neurological and orthopedic disorders. The hospital is part of the non-profit Warm Springs Rehabilitation System, which also operates hospitals in Gonzales and San Antonio.

Their treatment method is an interdisciplinary team approach involving physical and occupational therapy, physical medicine and rehabilitation physicians, rehabilitation nursing, speech therapy, social services and rehabilitation psychology. The hospital employs about 75 people.

It also operates four outpatient treatment centers in the Coastal Bend. They are: Warm Springs Rehabilitation Center, (512) 887-1919, 1521 S. Staples Street, Suite 501, Corpus Christi; Warm Springs Lifestyle and Rehabilitation Center, (512) 729-9799, 2600 Lakeview Drive, Rockport; Warm Springs Rehabilitation Center-Alice, (512) 668-6000, 65 N. Wright Street, Suite A, Alice; and Warm Springs Rehabilitation Center-Falfurrias, (512) 325-2511, 1400 S. St. Mary's Street, Falfurrias.

Driscoll Children's Hospital
3533 S. Alameda St., Corpus Christi
• **(512) 694-5000**

This 188-bed hospital is a private, nonprofit tertiary-care referral center serving children in a 32-county South Texas area. Its philosophy is that children are not small adults, and they have health needs requiring different services, care and resources.

It maintains 128 acute-care beds, 40 intensive-care beds for premature newborns and 20 intensive-care beds for children with a wide variety of medical and surgical abnormalities. Driscoll was the first hospital in South Texas to provide emergency services exclusively for children. The hospital's critical-care transport service provides immediate 24-hour-a-day response, transferring children who need specialized medical and surgical care by airplane, helicopter or ground transport vehicle to Driscoll's emergency room and intensive-care units.

Driscoll employs more than 1,200 people in its hospital and adjacent rehabilitation center. A three-year pediatric residency program offering training for physicians specializing in pediatric medicine is fully accredited by the American Council of Graduate Medical Education.

Driscoll Children's Rehabilitation Center of South Texas
3511 S. Alameda St., Corpus Christi
• **(512) 694-4380**

This hospital, adjacent to Driscoll Children's Hospital, began in 1939 as the Ada Wilson Children's Center for Rehabilitation and operated independently until merging with Driscoll Hospital. It offers outpatient services for children and young adults ranging from those with mild developmental delays to people with multiple handicaps.

The facility houses Driscoll's rehabilitation department, day surgery unit and Neuromuscular Institute, which includes orthopedics, neurology and neurosurgery. Outpatient services include physical therapy, occupational therapy, speech therapy, audiology, hyppotherapy, medical specialty clinics and case management services.

Specialty Hospital of Corpus Christi
1310 Third St., Corpus Christi
• **(512) 888-4323**

Specialty Hospital provides both complex-acute medical care and comprehensive physical rehabilitation services to inpatients. It's licensed by the state of Texas as a long-term acute-care hospital, and it's the only facility of its type in the Coastal Bend.

The 31-bed hospital takes patients from hospital intensive-care units and other patients needing acute care. The staff provides ventilator care, in-house dialysis and wound care.

Specialty Hospital has more than 75 employees and 50 physicians specializing in individualized care and complements services offered by other hospitals.

The Heart Hospital of South Texas
7002 Williams Dr., Corpus Christi
• (512) 980-1800
Situated next door to Columbia Bay Area Medical Center, The Heart Hospital is the most recent addition to the family of Corpus Christi hospitals. Opened in January 1998, this Columbia-owned hospital is dedicated solely to cardiac care in the area. State-of-the-art prevention, treatment, surgery and support services are available. The hospital's all-nurse management system is designed to view every aspect of patient care through the patient's point of view.

Referral Services

Corpus Christi has several medical referral services, which provide callers with information on physicians and services available in the area. These include Bay Area Medical Center, (512) 857-1503; Columbia Physician Referral, (800) 265-8624; Driscoll Physician Referral, (512) 694-5437; and Spohn Healthline, 5920 Saratoga Boulevard, Corpus Christi, (512) 881-3103 or (800) 247-6574.

Numbers to Call

When an emergency arises or you need general information or direction to community resources, refer to this list. For emergencies requiring ambulance, police or fire departments, call 911.

800 Cocaine Info Hotline, (800) 262-2463
AIDS Information Hotline, (800) 590-2437
AIDS Services of the Coastal Bend 24-Hour Hotline, (512) 814-7001
AIDS Testing-Fast, (800) 584-8183
Area Agency on Aging of the Coastal Bend, (512) 883-5743
Coast Guard Marine and Air Emergency, (512) 937-1898

Corpus Christi-Nueces County Health Department, (512) 851-7200
Medic Alert Foundation, (800) 344-3226
National Council on Compulsive Gambling, (800) 522-4700
National Child Abuse Hotline, (800) 422-4453
Nueces County Community Action Agency, (512) 883-7201
Nueces County Medical Society, (512) 884-5442
Nueces County Psychological Association, (512) 991-5915
Poison Center, (800) 764-7661
Texas Aged and Disabled Services, (512) 878-3426
Texas Department of Health, Environmental & Consumer Health Protection, (512) 888-7762
Texas Health Professions Council (For complaints against a health professional), (800) 821-3205
Texas Medical Examiners Board, Consumer Complaint Hotline, (800) 201-9353
Texas Mental Health and Mental Retardation Department, (512) 888-5301
Tri County Emergency Medical Service, (512) 776-0025
United Way Info-Line, (512) 882-4636

Walk-In Clinics

The only thing worse than getting sick while on vacation is not knowing where to find a doctor. For emergencies, you can turn to any of the full-service hospitals in the area. But what if your ailment doesn't warrant a trip to the emergency room? For those occasions you might, instead, turn to one of the Coastal Bend's walk-in clinics, which handle minor emergencies and illnesses.

Walk-in clinics generally can treat minor injuries like sprains, cuts, minor burns, whiplash and flu-like symptoms. Many have X-ray equipment and on-site diagnostic labs.

Most operate during typical business hours, although a few offer evening and weekend hours. They accept insurance, credit cards, cash, Medicare and Medicaid. Below you'll find the names, addresses, phone num-

Photo: Daniel Fielder

Spohn Hospital South is conveniently located near most of Southside
Corpus Christi's growing neighborhoods.

bers and office hours of several walk-in clinics in the area. Because hours are often subject to change, be sure to call the clinic to confirm the information or to ask additional questions.

North Bay Area

Gulf Coast Medical Clinic
**Texas Hwy. 35 at Henderson Rd.,
Rockport • (512) 729-9811**
Hours are 8 AM to noon and 1 to 5 PM Monday through Friday. The clinic is closed weekends and major holidays.

Corpus Christi

Bayside Family Medicine
**3817 S. Padre Island Dr., Corpus Christi
• (512) 857-0178**
Bayside is open 8 AM to 8 PM Monday through Friday and 8 AM to 4:45 PM on weekends.

Urgent Care Clinic
**3434 Saratoga Blvd., Corpus Christi
• (512) 852-3938**
Monday through Friday, this clinic is open 9 AM to 6 PM. On Saturday, hours are 8 AM to noon.

Port Aransas
to Padre Island

Port Aransas Health Clinic
**738 Tarpon St., Port Aransas
• (512) 749-5524**
Hours here are 8 AM to 11:30 AM and 1 to 4:30 PM Monday through Friday.

Spohn Neighborhood Care Center
**14202 S. Padre Island Dr., Corpus Christi
• (512) 949-7660**
This care center is open 8 AM to 7:30 PM Monday through Friday and noon to 6 PM on weekends.

Kingsville Area

Spohn Bishop Family Health Clinic
301 W. Main St., Bishop • (512) 584-2563
Spohn Kingsville Family
Health Clinic
915 S. Ninth St., Kingsville
• (512) 592-6456

Both clinics are open Monday through Friday from 8 AM to 5 PM. They're closed on weekends.

Mental Health

Corpus Christi

Charter Behavioral Health System of Corpus Christi
3126 Rodd Field Rd., Corpus Christi
• (512) 993-8893, (800) 843-1020

Formerly known as Charter Hospital, Charter Behavioral Health System offers a variety of psychiatric and addiction-behavioral services at several locations throughout the Coastal Bend. The main facility in Corpus Christi offers psychiatric and addiction services on an inpatient basis for children, adolescents and adults. Intensive outpatient and partial programs on weekends, evenings and days help people with general psychiatric and eating disorders, pain management, sexual abuse, family conflict and geriatric and anxiety issues.

Charter Behavioral Health System also offers the Sedona Women's Wellness Program, which provides a range of therapies oriented toward women's issues. Education also is provided on topics ranging from stress management to employer-employee relations.

Charter also provides outpatient counseling in Aransas Pass, Ingleside and Kingsville.

Columbia Bayview
Psychiatric Center
6226 Saratoga Blvd., Corpus Christi
• (512) 993-9700, (800) 265-8621

Columbia Bayview Psychiatric Center specializes in the treatment of alcohol and chemical dependencies, behavioral disorders, emotional wellness for women and the psychiatric needs of children, adolescents and adults. Outpatient counseling also is available at several locations in the Coastal Bend. Physicians, psychologists, social workers, registered nurses and educators provide treatment and counseling. Day and evening programs are available.

The center's campus is home to the Cimarron Center for Women's Wellness, designed to help women 18 and older find relief from depression, anxiety, panic attacks, abuse, co-dependency, alcoholism, loss, grief and eating disorders.

Community Mental Health Center of Corpus Christi
226 Enterprize Pkwy., Ste. 104, Corpus Christi • (512) 299-1933

The Community Mental Health Center of Corpus Christi's partial hospitalization program treats patients who are unable to function mentally on a day-to-day basis or have chronic psychiatric conditions who need intensive daily services to prevent full-time hospitalization. It treats patients who require more intensive outpatient therapy to prevent full-time hospitalization or whose level of functioning or psychiatric symptoms have not been maintained or improved by outpatient treatment.

Seaview Mental Health Center
4529 Weber Rd., Corpus Christi
• (512) 852-3994

Seaview Mental Health Center is a sister-center to the Community Mental Health Center of Corpus Christi, offering the same partial hospitalization program listed above.

Southside Health Center
4626 Weber Rd., Corpus Christi
• (512) 854-2031

Southside Health Center, at the site of the former Southside Community Hospital, is home to the Nueces County Hospital District's 42-bed Behavioral Medicine Unit. This unit provides short-term acute psychiatric care. Also on site is the Nueces County Mental Health Mental Retardation's 15-bed Geropsychiatric Triage Unit and Spohn Memorial Hospital's Home Health Agency.

Hospices

North Bay Area

Aim Hospice
703 E. Concho St., Rockport
• (512) 729-0507, (800) 854-2674

This nonprofit hospice has been in business here for 10 years, serving people with terminal illnesses with a life expectancy of six months or less. All hospice care is provided in the patient's home or nursing home, with family, friends or paid caregivers caring for them.

The hospice staff teach families to provide nursing assistance and provide a social worker, pastoral worker and bereavement counseling for a year after the death. Aim Hospice serves clients within a 70-mile radius of Rockport.

Corpus Christi

Spohn Hospice
1660 S. Staples St., Corpus Christi
• (512) 881-3159

Spohn Hospice, in business since 1983, provides home care for terminally ill patients who prefer to die at home surrounded by loved ones instead of in a hospital hooked up to medical equipment. To qualify, patients must have accepted their impending death and stopped all curative treatments. Spohn Hospice provides a team of nurses, a medical director, nurses aids, a social worker, chaplain and a counselor who work together to keep the patient comfortable at home or in the nursing home in which they reside.

The staff work to control symptoms and pain and help the family deal with the sorrow of losing loved ones. They help the family get their finances in order and prepare for death. They strive to keep patients at home and pain-free and work with their doctor and family in caring for them.

Spohn Hospice serves clients within a 100-mile radius of Corpus Christi. It has 16 full-time and two part-time employees.

VistaCare
5151 Flynn Pkwy., Ste. 304, Corpus Christi • (512) 854-1540, (888) 878-1540

VistaCare, based in Arizona, has two locations in Texas, including its newest one in Corpus Christi. This Medicare-certified hospice program provides a full range of comfort care to people with terminal illnesses and their loved ones. This includes skilled nursing, home-health

Photo: Daniel Fielder

Corpus Christi's Driscoll Children's Hospital offers specialty fields in a variety of neonatal and pediatric areas.

aids, specially trained volunteers, chaplains, social workers and 13 months of bereavement followup for families. The staff work in conjunction with their primary-care physician and the VistaCare medical director. They serve clients within a 100-mile radius of Corpus Christi.

People receiving hospice care elsewhere who wish to move to or visit the Corpus Christi area can do so without losing benefits. Call VistaCare's toll-free number for a free video.

Alternative Healthcare

Corpus Christi

Angel Light Center for the Healing Arts
5301 Everhart Rd., Corpus Christi
• **(512) 854-6563**

Angel Light is an alternative health and education center providing products with an angelic theme. Its mission is "to create a safe place of beauty and light where one can enlighten one's mind, whole one's body, and renew one's spirit."

Here you'll find self-help and transformational books, tapes and CDs, candles, herbs, beauty products, art and jewelry. Angel Light features practitioners in massage, reflexology, hypnotherapy, herbology and card reading. It also hosts classes in yoga, Tai Chi and meditation.

Retail business hours are 10 AM to 7 PM Monday through Friday and 10 AM to 4 PM on Saturday.

Christi Center for Attitudinal Healing
909 Ayers St., Corpus Christi
• **(512) 882-4820**

The Christi Center provides one-on-one counseling and support groups at no cost. The center sponsors groups for attitudinal healing, grief, divorced and separated adults, and a group for the children of divorced and separated adults.

Attitudinal Healing is an approach to facing conflict, fear and separation. It is based on the premise that it is possible to let go of painful, fearful thoughts and attitudes and to choose peace rather than conflict and love rather than fear.

As in most rural areas,
weeklies and biweeklies
abound in the Coastal
Bend, with one or more
newspapers published
in small towns
throughout the area.

Media

The Coastal Bend is served by one large daily newspaper, several weekly and biweekly newspapers, seven TV stations and about 30 radio stations. Local news coverage ranges from good to comical depending on the source, and hard-hitting investigative pieces are less common than in urban areas. The *Corpus Christi Caller-Times* is the only daily newspaper published in the area, although the *San Antonio Express News*, *Houston Chronicle* and *Dallas Morning News* circulate here.

As in most rural areas, weeklies and biweeklies abound, with one or more newspapers published in small towns throughout the Coastal Bend. Corpus Christi lacks a city magazine of the sort found in many urban areas as attempts at establishing one over the years have failed. Instead the market is blanketed with specialty publications (aimed at lawyers, Catholics and seniors, for example) and publications targeted at tourists. Most publications are available in grocery stores, convenience stores and restaurants in the areas they serve.

Publications

Daily Newspapers

Corpus Christi Caller-Times
820 Lower N. Broadway, Corpus Christi
• (512) 884-2011

It seems only fitting to begin our section on the media with the Coastal Bend's primary source for news. Although the San Antonio, Houston and Dallas newspapers circulate here, and four local TV stations and several radio stations broadcast news reports, the *Caller-Times* leads the way in local coverage. Like many newspapers with hyphenated names, the *Caller-Times* began as two newspapers, first as competitors and later as part-

ners in a joint-operating agreement for the same company.

The *Caller* served morning subscribers while the *Times* kept afternoon readers informed. The *Corpus Christi Caller*, at the time a weekly, rolled off the presses for the first time on January 21, 1883, on a rare below-freezing day. The birth of triplets to Mrs. Mark Downey was among the big stories of the day, and the 849 subscribers in the town of 3,257 read all about it.

The *Corpus Christi Times* (operating as the *Corpus Christi Democrat* until 1917) was founded in 1911 by J.W. Bauerfeind and a man named O'Flaherty. (As far as is known, history has not recorded his first name.) For years the two papers battled for subscribers, with the *Caller* having the advantage of a larger staff and greater resources. Although the *Times* operated with only one reporter for many years, it benefited from the ability to steal stories from its morning competitor.

In 1924 Bernard Hanks, publisher of the *Abilene Reporter-News*, and Houston Harte, publisher of the *San Angelo Standard-Times*, formed a partnership to buy newspapers. They bought the *Corpus Christi Times* in 1928 and the *Corpus Christi Caller* in 1929. For the next 58 years the two papers operated jointly but published separate newspapers. The *Caller* served morning readers, and the *Times* kept afternoon readers informed. On May 29, 1987, the *Times* published its last afternoon edition.

On June 1, 1987, the first edition of the new combined morning paper, the *Corpus Christi Caller-Times*, hit the streets. During the past several years the paper has won numerous journalism awards and has bucked an industry-wide trend toward lower or stagnant circulation growth. On May 20, 1997, long-time publisher and media conglomerate E.W. Scripps Company, announced plans to buy the *Caller-Times* after the paper's parent company announced its intention to concentrate on shopper publications and direct market-ing. The sale became final in October 1997.

The *Caller-Times* usually publishes stand-alone local, sports and classified sections. The "Weekend" section published every Friday de-tails recreational and entertainment activities throughout the Coastal Bend, and the Sunday edition includes the *TV Channels* magazine, ad-vertising inserts and an expanded "Help Wanted" section. Other features include: a sec-tion each Monday on financial planning, a tab-loid focusing on local people published each Thursday and a monthly tabloid devoted to His-panic issues. The *Caller-Times* circulation is more than 64,000 daily and more than 88,000 on Sundays.

www.insiders.com

See this and many other
Insiders' Guide® destinations
online — in their entirety.

Visit us today!

Weekly and Biweekly Newspapers

Weekly and biweekly newspapers are avail-able by subscription or can be purchased at convenience stores, grocery stores and, oc-casionally, newspaper racks in their coverage areas. Generally speaking, a weekly or bi-weekly devoted to a particular town cannot be found in other towns.

Aransas Pass Progress
346 S. Houston St., Aransas Pass
• (512) 758-5391

The *Aransas Pass Progress*, one of the old-est businesses in the Coastal Bend, was founded in 1909 for the sole purpose of pro-moting a land sale. It all began when J.W. Vernor, a 24-year-old printing equipment sales-man from Dallas, moved to Aransas Pass at the request of a local real estate firm to pro-mote a land auction involving hundreds of acres of city lots. Vernor's job was to attract prospective buyers by touting the auction.

When the auction was over, Vernor contin-ued publishing the *Progress* until 1911. The current publisher is Richard P. Richards, whose father, J.G. Richards, purchased a half inter-est in the paper in 1946. The *Progress*, pub-lished every Wednesday, has 2,806 paid sub-scribers. The Progress usually publishes

around 16 pages, and, like most small-town newspapers, concentrates coverage on local issues such as fishing, the shrimping indus-try, local residents and Aransas Pass schools.

Each year the *Progress* and its sister pa-per, *The Ingleside Index*, publish *The North Bay Area Visitors & Newcomers Guide*.

Christian Metro Times Newspaper
Corpus Christi • (512) 855-5343

Publisher Belma Fussell describes the *Christian Metro Times Newspaper* as providing local, national and inter-national news on issues important to Christians that would otherwise be unavailable. The *Metro Times* also provides a forum for local minis-ters to share their ministries' events with other Christians and provides information on Chris-tian-owned businesses in the Coastal Bend. The *Metro Times* publishes in the middle of each month. Between 15,000 and 20,000 free copies are distributed to churches, stores and restaurants throughout the Coastal Bend.

The Coastal Bend Herald
1114 Main St., Rockport • (512) 729-1828

The Coastal Bend Herald may well be the most ambitious weekly in the Coastal Bend, covering an area from Rockport to the north side of Corpus Christi. Publisher Kerry Riley bought the paper, established 15 years ago, in October 1996. *The Herald* and its more es-tablished competitor, *The Rockport Pilot*, com-pete for advertisers and readers in an old-fash-ioned newspaper war. The Herald strives to cover a broader area than the Pilot, which fo-cuses its reporting on the Rockport/Fulton area.

The Herald is published on Thursdays and is distributed to more than 4,000 paid sub-scribers. It usually runs about 18 pages, with news and sports in separate sections. *The Herald* also publishes a weekly TV listing.

Coastal Bend Sun
427 Naval Air Station Dr., Corpus Christi
• (512) 939-7885

Seventy-six-year-old publisher Marie Speer has three Coastal Bend publications in her fold, including the *Coastal Bend Sun*, which she began publishing in 1994. Her other publications are the *Flour Bluff Sun* and the *Seaside Sun*. Published each Saturday, the *Coastal Bend Sun* is a general-interest tabloid that reports on municipal and state issues affecting Coastal Bend residents.

By virtue of the weekly's size and location, coverage tends to focus largely on Corpus Christi. (Many stories that appear in the *Coastal Bend Sun* also can be found in the *Flour Bluff Sun*.) The *Sun*'s slogan — "We tell the truth" — is a not-so-subtle jab at the *Corpus Christi Caller-Times*, which Speer believes often slants its coverage to support its opinion on a particular issue. "We don't give any window dressing," she says. "We tell it like it is." The *Coastal Bend Sun* has a circulation of about 2,500.

Flour Bluff Sun
427 Naval Air Station Dr., Corpus Christi
• (512) 937-4584

The *Flour Bluff Sun*, another Speer publication (see the previous listing), is the community newspaper for Flour Bluff, a Corpus Christi neighborhood on the city's south side.

The *Flour Bluff Sun*, which began publishing in 1976, publishes each Friday and is delivered to its 2,500 subscribers.

Flightline/Aircraftsman Newspaper
4455 S. Padre Island Dr., Ste. 45, Corpus Christi • (512) 814-0866

The *Flightline/Aircraftsman Newspaper* is the general-interest newspaper for Naval Air Station Corpus Christi and the Corpus Christi Army Depot (on the naval air station) on the city's south side. Articles cover base news and news from the Navy. The paper is distributed at Naval Air Station Corpus Christi, Naval Air Station Kingsville, Naval Station Ingleside and some nearby restaurants.

The Flying K
554 McCain St., Ste. 309, Kingsville
• (512) 516-6146

Articles for this 1,500-circulation newspaper at Naval Air Station Kingsville are submitted by the training squadrons and other departments at the base. Published every other week, it is produced by the public affairs office and distributed free on the base.

The Foc'sle
1455 Ticonderoga Rd., Ingleside
• (512) 776-4206

Featuring articles of interest to the Navy's mine warfare community, this newspaper at Naval Station Ingleside has a circulation of 10,000 active duty and retired military readers here as well as overseas. It is produced by the base public affairs office every other week, and is distributed free at Naval Station Ingleside, Naval Air Station Corpus Christi and the Family Service Center at Bay Vista Shopping Center, 2370 Texas Highway 361.

The Ingleside Index
346 S. Houston St., Aransas Pass
• (512) 758-5391

In contrast to its nearest neighbor, *The Aransas Pass Progress*, the *Ingleside Index* is a relatively young creature, having sprung into existence in early 1951 at the hands of local newspapermen Carter Snooks and Bill Kennedy. The duo operated *The Index* until J.G. Richards, publisher of *The Aransas Pass Progress*, bought it on March 21, 1973. *The Index* and *The Progress* share similar layouts, news philosophies, staffs and facilities. *The Ingleside Index* focuses on Ingleside people and issues and military stories of interest to the many people stationed at Naval Station Ingleside, the center for the Navy's mine warfare fleet and equipment.

Published on Thursdays, *The Index* usually runs about 10 pages. It has more than 850 paid subscribers. Each year the *Index* and *Progress* publish *The North Bay Area Visitors & Newcomers Guide*.

The Kingsville Record and Bishop News
105 S. Fifth St., Kingsville
• (512) 592-4304

The Kingsville Record and Bishop News is one of the largest small-town newspapers in the Coastal Bend. Published on Wednesdays and Sundays, *The Record* boasts an average of 20 to 30 pages per issue. The paper is owned by the King Ranch Inc. and has been in business since 1906 when the Kingsville Publishing Company formed *The Kingsville Record*. Recently it merged with another newspaper, *The Bishop News*, expanding its coverage area to include the town of Bishop.

The Kingsville Record and Bishop News now has about 6,200 paid subscribers and covers news in Kingsville, Bishop, Riviera, Driscoll, Ricardo and surrounding areas. The paper is divided into several sections — news, sports, society, classified and a Sunday entertainment tabloid with articles on restaurants, music and other entertainment-related subjects. It also includes local TV listings and a page devoted to subjects of interest to children.

Port Aransas South Jetty
141 W. Cotter Ave., Port Aransas
• (512) 749-5131

The *South Jetty* began in 1971 with a shoestring budget and a cause. Publishers Suzanna Reader and Steve Frishman convinced Reader's father to donate $1,000 to start up a newspaper to fight a proposed deepwater port near Port Aransas that would allow tankers to dock and unload crude oil for refining in Corpus Christi. Reader and Frishman, along with others fond of Port Aransas's laid-back lifestyle, railed against the proposal in the *South Jetty*'s pages. So far, their efforts have paid off: The deepwater port, now labeled Safe Harbor, has yet to be built.

Current editor Mary Judson thinks the *Jetty*'s history is special. In the old days, before newspapers became profit centers and journalists claimed to be objective, newspapers generally were started by nonjournalists to promote a cause. The *South Jetty*, Judson says, was founded in that same spirit. Judson and her husband, publisher Murray Judson, bought the *South Jetty* in 1981 and published their first edition in January of that year. The paper is published every Thursday.

As evidence of the city's status as a tourist destination, about 2,500 of the *South Jetty*'s 4,000 subscribers live outside Port Aransas. The *South Jetty* is mailed to subscribers in 49 states and several foreign countries. Its 16- to 18-page editions boast more fish photos than any newspaper in the Coastal Bend. Deep-sea fishing is big business in Port Aransas, so it's not unusual to see the *South Jetty*'s pages

plastered with photos of smiling tourists displaying their catches.

The *South Jetty* covers Port Aransas and Mustang Island and publishes visitors guides in August, November, February and May.

Portland News
101 Cedar Pl., Ste. G, Portland
• (512) 643-1566

Several Portland newspapers bit the dust in the hundred or so years before the Guthrie Publishing Company founded the *Portland News* in 1964. In 1971 Guthrie Publishing sold the *News* to James F. Tracy Jr., who now publishes the weekly with his son, John H. Tracy. The *News* focuses its coverage on Portland, a few miles from Corpus Christi on the north side of the Nueces Bay Causeway. The *News* has about 2,500 paid subscribers and publishes about 12 pages each week.

The Rockport Pilot
1002 Wharf St., Rockport
• (512) 729-9900

The Rockport Pilot is one of the older publications in the Coastal Bend and more than a century older than its Rockport rival, *The Coastal Bend Herald*. The *Pilot*, which publishes on Wednesdays and Saturdays, started in 1869 and is owned by Hartman Newspapers with Mike Probst as publisher.

More than 4,800 people subscribe to *The Pilot*, which normally runs about 16 pages. *The Pilot* covers Rockport and Fulton schools and city governments, along with the Aransas County government and the Aransas County Navigation District. It's interesting to note that back editions of this and other area newspapers are rare because hurricanes and other storms have destroyed them.

Seaside Sun
427 Naval Air Station Dr., Corpus Christi
• (512) 937-4584

A third Marie Speer publication, the *Seaside Sun*, has been guiding Coastal Bend tourists to a good time since 1976. This small tabloid gives tourists information on local fishing, entertainment and tourism-related activities in the area. The *Seaside Sun* is free and published every Thursday.

Photo: Daniel Fielder

CBS affiliate KZTV-TV is located in uptown Corpus Christi.

Specialty Newspapers

South Texas Catholic
Corpus Christi • (512) 289-1752

The Catholic community keeps up to date on news of the Diocese of Corpus Christi through this monthly newspaper published by the diocese and circulated to church members. Topics include official diocesan news, local news about the Catholic community and national and international news from a Catholic news service. The *South Texas Catholic* is a mixture of news stories and columns of interest to Catholics in the 16-county area from Corpus Christi to Laredo that is served by the diocese. It's available by paid subscription or free at local Catholic churches. It's published on or near the last Friday of the month.

Magazines and Other Print Media

Arts and Attractions in Corpus Christi
710 Buffalo St., Ste. 810, Corpus Christi • (512) 882-2250

The title of this annual, four-color magazine tells you exactly what you'll find between its 40 or so pages. The local advertising firm that publishes this glossy magazine describes it as the "definitive guide" to art organizations and events taking place in the Coastal Bend. Features run the gamut from artists and art organizations to dance, music and sculpture. Each edition carries about 18 features, an events calendar and a directory of arts organizations. This free publication is published each spring and is available at Coastal Bend hotels and local tourist bureaus.

Corpus Christi Lawyer
520 Cut Off Rd., Ste. 4, Port Aransas • (512) 749-5955, (800) 330-8069

This quarterly publication of the Corpus Christi Bar Association is published by Anaqua Publishing Inc. in Port Aransas. Publisher Rick Thomas says the four-color, glossy magazine is mailed to about 2,000 bar members, doctors, CPAs and other professionals. Articles on legal issues are written by attorneys and law professors. The *Lawyer* is mailed to bar members and is available at the Nueces County Bar Association office in the Nueces County Courthouse.

Explore the Texas Coastal Bend 1998 Information Guide
520 Cut Off Rd., Ste. 4, Port Aransas • (512) 749-5955, (800) 330-8069

This glossy tourist guide is produced by Anaqua Publishing Inc. in Port Aransas for the

Texas Coastal Bend Regional Tourism Council. Its small pages are stuffed with all sorts of Coastal Bend tourism information, including a calendar of events, Coastal Bend tours and a buyer's guide. This annual publication is available free all over the Coastal Bend, including local chambers of commerce.

South Texas Women's World
Corpus Christi • (512) 939-7599

Publisher Mary Weaver describes *South Texas Women's World* as a publication with a "positive outlook that gives readers something enjoyable to read." As the name suggests, this monthly tabloid focuses on women and women's issues. Already in its fourth year, this free publication is published on the 10th of each month and has a circulation of about 40,000.

The Real Estate Book
4942 Arlene Dr., Corpus Christi • (512) 851-9250

Chances are you've seen the local version of *The Real Estate Book* in your hometown or some other city you've visited. That's because the Atlanta-based publisher has more than 300 franchises throughout the United States. The concept is straightforward enough: Take pictures of homes for sale throughout the Coastal Bend and put them in a small book with brief descriptions and prices. Tom Dunovan, owner of the local franchise, has produced the Coastal Bend book since 1984. Twenty-five thousand copies of the monthly publication are available for free at retail outlets throughout the Coastal Bend.

Local TV
Stations and Networks

Take our advice: Get cable. Without it you'll spend most of your time trying to decipher a fuzzy screen. Only one of the seven local TV stations comes through clear enough to make TV viewing enjoyable unless you have cable.

Because the area is served by five cable companies, (see the following section for information on cable providers) you'd be wise to consult the cable conversion chart in the *Caller-Times*' *TV Channels* magazine. Find your city, locate the network you want to watch and follow your fingers to find the correct number to which to tune your set. To avoid confusion, ignore the numbers broadcast by the local TV stations because they won't coincide with the number on your TV dial. For instance, KIII-TV, the ABC affiliate in Corpus Christi, promotes itself as Channel 3, which is where you'd find it if you didn't have cable. Cable subscribers in Corpus Christi will find the station on Channel 5; cable subscribers in other areas will find it on channels 2, 3 or 4.

Corpus Christi is the 128th-largest TV market in the United States. The five major networks — ABC, CBS, NBC, PBS and Fox — each has an affiliate here. Two Spanish-language TV stations serve as affiliates to the Spanish-language networks Telemundo and Univision. All TV stations and the one network listed here are based in Corpus Christi.

Catholic Communications Network
1200 Lantana St., Corpus Christi • (512) 289-6437

You need no more evidence of the heavy influence of Catholicism in the Coastal Bend than the existence of the Catholic Communications Network, a product of the Diocesan Telecommunications Corp. (DTC), a nonprofit entity that operates radio station KLUX 89.5 FM and the Catholic Communications Network. Network is perhaps too strong a word for what the DTC does. The DTC airs programming provided by the Eternal Word Television Network over Channel 27 to Heartland Wireless Cable subscribers.

Programs cover topics pertaining to and of interest to Catholics. Most programming comes from Eternal Word Television with a few locally produced shows thrown into the mix. The DTC has the right to inject its own programming whenever it wants. Local shows include *Our Shepherd's View* with Bishop Roberto Gonzalez.

KIII-TV, Channel 3
4750 S. Padre Island Dr., Corpus Christi • (512) 855-6397

KIII-TV is the No. 1 TV station in the Coastal Bend, having topped the news ratings for the past 15 years. The ABC affiliate is owned by Mike McKinnon, who has headed the station since it went on the air in 1964. Much of KIII's success is attributed to the appeal of anchorman Joe Gazin, who joined the station in 1977 after working as a news anchor in Madison, Wisconsin. His easygoing style and smooth delivery seem to appeal to area viewers who have tuned in to Joe night after night for years.

KZTV-TV, Channel 10
301 Artesian St., Corpus Christi
• (512) 883-7070

KZTV-TV, the local CBS affiliate, runs a distant third to the top-two stations in the local news ratings and shows no signs of climbing out of the cellar. The station began in 1956 as KSIX-TV, with Vann M. Kennedy as the station's president, a title he continues to hold today. In the days before cable the station dubbed itself "the clear channel" because of its unfuzzy signal. For years its newsroom was in Corpus Christi while its studio and transmitting tower remained in Robstown, which meant anchormen had to spend 30 minutes before each newscast on the road.

Kennedy is known as a conservative businessman who runs a tight ship, budget-wise. News reporters are generally young, and production quality is sometimes lacking.

KEDT-TV, Channel 16
4455 S. Padre Island Dr., Corpus Christi
• (512) 855-2213

KEDT is the Coastal Bend's Public Broadcasting System affiliate. It went on the air on October 15, 1972, after a local grocery store tycoon took a liking to Public Broadcasting System programs during his travels. He said the programs inspired and challenged viewers to be participants in their communities. He and another Corpus Christi resident decided to bring public broadcasting to the city.

The station had its share of problems in the beginning, namely the fact that most local residents didn't know it existed. But Richard Nixon saved the day when he got into trouble and KEDT decided to televise gavel-to-gavel coverage of the Senate Watergate hearings. The public (most of whom voted Democratic) loved it.

Like many public TV stations KEDT has experienced its share of struggles related to limited funding. As recently as five years ago the TV station and its sister radio station, KEDT-FM, were on the brink of shutting down. The

TV station owed creditors $1.1 million and some bills were running 90 days past due. A new station manager, who has since left for greener pastures, substantially reduced the debt and moved the station into larger, more attractive offices. Outdated equipment has been replaced and staff morale repaired. The station is now a stable PBS affiliate. KEDT airs PBS and local instructional programs.

KORO-TV, Channel 28
102 N. Mesquite St., Corpus Christi
• (512) 883-2823

The Coastal Bend's first Spanish-language TV station went on the air on April 19, 1977. It broadcast a San Antonio TV station's signal and gradually inserted local ads and programs as they came along. The station has grown along with the Spanish-language market nationwide. KORO is now an affiliate of Univision, a Spanish-language network based in Miami. KORO airs both a 5 PM and 10 PM local newscast in Spanish.

KDF-Fox, Channel 47
2209 N. Padre Island Dr., Corpus Christi
• (512) 289-7451

KDF-Fox, as the name suggests, is the local affiliate of the Fox Broadcasting Company. It became the 143rd Fox affiliate on April 10, 1994, despite Fox's reservations about KDF's status as a low-power TV station. A Fox official said at the time that only two other low-power stations had been chosen as Fox affiliates. She said KDF's aggressive programming and the addition of a nightly newscast helped convince them to take KDF on as an affiliate.

Paloma Broadcasting Corp., whose stockholders included the Catholic Diocese of Corpus Christi's Diocesan Telecommunications Corp., originally owned the station, but financial troubles and Chapter 11 bankruptcy forced Paloma to sell the station to a group of KRIS-TV executives under the name Miramar Broadcasting Company. Miramar then sold the station to South Carolina-based Evening Post Publishing Co. in February 1998.

KAJA-TV, Channel 68
2209 N. Padre Island Dr., Corpus Christi
• (512) 289-2826

KAJA is the sister station of KDF-TV, operating out of facilities in the same building and owned by Evening Post Publishing Co. of South Carolina. KAJA is an affiliate of the Spanish-language network, Telemundo. Like KDF, KAJA was previously owned by Paloma Broadcasting Corp. and was sold to Miramar Broadcasting Company when Paloma ran into financial problems.

KAJA is a low-power station distributed mostly by cable systems in Nueces and San Patricio counties. Telemundo, the nation's second-largest Spanish-language TV network, took KAJA on as an affiliate in October 1993. Programming includes talk shows, soap operas, variety shows, dramas, comedies and news. A majority of Telemundo's programs are produced in the United States. The rest come mainly from Latin America and Spain.

KRIS-TV, Channel 6
409 S. Staples St., Corpus Christi
• **(512) 886-6100**

The perennial bridesmaid among Corpus Christi TV stations is KRIS-TV. Although ratings for its newscasts have seldom topped KIII-TV during the past 15 years, the NBC affiliate's hard work and a willingness to try new things has narrowed the gap between the No. 1 and No. 2 stations. KRIS prefers cleanly written, well-reported TV news stories to the flashier style favored by so many local news teams. Former longtime owner T. Frank Smith Jr. sold the station to South Carolina-based Evening Post Publishing Co. in February 1998.

Cable Providers

The Coastal Bend is served by five cable television stations, including two in Corpus Christi. Prices and packages vary from company to company and even from city to city. Call the cable company that serves your area of interest for information on prices and services.

Coastal Bend Cablevision
316 S. Commercial St., Aransas Pass
• **(512) 758-7621, (800) 242-2039**

Coastal Bend Cablevision serves Aransas Pass, Ingleside and Gregory. It offers 34 channels on its standard basic service. Cinemax, HBO, Showtime, The Movie Channel, pay-per-

view services and Sega Channel are available at additional cost.

Crown Cable
415 S. Sixth St., Kingsville
• **(512) 595-5726**

Crown Cable in Kingsville serves residents within the city limits of Driscoll, Kingsville and Agua Dulce. It offers basic service with 12 channels and expanded service with 32 channels. Cinemax, HBO, Showtime and The Disney Channel are available at additional cost.

Falcon Telecable
822 Market St., Portland
• **(512) 643-8588, (800) 873-9395**

Falcon Telecable provides service in Port Aransas, Portland and Rockport.

Port Aransas residents receive standard basic service with 33 channels. Cinemax, Encore, HBO, Showtime and The Movie Channel are available at additional cost.

Portland residents can choose from standard basic with 38 channels and extended basic with 42 channels. Cinemax, Encore, HBO, The Playboy Channel, Showtime and The Movie Channel are available at additional cost.

Rockport residents can choose from standard basic service with 39 channels or extended basic with 45 channels. Cinemax, HBO, The Playboy Channel, Showtime and The Movie Channel are available at additional cost.

Heartland Wireless Communications
5541 Bear Ln., Corpus Christi
• **(512) 289-0000**

Heartland Wireless Communications is Corpus Christi's wireless cable television company. Its signal is broadcast via the airwaves to antennas placed atop subscribers' homes. Their signal covers a 25-mile radius of downtown Corpus Christi. Heartland offers basic service with 28 channels. Cinemax and HBO are available at additional cost.

TCI Cablevision
4060 S. Padre Island Dr., Corpus Christi
• **(512) 857-5000**

TCI Cablevision offers basic service with 18 channels and expanded basic with 35, including The Disney Channel. Cinemax, Encore, HBO, Showtime and Starz are available at additional cost.

Radio

The Coastal Bend radio market is surprisingly diverse for a relatively unpopulated area. About 30 radio stations broadcast here compared to about 20 in the much larger Austin area. Rock 'n' roll, country, Christian and Spanish-language stations dominate.

In one Arbitron radio survey, contemporary hits station KZFM 95.5 FM ranked first among listeners 12 and older. Country station KRYS 99.1 FM took second, followed by Spanish-language station KSAB 99.9 FM.

Four stations in the Corpus Christi market are owned by the same company. Gulfstar Communications Inc. of Austin owns stations KRYS 1360 AM, KRYS 99.1 FM, KMXR 93.9 FM and KNCN 101.3 FM.

Contemporary
KLUX 89.5 FM (Easy listening)
KMXR 93.9 FM (Adult contemporary)
KZFM 95.5 FM (Contemporary hits)

Children
KRYS (1360) Radio Disney

Christian
KBNJ 91.7 FM
KCCT 1150 AM
KCTA 1030 AM
KFGG 88.7 FM

Classical
KEDT 90.3 FM (Jazz, blues, NPR news)

Country
KFTX 97.5 FM
KOUL 103.7 FM
KRYS 99.1 FM

International (Spanish Top 40)
KUNO 1400 AM

News/Talk
KEYS 1440 AM
KSIX 1230 AM (CBS Radio Network, Astros baseball)
KTKY 106.1 FM
KTSA 550 AM (From San Antonio)
WOAI 1200 AM (From San Antonio)

Nostalgia
KCCG 107.3 FM
KDAE 1590 AM

Rock
KBBA 92.7 FM (Soft rock hits: '70s, '80s)
KBTE 102.3 FM (Classic rock)
KLTG 96.5 FM (Soft rock hits)
KNCN 101.3 FM (Album-oriented rock)
KRAD 105.5 FM (Album-oriented hard rock)

Tejano
KBSO 94.7 FM
KLHQ 98.5 FM
KNDA 102.9 FM
KSAB 99.9 FM

The strong showing among Catholics in Corpus Christi is due in part to the area's large Hispanic population and its ties to Roman Catholicism.

Worship

Take a spin down Corpus Christi's Shoreline Boulevard and you'll soon realize the importance religion plays in the lives of Texas Coastal Bend residents. A 15-foot, 6-inch statue of Jesus entitled *It Is I* towers over the roadway in front of First United Methodist Church. (For more information on the statue and artist see the Closeup in this chapter.) The city itself has a religious meaning. Corpus Christi is Latin for "Body of Christ," a name given it by Alonzo Álvarez de Piñeda, who is said to have discovered Corpus Christi Bay on the Roman Catholic Feast Day of Corpus Christi.

The Hispanic influence on the Texas Coastal Bend, which touches so many aspects of life here, is especially evident in the region's religious makeup. A 1995 poll conducted by the *Corpus Christi Caller-Times* newspaper revealed that half the city's residents were Catholic, while another poll, The Harte-Hanks Texas Poll, showed that only 27 percent of residents statewide were Catholic. The strong showing among Catholics in Corpus Christi is due in part to the area's large Hispanic population and its ties to Roman Catholicism. According to the *Caller-Times* poll, 63 percent of the city's Catholics, or 80,000 people, are Hispanic.

As of August 1995, approximately 35 percent of the population was Protestant, including 13 percent Methodist, 6 percent Presbyterian, 3 percent Lutheran, 3 percent Episcopalian and 1 percent Church of Christ.

In Corpus Christi the Catholic church influences religion, politics, social issues and entertainment. The city is home to the Catholic Diocese of Corpus Christi, founded as a mission field in 1874 and established as a diocese in 1912. It includes all or part of 16 South Texas counties covering 17,000 square miles from Corpus Christi to Laredo, not including the Rio Grande Valley in far South Texas. According to church estimates, the diocesan population totals more than 350,000 people.

Before it became a republic, the area that is now Texas belonged to Mexico. The government encouraged Roman Catholics to settle the area by awarding them land. Empresarios were people who contracted with the Mexican government to bring Roman Catholic settlers to Texas in exchange for 23,000 acres for each 100 families. Their descendants (many of whom are no doubt Catholic) inhabit the area today.

The Bishop of Corpus Christi is the Most Rev. Roberto Gonzalez, who serves as pastor of the Corpus Christi Cathedral, an architecturally and historically significant church that sits on a bluff overlooking Corpus Christi Bay (see our Attractions chapter). Gonzalez succeeded the Most Rev. René Gracida, who retired on April 1, 1997.

The diocesan offices are located throughout the city. The chancery office, (512) 882-6191, is at 629 Lipan Street in the city's uptown region. Diocesan facilities include retreat centers, a newspaper and TV network and a Catholic school system. The Diocese of Corpus Christi is known as a conservative diocese, especially under the direction of former Bishop René Gracida, who in 1990 became the nation's first and only Catholic bishop to excommunicate several Catholics who administered abortion clinics or performed abortions.

In recent years anti-abortion protests have led to pickets, lawsuits and arrests when anti-abortion activists (made up of Catholics and Protestants alike) blocked access to abortion clinic entrances.

Catholic Social Services, (512) 884-0651, which operates as an affiliated corporation of the diocese, runs several charitable programs in Corpus Christi. It provides emergency aide for poor and indigent individuals and families with immediate needs that cannot be met by state or federal assistance. Help includes cash, food, clothing, furniture and other household goods. Each year the agency serves about 20,000 people in Corpus Christi.

Kent Ullberg and the Christ Statue

For more than 65 years, the Christian community in Corpus Christi, which means "body of Christ" in Latin, had discussed the possibility of a Christ statue overlooking Corpus Christi Bay. Several memorials were proposed, including the commissioning of Gutzon Borglum, the sculptor of Mount Rushmore, to create such a piece. None of the projects succeeded.

Retired schoolteacher Dorothy McCoy prompted interest again when she searched for ways to memorialize her son, Bob, who was killed in a 1991 auto accident. She sent a check to the First United Methodist Church, 900 S. Shoreline Boulevard, and a letter outlining her vision for a Christ statue "stilling the waters."

Close-up

With McCoy's initial contribution, a fund drive was started to make the statue a reality. In 1993, Corpus Christi sculptor Kent Ullberg was commissioned by the church to produce the statue.

Unveiled in October 1995, Ullberg's $100,000 sculpture depicts Christ with uplifted arms standing in the bow of a boat in rough waters. The scene represents the time Jesus calmed his disciples' fears amidst a storm on the Sea of Galilee by rebuking the

— continued on next page

Photo: First United Methodist Church

Artist Kent Ullberg stands next to the 15 1/2-foot sculpture of Jesus he created for First United Methodist Church in Corpus Christi.

wind and stilling the waters. The details were researched for historical accuracy, including the sandals Jesus is wearing and the boat's design.

Called *It is I*, the bronze sculpture is 15 feet, 6 inches tall and rests on an 8-foot granite base. The statue is outside the entrance to the church sanctuary, facing the bay.

Ullberg has created and installed more than 40 monumental sculptures worldwide. His work has been shown at the National Museum of Natural History in Stockholm, Sweden; the Exhibition Hall in Beijing, China; and the Salon d'Automne in Paris, France.

His other sculptures in the Coastal Bend include *Leaping Marlin* at the entrance to Padre Island and *Spring Plumage* at the Texas State Aquarium.

The Jewish Community Council of Corpus Christi, (512) 855-6239, 750 Everhart Road, serves the area's Jewish community as well as people of other faiths. It operates the Jewish Community Center and a preschool program for children age 2 through kindergarten age. It also provides meeting space for the community and maintains an indoor swimming pool. Anyone can become a member of the Jewish Community Center for a fee ranging from $50 to $190 a year. Membership entitles you to pool privileges, school discounts, a newsletter and retail discounts.

Corpus Christi's small Muslim community worships at 7341 McArdle Road. Members, who built the mosque in 1998, raised the money needed to build it from local and out-of-town sources. The organizational wing of the mosque, the Islamic Society of South Texas, can be reached at (512) 992-8550.

The Christian Business Men's Committee, (512) 851-1605, 5205-A Embassy Drive, Corpus Christi, is a Christian outreach to the business community. The committee, one of about a thousand throughout the country, hosts monthly speaker luncheons at the Holiday Inn-Padre Island Drive, 5549 Leopard Street, and weekly scripture studies. Scripture studies are held five times a week at various times and sites. Although the committee is Protestant in terms of teachings and use of scripture, participation is open to people of all faiths. The committee hosts an annual Leadership Prayer Breakfast in which members pray for local elected officials.

The Corpus Christi Baptist Association, (512) 853-2555, 4301 Ocean Drive, Corpus Christi, helps Southern Baptist Churches in the Corpus Christi area with religious education and weekday ministries (helping the poor, fighting illiteracy, etc.). It also helps start new churches and directs callers to a Southern Baptist Church that is right for them.

You won't find many mosques or Buddhist or Hindu temples in the area, but you will find a surprising variety of churches and temples here. For a complete list of churches and services in Corpus Christi turn to the Saturday religion page of the *Corpus Christi Caller-Times*. Many newcomers to the area say the extensive listing of worship services helped guide them in choosing a church. For a list of churches and services in other parts of the Coastal Bend, check the weekly newspaper serving the area in which you are staying. See our Media chapter for information on newspapers.

Index

C